P9-CCQ-650

The NOLO *News*—

Our free magazine devoted to everyday legal & consumer issues

To thank you for sending in the postage-paid feedback card in the back of this book, you'll receive a free two-year subscription to the **NOLO** *News*—our quarterly magazine of legal, small business and consumer information. With each issue you get updates on important legal changes that affect you, helpful articles on everyday law, answers to your legal questions in Auntie Nolo's advice column, a complete Nolo catalog and, of course, our famous lawyer jokes.

Legal information online–24 hours a day

Get instant access to the legal information you need 24 hours a day.

Visit a Nolo online self-help law center and you'll find:

- hundreds of helpful articles on a wide variety of topics
- selected chapters from Nolo books
- online seminars with our lawyer authors and other experts
- downloadable demos of Nolo software
- frequently asked questons about key legal issues
- our complete catalog and online ordering info
- our ever popular lawyer jokes and more.

Here's how to find us:

America Online Just use the key word Nolo.

On the **Internet** our World Wide Web address (URL) is: http://www.nolo.com.

Prodigy/CompuServe Use the Web Browsers on CompuServe or Prodigy to access Nolo's Web site on the Internet.

OUR SPECIAL UPGRADE OFFER
It's important to have the most current legal information. Because laws and legal procedures change often, we update our books regularly. To help keep you up-to-date we are extending this special upgrade offer. Cut out and mail the title portion of the cover of your old Nolo book and we'll give you 25% off the retail price of the NEW EDITION when you purchase directly from us. For details see the back of the book.

OUR NO-HASSLE GUARANTEE
We've created products we're proud of and think will serve you well. But if for any reason, anything you buy from Nolo Press does not meet your needs, we will refund your purchase price and pay for the cost of returning it to us by Priority Mail. No ifs, ands or buts.

SEP 1997

FIRST EDITION

FORM YOUR OWN

LIMITED LIABILITY COMPANY

BY ATTORNEY ANTHONY MANCUSO

EDITED BY LISA GOLDOFTAS

NOLO PRESS  BERKELEY

g346.066
IN

Your Responsibility When Using a Self-Help Law Book

We've done our best to give you useful and accurate information in this book. But laws and procedures change frequently and are subject to differing interpretations. If you want legal advice backed by a guarantee, see a lawyer. If you use this book, it's your responsibility to make sure that the facts and general advice contained in it are applicable to your situation.

Keeping Up to Date

To keep its books up to date, Nolo Press issues new printings and new editions periodically. New printings reflect minor legal changes and technical corrections. New editions contain major legal changes, major text additions or major reorganizations. To find out if a later printing or edition of any Nolo book is available, call Nolo Press at 510-549-1976 or check the catalog in the *Nolo News,* our quarterly newspaper.

To stay current, follow the "Update" service in the *Nolo News*. You can get a free two-year subscription by sending us the registration card in the back of the book. In another effort to help you use Nolo's latest materials, we offer a 25% discount off the purchase of the new edition of your Nolo book when you turn in the cover of an earlier edition. (See the "Recycle Offer" in the back of the book.)

This book was last revised in: May 1996.

First Edition	May 1996
Editors	Lisa Goldoftas
	Ralph Warner
Book & Cover Design	Jackie Mancuso
Index	Sayre Van Young
Proofreader	Dahlia Armond
	Robert Wells
Printing	Delta Lithograph

Mancuso, Anthony.
Form your own limited liability company / by Anthony Mancuso.
p. cm.
Includes index.
ISBN 0-87337-307-3
1. Limited partnership—United States—Popular works. 2. Private companies—United States—Popular works. I. Title.
KF1380.Z9M36 1996
346.73'0668–dc20
[347.306668] 96-17358
CIP

ALL RIGHTS RESERVED. Printed in the U.S.A.
Copyright © 1996 by Anthony Mancuso
No part of this publication may be reproduced, stored in a retrieval system, or transmitted in any form or by any means, electronic, mechanical, photocopying, recording or otherwise without the prior written permission of the publisher and the author.

For information on bulk purchases or corporate premium sales, please contact the Special Sales department.

For academic sales or textbook adoptions, ask for Academic Sales. 800-955-4775, Nolo Press, Inc., 950 Parker Street, Berkeley, CA 94710.

Acknowledgements

The author thanks Lisa Goldoftas for a superb job of editing and organizing this material, Jake Warner for being backup editor and providing his usual keen insight in making this a better book, Steve Elias for his helpful suggestions on intellectual property law issues, Jackie Mancuso for her fine design and production of this book, Stan Jacobsen for his research help, and all the other hard-working people at Nolo Press.

CREATE A LEGAL PARTNERSHIP AGREEMENT ON YOUR COMPUTER

Nolo's Partnership Maker allows you to quickly and easily prepare a legal partnership agreement on your computer. Using the step-by-step legal help, you can select and fill in clauses, print an agreement and show it to your partners for feedback. Repeat the process until you settle on a final agreement. Once you are satisfied, you can print out the agreement and have it signed by all the partners. And, you can change or revise your agreement at any time.

Nolo's Partnership Maker provides:

- 84 standard and alternative clauses
- on-line, step-by-step legal help for understanding each clause and filling in each blank
- an on-line editor that allows for customizing your agreement

Using *Nolo's Partnership Maker*, you and your partners decide:

- who contributes what to the venture
- what happens if a partner fails to contribute agreed upon money or services
- how profits and losses get divided
- how partners will be compensated
- how a partner can sell out or leave the partnership
- how to handle disputes without paying costly legal fees

System Requirements

Dos 3.0 or higher, 512K Ram.

Free Technical Support

Nolo Press offers free technical support to all registered owners.

Unconditional Guarantee

All Nolo products have an unconditional guarantee. If for any reason you are unhappy with *Nolo's Partnership Maker*, simply return it to us for a refund.

To Order call 800-992-6656 or use the order form in the back of the book.

All the forms you need to conduct and document corporate business!

Includes forms on disk

Taking Care of Your Corporation, Vol. 1

Director & Shareholder Meetings Made Easy

This book takes the drudgery out of the necessary task of holding meetings of the board of directors and shareholders. It shows how to comply with state laws for holding meetings, how to prepare minutes for annual and special meetings, take corporate action by written consent, hold real or paper meetings and handle corporate formalities using e-mail, computer bulletin boards, fax, telephone & video conferencing. Includes all corporate forms on disk.

$26.95/CORK • Book with PC disk • Attorney Anthony Mancuso • Nat'l 1st ed. • ISBN 0-87337-223-9

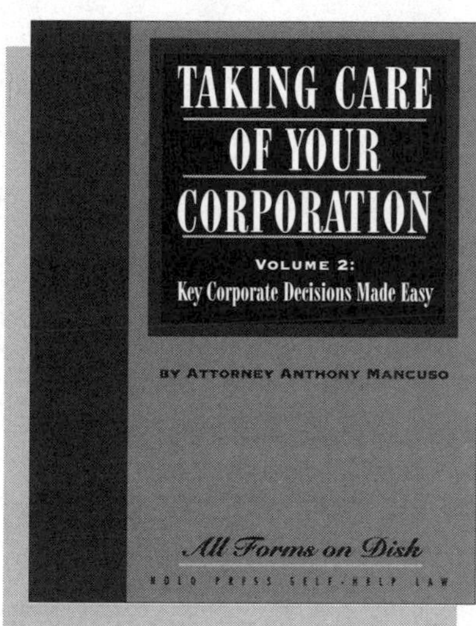

Taking Care of Your Corporation, Vol. 2

Key Corporate Decisions Made Easy

Running a corporation successfully involves making—and documenting—many ongoing business, legal and tax decisions. This book explains the practical, legal and tax aspects of important corporate decisions and provides all the instructions and forms necessary to approve corporate resolutions. Provides over 80 corporate resolutions with the legal language necessary to undertake and approve major corporate business and tax decisions such as electing S corporation tax status, adopting pension and profit-sharing plans, setting up employee benefit plans and much more.

$39.95/CORK2 • Book with PC disk • Attorney Anthony Mancuso • Nat'l 1st ed. • ISBN 0-87337-276-X

To Order call 800-992-6656 or use the order form in the back of the book.

Table of Contents

Introduction

CHAPTER 1

Overview of the LLC

CHAPTER 2

Basic LLC Legalities

CHAPTER 3

Pass-Through Tax Status for Your LLC and Other Tax Issues

CHAPTER 4

How to Prepare LLC Articles of Organization

CHAPTER 5

Prepare an LLC Operating Agreement for Your Member-Managed LLC

CHAPTER 6

Prepare an LLC Operating Agreement for Managers

CHAPTER 7

After Forming Your LLC

CHAPTER 8

Lawyers, Tax Specialists and Legal Research

APPENDIX A

State Sheets

APPENDIX B

Revenue Rulings and Notices

APPENDIX C

Tear-Out LLC Forms

Introduction

This book shows you how to form one of the newest and most exciting kinds of business entities available in the U.S.: the limited liability company (LLC). LLCs give business owners two main benefits. First, owners receive the tax advantages and capital flexibility of a partnership. Second, owners enjoy the limited liability protection previously unique to the corporation—that is, personal protection from business debts and claims.

The unique tax and legal benefits of this emerging business form, which at this writing is legal in all U.S. states except for Hawaii and Vermont, makes it essential that every small business person gain at least a passing familiarity with LLCs. A large number of small business owners currently operating as sole proprietorships or partnerships will conclude that they absolutely must form or convert to an LLC. In fact, the legal protection an LLC offers almost always makes it preferable to a partnership.

Are there any disadvantages to forming an LLC? Not many. True, LLCs are a relatively new legal entity and, as a result, you might run into some minor hassles with some state and local bureaucracies and commercial institutions. Fortunately, the passage of LLC-enabling legislation has received reams of favorable publicity, so by and large you shouldn't expect any major red tape. In a later chapter, we'll show you how to assure outside institutions and businesses that yours is a validly-formed legal entity, operating under an established set of rules. For now, read on to gain an appreciation of this fledgling business entity that promises to change the face of small business throughout the U.S.

An existing partnership may use this book to convert to an LLC. If you and your business associates are already doing business as a general or limited partnership, you can use this book to convert your partnership to an LLC. In some states, you may need to perform one or two additional simple tasks—for example, you may need to file a special form of LLC Articles of Organization to convert a partnership to an LLC. The procedures are, however, essentially the same as those followed by a start-up LLC. (We discuss the special steps that may be necessary to convert an existing partnership to an LLC in Chapter 7, Section A2.)

A. Who May Form an LLC?

The typical candidates for forming an LLC are two or several business associates, friends or family members who decide to pool energies and resources to own and operate a business.

If you're contemplating an LLC, take into account two overriding rules that could limit the scope or usefulness of the LLC form for your particular circumstances:

- *Rule 1: You normally need at least two people to set up an LLC.* This minimum number is a legal requirement in most states, and a basic federal tax law requirement to obtain the LLC tax benefits discussed in this book.
- *Rule 2: LLCs work best for smaller businesses.* Generally LLCs are suitable for businesses with no more than 35 or so owners and investors (this is our ballpark figure—not a hard and fast legal rule). To qualify for partnership tax status for your LLC, you will also need to set limits—albeit very reasonable ones—on your LLC's ability to have new members (owners) join and old members leave the LLC.

With few exceptions, LLCs may be formed for all types of businesses. You may even form one LLC to engage in several businesses—for example, furniture sales, trucking and redecorating all under one legal, if not physical, roof.

BUSINESSES THAT MAY NOT FORM REGULAR LLCs

Depending on state law, certain kinds of businesses may either be restricted or prohibited from setting up an LLC. State laws often have special restrictions for:

- businesses formed to engage in banking, trust or insurance transactions—these normally can't do business as an LLC, and
- businesses formed to practice a licensed profession such as medicine, law or accounting. In some states, these professions cannot form LLCs, although they may be able to obtain some of the benefits that LLCs enjoy by forming a special type of entity called a professional limited liability company or a limited liability partnership. (We discuss how to form this kind of professional practice in Chapter 4, Section D2.)

B. How to Use This Book

This book gives basic background legal and tax information that applies to LLCs. It covers all the information you need to make an informed choice on whether to form an LLC. It also provides helpful information and forms for existing LLCs, such as information on ongoing legal formalities and instructions for preparing minutes of LLC meetings.

If you decide to set up your business as an LLC, either from scratch or by converting an existing partnership, this book will also give you the step-by-step information you need to form an LLC in your state. Specifically, you'll find out:

- which state administrative offices to contact
- how to prepare standard organizational and operational documents to get your LLC started, including LLC Articles of Organization and an LLC operating agreement, and
- how to comply with legal rules for your state. The state sheets in Appendix A will help you follow your state's particular legal requirements.

In general, we recommend checking with a small business tax or legal advisor before taking the plunge and filing your papers with the state. Consultations of this sort are invaluable to make sure that an LLC is your best choice, that you have up-to-date state-specific information and that you have considered all legal and tax angles that apply to your particular business. Although you'll have to pay for an initial consultation with a tax or legal advisor, you'll save quite a bit by not handing over all your paperwork to a professional. We believe it is well worth the price in terms of the peace of mind you'll get knowing you've reached the right business conclusions. In Chapter 8, we discuss how to find a legal "coach"—a helpful legal professional who will work with you, review your papers and augment (not redo) your self-help legal efforts in organizing and operating your LLC.

We are confident that a careful reading of this book can help make you an informed LLC organizer, manager and member. We wish you all the best on the road to forming and running a successful LLC.

NOTES AND ICONS

Throughout this book, we have included special notations and icons to help organize the material and underscore particular points:

A legal or commonsense tip to help you understand or comply with legal requirements.

A caution to slow down and consider potential problems.

A suggestion to seek the advice of a professional.

An indication that you may be able to skip some material.

A cross-reference to another section of this book, or a suggestion to consult another book or resource.

CHAPTER 1

Overview of the LLC

In this chapter, we briefly trace the history of the limited liability company (LLC), discuss its legal and tax characteristics and compare it to the traditional ways of organizing and doing business in the U.S. We'll delve more into the specific legal and tax characteristics of LLCs in the next two chapters.

If you are familiar with LLCs. If you have followed the development of the LLC over the last few years and know its general legal and tax characteristics (or you simply want to look at the specifics of forming an LLC right now), you can skip the introductory material in this and the following two chapters. Move right ahead to Chapter 4, where you'll learn how to prepare LLC Articles of Organization.

A. Development of the LLC

The LLC is a relatively recent version of a type of business organization that has existed for years in other countries. It resembles the German *GmbH*, the French *SARL* and the South American *Limitada* forms of doing business, all of which allow small groups of individuals to enjoy limited personal liability while operating under partnership-type rules (rather than the complex rigmarole that applies to corporate-type structures).

The Wyoming legislature enacted the first state LLC legislation in 1977, eventually followed by Florida in 1982. In those early days, this new type of business entity was a risky proposition, because no one knew whether the IRS would tax an LLC as a corporation or a partnership. Because the idea behind forming an LLC—to enjoy the tax status of a partnership without the legal liabilities—seemed almost too good to be true, few business people were brave enough to avail themselves of this new business model without clarification from the IRS. Similarly, other states were unwilling to jump in with LLC legislation of their own.

The first big break in the LLC stalemate came in 1988, when the IRS ruled on the tax treatment of Wyoming LLCs in Revenue Ruling 88-76. (A copy of this ruling is in Appendix B.) To the surprise of many tax practitioners, the IRS agreed that an LLC formed under the Wyoming statute was eligible for partnership tax status. The IRS's nod of approval created huge amounts of enthusiasm for LLCs, ultimately resulting in all states plus the District of Columbia introducing LLC legislation. All states have approved this legislation at the time of this printing with the exceptions of Hawaii and Vermont; these holdout states are expected to pass pending LLC laws soon. (If you live in Hawaii or Vermont, call the state LLC filing office telephone number listed on your state sheet in Appendix A).

B. LLCs at a Glance: The Best Thing Since Sliced Bread?

In the U.S., the LLC stands as a unique alternative to five traditional legal and tax ways of doing business: sole proprietorships, general partnerships, limited partnerships, C (regular) corporations and S corporations. The business press has heralded the arrival of the LLC with enthusiasm and hyperbole. Finally, you can establish a business entity with the limited liability of a corporation while retaining a level of tax simplicity that resembles a partnership. Is this fanfare justified? In large part, we think so, at least for smaller startup businesses and existing partnerships. It doesn't often happen that a new business form comes along, particularly one that is blessed by the IRS with the favorable tax ruling bestowed upon the LLC.

THERE'S NEVER LIMITED LIABILITY FOR PERSONALLY-GUARANTEED DEBTS

No matter how a small business is organized (LLC, corporation, partnership or sole proprietorship), its owners must normally co-sign business loans made by banks—at least until the business establishes its own positive credit history.

When you co-sign a loan, you promise to voluntarily assume personal liability if your business fails to pay back the loan. In some cases, the bank may ask you to pledge all your personal assets as security for repayment of the guaranteed loan; in others, it may require you to pledge specific personal assets—for example, the equity in your home—to secure repayment of the loan.

Example: A married couple owns and operates Books & Bagels, a coffee shop *cum* bookstore. In need of funds (dough, really) to expand into a larger location, the owners go to the bank to get a small loan for their corporation. The bank grants the loan on the condition that the two owners personally pledge their equity in their house as security for the loan. Because the owners personally guaranteed the loan, the bank can seek repayment from the owners personally by foreclosing on their home if Books & Bagels defaults. No form of business ownership can insulate them from the personal liability they agreed to.

If you want more information about pledging personal assets to secure business loans, see *The Legal Guide for Starting and Running a Small Business*, by Fred Steingold (Nolo Press).

1. Limited Liability Status

The legal characteristic most interesting to the business world is undoubtedly the limited liability status of LLC owners. With the exception of corporate entities, the LLC is the only form of legal entity that lets *all* of its owners off the hook for business debts and other legal liabilities, such as court judgments and legal settlements obtained against the business. Another way of saying this is that an investor in an LLC normally has at risk only his or her share of capital paid into the business.

2. Business Profits and Losses Taxed at Individuals' Income Tax Rates

The LLC is recognized by the IRS as a "pass-through" type of tax entity. That is, the profits or losses of the LLC pass through the business and are reflected and taxed on the individual tax returns of the owners, rather than being reported and taxed at a separate business level. (Other pass-through entities include general and limited partnerships, sole proprietorships and S corporations—those that have elected S corporation tax status with the IRS. A detailed discussion is in Section D, below.)

3. Flexible Management Structure

LLC owners are referred to as members. A member may be an individual or, generally, a separate legal entity, such as a partnership or corporation. Members invest in the LLC and receive a percentage ownership interest in return. This ownership interest is used to divide up the assets of the LLC when it is sold or liquidated, and is typically used for other purposes as well—for example, to split up profits and losses of the LLC or to divide up its voting rights.

LLCs are run by their members unless they elect management by a management group, which may consist of some members and/or nonmembers. Small LLCs are normally member-managed—after all, most small business owners want and need to have an active hand in the management of the business. However, this isn't always true. Especially with a growing business or one that makes fairly passive investments, such as in real estate, investors may not want a day-to-day role. Fortunately, an LLC can easily adopt a management-run structure in situations such as these:

- the members want the LLC to be managed by some, but not all, members
- the members decide to employ outside management help, or
- the members choose to cater to an outsider who wishes to invest in or loan capital to the LLC on condition that he or she be given a vote in management.

UNIFORM LLC LAWS

For many years, legal scholars and state legislators have worked hard to have all states adopt the same (or very similar) laws affecting key areas of American business and life. A bit belatedly, efforts are being made to adopt a national model LLC act that can be used by individual state legislatures to pass future LLC legislation. One model is the Prototype Limited Liability Company Act, sponsored by the American Bar Association's Section of Business Law. Another is the Uniform Limited Liability Company Act, developed by the National Conference of Commissioners on Uniform State Laws.

Both of these acts are still in development, and there is justified skepticism as to whether states will replace current LLC laws with either model act. More likely, states probably will adopt portions of the model acts to supplement their current LLC statutes. In short, while LLC laws are fairly similar (they generally try to conform to IRS regulations and to LLC statutory schemes in other states), state-by-state differences are likely to remain.

4. Flexible Distribution of Profits and Losses

Business owners may want flexibility in how they split their profits and losses. An LLC allows you to decide what share of the LLC profits and losses each owner will receive. Rather than being restricted to dividing up profits proportionate to the members' capital contributions, you may split up LLC profits and losses any way you wish (this flexibility is afforded partnerships as well).

Example: Steve and Frankie form an educational seminar business. Steve puts up all the cash necessary to purchase a computer with graphics and multimedia presentation capabilities, rent out initial seminar sites, send out mass mailings and purchase advertising. As the traveling lecturer, cash-poor Frankie will contribute services to the LLC. Although the two owners could agree to split profits and losses equally, they decide that Steve will get 65% for the first three years as a way of paying him back for taking the risk of putting up cash.

By contrast, rules governing the distribution of corporate profits and losses are fairly restrictive. A regular (C) corporation cannot allocate profits and losses to shareholders at all—shareholders get a financial return from the corporation by receiving corporate dividends or a share of the corporation's assets when it is sold or liquidated. In an S corporation (a corporation that has made a special tax election with the IRS, covered in Section D5, below), profits and losses pass through to the owners and profits and losses generally must follow shareholdings. For example, an S corporation shareholder holding 10% of the shares ordinarily must be allocated a 10% share of yearly profits and losses.

There are a few wrinkles in the flexibility afforded to LLCs. Because LLCs are treated like partnerships for tax purposes, LLCs must comply with technical partnership tax rules:

- *Special (disproportionate) allocations of LLC profits or losses are subject to rules that require such allocations to have "substantial economic effect."* Generally, they must reflect some economic reality of the business—for example, the member with the greater share of profits should also be at risk for a greater share of losses. Rather than squabble with the IRS on this issue, LLCs that make special allocations usually have their tax advisor add technical provisions to their operating agreement to make sure their allocations will be respected by the IRS. (See the discussion in Chapter 3, Section D2.)
- *Members contributing future services to the LLC may be subject to income taxes on the value of their services.* A member promising to contribute services to the LLC may face personal income tax liability on the value of those services—although there are some ways around this. (We'll have more to say about the tax problems associated with a member's contribution of services in Chapter 3, Section D1.)

C. Which Businesses Would Benefit as LLCs?

Here is an overview of the types of persons and businesses for which the LLC form makes the most and least sense. Bear in mind that this discussion is not meant to be set in stone—certainly you may find that your business breaks the mold.

1. Businesses That Benefit From the LLC Structure

LLCs generally work best for:

- *Actively run businesses with a limited number of owners.* Owners numbering between two and about 35 keep the logistics of making collective business decisions manageable. With the LLC form, all owners of the business enjoy limited liability and the flexibility of pass-through (partnership) tax treatment.
- *Small start-up companies.* New businesses generally wish to pass possible early-year losses along to owners to deduct against their other income (usually salary earned working for another company or income earned from investments).
- *Anyone thinking of forming an S corporation.* An S corporation is a corporation formed under state law, which files a special IRS tax election to have corporate profits pass through the business and be taxed only at the shareholder level (similar to the tax treatment of LLCs, but less flexible, as discussed below). Like LLCs, S corporations also provide limited liability protection to all owners. The S corporation tax election comes at a fairly heavy price: S corporations must limit the number and types of shareholders. They are restricted as to how they allocate profits and losses among owners, the types of losses they can pass along to owners to ease their income tax burden, and the kinds of stock they can issue to investors. Even if a business meets the S corporation tax requirements, it can inadvertently lose its eligibility—

for example, when a disqualified shareholder inherits or buys the stock—resulting in a big tax bill. (For more on S corporations, see Section D5, below.)

- *Existing partnerships.* Only the LLC provides pass-through tax treatment of business income while insulating *all* owners (not just limited partners as in the case of a limited partnership) from personal liability for business debts.
- *Businesses planning to hold property that will appreciate, such as real property.* Regular corporations (also called C corporations) and their shareholders are subject to a double tax on this appreciation when assets are sold or liquidated—in other words, taxation occurs at both the corporate and individual level. S corporations that were organized as C corporations prior to making an S corporation tax election also may be subject to a double tax on "built-in gains" from asset appreciation, as well as a penalty tax if their passive income (money from rents, royalties, interest, dividends) gets too high. Because the LLC is a true pass-through tax entity, it allows a business that will hold appreciating assets to avoid double taxation.

2. Businesses That Should Normally Not Form an LLC Using This Book

The LLC is not normally suitable for:

- *One-owner businesses.* Even in the handful of states that allow one-person LLCs (Arkansas, Idaho, Indiana, Montana, New Hampshire, New Mexico, New York and Texas), it's rarely a sensible choice. Under current IRS rules, LLCs need at least two owners (members) to obtain the benefits of pass-through tax treatment. Some small business owners choose to form an LLC with their spouse, which automatically gets the business going with the required two owners. At this point, it's not absolutely clear how the IRS will treat a one-person LLC. It's possible that the IRS will tax a one-person LLC as a separate taxable association, but it will most likely be treated as a sole proprietorship. The IRS promises to clarify the tax status of one-person LLCs in a future ruling, so we'll need to wait to obtain definitive answers to this tax question.
- *Owners who wish to split income between their business and themselves.* Business owners sometimes want a portion of business profits taxed at initially low corporate rates, with the remainder taxed at the owners' individual rates. The C corporation is the only business form that allows this splitting of income and bifurcation of business income tax rates. (See Section D3, below.)
- *Existing S or C (regular) corporations.* The tax cost of converting a corporation to an LLC, as well as security law uncertainties, are problematic. It may be possible to convert an existing corporation to an LLC without hefty tax or legal costs, but you'll need the help of a lawyer and a tax advisor to make sure you don't get stung.
- *Highly profitable LLCs in certain states.* In states with a graduated LLC license fee schedule, the more profitable the LLC, the higher the tax. In California, for example, LLCs with reportable income over $5 million must pay an annual fee of $4,500. Such a stiff tax is unusual; check your state sheet in Appendix A or ask your tax advisor to be sure you understand whether you face the unpleasant prospect of paying excessive state LLC fees. Of course, in states with a high LLC fee or tax, chances are good that the state also has enacted fees that apply to other pass-through tax entities (limited partnerships and S corporations). In these states, you may decide that forming a general partnership, which isn't taxed separately, is the least expensive way to go—but you won't qualify for limited liability for business debts.

D. Comparison of LLCs and Other Business Forms

Anyone considering an LLC will want to compare this business form to the three traditional ways of doing business:

- sole proprietorships
- partnerships, and
- C (regular) corporations.

In addition, to fully understand the pros and cons of LLC status, you'll need to compare the LLC to two variants on these traditional business forms that come closest to resembling the legal and tax characteristics of the LLC:

- limited partnerships, and
- S corporations.

This section provides general information on the characteristics of each type of legal entity, focusing on the main reasons why business people adopt one form over another. Our aim is to explain most of the information you'll need to make an informed decision as to whether the LLC is right for you. However, please realize that we can't cover every nuance of tax and business organization law as it applies to your business, especially if yours involves a number of owners with different and complicated personal tax situations. Furthermore, the area of pass-through taxation is no piece of cake, even to tax specialists. You will need to check with a tax advisor to make sure the LLC makes sense to you from a tax standpoint, and to learn about any of the special tax areas that may have special relevance to your business (some of which are covered in Chapter 3).

OTHER WAYS OF DOING BUSINESS: MORE INFORMATION FROM NOLO PRESS

For a more complete examination of the legal and tax characteristics of the various ways of doing business, see the following Nolo Press titles:

- *Legal Guide for Starting and Running a Small Business*, by Fred Steingold. This book provides a thorough summary of the legal and tax characteristics of sole proprietorships, partnerships, corporations and LLCs.
- *The Partnership Book*, by Denis Clifford and Ralph Warner, and *Nolo's Partnership Maker* (interactive software to easily set up a general partnership using any IBM or compatible computer). Both resources discuss general partnerships and show you step-by-step how to prepare a general partnership agreement.
- *How to Form Your Own Corporation*, by Anthony Mancuso. This state-specific series for California, Florida, New York and Texas provides an in-depth treatment of the corporate structure and shows you how to incorporate in each of the covered states. Incorporation forms are included as tear-outs and on computer disk.
- *California Incorporator*. This stand-alone software package steps you through the California incorporation process and form preparation on your IBM or compatible computer.

1. Sole Proprietorship

The simplest way of being in business for yourself is as a sole proprietor. This is just a fancy way of saying that you are the owner of a one-person business. There's little red tape and cost—other than the usual business licenses, sales tax permits and local and state regulations that any business must face. As a practical matter, most one-person businesses start out as sole proprietorships just to keep things simple.

a. Sole Proprietorship Is Limited to One Person

If your sole proprietorship grows, you'll need to move to a more complicated type of business structure. Once you decide to own and split profits with another person (other than your spouse), by definition, you have at least a partnership on your hands.

b. Sole Proprietor Is Personally Liable for Business Debts

Unfortunately, although a sole proprietorship is simple, it can also be a dangerous way to operate, especially if your business may result in debts or liabilities from lawsuits. The sole proprietor is personally liable for all debts and claims against a business. For example, if someone slips and falls in a sole proprietor's business and sues, the owner is on the line for paying any court award (if commercial liability insurance doesn't cover it). The owner's personal assets, such as a home, car and bank accounts, are fair game for the repayment of these uncovered amounts. Similarly, if the business fails to pay suppliers, banks or other businesses' bills, the owner is personally liable for the unpaid debts.

c. Sole Proprietor's Taxes

Sole proprietors report business profits or losses on an *IRS Schedule C, Profit and Loss From Business (Sole Proprietorship)*, included with a *1040* individual federal tax return. Profits are taxed at the owner's individual income tax rates.

Because the owner is self-employed, he or she must pay an increased amount of self-employment (FICA) tax based upon these profits—about twice as much as an incorporated business or corporate employee would pay. This increased FICA tax doesn't necessarily mean that sole proprietorships are more expensive tax-wise than other business forms. In fact, if you are both a corporate shareholder and employee, as is the case for the owner/employees of most small corporations, you end up paying close to the same total FICA taxes.

d. Sole Proprietorships Compared to LLCs

The LLC requires more paperwork to get started and is more complicated than a sole proprietorship from a legal and tax perspective. Although LLC owners, like sole proprietors, report business profits on their individual tax returns, the LLC itself is treated as a partnership and must prepare its own annual informational tax return. The payoff of the LLC for this added complexity is that owners are not personally liable for business claims or debts (unless personally guaranteed, as with a personally guaranteed bank loan).

Do you really want to share ownership? The LLC does require at least two owners, which means sharing power and profits with a second person. If you are set on keeping your business all to yourself, you probably won't want an LLC (unless perhaps you want to include your spouse as the second LLC member).

2. General Partnerships

A partnership is a business in which two or more owners agree to share profits. If you go into business with at least one other person and you don't file formal papers with the state to set up an LLC, corporation or limited partnership, the law says you have formed a general partnership. A general partnership can be started with a handshake (a simple verbal agreement or understanding) or a formal partnership agreement.

Partners should always create a written partnership agreement. Without an agreement, the default rules of each state's general partnership law apply to the business. These provisions usually say that profits and losses of the business should be split up equally among the partners, regardless of the amount of capital contributed to the business by each partner. Rather than relying on state laws, general partners should prepare an agreement that covers issues such as the division of profits and losses, the payment of salaries and draws to partners and the procedure for selling partnership interests back to the partnership or to outsiders.

a. Number of Partners in a General Partnership

General partnerships may be formed by two or more people; there is no such thing as a one-person partnership. Legally, there is no upper limit on the number of partners who may be admitted into a partnership, but general partnerships with many owners may have problems reaching a consensus on business decisions and may be subject to divisive disputes between contending management factions.

b. General Partnership Liability

Each owner of a general partnership is individually liable for the debts and claims of the business. In other words, if the partnership owes money, a creditor may go after any member of the partnership for the entire debt, regardless of his or her ownership percentage (although one partner can sue other partners to force them to repay their shares of the debt).

Legally, each partner may bind the partnership to contracts or enter a business deal that binds the partnership, as long as the contract or deal is generally within the scope of business undertaken by the partnership. In legal jargon, this authority is expressed by saying that each partner is an agent of the partnership. If the partnership can't fulfill a contract or other business deal, each partner may be held personally liable for the amount owed. This personal liability for partnership debts, coupled with the agency authority of each partner, makes the general partnership riskier than limited liability businesses (corporations, LLCs and limited partnerships).

c. General Partnership Taxes

A general partnership is not a separate taxable entity. Profits (and losses) pass through the business to the partners, who pay taxes on profits at their individual tax rates. Although the partnership does not pay its own taxes, it must file an information return each year, IRS Form 1065, *U.S. Partnership Return of Income*. This includes an IRS Form K-1 (1065), *Partner's Share of Income, Credits, Deductions* for each partner, which shows the proportionate share of profits or losses each person carries over to his or her individual *1040* tax return at the end of the year.

d. General Partnerships Compared to LLCs

General partnerships are less costly to start than LLCs because most states do not require a state filing (and fees) to form general partnerships. The major downside to running a general partnership over an LLC is the exposure to personal liability by each of the general partners. Although a general business insurance package (possibly supplemented by more specialized coverage for unusual risks) can mitigate possible effects, each partner is still personally responsible for any liabilities and debts not picked up by the business's insurance policy. LLC owners, on the other hand, avoid this personal liability problem altogether.

General partnerships and LLCs come out about even on a couple of important issues:

- *Partnership agreement or operating agreement.* Even a small general partnership should start off with a good written general partnership agreement. This, of course, takes time and, if you don't do the work yourself, is likely to cost $1,000 to $5,000 in legal fees, depending on the complexity of your partnership and the thickness of your lawyer's rug. You'll also need to draw up an operating agreement if you form an LLC; this agreement is similar in scope to a partnership agreement. (We take you through the steps involved in preparing an operating agreement in Chapters 5 and 6 of this book.)
- *Taxes.* General partnerships and LLCs can count on about the same amount of tax complexity, preparation time and paperwork. Even though you'll probably turn over most year-end tax work to a tax advisor to prepare a partnership return, understanding and following basic partnership tax procedures takes a fair amount of time and effort.

3. C (Regular) Corporations

To establish a C (regular) corporation, you prepare and file formal Articles of Incorporation papers with a state agency (usually the Secretary of State) and pay corporate filing fees and initial taxes. A corporation assumes an independent legal and tax life separate from its owners, with the result that it pays taxes at its own corporate tax rates and files its own income tax returns each year (IRS Form 1120).

Corporations are owned by shareholders and managed by a board of directors. Most management decisions are left to the directors, although a few must be ratified by the shareholders as well, such as the amendment of corporate Articles of Incorporation, sale of substantially all of the corporation's assets or the merger or dissolution of the corporation. Corporate officers are normally appointed by the board of directors to handle the day-to-day supervision of corporate business, and usually consist of a corporate President, Vice President, Secretary and Treasurer.

"C" corporation is nothing more than a regular corporation. The letter "C" simply distinguishes the regular corporation (one taxed under normal corporate income tax rules) from a more specialized type of corporation regulated under Subchapter "S" of the Internal Revenue Code. The latter type of corporation, the S corporation, makes a special tax election and is treated differently under the Internal Revenue Code. (We compare the LLC to the S corporation in Section D5, below.)

a. Number of Corporate Shareholders and Directors

In most states, one or more persons can form and operate a corporation. In a few states, the number of persons necessary to manage a multi-owner corporation (that is, the number of directors) is directly proportionate to the number of shareholders. For example, if there are two shareholders, two or more directors must be named; if three shareholders, then three or more directors are necessary.

b. Corporate Limited Liability

As we have mentioned, a corporation provides all its owners (shareholders) with the benefits of limited liability—traditionally, a major reason why many businesses have organized as corporations. The LLC is the latest arrival on the legal and business scene that also gives all business owners this significant legal advantage.

LIMITED LIABILITY FOR THE MASSES: THE TREND CONTINUES

Historically, it was the development of the corporation and the concept of limited liability that made it possible to capitalize large corporations and create modern capitalism. This same sort of revolution has taken place on a small scale among successful small business people. Surely, the great majority of America's 50,000 most successful smaller businesses are incorporated. Extending the concept of limited liability to the small business world has produced amazing results, and we're sure the momentum of the LLC as an emerging business vehicle is bound to continue this trend.

c. Corporation's Separate Legal and Tax Existence

The remaining significant difference between the C corporation and the LLC is that the corporation has a legal and tax existence separate from its owners. This leads to the following corporate characteristics:

- *Separate taxes.* A corporation files its own income tax return and pays its own income taxes. LLCs (like partnerships) file an informational return only and do not pay their own income taxes.
- *Tax benefits of employee fringe benefits.* Even small corporations have the opportunity to offer their employees unique fringe benefits. The corporate form allows owner-employees (shareholders who also work in the business) to deduct a number of corporate fringes paid to them as employees from corporate income, such as the 100% deductibility of health insurance premiums. Other corporate fringes include the direct reimbursement of medical expenses and stock bonus and stock option plans. There is not much difference between corporate and noncorporate pension and profit sharing plans, but corporate defined benefit plans usually afford better retirement options and benefits than those available under a noncorporate (Keogh) plan.
- *Legal formalities.* Because a corporation has a separate legal existence, you must pay more attention to its legal care and feeding. This means you must don directors' and shareholders' hats and hold and document annual meetings required under state law. You must keep minutes of meetings, prepare other formal documentation of important decisions made during the life of the corporation and keep a paper trail of all financial dealings between the corporation and its shareholders. You also need to tend to other formalities, such as appointing officers required under corporate statutes. A corporation should issue stock to its shareholders and keep adequate capitalization on hand to handle foreseeable business debts and liabilities.

Problems with shoddy corporate procedures. There are dangers if you set up a thinly capitalized corporation, treat corporate coffers as an incorporated pocketbook for your personal finances, fail to issue stock, neglect to hold meetings or overlook other formalities required under your state's corporation code. If you do (or don't do) these things, a court or the IRS may "pierce the corporate veil" (a mixed metaphor carried over from a long line of court cases) and decide that the corporation is simply an "alter ego" of the shareholders of a small corporation. If this happens, the business owners (shareholders) can be held personally liable for any money awarded by a court against the corporation.

Help with corporate forms and formalities. For those who wish to explore more fully the formalities (holding annual and special meetings) and ins and outs of doing business as a corporation (approving contracts, leases, promissory notes and numerous other important legal, tax and business decisions), see Volumes 1 and 2 of *Taking Care of Your Corporation*, by Anthony Mancuso (Nolo Press).

d. Corporations Compared to LLCs

Corporations are similar to LLCs in the types of paperwork and fees necessary to get them started with the state. Both must prepare and file organizational papers with the Secretary of State and pay filing fees. Both should adopt a set of operating rules that set out the basic legal requirements for operating the business under state law—corporations adopt Bylaws; LLCs adopt operating agreements.

What sets the corporate form apart from LLCs is how they are taxed. Corporations are taxed separately from their owners at corporate income tax rates. While this does result in extra complexity, because separate accounting must be made of corporate profits and losses, it can also result in a tax advantage. This advantage stems from the fact that the separate tax rates applied to corporate income allow business owners who work in the business (shareholder-employees) to split income between themselves and their corporation.

Example: Justine and Janine own and operate Just Jams & Jellies, a specialty store selling gourmet canned preserves. Business has boomed and their net taxable income, split equally by the partners, has reached a level where it is taxed at the highest individual tax rate of 39.6%. If the owners incorporate, they can keep money in their corporation that is taxed at the lower corporate tax rates of 15% and 25%, saving overall tax dollars on business income. Also, because the owners will receive less personal income as a corporate salary, their top individual tax rate will drop to 31%.

No other type of business structure lets you split business income between yourself and your business. Realize that many smaller businesses start plowing money back in the business from the get-go, before the owners are able to pay themselves a wage comparable to what they would receive if employed by another company. If these retained earnings are kept in a corporation, they may be taxed at the lower (15% and 25%) corporate tax rates.

WHAT ABOUT THE DOUBLE TAXATION OF CORPORATE PROFITS?

We're sure you've read about the awful consequence of double taxation when a corporation makes money. Specifically, the tax law says that corporate profits are first taxed at the corporate level, then any profits paid out as dividends to shareholders are taxed at each shareholder's individual income tax rate. Doesn't this result in a big comparative benefit to LLC businesses (and other pass-through entities such as partnerships and sole proprietorships), where the owners just pay taxes once on business income at their personal rates?

For small, actively run corporations, we say no—this comparative advantage of the LLC is just a technicality and, in our opinion, doesn't deserve all the hoopla it gets in the business press. Here's why. To avoid the penalty of double taxation, smaller corporations rarely pay dividends to the owners. Instead, the owner-employees are paid salaries and fringe benefits that are tax deductible to the corporation. As a result, only employee-shareholders pay income taxes on this business income.

So cast a critical eye on any article decrying the double taxation of corporate profits. Unless you are forming a corporation with passive investors who expect to receive regular dividends as a return on their investment in your corporation, double taxation will generally not be a big deal.

There may be other reasons to favor the corporate form over the LLC. Some are the increased deductibility of corporate-employee fringes, better retirement benefits or options under a corporate retirement plan. The increased respectability of doing business as a corporation may seem overrated, but a number of people—perhaps including persons you may wish to hire as key employees and reward with stock option and stock bonus incentives—associate the corporate form with an added degree of formality and solidity. And, of course, the ability to go public (make a public offering of corporate shares) is a traditional feature of the corporate form that more successful small businesses may be able to capitalize on. (Forget about going public with an LLC; the legal and tax restrictions on transferring membership interests rule out this possibility.)

There are several downsides to corporate life. We've already mentioned the complexity of complying with state law corporate procedures by preparing annual and special director and shareholder meetings. (Some states have tried to lessen the impact of these state-mandated formalities with the creation of the close corporation form—see the sidebar on the following page, "A Look at Close Corporations.") Also, the corporate form often complicates tax accounting and reporting without providing a corresponding tax savings. Many smaller businesses find that they pay the same or less taxes if all business income and expenses are reported and taxed to them as individuals (as is the case for sole proprietors, partners and LLC members).

4. Limited Partnerships

To get this special type of partnership started, you must file papers (Certificate of Limited Partnership) with the state and pay an initial filing fee. Legally, a limited partnership is similar to a general partnership (discussed in Section D2, above), except that instead of only being comprised of general partners, it has two types:

- *Limited partners.* One or more partners contribute capital to the business. Limited partners neither participate in its day-to-day operations nor have personal liability for business debts and claims.
- *General partners.* One or more partners manage business operations and have personal liability for business debts and claims.

a. Number of Partners

Limited partnerships must be formed by two or more people, with:

- at least one person acting as the general partner, who has management authority and personal liability, and
- at least one person in the role of limited partner.

b. Limited Liability Only for Limited Partners

Limited partners enjoy the same kind of limited liability for the debts and liabilities of the business as do the shareholders of a corporation and the members of an LLC. General partners of limited partnerships, on the other hand, have the same personal liability described above for general partnerships. (See Section D2.)

c. Limited Partnership Taxes

For tax purposes, limited partnerships normally are treated like general partnerships, with all owners having to report and pay taxes personally on their share of the profits each year. The limited partnership files an informational tax return only, and is not subject to an entity level federal income tax.

A LOOK AT CLOSE CORPORATIONS

Several states have enacted special corporate statutes that allow corporations to dispense with normal operating rules. These corporations, called "close" or "statutory close" corporations, generally must meet a number of legal requirements:

- The corporation must have a limited number of shareholders, usually no more than 35.
- Shares of stock must not be sold or transferred to outsiders unless approved by all shareholders.
- The corporation must elect close corporation status in its formation documents or an amendment to these papers.
- The corporation must operate under partnership-type rules specified in a shareholders' agreement. (The drafting of this agreement is time-consuming and can involve fairly high attorney fees.)

Ten to 15 years ago, legislators in corporately-active states, including California, Delaware, Illinois and Texas, expected business organizers to line up to form close corporations under recently enacted state laws, but few were formed. The close corporation's failure to spark the interest of business organizers was caused by reasons such as the following:

- Few corporations want to forego the customary formality of appointing a board of directors, electing officers and assuming the other traditional accoutrements of corporate life.
- Management of a corporation by its shareholders is normally seen as novel and potentially chaotic.
- Preparation and adoption of a custom-tailored shareholders' agreement is a time-consuming incorporation step most organizers want to avoid.
- Shareholders do not want restrictions on their right to sell or transfer shares, which are mandatory under typical close corporation statutes.

In many ways, the close corporation resembles the LLC by giving owners the protection of limited liability while allowing them to operate under partnership-type legal rules. The big difference is that unlike LLCs, the IRS never bestowed the general mantle of partnership tax treatment on close corporations. Had close corporations successfully obtained partnership tax treatment with the IRS and been able to operate informally without having to prepare a special shareholders' agreement, perhaps they would be vying today for the popular attention currently enjoyed by LLCs.

d. Limited Partnerships Compared to LLCs

There are two major differences between limited partnerships and LLCs. First, a limited partnership must have at least one general partner, who is personally liable for the debts and other liabilities of the business. This differs from LLCs, where all members are covered by the cloak of limited liability.

Second, limited partners are generally prohibited from managing the business. If a limited partner is active in the business of the limited partnership, he or she typically loses the limited partner status with its attendant limited liability protection. (There are exceptions to this ban under the newer Revised Uniform Limited Partnership Act, which has made the rounds through state legislatures and has been adopted, at least in part, in most states.) In contrast, LLC members are given a free hand in managing and running the business, either by themselves or in conjunction with outside managers.

This second restriction of the limited partnership makes it more of a gamble for investors, who must turn over management of the business to a general partner. Such an arrangement may work well for outsiders who want to invest a little cash or property in a business run by others, but it won't work well for businesses that are funded and run primarily by their owners. Investors in actively run businesses who want limited liability status for all owners generally benefit by forming an LLC or corporation; both of these entities permit investors to help run the business while enjoying the personal protection of limited liability.

5. S Corporations

Now we come to our last comparison, and the one with the nicest (that is, most picayune) technical distinctions: the S corporation versus the LLC. Below, we address the main similarities and differences, but you may need to ask your tax person for further particulars if you want to understand the ins and outs of comparing these two business forms.

For starters, an S corporation follows the same state incorporation formalities as a C (regular) corporation. Typically, this means filing Articles of Incorporation and paying a state filing fee. An S corporation also must make a special one-page tax election under Subchapter S of the Internal Revenue Code to have the corporation taxed as a partnership (by filing IRS Form 2553, the *S Corporation Tax Election* form, with the IRS).

a. Number of S Corporation Owners

Generally, an S corporation may have no more than 35 shareholders (who must be individuals or certain types of trusts or estates). In the future, this upper limit may change to a greater number, perhaps 50.

b. Limited Liability of S Corporation Shareholders

All S corporation shareholders are granted personal protection from the debts and other liabilities of the business, just like regular C corporation shareholders and LLC members.

c. Tax Election of S Corporation

Once a corporation makes a Subchapter S tax election, its profits and losses pass through the corporation and are reported on the individual tax returns of the S corporation's shareholders. This is the same basic pass-through treatment afforded partnerships and LLCs. The S corporation's profits and losses are generally not taxed at the business entity level (as is the case for a regular C corporation).

d. S Corporations Compared to LLCs

Like any other type of corporation, an S corporation requires some care and feeding—more than typically needed for an LLC. Regular and special meetings of directors and shareholders should be held and recorded to transact important corporate business or decide key legal or tax formalities. And although profits and losses of an S corporation are passed along to its shareholders, the S corporation must prepare and file an S corporation annual income tax return each year (IRS Form 1120S). This requirement is similar, from a time and energy standpoint, to the task of an LLC preparing its own informational tax return each year.

The main difference between S corporations and LLCs has to do with the requirements for electing S corporation tax treatment and some of the unique tax effects that result from this election. To be eligible to make an S corporation tax election with the IRS, the corporation and its shareholders must meet a number of special requirements. Here are a few of the S corporation tax requirements that can present a problem:

- *Individual shareholders of an S corporation must be U.S. citizens or have U.S. residency status.* If shares are sold, passed to (by will, divorce or other means), or otherwise fall into the hands of a foreign national, the corporation loses its S corporation tax status.
- *Shareholders must be individuals or certain types of qualified trusts or estates.* S corporations can't have partnerships or other corporations as shareholders. Under typical state statutes, LLCs may have both natural (individual) and artificial (corporate, partnership, trust and estate) members.
- *There can be no more than 35 shareholders in an S corporation.* Again, this limit may be increased in the future.
- *S corporations must have only one class of stock.* Different voting rights are permitted, meaning that S corporations may have one class of voting shares and another consisting of nonvoting shares. But all shares must have the same rights to participate in dividends and the assets of the corporation when the business is sold or liquidated. Having only one class of stock limits the usefulness of the S corporation as an investment vehicle. Investors typically like to receive special classes of shares that have preferences regarding corporate dividends and participation in the liquidation assets of the corporation when it is sold or dissolved.
- *An S corporation cannot own a subsidiary business.* This is defined as an 80% stake in another corporation.
- *An S corporation that loses its status cannot reelect it for five years.* An S corporation can lose its tax status—perhaps inadvertently, for example, if some shares fall into the hands of a disqualified shareholder. Even if the corporation again becomes qualified, it must wait until five years have elapsed from the year of the disqualification.

Two special tax effects not suffered by other pass-through tax entities, such as LLCs and limited partnerships, often present problems for S corporation shareholders:

- *S corporation shareholders can't receive special allocations of profits and losses.* Corporate profits and losses must be split up proportionately to the percentage of shares owned by each shareholder. This point may sound technical or theoretical, but even for smaller businesses it has practical—and sometimes negative—significance.

Example: Ted and Natalie want to go into business designing solar-powered hot tubs. Ted is the "money" person and agrees to pitch in 80% of the first-year funds necessary to get the business going. Natalie is the hot tub and solar specialist and will contribute her skills as a solar systems and hot tub designer in overseeing the design and manufacture of the tubs. Ted and Natalie want a portion of her first-year salary to go toward paying for her initial shares in the enterprise. They also want Ted to get a disproportionate number of shares in recognition of the extra risk associated with putting cash into the business up-front. Instead of getting two shares for every one of Natalie's shares, which reflects the ratio of Ted's cash to the value of Natalie's services, they want him to receive four shares for every share that she gets. Unfortunately, while this disproportionate doling out of shares may make a lot of practical sense, it is not permitted under S corporation rules.

- *S corporation entity-level debt can't be passed along to shareholders.* An S corporation generally can't pass the potential tax benefits of borrowing money along to its shareholders. Here's a short run-down of this issue. In other pass-through entities, such as partnerships and LLCs, business debt (money borrowed by the business) increases the tax basis of the owners. This is good for a couple of reasons. First, the owners can deduct more losses from the business on their tax returns. Second, the higher the basis, the less gain—and the lower the taxes due—when owners sell their interests or the business itself is sold. This technical tax point is illustrated in the following example.

Example: Mitch's Barbecue Pit Corp., organized as an S corporation, is a promising business in search of outside capital for expansion. A special blend of seasonings in Mitch's secret rib sauce consistently brings in overflow crowds to his two downtown locations. A number of people have expressed interest in investing in Mitch's expansion into other cities. It's expected that the venture will generate business losses in its first years immediately following the capital infusion. Mitch's will borrow funds from banks to supplement cash reserves and working capital. At first, interested investors plan to simply use the early S corporation losses to offset other income on their personal tax returns. However, the investors' tax advisors warn that because S corporation debt cannot be used to increase the tax basis of the shares held by the investors (as it could in a partnership or LLC) investors won't get to write off all the expected business losses on their individual tax returns. This technical tax disadvantage of the S corporation ultimately results in Mitch having difficulty finding investors to fund his planned business expansion.

We won't go into this technical point further. Just realize that an S corporation has less flexibility than other pass-through entities to use borrowed money of the business to increase the tax deductions of the owners on their annual individual tax returns and lower the tax bite when the business or their interests in it are ultimately sold. These technical considerations can have important real-world effects. Your tax advisor can fill you in on the details if you want more information.

To summarize, even if S corporation status makes sense to gain the benefits of limited liability for the owners but keep the pass-through tax status for business income and losses, it is often inconvenient or uncertain because of the requirements for adopting and keeping S corporation tax eligibility. By comparison, the tax status of an LLC is sustained and certain throughout the life of the business. Further, the above technical tax considerations make the S corporation less attractive to investors seeking to maximize the deductions and losses they can pass through the business and claim on their individual tax returns.

E. Business Entity Comparison Tables

In the tables below, we highlight and compare general and specific legal and tax traits of each type of business entity. We include a few technical issues in our chart (partially covered in Section D, above) to tweak your interest. Should any of the additional points of comparison seem relevant to your particular business operation, we encourage you to talk them over with a legal or tax professional.

BUSINESS ENTITY COMPARISON CHART—LEGAL CHARACTERISTICS

	Sole Proprietorship	General Partnership	Limited Partnership	C Corporation	S Corporation	LLC
Who owns business?	sole proprietor	general partners	general and limited partners	shareholders	same as C corporation	members
Personal liability for business debts	sole proprietor personally liable	general partners personally liable	only general partner(s) personally liable	no personal liability of shareholders	same as C corporation	no personal liability of members
Restrictions on kind of business	may engage in any lawful business	may engage in any lawful business	same as general partnership	some states prohibit formation of banking, insurance and other special businesses	same as C corporation —but excessive passive income (such as from rents, royalties, interest) can jeopardize tax status	same as C corporation
Restrictions on number of owners	only one sole proprietor	minimum two general partners	minimum one general partner and one limited partner	most states allow one-person corporations; some require two or more shareholders	same as C corporation, but no more than 35 shareholders permitted	at least two members for tax purposes (although some states allow one-person LLCs)
Who makes management decisions?	sole proprietor	general partners	general partner(s) only (not limited partners)	board of directors	same as C corporation	ordinarily members; or managers if manager-managed LLC
Who may legally obligate business?	sole proprietor	any general partner	any general partner (not limited partners)	directors and officers	same as C corporation	ordinarily any member; or any manager if manager-managed LLC
Effect on business if an owner dies or departs	dissolves automatically	dissolves automatically unless otherwise stated in partnership agreement	same as general partnership	no effect	same as C corporation	dissolves unless remaining members vote to continue business

	Sole Proprietorship	General Partnership	Limited Partnership	C Corporation	S Corporation	LLC
Limits on transfer of ownership interests	free transferability	consent of all general partners usually required under partnership agreement	same as general partnership	transfer of stock may be limited under securities laws or restrictions in Articles of Incorporation or Bylaws	same as C corporation —but transfers limited to persons and entities that qualify as S corporation shareholders	unanimous consent of nontransferring members usually required under state law or operating agreement
Amount of organizational paperwork and ongoing legal formalities	minimal	minimal; partnership agreement recommended	start-up filing required; partnership agreement recommended	start-up filing required; Bylaws recommended; annual meetings of shareholders required	same as C corporation	start-up filing required; operating agreement recommended; meetings not normally required
Source of start-up funds	sole proprietor	general partners	general and limited partners	initial shareholders (in some states, cannot invest with promise to perform services or contribute cash in the future)	same as C corporation —but cannot issue different classes of stock with different financial provisions	members (may usually invest with promise to perform services or contribute cash in the future)
How business usually obtains capital, if needed	sole proprietor's contributions; working capital loans backed by personal assets of sole proprietor	capital contributions from general partners; business loans from banks backed by partnership and personal assets	investment capital from limited partners; bank loans backed by general partners' personal assets	flexible; outside investors (may offer various classes of shares); bank loans backed by shareholders' personal assets (if corporation has insufficient credit history); may go public if need substantial infusion of cash	generally same as C corporation—but can't have foreign partnership or corporate shareholders; must limit number of shareholders to 35; can't offer different classes of stock to investors except for shares without voting rights	capital contributions from members; bank loans backed by members' personal assets (if LLC has insufficient credit history)

	Sole Proprietorship	General Partnership	Limited Partnership	C Corporation	S Corporation	LLC
Ease of conversion to another business form	may change form at will; legal paperwork involved	may change to limited partnership, corporation or LLC; legal paperwork involved	may change to corporation or LLC; legal paperwork involved	may change to S corporation by filing simple tax election; change to LLC can involve tax cost and legal complexity	generally same as C corporation—may terminate S tax status to become C corporation but cannot reelect S status for five years after	may change to general or limited partnership or corporation; legal paperwork involved
Is establishment or sale of ownership interests subject to federal and state securities laws?	generally not	generally not	issuance or sale of limited partnership interests must qualify for securities laws exemptions, otherwise must register with federal and state securities laws offices	issuance or transfer of stock subject to state and federal securities laws or must qualify for securities laws exemptions	same as C corporation	probably not, if all members are active in business
Who generally finds this the best way to do business?	owner who wants legal and managerial autonomy	joint owners who are not concerned with personal liability for business debts	joint owners who want partnership tax treatment and some nonmanaging investors; general partners must be willing to assume personal liability for business debts	owners who want limited liability and ability to split income between themselves and a separately taxed business	owners who want limited liability and individual tax rates to apply to business income; must be willing to meet initial and ongoing S corporation requirements	owners who want limited liability and full benefits of pass-through taxation; particularly beneficial for smaller, privately held businesses

BUSINESS ENTITY COMPARISON CHART—TAX CHARACTERISTICS

	Sole Proprietorship	General Partnership	Limited Partnership	C Corporation	S Corporation	LLC
How business profits are taxed	individual tax rates of sole proprietor	individual tax rates of general partners	individual tax rates of general and limited partners	split up and taxed at corporate rates and individual tax rates of shareholders	individual tax rates of shareholders	individual tax rates of members—as long as LLC meets IRS rules (has no more than two corporate characteristics)
Tax-deductible fringe benefits available to owners who work in business	sole proprietor may set up IRA or Keogh retirement plan; may deduct a portion of medical insurance premiums	general partners and other employees may set up IRA or Keogh plans; may deduct a portion of medical insurance premiums	same as general partnership	full tax-deductible fringe benefits for employee-shareholders; may fully deduct medical insurance premiums and reimburse employees' medical expenses	same as general partnership, but employee-shareholders owning 2% or more of stock are restricted from corporate fringe benefits under partnership rules	same as general partnership
Automatic tax status	yes	yes	yes, upon filing certificate of limited partnership with state corporate filing office	yes, upon filing Articles of Incorporation with state corporate filing office	no; must meet requirements and file tax election form with IRS (and sometimes state); revoked or terminated tax status cannot be re-elected for five years	no; state law or provisions of operating agreement must result in LLC meeting IRS rules (has no more than two corporate characteristics)
Are taxes due when business is formed?	generally tax-free to set up	generally tax-free to set up; individual income taxes may be due if a general partner contributes services as capital contribution	usually same as general partnership	generally not taxable unless existing business is incorporated and new owners are brought into the business	same as C corporation	generally tax-free to set up; individual income taxes may be due if a member contributes services as capital contribution

	Sole Proprietorship	General Partnership	Limited Partnership	C Corporation	S Corporation	LLC
Deductibility of business losses	owner may use losses to deduct other income on individual tax returns (subject to active-passive investment loss rules that apply to all businesses)	partners may use losses to deduct other income on individual tax returns if "at risk" for loss or debt	same as general partnership, but limited partners may only deduct "nonrecourse debts" (for which general partners are not specifically liable)	corporation may deduct business losses (shareholders may not deduct losses)	shareholders may deduct share of corporate losses on individual tax returns, but must comply with special limitations	generally members entitled to deduct losses (subject to active-passive investment loss rules that apply to all businesses)
Tax level when business is sold	personal tax level of owner	personal tax level of individual general partners	personal tax level of individual general and limited partners	two levels: shareholders and corporation may be taxed on liquidation if it includes sale or transfer of appreciated property	normally taxed at personal tax levels of individual shareholders, but corporate level tax sometimes due if S corporation was formerly a C corporation	personal tax levels of individual members

CHAPTER 2

Basic LLC Legalities

This chapter examines legal issues and procedures involved in setting up and running an LLC. Here you'll find chunks of information not presented elsewhere on a number of important LLC legal issues. If a particular legal area provokes special questions or concerns that you think apply to your LLC, you may wisely choose to do additional reading. (Check with a legal coach or tax advisor.)

A. At Least Two People Must Be Members of an LLC

As we've pointed out earlier, a minimum of two people must be members (owners) of an LLC under most state statutes. A sole member is permitted in a handful of states: Arkansas, Idaho, Indiana, Montana, New Hampshire, New Mexico, New York and Texas. However, you will need at least two members—even in those states—to qualify for pass-through (partnership) tax status for your LLC (which allows LLC profits and losses to be reported on the owners' individual tax returns).

Some states specify that a husband and wife are to be counted as separate members of an LLC, but most states are silent on this issue. We believe that the law is fairly clear that spouses are counted separately as long as each is listed as a member with separate ownership interest percentages in the LLC. (You indicate the ownership percentages of each member in your operating agreement, discussed in Chapters 5 and 6.)

Example: Nathan and Sheila Myers form Shady Oak Furniture, LLC. They list themselves as the two initial members of the co-owned LLC in their LLC operating agreement, each with a 50% ownership interest in the company.

B. Paperwork Required to Set Up an LLC

Let's look at the basic legal documents and procedures involved with starting your own LLC. Fortunately, it's a simple process, meaning that it should take you relatively little time to turn your idea of forming an LLC into a legal reality.

One person may prepare and file the paperwork. Generally, one person may prepare, sign and file the basic documents to set up an LLC. This person need not be a member of the LLC, but must turn the reins of management over to LLC members or a management team after the LLC is formed. Of course, what the legislatures have in mind is that a lawyer can do the filing for you—which is fine if that's what you want. Normally, you can just as well prepare the paperwork yourself and drop it in the nearest mailbox.

1. LLC Articles of Organization

The only formal legal step normally required to create an LLC is to prepare and file LLC Articles of Organization with your state's LLC filing office. A few states require an additional step: the publication in a local newspaper of a simple notice of intention to form an LLC prior to filing your Articles. (See your state sheet in Appendix A for particulars.)

The LLC filing office is usually the same one that handles your state's corporate filings, typically the Department or Secretary of State's office, located in each state's capitol city. Larger states usually have branch filing offices in secondary cities as well.

LLC Articles of Organization don't have to be lengthy or complex. In fact, you can usually prepare your own in just a few minutes by filling in the blanks and checking the boxes on a relatively simple form provided by your state's LLC filing office. Typically, you need only specify a few basic details about your LLC, such as its name, principal office address, agent and office for receiving legal papers, and the names of its initial members (or managers, if you're designating a special management team to run the LLC).

Instructions for completing Articles of Organization. We provide a sample LLC Articles of Organization form with instructions, and show you how to get your state's form to fill in and file in Chapter 4.

2. LLC Operating Agreement

An LLC should always create a written operating agreement to define the basic rights and responsibilities of LLC members (and managers, if you decide to form a manager-run LLC—more on this option later). An operating agreement is also of crucial importance because it helps establish that the LLC qualifies for favorable (pass-through) tax status with the IRS. (Refer to Chapter 3, Sections A and B for more on this tax point.)

Although not advisable, an LLC that is registered with your state may be operated on a handshake without a formal operating agreement among the owners. No matter how busy you are, we believe it's a big mistake to delay preparing an operating agreement. Without a written agreement to refer to, you may get stuck in a crisis trying to answer such questions as:

- When members are faced with an important management decision, does each get one vote, or do they vote according to their percentage interests in the LLC?
- Are owners expected to make additional capital contributions (the money invested in the business) if the LLC needs additional operating capital?
- Are owners entitled to periodic draws from the profits of the business?
- Will interest be paid to the owners on their capital contributions?
- May members leave the LLC any time they wish and expect an immediate payout of their capital contributions?
- How much should an owner be paid when he or she decides to leave the business?
- Is a departing owner allowed to sell an interest to an outsider?

Please believe us when we say that these kinds of unanswered questions can, and frequently do, come back to haunt small businesses. They are far better addressed in a written operating agreement, signed around the time your new LLC entity is created.

Instructions for completing LLC operating agreements. Chapters 5 and 6 provide instructions for completing two different types of operating agreements included in Appendix C.

LLC LACKING OPERATING AGREEMENT IS CONTROLLED BY STATE LLC STATUTES

If you run your LLC without an operating agreement, your state's LLC statute will control basic elements of how your LLC is run and terminated. The default state LLC rules usually qualify the LLC for pass-through tax status with the IRS, but this is not always a sure bet. Obviously, obtaining favorable pass-through tax treatment is an important goal when setting up an LLC. Because the options you can select to achieve this result can have important consequences on how you run your LLC, we think it is essential for you to spell out how you qualify for pass-through tax treatment in a written operating agreement. (We discuss these tax options in Chapter 3, Section B, and show you how to choose among them when preparing your operating agreement as part of Chapters 5 and 6.)

Your state's LLC statutes may not reflect the choices you want to make for your LLC. For example, typical state statutes specify that an LLC is managed by the members (owners). In addition, most states establish that profits and losses are to be divided up among the members equally, regardless of each member's capital contribution.

Example: Yvonne and Joe form an LLC with Yvonne contributing 30% of the capital to get started and Joe contributing 70%. Under their state's default rule, Yvonne and Joe each would be entitled to receive one-half the profits of the LLC each year, even though they pay disproportionate amounts to get the LLC up and running. If Yvonne and Joe prepare their own operating agreement, however, they can divide profits in a way they consider more equitable.

C. Responsibility for Managing an LLC

At least one person needs to be responsible for overall management of a business, and the LLC is no exception. Under most states' default legal rules, all members (owners) are automatically responsible for managing the business, unless they choose to select a separate management team. An LLC that is managed exclusively by all its members is referred to as "member-managed"; LLCs with other management arrangements are known as "manager-managed."

1. Member-Managed or Manager-Managed LLC?

Most LLC owners will choose member-management, not manager-management, for two basic reasons. First, most smaller LLCs won't want an extra (management) level of bureaucracy; they'll want to let the LLC members run the business they own without oversight by or interference from a separate management team. Second, a member-managed LLC has more flexibility under the tax rules in qualifying for pass-through taxation because it avoids the corporate characteristic of centralized management. (This technical point is covered in Chapter 3, Section B2.)

Don't get too distracted by manager-management possibilities. Unless you are planning to bring in outside investors who want a management role in your business, which might be appropriate if you own an interest in a sideline business that you prefer be operated by others, it's likely that you'll naturally decide to let all of your members run your LLC.

2. Selection and Removal of Members and Managers

Initial members or managers of the LLC are usually named in the Articles of Organization filed with the state LLC filing office. As a default rule in most states, which operates unless your operating agreement says something else, new members can only be admitted by the vote of all members of the LLC. If your LLC has chosen manager-management, the default rule is that anyone selected to replace an initial manager must be voted in by a majority of the members. But you can vary this latter rule to let the managers (by a majority or greater vote), rather than the members, vote to fill a manager vacancy.

State law is usually silent on the issue of how and why members or managers of an LLC may be removed. Under typical provisions found in LLC operating agreements, members cannot be removed from the LLC member roster except for specific reasons, such as bankruptcy, insanity or another listed reason, and then only with the vote of all other members.

Manager removal is usually easier under most operating agreements, and often is allowed "without cause" (for any or no particular reason) upon a vote of the membership. Managers are also typically elected by the members to specific terms of office—in other words, they can be voted out of office at the expiration of their management term if the members elect someone else in their place.

MANAGER-MANAGED LLC OPTIONS

If all members of the LLC do not assume exclusive management power in the LLC, a group of managers must be selected. These are the options when selecting managers in a manager-managed LLC:

- Select some, but not all, LLC members. Some larger LLCs—for example, those with passive investors who will not work in the business—may decide to delegate management to a few members.
- Select only outsiders. Some LLCs decide that management should consist exclusively of outsiders with particular expertise in the business of the LLC. (For purposes of qualifying for pass-through tax status, such an arrangement can sometimes be problematic; see Chapter 3, Section B.)
- Select some or all LLC members, plus people from outside the LLC. Still other LLCs may settle for a combination of members, investors and outside managers.

3. Legal Authority of LLC Members and Managers

Generally, any one of the members or managers of the LLC can legally bind the LLC to a contract, business transaction or course of action, as long as the transaction is within the LLC's normal scope of business. In other words, one person has the unfettered right to commit the LLC to a loan, debt or other obligation. A common legal exception states that a contract with an outsider who knows, or should have known, that the LLC member or manager does not have specific authority for a transaction is not binding on the LLC. Unfortunately, this type of knowledge is hard to prove.

Example: Gary is a member and VP of Fish and Fritters Fast Foods, LLC ("4F"). He orders $500 in stationery from Joe's Stationery Supply Company, a local merchant, consisting of $400 of LLC stationery and $100 of personal letterhead. When he places the order, he does so on behalf of his LLC, and charges the bill to his LLC's account. Joe gets a check from 4F for $400, with a note from the LLC accounts payable officer advising Joe to collect the $100 balance from Gary because the order for personal letterhead was not approved by the LLC. Would a small claims court let Joe recover the $100 balance from the LLC itself? Probably. Joe would normally be justified in believing that an officer of the LLC had authority to place the full order on behalf of the LLC, unless Gary specifically told Joe that the extra stationery should be billed to him alone.

Generally, it's safest to assume that any contract or transaction signed on behalf of your LLC by anyone in management will be legally binding. This legal authority should not present a problem if you make sure you choose the right people to be members or managers of your LLC.

If you're uncomfortable with the idea that others could obligate your business. An LLC is probably not the right form of business for you. You may want to stick to a sole proprietorship, where you have the only say, or to a limited partnership, where you can get full management authority if you become the only general partner.

4. Member and Manager Voting Rules

The default laws of most states (those that apply unless your operating agreement says otherwise) specify that members' voting rights are allocated according to the capital contributions made by each. In other words, a member contributing 50% of the capital to the LLC usually gets 50% of the voting power of the LLC. Only Arizona, Kansas and Louisiana buck this trend and allocate member's voting rights on a per capita system (one person, one vote) if the LLC operating agreement doesn't set a different standard.

Under state default rules, most LLC matters brought to a vote of the members must be approved by at least a majority of the LLC's voting power—that is, by more than 50% of the full voting interests of the members.

Example: Sit-u-ational Awareness, LLC, a three-member computer furniture ergonomics consulting firm, has parceled out its voting interests to the three owners as follows: Kathlyn—30%, Evan—25% and Alyson—45%. The vote of at least two of the three members is necessary to obtain a majority and decide an issue brought to the membership for resolution.

If the LLC is manager-managed, states typically give managers one vote each, with a majority-manager vote required to approve a decision.

Example: Dollars to Donuts, LLC, an emerging franchiser and promoter of the one-buck-per-dozen-donut discount offer on every tenth purchase, is owned by four entrepreneurs, but managed by a team of five persons consisting of the four members and an outside pastry chef, Pierre (who brings the recipe for a delectable French twist pastry—the hallmark of the enterprise—to the business). When an important management vote needs to be made, each manager gets one vote, and the vote of at least three of the five managers is required to resolve the matter. Pierre doesn't function as a fifth-wheel on the management team—he becomes the all-important deadlock-breaking vote whenever the four owners don't see eye-to-eye and split their votes two-to-two.

Remember, as with most state law rules mentioned in this chapter, these are default member and manager voting rules. You can override them by defining voting rights any way you wish in your operating agreement.

Special voting rules for certain important LLC matters. To qualify for pass-through taxation for your LLC, you will probably need to establish a number of special voting rules. Key matters include the membership vote required to admit members into the LLC who have been transferred an LLC membership interest from a former member, and the vote necessary to continue the LLC after a member dies, resigns or is expelled. To be sure you will specify voting rules that meet IRS requirements for pass-through tax status, read Chapter 3, Sections A, B and C.

5. Membership and Management Meetings

Most states do not give mandatory rules for when and how membership meetings should take place. It's ordinarily up to you to come up with your own rules for the frequency, notification procedures and conduct of membership meetings.

Regular LLC meetings are not required using the forms in this book (although you can require meetings if you're so inclined), because we believe most smaller LLCs are better off spending their time taking care of business and making money, rather than filling up their records books with page upon page of formal LLC meetings. Ordinarily, you should need to meet for formal LLC meetings (which are recorded in written minutes) only in situations such as these:

- An important legal or tax formality needs to be approved and recorded (the LLC is undertaking a legal or tax election that should be documented in your LLC records, such as approving the buy-back of a departing member's interest in the LLC).
- You need to meet face-to-face with your full membership and formally approve an out-of-the-ordinary or disputed business decision (sell important LLC assets or dissolve the LLC contrary to the wishes of some of the members).
- You have elected a management team and need to reelect them to another term (more on this just below).

Meeting to elect managers if LLC is manager-managed. States typically say that members must elect the managers at a membership meeting, without specifying terms of office for managers or how often members should meet to elect or reelect managers. Some states do limit the term for managers to one year unless you override it in your operating agreement. If your LLC is manager-managed and you adopt a one-year term for your managers, you will want to hold annual membership meetings to reelect your managers. Generally, the appointment of managers is a routine task for most LLCs unless a manager is withdrawing or is not performing satisfactorily.

D. Member and Manager Liability to Insiders and Outsiders

One of the nicest parts of forming an LLC is the general immunity from personal liability the members and managers enjoy. But it's important to realize that this immunity has its limits; there are some situations in which a person acting as an LLC member or manager may end up liable to the LLC, other members or managers, or even outsiders. We discuss these exceptions below.

1. LLC Members and Managers Must Act in Good Faith Towards Each Other

LLC members and managers have a legal obligation to act in good faith, in the best interests of other members and of the LLC itself. In legal jargon, this duty is known as their "duty of care." It is similar to the obligation corporate directors have to a corporation.

Courts have interpreted this duty in the corporate context by promulgating the "business judgment rule." This says that in making management decisions, honest business mistakes will not subject managers and members to personal liability. Another way of saying this is that, under this rule, decisions that have some rational basis—based upon facts known to managers and members or presented to them in a report from someone else with superior knowledge—should not give rise to personal liability if they turn out to be wrongheaded and result in financial loss to other members or to the LLC.

Example: Robert and Juliet are two of three owners of the Lucky Lock Company LLC. They vote at a management meeting to use one-quarter of the company's accumulated earnings to market and sell Bob's Big-Lock, a unique, three-by-five-foot lock plate with a neon clock display that Bob invented. Greg, the third owner at the meeting, is against the idea of committing company funds to promote a device with such an uncertain future. The uncertainty of the profitability of Bob's Big-Lock is fully discussed at a membership meeting, but Greg is outvoted two-to-one by his co-owners. The clock-lock idea catches on slowly, and the project loses money big-time. Can Greg sue the other owners personally for their bad business judgment? As long as Bob and Juliet made a bad business decision without underhandedness, concealment or misrepresentation of facts, or other fraud or illegality, the answer should be "no" under the business judgment rule. But let's say Bob and Juliet knew that certain features of the purported master-timepiece would be difficult to produce, yet kept this knowledge from Greg when they pitched Bob's Big-Lock idea. Greg may be able to recover some or all of the clock-loss money personally from Bob and Juliet for failing to disclose all material facts at the management meeting.

The above example points out a basic LLC legal rule: Full and fair disclosure of facts is part and parcel of an LLC member/manager's duty to the LLC—a duty that isn't mitigated or otherwise lessened by the business judgment rule.

2. Liability to Other Members for Unjustifiable Loss

Most states have provisions in their LLC act that permit members to sue other members or managers on behalf of (in the name of) the LLC. Often called "derivative actions" in legal lingo, these can occur if a member feels that other members or managers caused unjustifiable financial loss to the LLC.

Example: Let's use the same Lucky Lock Company LLC described above. But this time, members Bob and Juliet siphon off some of the funds for themselves, personally, rather than using them to prototype and sell Bob's Big-Lock. Bob and Juliet can expect to be sued by and be held personally liable to the LLC and/or to Greg for the amount of the diverted funds.

Many states have indemnification provisions in their LLC laws. This fancy legal word means that the LLC will pay the legal expenses, settlements, court judgment awards, fines, fees and other liabilities personally assessed or awarded against an LLC member or manager for ill-advised management decisions or other liability-causing events. Generally, state rules say that the person to be indemnified must have acted in good faith, in the best interests of the LLC, before he or she can be reimbursed or advanced legal expenses or receive other indemnification. And, as you might guess, intentional misconduct, fraud and illegal acts normally can't be covered under these statutes. Indemnification provisions vary and are technical, so check with an LLC legal coach or take a closer look at your state's LLC indemnification statute if this area of LLC law interests you.

3. Member and Manager Liability to Outsiders

No matter how an LLC is managed—whether by LLC members or a management team—one basic limited liability rule applies. LLC members and managers are not normally personally responsible to outsiders for any mistakes in management that they make.

Example: A customer of Jen & Len's Computers LLC sues the company, as well as each owner personally, for not fixing a problem with his two-gigabyte hard drive, resulting in 40 hours of extra work for her to get the data back on line. Are Jen and Len personally liable to the customer? No. Limited liability should protect them.

But what about torts? (Here we're talking about the legal, not comestible, kind.) Basically, a tort is a negligent act that harms another person and causes monetary loss—for example, running a red light, which causes an accident and damages another automobile. Members of an LLC, like corporate directors, partners and all other business managers, can be personally liable for financial loss caused by their tortious behavior. Whether working for an LLC as an employee or acting in the capacity as a member, if a member does something negligently, and the action causes harm to another person or that person's property, the member can be held personally liable for the damage.

Example: Otto, one of the two employee/members of Otto's Oughto Order Auto Parts Supply LLC, gets in his Mazda Miata to pick up a throwout bearing for a customer's Mercedes station wagon. On the way, he negligently sideswipes a slow-moving Geo, a stunt that results in a $5,000 repair bill to the Geo owner and a $25,000 medical claim for whiplash to George, the Geo driver. Otto can be held personally liable for $30,000.

Of course, insurance—commercial, automotive, workers' compensation or even the employee's individual homeowner policy—may cover some or all damage caused by LLC manager or worker torts. Check LLC and personal insurance policies to see what protection may be available to you in the event of an accident.

LLCs SHOULD HAVE LIABILITY INSURANCE COVERAGE

Our advice is to get reliable liability insurance to cover potential personal and business liabilities arising from the LLC's operations. Typically, a commercial general liability insurance policy will cover:

- tort liability (bodily injury and property damage, so called "slip-and-fall" coverage) caused by business owners and employees in the course of business or on the business premises, and
- fire, theft, catastrophe and the like.

Most smaller LLCs, at least to begin with, rely primarily on their commercial liability insurance to protect them in the event of lawsuits brought by outsiders. They may go beyond this basic coverage later if they can afford to supplement it with personal liability policies for members or other managers. Such policies can protect members and managers from personal liability for torts to outsiders as well as inside liability to the LLC for losses caused by members' or managers' faulty decisions.

Make sure you look for newer policies that recognize the legal status of your LLC and its members. Because LLCs are relatively new, insurance companies may need to adapt their current corporate director and officer errors and omissions policies for use by LLC members and managers.

E. Are LLC Membership Interests Considered Securities?

When someone buys into or invests in an LLC, they are being sold an interest in the business. Is this sale of an LLC interest the sale of a "security" within the meaning of state or federal law? If it is, it must either be registered at the federal level—with the Securities and Exchange Commission—and with the state securities office, or it must be eligible for an exemption from these federal and state securities registration requirements.

The question of whether and under what circumstances LLC memberships may be a security interest is too new to provide a black-and-white analysis, but we'll mention a few basic expectations of the securities law treatment of LLCs. A helpful generalization is that when the owner of an interest in a business relies on his or her own efforts to make a profit, the interest normally is not a security interest under federal and state law. Conversely, if a person invests in a business with the expectation of making money from others' efforts, federal and state statutes as well as the courts usually treat the interest purchased with the investment as a security.

1. Member-Managed LLCs and Securities Laws

If you and your co-owners plan to set up a member-managed LLC in which all members run the LLC, it is likely that your membership interests will not be treated as securities. Why? Because all members plan to make a profit in the business from their own individual efforts, not the efforts of others. California is one state that has enacted legislation that says that membership interests in an LLC where all members actively participate in the business are not securities under state law. We'll have to wait and see if the other states and the federal government follow suit and adopt similar exemption legislation.

2. Manager-Managed LLCs and Securities Laws

If you set up a manager-managed LLC, it is likely that the interests of at least the nonmanaging members will be treated as securities under state and federal law. It's even possible that the feds and the state will treat all membership interests as securities (securities agencies have been known to take an "all-or-none" position—either all LLC memberships are exempted from the definition of securities or none are).

Don't give up even if you decide to form a manager-managed LLC or your LLC membership interests fall within the definition of "securities." There are other exemptions from securities that your LLC may qualify for if it is a one-state operation or it has a limited membership. Below is a summary of the most commonly relied upon federal securities law exemptions that may apply to your LLC. Many states either defer to or adopt one or more of these federal exemptions in their securities statutes and regulations. Note that the first two exemptions do not require the filing of any paperwork—you informally rely on them without notification to any securities agency.

- *Private placements*. Under federal statutes and case (court-developed) law, the selling of securities privately—without advertising or promotion—to a limited number of people may be eligible for the private placement exemption contained in Section 4(2) of the federal Securities Act of 1933. You stand a better chance of getting this exemption if transfers of the securities—memberships—are restricted (for example, language restricting transfer of the stock is placed on all membership certificates and a conspicuous notation is made in the LLC membership book that memberships are nontransferable) and if persons buying memberships are doing so for themselves (that is, not for resale to other investors). Many smaller LLCs will neatly fit within this traditional securities law exemption because memberships are issued to a limited number of people (the number 35 is often used, but not written into this section of law), memberships are a personal investment and transfer of memberships to outsiders is restricted to satisfy tax requirements (for more on this point, see Chapter 3, Section B4).

- *One-state sales.* Another federal exemption, the intrastate offering exemption contained in Section 3(a)(11) of the Securities Act, exempts from registration the offer and sale of securities made within one state only. If you privately offer and sell memberships within one state to residents of that state only, you may qualify for this exemption from federal registration of your memberships.
- *Regulation D.* Regulation D is a formal process. It requires that you follow specific requirements contained in the Regulation D statutes and file a Form D with the Securities and Exchange Commission (SEC). When using Regulation D, you can seek an exemption under one of three rules: Rules 504, 505 or 506. We won't cover the requirements of each rule, but offer the following gloss: You stand a good chance of qualifying under one of the Regulation D rules if you privately offer and sell a small (measured in dollar value; the limits vary from $1 million to $5 million, although Rule 506 does not have a monetary limit) amount of memberships to 35 or fewer people, each of whom is a close personal friend, family member or business associate or has the capability to protect his or her own interests (because of past investment history or current and anticipated net worth and income earning capacity). In addition, you must place restrictions on the transfer of your LLC memberships (language on membership certificates and in LLC membership records that limits transfers), as explained in the discussion above of the Section 4(2) private placement exemption.

Again, state law securities exemptions tend to parallel one or more of the federal exemptions. For example, a state may exempt from registration the private sale of securities solely within the state or to a limited number of persons, such as 10 or 35. In some states, you may need to file an exemption form, sometimes along with a filing fee.

3. How Should You Handle Securities Law Issues?

Securities laws are meant to protect investors from unscrupulous operators, not active business owners from the results of their own business decisions. Your decision on how to approach securities law issues will be a personal decision, based upon the particular facts of your LLC formation and your own personal comfort level in this unsettled area of law. For example, if you're setting up a small LLC with your spouse and you plan to actively run the business yourself (say a car repair service, retail outlet or consulting business), you will very likely decide that you are exempt from securities laws and need not file paperwork. Similarly, if you are setting up your LLCs with a handful of owners who know and have worked together in the past and who will actively run the LLC, you may likely conclude that you are also on safe legal ground if you do not treat your memberships as securities.

If, however, you bring in outside LLC members who are not active in the day-to-day business of the LLC, or if you bring in outside managers, we strongly recommend making sure your LLC qualifies from exemptions from both federal and state securities laws. You can do your own research in this area, but the securities laws are murky, and the newness of the LLC throws a little extra mud in the water.

See a lawyer to ensure compliance with securities laws. Brainstorming with an LLC legal coach to learn the latest legal rules and come up with a safe securities law approach should be well worth the estimated one to three hours' worth of legal fees necessary to put this technical issue to rest. (See Chapter 8, Section B, for guidelines to follow when searching for an LLC legal coach.)

THE MOST IMPORTANT SECURITIES LAW RULE OF ALL: DISCLOSE, DISCLOSE, DISCLOSE!

One important securities law rule always applies to any business venture: Always fully disclose all pertinent facts to potential investors. Let everyone know all known and foreseeable risks of investing in your enterprise, and make all financial records available to prospective purchasers. If you go out of your way to disclose all possible risks of investment, you'll stand a much better chance of fending off securities law problems later if a member or investor starts feeling surly about lower-than-expected profits or returns from the LLC.

CHAPTER 3

Pass-Through Tax Status for Your LLC and Other Tax Issues

This chapter covers the rules for obtaining pass-through tax status—a primary objective when forming an LLC. At the end of this chapter, we also touch upon a few additional tax matters you should consider when setting up your LLC.

You'll see that most LLC tax rules are technical, plus a bit silly because you are expected to first adopt the rules and then do your best to get around them. This two-faced approach to taxation is neither new nor underhanded—it's built into the system. So read on to understand the technical tax rules important to LLCs and how to make them work to your best advantage.

PROPOSED IRS CHECK-THE-BOX TAX CLASSIFICATION SCHEME

Even the IRS has come to realize that the technical tax rules for distinguishing between corporations and pass-through tax entities (partnerships and LLCs)—the very rules discussed in this chapter—do not serve their purpose of drawing a distinct tax line between different business forms. It is clear that lawyers, accountants and informed business owners (including readers of this book) can structure an unincorporated business to meet the tax definition of either a corporation or a partnership under these rules.

In recognition of this tax practice reality, the IRS has issued Notice 95-14, which announces that the IRS is considering adopting a simple check-the-box tax classification system for U.S. and foreign businesses. With this approach, a business simply checks a box on an IRS tax form to elect how it will be treated under the federal tax scheme: either as a corporation or as a pass-through (partnership-like) tax entity. This tax election could be made by any co-owned business no matter how it is structured or labeled under state law (corporation, partnership or LLC). We include this tax notice in Appendix B.

Even if this new classification system is implemented, some provisions in your operating agreement designed to satisfy the current federal rules may continue to be required under state law, or you may wish to keep once originally tax-driven provisions in your agreement for nontax, practical reasons. For example, the tear-out operating agreements in Appendix C require a membership vote to approve the transfer of memberships and to avoid dissolution of the LLC after a member departs. These procedures are currently required for pass-through tax status under the tax classification rules discussed in this chapter, but should continue to be useful to your LLC even if they eventually lose their tax relevance.

The business press and your accountant can keep you informed of the progress of this federal check-the-box tax proposal. When updated information on this issue is available, it will be published in the *Nolo News*, a quarterly newspaper published by Nolo Press (see registration card in this book for a free two-year subscription). In addition, new editions of this book will reflect future changes, so also keep an eye on the catalog included as part of the Nolo News to keep your LLC and its paperwork in tune with future tax developments.

A. Benefits of Pass-Through Tax Status

We've already discussed the importance of pass-through tax classification for your LLC earlier in this book, but let us repeat our basic points. Pass-through tax status will allow you to enjoy the tax advantages of a partnership. If you fail to qualify for pass-through tax status, your LLC will be taxed as a corporation, and you will lose the main tax advantage associated with this way of doing business.

It follows that your most important tax planning task is to make sure your LLC will be treated by the IRS (and, if applicable, the state) as a pass-through tax entity. Frankly, this task will also require you to expend the most cerebral calories (brainwork) in the LLC formation process. Fortunately, the rest of the job primarily consists of routine legal paperwork.

Consider seeing an LLC tax or legal advisor. Every business has unique tax circumstances, and the tax information in this chapter is subject to change (see the sidebar titled "Proposed IRS Check-the-Box Tax Classification Scheme"). For these reasons, it's a good precaution to have your LLC tax or legal advisor review your LLC plan—particularly your tax choices (discussed further below)—before you file your Articles of Organization. (You'll learn how to file LLC Articles as part of Chapter 4.)

B. How to Qualify for Pass-Through Tax Status

The key to having your LLC treated by the IRS as a pass-through tax entity is to make sure it doesn't resemble a corporation for tax purposes. Specifically, your LLC must have no more than two out of four traditional tax characteristics associated with corporations. (To read the technical language of each characteristic, see Income Tax Regulation §301.7701-2.) The four corporate characteristics are:

1. *Limited liability.* Under state law, no owner is personally liable for the debts of the business. Traditionally, this has been the big advantage of the corporate form.
2. *Centralized management.* Less than all of the owners are in charge of managing the business. Typically, corporations are managed by a select few, often nonowners in larger corporations, known as directors.
3. *Continuity of life.* The departure of an owner—due to retirement, death or other reasons—does not cause the business to dissolve. Corporations continue despite sales of shares or the loss of individual owners.
4. *Free transferability of interests.* Each owner may transfer his or her interest in the business to an outsider without obtaining approval of the other owners. Except for closely held (very small) corporations, most corporations allow shares to be sold by the owners at will.

DO YOU NEED A TAX RULING FROM THE IRS?

Much of the tax information concerning LLCs in this chapter is taken directly from IRS Revenue Procedure 95-10, designed to show you how to comply with technical IRS requirements. We include a copy of Revenue Procedure 95-10 in Appendix B. If you glance through this Revenue Procedure, you'll notice that it discusses the circumstances under which the IRS will issue a ruling on—that is, tell you ahead of time—whether your LLC will be treated by the IRS as a partnership pass-through tax entity (this is what you want) or as a corporation (what you don't want).

Most people who form LLCs will not need an IRS ruling, because the information contained in IRS Revenue Procedure 95-10 clearly spells out rules that should guarantee pass-through tax status. Obtaining a ruling from the IRS is usually only necessary for those adventuresome few who wish to structure their LLCs so as to push the edge of the tax and legal envelopes. Not surprisingly, people in this group usually work with a lawyer or tax advisor to think up a particularly inventive or convoluted structure for their LLCs.

For your LLC to be treated by the IRS (and most state tax departments) as a pass-through entity, it must have less than a majority of the above corporate characteristics. In other words, *two out of four is OK—but absolutely no more.* If, like most LLCs, you can avoid three out of the four (this isn't necessary, but it may help you feel safer in case the IRS decides that your LLC has a corporate characteristic you didn't think it had), then you're batting 100%. (Mathematically it's 75%, we know, but the kind of LLC we're talking about almost always will choose to have the corporate characteristic of limited liability, so restricting yourself to this one corporate characteristic is usually the best you can do.)

In the sections below, we discuss ways to help maximize your chance of getting pass-through tax status for your LLC. We take a conservative approach, showing you how to avoid the maximum number of corporate characteristics based upon the sure-fire "safe-harbor" (recognized rules that show you one way to obtain a desired tax status or result) provisions of IRS Revenue Procedure 95-10. But realize that, if necessary, you may be able to wander fairly far from the shores of this safe-harbor procedure and still qualify for LLC pass-through tax status. You are free to try other—often less certain—paths to setting up your LLC. Again, to protect your interests, any variances to our approach should be under the guidance of an LLC tax or legal advisor.

Special rules for manager-managed LLCs. Under special tax rules in Revenue Procedure 95-10, manager-managed LLCs can decide to vote to continue the LLC only after a member-manager (not just any member) leaves the LLC. They can also decide to have the membership vote to approve transfers of memberships by member-managers only. We show manager-managed LLCs how to adopt these special voting rules in Chapter 6. For now, we just want to warn you that if you set up a manager-managed LLC and adopt either of these special rules, you must have at least one member on your management team. We repeat this advice in the appropriate sections of Chapter 6 as well. (By the way, not having at least one member on a management team is unlikely for smaller LLCs—after all, would you really want your LLC completely managed by outsiders with no input from the owners? We think not.)

"BULLETPROOF" AND "FLEXIBLE" STATE LLC STATUTES

Business and legal articles covering LLCs often use the terms "bulletproof" and "flexible" to refer to state LLC laws. For our purposes, these labels are inexact and potentially confusing, so we neither use nor place much significance on them. However, here's what you can usually expect these terms to mean if you encounter them in other LLC materials:

- *Bulletproof states.* When you form an LLC in a "bulletproof" state, you automatically avoid two of the four corporate characteristics. State statutory rules qualify your LLC for pass-through tax treatment with the IRS, and you are not allowed to vary these rules in your operating agreement.
- *Flexible states.* In other states, known as "flexible" states, state LLC statutes provide leeway for LLC owners to decide how to handle some or all of the characteristics treated in IRS guidelines. Of course, this increases the possibility that you'll end up choosing options that do not avoid at least two corporate characteristics—in which case, you will not be eligible for pass-through tax treatment.

As mentioned, we don't adopt these terms in this book because they mean different things to different LLC analysts. For example, a "bulletproof" state may refer to one whose statutes follow the minimum or the maximum requirements of the IRS procedure to qualify for favorable pass-through tax status. Similarly, the "flexible" label can mean you may vary the state rules for all corporate characteristics or just some of them.

1. Limited Liability

As a matter of state law, LLC members enjoy limited liability: protection from personal liability for the business's debts and claims. This characteristic is one of the big benefits of forming an LLC, and we suggest you keep and make the most of this valuable LLC trait.

Exceptionally few LLCs want any members to be personally liable for business debts. Except for the oddball exception, all small LLC owners want personal limited liability status for all members and can skip to Section B2, below. Only a very, very few would even consider the possibility of making any LLC members personally liable for LLC operations and liabilities, and may be interested in reading the special rules below on making one person personally liable for LLC debts.

In an effort to entice investor-owners to feel more comfortable putting funds into the LLC enterprise, some LLC promoters may be willing to accept personal liability for business debts and obligations, much like a general partner of a limited partnership. Here are some legal and tax questions to consider if you are asked to take this approach with your LLC:

- *Does your state law permit one or more LLC members to disclaim limited liability in LLC documents?* Only Delaware, Florida, Iowa, Texas and Virginia will let you form an LLC without limited liability by allowing members to disclaim it in the LLC's Articles of Organization or operating agreement. It's not clear whether members in other states can disclaim limited liability. If this interests you, consult a lawyer.
- *Is one member willing to accept all liability?* IRS Revenue Procedure 95-10 allows an LLC to tinker with, and still avoid the corporate characteristic of, limited liability by having one member assume all of the LLC's liabilities. This member must maintain at least a 1% interest in the LLC and have a minimum capital account balance in the LLC of at least 1% of all LLC capital account balances or $500,000, whichever is less. (There are other requirements; see Revenue Procedure 95-10 in Appendix B for additional details.)

Example: Career Caterers, an LLC, wants to make one of its members exclusively liable for LLC debts and claims. It also wants to avoid the corporate characteristic of limited liability, having concluded that it's more important to have two of the other three corporate characteristics in its quest to qualify for pass-through tax treatment. One of Career Caterers' organizers checks with a small business lawyer with LLC experience to be sure it's legal under the state's LLC act for one member to be made liable for all LLC debts in the Articles of Organization. The LLC's tax advisor agrees that this can be done in compliance with IRS Revenue Procedure 95-10 and makes sure that the member qualifies under the specific rules of this tax procedure so that the LLC will avoid the corporate characteristic of limited liability.

Lack of limited liability does not necessarily eliminate the LLC as the business entity of choice. For instance, an LLC without limited liability may still be preferable to a limited partnership. Even if an LLC member agrees to be personally liable for business debts (like the general partner in a limited partnership), all other LLC members can still participate in management—an option not generally available to limited partners, where anyone who participates in management ordinarily loses limited liability status. (Limited partnerships are covered in Chapter 1, Section D4.)

2. Centralized Management

Under most state LLC acts, all members are responsible for managing the LLC unless a special management team is selected in the LLC's Articles of Organization or operating agreement. This means you automatically avoid the corporate characteristic of centralized management unless you go to the trouble of selecting a management team. Most smaller LLC owners will accept this every-owner-a-manager rule without modification, because it corresponds with the natural desire of owners to actively participate in running their LLC.

Exception for Minnesota. The Minnesota LLC Act (Section 322B.606) requires the management of a Minnesota LLC by a board of governors. Presumably, if you appoint all your members (and no one else) to the board of governors, your Minnesota LLC will be treated by the IRS as a member-managed (not manager-run) LLC, without centralized management.

Some larger LLCs may want to adopt a centralized management structure by making their LLC manager-managed. Picking a special management team normally only makes sense for LLCs with a large number of members who cannot all participate in running the LLC, or LLCs with passive investors who wish to contribute capital as members but don't want to make decisions or commit time to running the LLC.

If you have a good reason to select managers, you probably want to know if there is any way to select a management team and still avoid the corporate characteristic of centralized management. The equivocal answer is "maybe." Under Revenue Procedure 95-10, the IRS may say yes—you avoid the characteristic of centralized management—if the managers collectively own at least 20% of the interests of the LLC (in other words, the more *member-managers* on your management team, the better). The idea is that the greater the ownership interests of managers, the more the LLC avoids looking like a corporation, where nonowner directors often run the show (at least in larger, publicly held corporations).

To decide whether or not your LLC has centralized management, the IRS will assess all the facts and circumstances of its structure and operation. The IRS will pay special attention to whether the positions of member-managers in management are secure. The LLC starts to look more like a corporation as far as centralized management if member-managers' positions are relatively insecure—for example, if:

- members can vote member-managers in and out of office, or
- nonmanager members (those members who do not also serve as managers) have authority to remove the member-managers on their own.

If your situation resembles either of the above, there is no safe-harbor rule that you can absolutely rely on ahead of time to avoid the corporate characteristic of centralized management.

Example: Fred, Herb's father-in-law, agrees to invest $50,000 for a 75% interest in Herb's business venture, Ends of the Earth Tours & Travel LLC, as long as Fred will not be asked to get involved in any decision-making. Herb, the only other member, owns 25% of the LLC, which will be managed by Herb and two nonmember managers. Ends of the Earth may be able to rely on Revenue Procedure 95-10 to avoid the corporate characteristic of centralized management, since Herb owns more than a 20% stake in the LLC. But this beneficial tax result will not be possible if Fred, a nonmanager member, is allowed to oust Herb from the management team, or if an at-large membership vote is taken to periodically reelect the managers (including Herb, who is a member-manager). These special management rules can be tricky, and the application of the ruling to different scenarios is imprecise, so read Revenue Ruling 95-10 in Appendix B for more details, and check with your tax advisor if you face a situation similar to Herb's and Fred's.

How to set up a manager-managed LLC. In Chapter 6, we show you how to adopt an operating agreement with a management structure (instead of management by all LLC members, which we cover in Chapter 5).

3. Continuity of Life

Most LLCs will easily be able to avoid this corporate characteristic. Continuity of life means that the legal form of the business will continue despite changes in ownership, which pretty much describes the corporate form. By contrast, in a partnership, the departure of a general partner technically causes the partnership to legally dissolve. (As an aside, most partnerships get around this by including boilerplate language in their partnership agreements that says the partnership does not legally terminate when a partner leaves.)

Here's how the IRS frames the issue of continuity of life in Revenue Procedure 95-10. An LLC lacks continuity of life if the death, insanity, bankruptcy, retirement, resignation or expulsion of an LLC member will cause the dissolution of the LLC, unless a majority in interest of the remaining members votes to continue the LLC. (We explain what a majority in interest means in the context of preparing your operating agreement in Chapters 5 and 6.)

Example: Five people form Rotorheads Flying Corps LLC, a helicopter tour and sling-load contracting company. All members are high-time helicopter pilots who will manage and work in the business. Rotorheads' operating agreement specifies that the LLC will dissolve if any member dies, resigns, retires, is expelled, goes bankrupt or insane, or if a person's membership is cancelled for any other reason, voluntarily or involuntarily, unless a majority in interest of the remaining LLC membership votes to continue the legal life of the LLC. Rotorheads should avoid the corporate characteristic of continuity of life.

Most state statutes echo the IRS-specified circumstances that trigger the dissolution of an LLC—known as membership dissociation events—and require the vote of at least a majority in interest of the remaining members to continue the life of the LLC. In fact, most states require—at least as a default rule, which you can override in your operating agreement—the vote of *all* remaining members. (We'll have more to say about these state rules below, as well as in Chapters 5 and 6).

The safe-harbor rule in Revenue Procedure 95-10 does not contain the exclusive ways for your LLC to avoid having the characteristic of continuity of life. You could specify that your LLC will dissolve, unless a vote is taken to continue it, upon the happening of other significant events. The IRS should still agree that your LLC lacks the corporate characteristic of continuity of life as long as the terminating events have a reasonable chance of occurring. You cannot, however, use some contingency with a slim chance of happening—say a solar eclipse on January 1 or an earthquake during the seventh game of a world series two years in a row.

Example: The members of a car dealership LLC decide their LLC will dissolve unless they vote to continue it when and if the new car line they promote is discontinued by the manufacturer. Given the uncertainties of the automobile marketplace, the IRS should agree that dissolution is a real possibility in this particular circumstance.

a. LLC Does Not Have to Dissolve When a Member Departs

Probably one reason why so many people are disgusted with America's legal and tax systems is that they often create nonsensical rules—and then loopholes to avoid the rules. A good example in the world of LLCs is that an LLC can avoid the corporate characteristic of continuity of life (to qualify for pass-through tax status), without having to dissolve when a member leaves. Under this particular loophole, a member's departure must simply *trigger a voting procedure to extend the life of the LLC*. In that event, a majority in interest of the remaining membership votes is required to continue the LLC.

What's the bottom line? To avoid the corporate characteristic of continuity of life, your LLC operating agreement must require that your members vote to continue the LLC's legal life when a member (or a member-manager in a manager-run LLC, covered below) leaves due to the member's resignation, retirement, expulsion, death, bankruptcy or insanity. Although IRS rules require the vote of a majority in interest of the remaining members in these situations, we recommend that you have *all* remaining members vote to keep the LLC alive. This makes it simpler and safer, with no need to worry about the technical definition of a "majority in interest" when a membership vote is taken to continue the life of the LLC. This unanimous vote requirement also comports with the standard default rule found in state LLC Acts for handling continuity of life: most states say that a unanimous vote of the remaining members is necessary to continue the life of the LLC after a member is dissociated. (In the state sheets in Appendix A, we call this state LLC Act rule the "Default Continuation Rule" and tell you whether you are free to vary it—specify a lesser vote requirement—in your operating agreement.)

Example: Harley and two of his MBA business school buddies form Publications Trends Ltd. Liability Co. Their first endeavor is to publish Brew Scoop Monthly, *a magazine devoted to seeking out, sampling and reviewing the workproduct of micro beer breweries throughout the state. The magazine makes a very small splash among the brewery trade and public readership, and can't muster the advertising revenue necessary to continue monthly publication. At this point, the company is reorganized. Harley leaves to pursue other entrepreneurial opportunities, and his two co-owners buy out his share of the business, deciding to publish a business journal instead.* Hi-Tech Prognostics Quarterly *will provide analysis and opinion on upcoming initial public offerings by high-tech companies throughout the country, and hopefully achieve a wider readership and advertising revenue base than the LLC's previous publication effort. Following Harvey's resignation, the two remaining members follow the requirements of their operating agreement and sign a statement formally approving the continuance of the legal existence of the LLC. This document is placed in the LLC records book, and business life goes on at company headquarters.*

SOME STATES REQUIRE OR SPECIFY LLC ENDING DATE

In the "old days" (for LLC statutes, the distant past is the early 1990s), before the IRS made its position clear on how to avoid the corporate characteristic of continuity of life, many state LLC statutes took an extremely conservative approach in trying to limit the life of the LLC (intended to help the LLC qualify for partnership-type tax treatment). They did this in a couple of ways:

- The brute-force approach adopted by a few of the first LLC states automatically limited the life of LLCs formed in the state to a term of 30 years from the date of formation.
- A slightly less restrictive approach was followed by other states, requiring LLCs to limit their legal life in the Articles of Organization to any term of years or to any date in the future.

Today we know that neither of these approaches is necessary to avoid continuity of life with the IRS. So, if you live in a state that still asks you to specify a future date in your Articles of Organization when your LLC will legally terminate (many still do), you can make it a date so far ahead that it will have no practical effect—say December 31, 2099. If you have the good fortune to survive this date (those anti-oxidant supplement tablets may really work!), you can file an amendment of your Articles with your state's LLC filing office to "update" this provision. Similarly, if your Articles of Organization must state that your LLC legally terminates in 30 years, don't be concerned. If you are still in business, you can amend your Articles to extend the life of your LLC before it automatically self-destructs.

b. Special Rules for Continuing the Legal Life of a Manager-Managed LLC

If your LLC adopts a management structure, instead of management by all members, your LLC can choose to vote to continue the legal life of the LLC only when a member-manager (a member who is also one of the managers) dies, retires, resigns, goes bankrupt, goes insane, or is expelled—instead of having to vote when any member leaves.

There are a couple of additional requirements if your manager-run LLC adopts this alternate approach:

- *The LLC's dissolution provisions must be tied to the loss of membership of any member-manager (not just one or a select group of member-managers).* In other words, when the membership of anyone who is both a member and a manager is terminated, the remaining members must vote to continue the existence of the LLC or it will dissolve.
- *A majority in interest of the remaining members must vote to approve the continuance of the LLC after a member-manager leaves.* The vote cannot, for example, be confined to the remaining members who are also managers. (See Chapter 6, Section B3, Special Instruction Ⓜ, where we discuss how to set up your management operating agreement this way.).

Example: Too Cool Limited Liability Company ("TC") manufactures refrigeration equipment and is managed by Vince, one of its founding members, and by Janet, a nonmember who is also the general manager of NovelPro, a limited partnership investment group that supplied venture capital funds to the LLC. TC's operating agreement says that the LLC will dissolve when any member-manager loses his or her membership, unless all remaining members vote to continue the legal existence of the LLC. This arrangement should satisfy the requirements of the tax rules and enable TC to avoid the characteristic of continuity of life.

4. Free Transferability of Interests

Free transferability of interests refers to a member's right to freely and easily sell or otherwise transfer all ownership rights associated with membership in the LLC, including voting and management rights. (As discussed in Section B4a, below, this does not affect a member's right to sell or transfer *economic interests* only in the LLC.)

Most LLC owners will want to avoid this corporate characteristic—that is, they will want to limit the transferability of membership rights to help qualify for pass-through tax status, as well as to allow nonselling members the right to approve new members who are transferred interests in the LLC. IRS Revenue Procedure 95-10 has safe-harbor rules regarding free transferability of interests. Here's how this issue is addressed:

- *Member-managed LLCs.* If members owning more than 20% of all LLC interests (capital, income, gain, loss, credits and deductions) cannot transfer their membership rights without the consent of at least a majority of the nontransferring members, the LLC will lack this corporate trait. (Chapter 5, Section C, Special Instruction 36 explain the three formulas you can use to compute a majority of the nontransferring members—for now, it's enough to know that one of these definitions is "a majority of the number of nontransferring members.")
- *Manager-managed LLCs.* LLCs with appointed managers will lack free transferability of interests if any member owning more than 20% of all interests in the LLC is restricted from transferring his or her membership without the approval of a majority of nontransferring member-managers. That is, approval of the transfer must be made by one or more remaining members who are also managers.

What if sole member-manager is dissociated? Revenue Procedure 95-10 does not address what will happen if the sole member-manager of an LLC departs, dies or is otherwise dissociated. Arguably, as long as a vote would have been required to continue the LLC if there had been any nontransferring member-managers, no actual voting is necessary in this case. We don't like the way this sounds or looks, however, and we think it best under these circumstances to have the other members (the remaining nonmanaging members of the LLC) approve the transfer. If this is an issue for your LLC, ask your tax advisor for further clarification.

For the average LLC run by a small group of family, friends or business associates, limiting the sale and transfer of LLC voting and management interests by members (by requiring the approval of nontransferring members or member-managers) will not present a problem. For starters, members of smaller LLCs almost always prefer a rule that prevents an owner from transferring LLC management and voting rights to outsiders without the consent of other members. After all, most small business owners want co-managers with whom they have developed a personal and business relationship—and, at the very least, won't like the idea of having a stranger join their ranks without getting to vote "yes" or "no" to the new person. Finally, an interest in an LLC is not very marketable, anyway. It's not as though requiring a vote to admit a new member will discourage throngs of outsiders looking for an easy way to buy into your LLC.

a. Transfer of Economic Interests Not Restricted

The transferability of interest approval rules discussed above restrict the sale of *membership rights* only—namely, the right to manage and vote in the LLC. They do not restrict the transfer of *economic* rights attached to memberships in the LLC, which generally include the rights to receive profit and/or capital distributions from the LLC. In other words, members may be given free rein in your operating agreement to sell, pledge, transfer or otherwise dispose of their economic interests in the LLC without the approval of other members or member-managers, without affecting your LLC's ability to avoid the corporate characteristic of free transferability of interests.

Example: Marjorie is a one-fifth owner in Stolid Engineering Limited Liability Co. She signs an agreement with her daughter, Elizabeth, agreeing to give Elizabeth half of her annual LLC profits in any year that Elizabeth earns a 3.0 or better grade point average in college. This is a transfer of an economic interest only; Elizabeth does not get to vote or manage the LLC as a member. An agreement of this sort does not need to be approved by the other members in Marjorie's LLC to pass muster with the IRS and avoid the corporate characteristic of free transferability of interests.

b. If You Want Free Transferability of Interests

You can form an LLC without limiting the transfer or sale of membership interests and still qualify for pass-through tax status as long as you avoid two of the other three corporate characteristics set out in Sections B1, B2 and B3, above. If, however, you have not avoided at least two corporate tax aspects, or you simply want an extra measure of safety in qualifying for pass-through tax treatment for your LLC (which we recommend), give some serious thought to this aspect of your LLC and discuss it with the other LLC members.

If you are set on starting a business where you want owners to have a free hand in transferring all incidents of ownership in the business—management and voting rights, as well as capital and profits interests—without approval by other members, you may need to rethink your decision to form an LLC. Tax angles aside, perhaps forming a regular C corporation with freely transferable shares of voting stock makes more sense for you and the other owners. It's also possible that you'd be more comfortable with a general or limited partnership. (We cover these different ways of doing business in Chapter 1, Sections D2, D3 and D4.)

Example: Henri and Mimeaux are in the process of organizing Francophilia Specialties LLC, with a proclaimed business purpose as "a retail outlet for all things French." On the Concorde jet that carries H & M back to France on an initial inventory shopping spree, Jacques, a fellow passenger and financial planner who forecasts profits of French start-up ventures, grills Henri on the specifics of the new business. By the time the trio deplanes at De Gaulle Airport, Jacques is sold on the profit potential of the company and is convinced he can round up an investment pool among his French business contacts. However, he wants H & M to assume all management and personal legal responsibilities for the business, and be willing to accede to the financial controls and fiscal oversight the investment group undoubtedly will require the duo to adopt in their business. H & M are delighted with the prospect of a large infusion of cash and decide to put their LLC plans on hold. Assuming Jacques and his associates come through with the francs, they decide a limited partnership venture will be best. This structure will give the investors a limited liability stake in their business, but no management votes. Sure, the couple will be personally liable as general partners for all business debts, but they think this is a reasonable risk to take, given the increased likelihood of success that should follow from the inflow of venture capital funds.

HOW STATES ADDRESS FREE TRANSFERABILITY OF INTERESTS

To help LLCs qualify for pass-through tax status, most states automatically limit the sale of LLC membership rights, saying that they can only be sold with the approval of all nontransferring members. Your state sheet in Appendix A shows your state's default legal rule for handling this issue under the item "Default Transfer Rule" in the "Operating Rules" section. Most states let LLCs change this rule in their Articles of Organization or operating agreement—namely, by allowing less than all members to approve a transfer of membership to a new member.

No matter what your state says, you should always be able to satisfy the IRS pass-through tax qualification requirements and comply with any state legal requirements by requiring the unanimous consent of all nontransferring members to admit a transferee as a new member in your LLC. You'll see in Chapters 5 and 6 that this is exactly the tack we take in our standard operating agreement provisions. (You can lower this unanimous consent requirement if your state sheet says that your state allows it.)

CORPORATE CHARACTERISTICS CHECKLIST

Will your LLC meet the two-out-of-four test? Check the box(es) below for every corporate characteristic your LLC is likely to have. No more than two boxes may be checked for your LLC to qualify for pass-through tax status.

My LLC is likely to have the corporate characteristics of:

☒ Limited Liability ❶

☐ Centralized Management ❷

☐ Continuity of Life ❸

☐ Free Transferability of Interests ❹

C. Will Your LLC Have No More Than Two Corporate Characteristics?

Now that you've read about the four corporate characteristics and recognize that you must avoid at least two of them (and preferably three), here's a Corporate Characteristics Checklist that will help you assess your own LLC. Follow the accompanying Special Instructions and check each box that applies.

SPECIAL INSTRUCTIONS

❶ *Limited Liability.* We've gone ahead and checked this box for you, since all but a very, very few LLCs will wish to take advantage of limited liability protection for their owners. (For special ways to avoid this characteristic and make one member liable for business debts, see Section B1, above.)

❷ *Centralized Management.* Don't check this box if *all* of your members will manage the LLC.

If you select managers for your LLC—consisting of some members and/or nonmembers—generally, you *should* check this box. However, if you select a management team consisting, in whole or in part, of members owning at least a 20% share in your LLC, you may be able to avoid this corporate characteristic—IRS Revenue Procedure 95-10 won't give you an absolute answer, so you will need to make an educated guess in these circumstances. (See Section B2, above, if you aren't sure whether to check this box.)

❸ *Continuity of Life.* Don't check this box if, like most smaller LLCs, your operating agreement will require the vote of *at least* a majority in interest (our tear-out agreements require unanimous approval) of your remaining members to continue the legal existence of your LLC after a member (or a member-manager) resigns, retires, dies, is expelled, or goes bankrupt or insane. (You may be able to substitute other termination events that will trigger a vote to continue the legal existence of the LLC and still be able to avoid this characteristic. See Section B3, above, for more information on this alternative.)

If you don't want the departure of members to trigger a vote to continue the LLC—that is, you want the LLC to continue after members or member-managers leave without the need for approval by remaining members, you will not avoid this corporate characteristic, and should check this box.

❹ *Free Transferability of Interests.* Don't check this box if your operating agreement will require the vote of a majority of nontransferring members (or nontransferring member-managers) for a transferee to be admitted as a new member into your LLC. Most smaller LLCs won't mind requiring this approval, and will leave this box blank. Remember, your operating agreement can allow members to transfer their *economic* rights to LLC profits or capital distributions to outsiders (our tear-out agreements do) without requiring the vote of nontransferring members or member-managers, and you can still leave this box blank. (Refer to the discussion on free transferability of interests in Section B4, above.)

If, on the other hand, you wish to allow your members to transfer their full membership rights (economic plus voting and management rights) to outsiders without getting permission from the other members or member-managers, you will not avoid this corporate characteristic and should check this box.

If you checked more than two of the four boxes. Don't form an LLC yet. You'll need to reevaluate the way you will handle each corporate characteristic—or at least review our earlier discussions and ask your tax advisor if you can meet one of the special rules for avoiding a corporate characteristic.

D. Other LLC Formation Tax Considerations

Now that we've warmed you up to think about tax technicalities, let's turn to two other tax issues that may arise when you're forming your LLC:

- tax liability for members who are interested in contributing services or property to start the LLC, and
- the division of LLC profits and losses among LLC members.

Specifically, we will focus on questions that are likely to arise as you fill in your LLC operating agreement (as part of Chapter 5 or 6).

Consult your tax advisor for help. Don't get too slowed down by this material. If any point is confusing or raises a red flag as far as organizing your LLC is concerned, ask your tax advisor for more information. There may be alternate ways you can accomplish your objectives without paying higher taxes or causing extra complications with the IRS. The types of questions raised here relate to partnership tax law (the LLC unfortunately inherits all the complexities associated with this pre-existing area). This field is a specialty all to itself, so if your questions are important enough, it makes sense to buy yourself some specialized legal or tax advice to find an answer. (See Chapter 8, and think about asking your regular LLC legal or tax advisor for a referral to a partnership tax specialist.)

1. Capital Contributions of Services or Property

Let's start with some background on how start-up LLCs are usually funded. The initial members, like partners in a partnership, ordinarily make financial contributions to the business. In return, each member normally gets a percentage (capital) interest in the LLC. This capital interest reflects how much of the assets a member is entitled to when the business is sold, and establishes a value for the membership interest when it is sold prior to a sale of the LLC itself. For example, a member having a 50% capital interest in an LLC receives $25,000 when the business (which has no bills to pay) sells for $50,000 (an over-simplified example, but one that makes our basic point).

In addition to receiving a stake in the LLC's assets upon distribution—a so-called capital interest—LLC members are also entitled to share in its profits and losses. Typically, divisions of profits and losses parallel LLC members' capital interests, although they may be distributed disproportionately. Disproportionate splitting of profits and losses is called "special allocations" under the tax law and is subject to special rules discussed below in Section D2.

Example 1: Tony and Lisa set up Elk-n-Stuff LLC. Both members contribute equal amounts of start-up capital. In their operating agreement, Tony and Lisa agree that each member has a 50% capital interest and will receive 50% of the business's profits (or losses, if antler-shaped back scratchers, wapiti-musk potpourri, coyote-call whoopee cushions and other mountain-state miscellany merchandised by the LLC don't sell as well as they expect).

Example 2: Tony and Lisa set up the same Elk-n-Stuff LLC, but this time Tony puts up the cash, while Lisa signs a promissory note to contribute cash in installments over the first two years of LLC life. They agree that Tony will have a 50% capital interest and will receive 75% of the business's profits (or losses) for the first two years. Lisa will have a 50% capital interest and will get 25% of the business's profits (or losses) during the business's initial two years—after that, both members will split LLC profits and losses 50-50.

Under most state statutes, members may make capital contributions of cash, property or services—or the promise to provide any of these in the future. As we discuss in the remainder of this section, any member who contributes property or services should take into account several important tax considerations. Your state sheet in Appendix A alerts you to any special contribution rules or restrictions in your state. For example, a few states prohibit or restrict capitalizing an LLC with (issuing memberships in return for) a promise to pay cash, property or services later, after the LLC is set up. If your state has such a rule, we list it under the item "Special Statutory Rules" in the "Operating Rules" section of your state sheet.

If all LLC members will contribute cash. When all members contribute cash, or a promise to contribute cash in the future (usually in the form of a promissory note—but check your state sheet in Appendix A to make sure your state does not prohibit or restrict the use of promissory notes to fund an LLC), there are no special tax consequences. Skip below to Section D2, to read about special profits and loss rules that may affect your LLC.

a. Contribution of Services

If a person is given a capital interest in an LLC in return for the performance of services, the IRS views the transaction as payment for personal services rendered. This means the member has to pay income taxes on the value of the membership, just as any other worker would upon receiving payment for services performed. In other words, the moment LLC members create and sign an operating agreement allocating capital contributions in exchange for a member's (generally future, unpaid) services, the member agrees to be hit with a personal income tax bill for the value of the services.

Example: Five Austin computer programmers start Future Tex LLC. Four put up $20,000 each as their 20% capital contributions. Cash-strapped Sharon is allotted her 20% membership in exchange for a promise to work for the company for six months without pay. The IRS considers this $20,000 allocation as Sharon's personal income. She will be liable for personal income taxes on the entire $20,000 (estimated and paid by her during the year).

Reporting and paying personal service income on the value of the capital interest in an LLC is normally doubly painful to the service-member, who generally has to wait to receive income from the LLC before he or she can afford to pay the taxes that result from joining the LLC. Fortunately, there are several ways around this income tax liability problem:

- *Member may be given a profits interest only.* If a member who's contributing services is given only an interest in the profits of the LLC, but not a capital (percentage) interest in LLC assets, income taxes normally are not due until profits are actually paid to the member. This may be easier for the member, who should at least receive some cash closer to the time when taxes must be paid.

Example: Hubert Allis Overalls, Ltd. Co., a supplier of denim fabric to clothes manufacturers, brings Hank Allis (son of founding member Hubert) to help run the LLC. Business is busting at the rivets, with HAO supplying fabric to all leading domestic brand-name jeans manufacturers. In return for signing a ten-year employment contract, Hank is given a 25% stake in LLC profits, plus a guaranteed annual salary. Because Hank does not receive a capital interest in the LLC, he will not be taxed up front on his promise to perform services for HAO.

- *Member may get a loan from the LLC, another member or an outside source to buy a capital interest for cash.* To help define and secure repayment of the loan, the member may be asked by the lender to sign a promissory note specifying repayment terms, including interest. He or she may also be required to pledge property as security for repayment.

Example: Bella and Xavier form Happy Hoofs Equestrian Academy and Stables LLC, with the idea of operating a horse-riding and boarding facility in the rolling foothills of Mesa de Oro, California. Bella can contribute $50,000 in cash and property as her stake in the new business—enough to finance a down-payment on a well-situated, if weather-worn, barn with surrounding acreage that can be converted to a stable with riding trails. Xavier is low on funds, but champing at the bit with energy that he'll use to fix up and convert the farm. Bella agrees to loan Xavier the money to become a cash member of the LLC at the start. Xavier will receive a capital interest without having to pay *taxes on the value of the future services he promises to perform for the LLC. Instead, as Xavier gets paid for his services, he can pay Bella back (of course, he'll also pay individual income taxes on the salary the LLC pays him).*

- *Member may buy into membership later.* Yet another approach is for a member wannabe to hold off joining the LLC until he or she has the cash to buy in. For example, a person can enter the LLC ranks as an employee, and buy a capital interest in the LLC (assuming the members agree) with savings the employee socks away out of earned LLC salary.

Example: Let's return to the Happy Hoofs Equestrian Academy and Stables LLC. Bella and her husband, Clyde, form the LLC as the two initial members. Xavier bides his time to buy into the LLC. He does not become a member right away, but simply works for the ranch as a regular employee and saves his money. When Xavier has sufficient cash, he buys out Clyde's capital interest in the LLC.

If you want to bring in members who will contribute services in return for a capital and/or profits interest in the LLC. One of the flexibilities granted LLCs is their ability to admit members who have worked or will work for the LLC. However, as highlighted above, there are tax issues to resolve first. Again, ask your tax advisor about the best way to handle each service member in your LLC.

b. Capital Contribution of Property to an LLC

Tax technicalities also arise when a member wants to contribute property to the LLC that has appreciated (increased in value) since the time he or she purchased, inherited or otherwise received title to the property. Ordinarily, this will involve real property—an interest in land or a building—although this discussion applies to any appreciated personal property (collectibles, airplanes, and so on). Below, we quickly look at a few of the tax issues involved with this kind of transaction and alert you to check the tax ramifications with a tax advisor before you set up your LLC with contributions of property.

First the good news. Contributions of property to an LLC are generally tax-free at the time they occur. The tax consequences are generally realized later when the LLC or a member's interest in it is sold. (By the way, this is one benefit of forming a pass-through tax business such as an LLC or partnership. Corporations are not so kindly treated; transfers of property to a corporation must pass muster under technical "control tests" required by Internal Revenue Code (IRC) Section 351 to be tax-free.)

The not-so-good news is that taxes on the appreciation (increase in value) that occurred prior to the property's transfer to the LLC must eventually be paid. The transferring member will be liable for taxes when the LLC is sold or when the member sells his or her LLC interest. This is accomplished by having the property owner's income tax basis (known simply as "basis") in the property carry over to his or her basis in the LLC. Only when the membership interest is sold will the basis of the membership be used to determine how much tax the owner must pay. The result is that taxes due from appreciation on the property transferred to the LLC are paid later by the member when he or she sells an LLC membership, not when it is contributed to the LLC. The following example illustrates how this works.

Example: Jim owns a building he bought for $20,000. It is worth $120,000 when he transfers it to his newly formed LLC (it has appreciated $100,000). For the transfer of this property, he receives a $120,000 capital stake in his LLC. Jim's "basis" in the property is $20,000 (his cost—we are being very simplistic and assuming there have been no adjustments to basis; in real life, basis increases with capital improvements and decreases as depreciation is taken on property). Jim pays no taxes at the time of transfer, but his basis in his LLC membership becomes $20,000 (again, his basis in the real property at the time of transfer).

Assuming no further adjustments to Jim's basis in his LLC (another unrealistic but convenient assumption), when the LLC is liquidated or sold, or when Jim sells his interest in the LLC to another person, his amount of gain—the amount he will have to pay taxes on—will equal the amount he receives for the sale of his LLC interest minus the amount of his basis in the interest. In other words, if Jim decides to retire from his LLC and sell his interest back to the other members for $120,000 (assuming his interest is worth the same amount when he sells as when he bought it), then he will have to report a gain of $100,000 and pay taxes on that amount at the time of sale. As you can see, Jim doesn't avoid taxes by selling his building to the LLC; he simply transfers his basis in the appreciated property to his LLC interest, and pays taxes on this appreciation later when his LLC interest is sold.

Be sure you understand the tax consequences before transferring real property to an LLC. There are additional complexities when real property is contributed to an LLC. For example, separate tax issues arise when real property is encumbered (subject to a mortgage or other debt), as it usually is. Not only does this liability need to be reflected as a liability on the LLC books, it also has bearing on gains or losses realized by LLC members when the business or membership interests are later sold. Before transferring property to your LLC, ask your tax advisor about any immediate and deferred tax consequences.

2. Special Allocations of LLC Profits and Losses

Like partnerships, LLCs are subject to special IRS rules if members decide not to follow the standard practice of splitting up profits and losses proportionately with each member's capital contribution. The disproportionate splitting of profits and losses is known as a "special allocation." For example, a special allocation would take place if an LLC allocates a member who contributes 10% of the initial LLC cash or assets a 20% share of profits and losses.

Although special allocations are perfectly legal, the IRS has pages upon pages of regulations designed to handle them. Basically, these regulations say that for special allocations of profits and losses to be valid (recognized and accepted by the IRS), they must have "substantial economic effect." This jargon refers to the fact that the IRS wants you to divide up profits and losses to reflect some economic reality of the enterprise. In other words, special allocations should not be made simply to lessen the tax burden of the owners. For instance, the IRS might balk if, without further justification, an LLC allocated all its losses to a member with significant income from non-LLC sources, simply so that member can fully deduct these losses and scale down on his or her personal income taxes.

Example: Up Up and Away Ventures, LLC, is a passive investment company that puts investors' money into business operations run by others. Its prime money-makers are multi-tiered car parking garages located in inner city business districts, plus a widely dispersed network of vending machines installed at suburban shopping malls. Joe and Kenneth have invested equally, and each holds a 50% capital interest in the business. Joe wants the parking lot income each year and Kenneth wants the vending machine profits (let's just say Joe likes cars and Ken has a thing for vending machines, or more likely, their accountants see this as the best way for each to maximize personal income and minimize taxes on their individual tax returns). Will the IRS object? Probably, unless there are additional facts we don't know about—or the LLC follows special IRS rules, discussed just below. Because neither Joe nor Kenneth is involved with either operation personally, and neither is specifically on the hook (at risk) for losses involved with a particular side of the business, there seems to be no reasonable business reason—no substantial economic reason or effect—associated with this allocation.

a. IRS Regulations Permit Special Allocations

Now that we've told you how the IRS rules are supposed to operate, we are going to turn the tables again and explain that you can allocate profits and losses any way you want and the IRS will still say that your allocations have substantial economic effect. How is this possible, you reasonably ask? Again, the simple answer is that complicated tax rules have been designed to be broken (by lawyers and accountants who charge handsomely to show you how).

Here's how this major loophole works. If your operating agreement recites special language taken from the 75 or so pages of special IRS regulations adopted under Section 704(b) of the Internal Revenue Code (these are the special allocations regulations), then all of your special allocations will have "substantial economic effect" under the Internal Revenue Code (even if they don't in real life) and will not be challenged by the IRS.

Example: Cuneiform Widgets Works Ltd. Liability Co. is founded by Sol Shimmaker. The business makes wedge-shaped objects of all descriptions, including a unique form-fitting door stopper named the Toe-Hold 2000. Expanding orders spur Sol on to seek additional capital to retool and expand CWW's fabrication facilities. Arnie and Lillian have the bucks, and agree to contribute an amount of cash equal to one-half of the existing capital of the enterprise. They insist, however, on receiving a five-year 65% profits interest in the Toe-Hold 2000, plus a 50% share of net profits derived from other CWW product sales. Is there any substantial economic reason for this special splitting of profits to the new investors? Let's assume there isn't. The LLC protects itself from IRS challenge to these special allocations of profits by asking its tax advisor to prepare and add the special Internal Revenue Code Section 704(b) language to its operating agreement.

b. Other Special Allocations Considerations

There are some real financial and tax consequences associated with adopting Internal Revenue Code Section 704(b) special allocation regulations in your LLC operating agreement. Generally, the lengthy series of provisions that you must adopt in your operating agreement to satisfy the IRS safe-harbor special allocations rules come down to three basic points:

1. The business's capital accounts must be carried and handled on the financial books under special rules based upon Section 704(b) of the Internal Revenue Code. These rules do *not* follow generally accepted accounting practices (known as "GAAP" in the trade) This is not a particular problem, just a quirk that must be taken into consideration by your tax person.
2. Distributions of cash or property to owners upon liquidation of the business must be made in accordance with capital accounts maintained under Internal Revenue Code Section 704(b), as mentioned just above.
3. When an owner leaves or the business is sold or liquidated, any partners or members with a negative capital account balance (capital accounts go negative if members are allocated losses in excess of their capital account balance) must restore the account to a zero balance. They do this by contributing cash or property equal to their negative capital account balance before their interest or the LLC itself is sold or liquidated.

If you want to make special (disproportionate) allocations of profits or losses in your LLC. Do what a big business would—hand your operating agreement over to a partnership tax specialist to insert the various technical provisions you'll need in order to rely on the IRS safe-harbor rules for special allocations. These rules are lengthy and subject to periodic change. For all these reasons, plus the fact that most smaller LLC owners will not wish to make special allocations of profits and losses, we don't include them in the operating agreements provided in this book.

CHAPTER 4

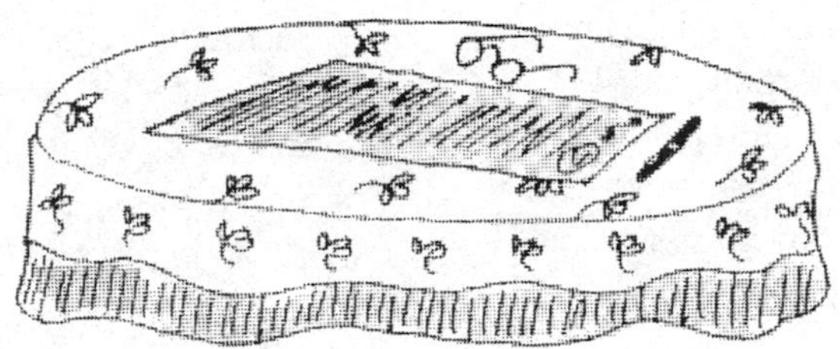

How to Prepare LLC Articles of Organization

In this chapter, we explain how to prepare Articles of Organization for your LLC and file them with your state LLC filing office. Once you perform this important task, your LLC will be a legal entity recognized by your state, as well as other states.

Don't be concerned if your state uses different LLC terminology. Different states use different legalese in their LLC statutes, regulations and bureaucracies. We have tried to use the most common terms to describe LLC documents and offices, but your state may use other language. For example, although we refer to the charter document used to form an LLC as the Articles of Organization, some states use a different name—for example, Delaware, New Hampshire and New Jersey refer to this document as a Certificate of Formation.

A. Read State Sheets and Order LLC Materials

Each state has its own requirements for preparing and filing LLC Articles of Organization. Make sure you follow the steps below to learn about your state's LLC rules. As you'll see, an important part of this process involves contacting your state's LLC filing office to obtain forms and state-specific information.

MATERIALS AVAILABLE FROM LLC FILING OFFICES

Each state's LLC filing office operates a little differently, but most states are likely to supply a number of helpful materials, including:

- fill-in-the-blank or sample LLC Articles of Organization with instructions
- a fee schedule showing current charges for filing, copying and certifying various LLC documents
- forms and instructions to check LLC name availability and reserve an LLC name for your use
- forms and instructions for post-formation procedures—these may include materials to amend LLC Articles, change the LLC's registered office or registered agent, or register an assumed or fictitious LLC name (one that is different from the official LLC name shown in the Articles of Organization), and
- a summary or complete collection of the state's LLC statutes (sometimes available for a small fee). Some states don't supply the statutes, but tell you how to obtain them from a commercial publisher. This material is usually worth having on hand to answer any LLC formation or operation questions that may arise (and eliminate the time necessary to go to the law library or the expense of asking a lawyer each time you need LLC statutory information). The statutes will also help you prepare your own LLC Articles if your state doesn't provide a form.

1. First Read Your State Sheet

Your first step is to locate and carefully read your state sheet in Appendix A. Among other valuable information, your state sheet provides the title, address and phone number of your state's LLC filing office. Most state LLC filing offices are part of the Secretary of State's Division of Corporations office located at the state capitol, but some are a division of the Department of State or a different state office. Many of the more populous states maintain LLC filing branch offices in several cities.

Most states provide their own fill-in-the-blank LLC Articles of Organization form. Some states give a sample form that is completed for a fictional or sample company; you retype the form and provide information that applies to your LLC. State forms are updated regularly, and their accompanying instructions contain the latest information on state filing procedures and fees.

We don't include copies of each state's Articles of Organization form. If your state provides fill-in-the-blank forms, you are better off getting the latest version from your state's LLC filing office when you decide to form an LLC. If your state does not provide its own form, we give information about how to find a ready-made form or how to use the sample Articles of Organization form in Appendix C to meet the requirements in your state.

2. Order LLC Materials

Usually, a phone call is the quickest way to get available LLC information. Your state's LLC filing office phone number is listed on your state sheet in Appendix A. Ask for the LLC materials we list in the sample LLC contact letter shown below.

Sometimes a letter gets better results—for instance, a clerk may be more thorough in sending you each item listed in a written request. In Appendix C, we provide a tear-out LLC contact letter you can use to request specific information on forming an LLC in your state. A sample letter with instructions follows.

SAMPLE LLC CONTACT LETTER

date ______________________

name and address of your state's LLC filing office ______________________

LLC Filings Office:

I am in the process of forming a domestic limited liability company (LLC). Please note:❶

☐ I am *or* ☐ I am not converting an existing **if applicable, specify "general" or "limited"** partnership to an LLC.

☐ I am *or* ☐ I am not forming an LLC to perform the professional services of **if applicable, specify name of profession**, which are licensed by the state.

Please send me the following forms, material and other information:

1. printed, sample or specimen LLC Articles of Organization, with instructions. If your office reviews Articles of Organization for correctness prior to filing, please advise me of the procedure I should follow to obtain this pre-filing review;

2. the telephone number or address I can contact to determine if a proposed limited liability company name is available for my use, plus any forms necessary to reserve an LLC name;

3. a current schedule of fees for LLC filings;

4. other LLC forms and publications provided by your office (or a list of these) for forming, operating and dissolving an LLC in this state; and

5. the name and price of a publication that contains the limited liability company statutes of this state. Please indicate whether it may be ordered from your office or, if applicable, another office or supplier.

If there is a fee for any of the above materials, please advise. Enclosed is a self-addressed, stamped envelope for your reply.

Thank you for your assistance,

your signature❷ ______________________

your name, address and phone number ______________________

____

Enclosure: self-addressed, stamped envelope

SPECIAL INSTRUCTIONS

❶ In the first paragraph, you'll need to check the appropriate boxes to indicate whether or not you are converting an existing partnership to an LLC and whether or not your LLC is being set up to perform state-licensed professional services. The state office will use this information to supply you with the proper form for Articles of Organization. Some states have a special form for forming an LLC that is converting from a general or limited partnership form; some have a separate form for forming a professional LLC.

Here's how to complete the blanks:

- If converting a partnership, insert whether you are converting a "general" or "limited" partnership in the first blank.
- If forming an LLC to practice a state licensed profession, insert the name of the profession in the blank in the second sentence, such as "law," "accounting," "medicine," "engineering" or "architecture."

❷ Sign the letter and fill in your name, address and telephone number in the space provided at the bottom. Enclose a self-addressed, stamped envelope and mail the letter to your LLC filing office, keeping a copy for your own files.

B. Review and Organize Your State's LLC Information

It typically takes about a week to receive materials from a state LLC filing office. Once your materials are in hand, take a little time to check them over. If a requested item is missing—for example, your state sheet shows that your state sends out a sample Articles of Organization form, but this form wasn't included—call the LLC office and ask for the missing item.

Next, get an accordion file or large file folder (or if you are an extra tidy sort, a number of folders) and place all forms, statutes and other legal material you receive from the filing office in it. You may want to organize this material with index tabs or dividers, separating out forms for Articles of Organization, name reservation, fee information and the like. You will need to refer to this information throughout your LLC formation process and don't want to misplace any of it. (We show you how to obtain and set up a formal LLC records book, including one available from Nolo Press, in Chapter 7, Section C4.)

C. Choose a Name for Your LLC

When you prepare your LLC Articles of Organization, you'll need to supply the name of your LLC. If your proposed LLC name, or one similar to it, is already in use by another LLC on file with the LLC filing office, your Articles of Organization will be returned unfiled to you. It pays, therefore, to plan ahead and check the availability of your proposed LLC name before you complete your Articles. Take a little time to read through the material in this section and to choose a good name for your LLC.

1. Important Legal Issues When Choosing an LLC Name

Our primary task is to show you how to choose a name that is acceptable to your state's LLC office when you file your Articles. We don't explore a number of additional potentially complicated and important legal issues that can come into play when you choose and use a business name. The material in this section should guide you in the right direction, but you'll have to go elsewhere for more thorough information.

a. Name Cannot Resemble Another Business's Name

Make sure your proposed name is not very similar to any famous business name (McDonald's, Procter & Gamble, The Quaker Oats Company, Honda and the like). If so, you shouldn't use the name, even if it is available for use by an LLC in your state. Companies with famous names and marks are fanatical about protecting them.

b. Name Cannot Infringe on Trademarks or Service Marks

If your LLC name will be used to identify and market goods and services sold by your LLC, and if this name is the same or similar to one already registered by another business (LLC or otherwise) as a federal or state trademark or service mark, the other business may be able to sue you for trademark or service mark infringement. The infringed business may also stop you from continuing to use your name to market your goods and services, and seek money damages from your LLC.

If you will use your LLC name to market goods and services, we show you several things you can do to help satisfy yourself that your proposed LLC name is not in use by others as a federal trademark or service mark in Section C4, below, but this is just a partial solution. Our best advice to those interested in using an LLC name to market products and services is to read other legal materials specifically written to cover this important area of business law.

How to learn more about trademark law. Our recommendation is to get a copy of *Trademark: How to Name Your Business and Product*, by Kate McGrath and Stephen Elias (Nolo Press), which you can find at the library or purchase using the order form at the back of this book. In addition to educating you about trademark law, the book will help you choose a strong marketing name, search for possibly conflicting trademarks and service marks, and, if the circumstances warrant, register your LLC name as a mark with state and federal trademark agencies. For a general overview of trademark law and other intellectual property law, you may be interested in *Patent, Copyright and Trademark: A Desk Reference to Intellectual Property Law*, by Stephen Elias (Nolo Press).

WHAT ARE TRADEMARKS AND SERVICE MARKS?

A trademark generally consists of a distinctive word, phrase, logo or graphic symbol that is used to identify a product and distinguish it from anyone else's. Well-known trademarks include Ford cars and trucks, IBM computers and Kellogg's cereal.

A service mark promotes services in the same way that a trademark promotes products. Some common service marks are Blue Cross (sells health insurance) and Greyhound (transports people by bus).

c. Other Considerations If Your LLC Name Will Identify Products or Services

Businesses often market goods or services using a name that is different from their company name—for example, Bausch & Lomb manufactures Renu® contact lens cleaner. Companies do, however, frequently use (and register) their business names as trademarks or service marks: The Rug Doctor (company) puts out The Rug Doctor® Steam Cleaner (product) and McDonald's Corp. uses "McDonald's" as a service mark. And of course, many companies use their business name together with additional words and symbols to make up trademarks and service marks for their products and services—for example, Apple Computer Corporation uses the name Apple® Macintosh for its personal computer line.

If your LLC decides to use its business name as, or as part of, a trademark or service mark to identify products or services, you will face a number of issues:

- *Does the name do a good job of marketing your goods or services?* To answer this question, you'll need to have a good idea of what makes a strong mark and what marks are considered legally weak—that is, not deserving of much protection against copiers. A strong mark will be unique, memorable or suggestive of your LLC's products or services.
- *Is the name identical or similar to any trademark or service mark being used on goods or services that are similar or related enough to yours to likely cause marketplace confusion?* To answer this you will need to 1) conduct what's called a trademark search, 2) understand more about when goods and services are considered related, and 3) be able to assess whether customer confusion is likely.
- *Assuming your name doesn't conflict with an existing mark, do the circumstances justify the time and expense involved in placing the name on the federal trademark register and/or your state's trademark register?* If you do the work yourself, you can easily keep costs to a minimum.

Don't overlook these important additional legal chores now, before you choose an LLC name, if you anticipate marketing goods or services later under your proposed LLC name. If you hastily choose a name for your LLC and later use it to promote products sales in a competitive market, you may face a legal conflict just when business is humming and your LLC and its product or service names are beginning to become known. (Again, for a discussion of these and other trademark related questions, as well as step-by-step instructions for registering a mark, see Nolo's *Trademark: How to Name Your Business and Product*, by Kate McGrath and Stephen Elias.)

2. State LLC Name Requirements

Your LLC name must conform to your state's legal requirements. Your state sheet in Appendix A summarizes these LLC name requirements, but it's a good idea to double-check this information against the materials you receive from your state LLC office before selecting a name. Most states' LLC name requirements usually incorporate the basic rules that follow.

a. LLC Designator Is Required in LLC Name

Your LLC name must normally include an LLC designator, such as "Limited Liability Company" or "Limited Company." Capitalization is normally not specified under state statutes—upper or lower case may generally be used for these words.

You must, however, follow your state's specific rules for abbreviations. Some states allow both "LLC" and "L.L.C." as acceptable abbreviations; others stick with one of these two forms. Further, the words "limited" and "company" can usually be abbreviated as "Ltd." and "Co., " but you normally can't abbreviate the word "liability"—for example, "Liab." is not a valid abbreviated form. The result is usually that the words "Limited Liability Company" can be abbreviated in most states to "Ltd. Liability Co."

Finally, realize that in a minority of states, you may be required to place the LLC designator—the words "Limited Liability Company" or one of the other approved LLC designators—at the end of your LLC name. For example, you'd have to settle on "Maladroit Ventures LLC," not Maladroit LLC Ventures." So be on the lookout for this requirement as you peruse your state sheet and state materials.

Example: Valid names for the ABC limited liability company would typically include one or more of the following:

- *ABC Limited Liability Company*
- *ABC Limited Liability Co.*
- *ABC Ltd. Liability Co.*
- *ABC Limited Company*
- *ABC Ltd. Co.*
- *ABC L.C.*
- *ABC L.L.C., or*
- *ABC LLC.*

Easy way to pick a required LLC designator. Ending your LLC name with the words "Limited Liability Company" will meet the name requirements of all states except Florida and Iowa—in these two states, "Limited Company" or "L.C." is required.

b. Certain Words Are Prohibited or Restricted in LLC Name

An LLC name usually cannot include words reserved for use by special businesses. In many states, prohibited words include references to banking, insurance, trust companies or similar financial service businesses.

Many states either prohibit regular (non-professional) LLCs from practicing certain state-licensed professions, or require that they set up professional LLCs and operate under special rules. Hence, words related to professions ordinarily cannot be included in a regular (non-professional practice) LLC's name, such as "law," "accounting," "medical," "engineering," "architecture," "real estate" and similar professional practice terms. Of course, if you want to organize an LLC for a licensed professional practice, you very well may want to use words that denote the profession.

What if you are forming an LLC that serves the needs of a licensed profession, but doesn't provide licensed services itself—such as a legal copying center, a medical supplies company, or a computer programming business for accountants—can you use the words "medical," "legal" or "accounting" in your name? We don't have a ready-made answer that applies in all states. If you want to use these words in an LLC name, call and ask the name section of the state LLC filing office if you will be allowed to do so. If you can't get a satisfactory answer over the phone, you can try reserving your name or filing Articles of Organization—the worst that can happen is that your paperwork will be returned unfiled if these words are not allowed in your LLC's name.

c. LLC Name Must Not Conflict With a Name Already On File

Another state LLC name requirement is that your LLC name must not be the same as, or too closely similar to, the name of an LLC already on file with the state LLC filing office. Another way to express this requirement is that your proposed LLC name must be available for your use with your state's LLC filing office. Names on file that are not available for your LLC may include the names of:

- domestic LLCs (those formed in the state)
- foreign LLCs (registered out-of-state LLCs that have qualified to do business in the state), and
- names on reserve for LLCs in the process of formation (names being held for 30 to 120 days by businesses planning to form or qualify LLCs in the state soon; see Section C5, below, for more on reserving names).

Some states also check proposed LLC names against other business forms. Some state LLC filing offices check proposed LLC names against names used in the state for corporations and limited partnerships, both of which must also file formation papers with the Department or Secretary of State. If your proposed LLC name is the same or similar to one in use by a corporation or limited partnership in these states, you will not be able to use it.

If your proposed LLC name is similar to another name already on file with the state LLC office, some states allow you to use it anyway if you can get the other business's written approval to use your similar name. But there are problems with this approach. For starters, the other business is likely to refuse to let you use the similar name unless you carefully limit or distinguish it in some way from its own name. Even if the other business does agree, it probably will ask you to pay big bucks to use any version of the name. In addition, it's messy to use a name already in use by others—even if you get their permission.

So, if you find that your proposed LLC name resembles one already on file with your state LLC office, or generally conflicts with a name discovered in your modest search efforts explained in Section C4, below, we recommend you come up with another name. We know that finding just the right sounding name for your business can be a chore, and that you may feel a little put out by having to select another name. With patience, however, and the usual amount of serendipity, you'll find that you can come up with two or three alternative names that suit your taste and your LLC business.

IMPORTANT BUSINESS NAME FACTS

There's a lot of misinformation and confusion about choosing names for LLCs and other businesses. Here are a few points of clarification:

- *Filing your LLC name with the LLC filing office does not guarantee your right to use it.* We've said this already, but it bears repeating: Another business may be able to prevent you from using the name if the other business is already using your LLC name (or one close to it) in a trademark or service mark to identify goods or services.
- *You are allowed to use a name that's different from the official name shown in your Articles of Organization.* If you do, this alternate name is known as an assumed or fictitious business name, and you will need to register it at the state and/or county level. (See Chapter 7, Section D3.)
- *You can change your official LLC name later by amending your Articles.* You may later decide to change the name of your LLC to a new name (again, which must be available for your use with the LLC filing office) by amending your Articles of Organization. Naturally, most LLC owners choose not to change their LLC name after they have been in business for a while, but this option is available if absolutely necessary.

3. Check Availability of LLC Name With the State

Let's say you've come up with a name or two that you'd like to use for your LLC. How can you find out if it is available for your use? Simple. Just call your state LLC filing office at the telephone number listed in your state sheet in Appendix A, and ask. The state LLC office will normally tell you over the phone, at no charge, whether one or two proposed names are available for your use. A few offices will ask you to send a written name availability request. If this happens, we suggest you use a written letter to request that your proposed LLC name be reserved for your use if it is available. (We show you how to reserve a proposed LLC name in Section C5, below.)

Don't count on using a name that you haven't reserved or filed. A telephone (or written) name check is just a preliminary indication of the availability of your proposed LLC name. Unless you formally reserve your name (as explained in Section C5, below), you do not secure your right to use your name with the state LLC office until you file your Articles of Organization. So don't order your business stationery, cards, signs or anything else until your name has been secured for your use (after your Articles have been filed with the LLC filing office, or after reserving your name if you are absolutely certain that you will file your Articles within the reservation period).

4. Consider Performing Your Own Name Search

There are a few simple business name searching procedures you can use, in addition to checking the availability of your name with the state LLC office, to get a sense of whether your proposed LLC name is in use by other businesses. Why is this important to know? For one thing, most business owners would like their names to be as unique as possible.

Another reason, mentioned earlier, is that you'd like to stay as clear as possible from names already being used by other businesses to market their goods and services. This not only helps you avoid names that others will lay legal claim to as trademarks and service marks, but can help you if you wish to use your LLC name yourself as a registered state or federal trademark or service mark (to identify and market your LLC's goods and services).

Below are several self-help search techniques you can employ to see if others are using a name similar to your proposed LLC name. If you are interested in performing any of these steps, it makes sense to do so before filing your LLC Articles—to avoid having to amend your Articles to change your name if you find your proposed name is already in use by another business.

- *Check state and county assumed business name files.* Your state LLC materials should indicate whether assumed (or fictitious) business names are registered with your Secretary of State's office, at the county level, or both. If they are registered at the state level, call the assumed or fictitious business name section of the Secretary of State's office and ask if your proposed LLC name is the same or similar to a registered assumed or fictitious name. Also call your local county clerk's office to ask how you can check assumed business name filings; in most states, assumed or fictitious business name statements, or "doing business as" (dba) statements, are filed with the county clerk's office. Generally, you must go in and check the assumed business name files in person—it takes just a few minutes to do this.

- *Check business directories.* Check such sources as major metropolitan phone book listings, business directories and trade directories to see if another company or group is using a name similar to your proposed LLC name. Larger public libraries keep phone directories for many major cities throughout the country, as well as trade directories. A local business branch of a public library may have a special collection of business research materials—check these first for listings of local and national trade and business groups.
- *Check state trademarks and service marks.* Call the trademark section of your Secretary of State's office and ask if your proposed LLC name is the same or similar to trademarks and service marks registered with the state. Some offices may ask for a written request and a small fee before performing this search.
- *Check the federal Trademark Register.* Another logical step is to check federal trademarks and service marks. Go to a large public library or special business and government library in your area that carries the federal *Trademark Register.* This consists of a listing of trademark and service mark names broken into categories of goods and services.

Using a computer to speed and simplify your self-help name search. Most of the business name listings mentioned above, including yellow page listings, business directory databases and federal and state trademark registers, are available as part of various commercial computer databases. For example, the federal and state trademark registers can be accessed through TRADEMARKSCAN®, which is part of the Dialog™ database. The federal register is also available through the Compu-Mark® database, which can be accessed if you are a member of the CompuServe™ service. (For information on subscribing and logging onto these online services, call 800- information and ask for each company's toll-free number.)

5. Reserve Your LLC Name

Let's say you have decided on an LLC name and checked that it is available by making a phone call to your LLC filing office as explained in Section C3, above. Most states allow you to reserve available LLC names. During the reservation period, only you—the person who reserved a name—may file Articles of Organization using this name. The reservation period and the fees vary, but generally an available LLC name can be reserved for 30 to 120 days for $10 to $50. In many states, you can reserve the same name more than once if you don't get around to filing your Articles of Organization during the first reservation period. We show your state's LLC name reservation rules in your state sheet in Appendix A.

It makes sense to reserve your name if you will not be filing your Articles of Organization immediately. Start by checking the materials received from your state LLC filing office. A sample or fill-in-the-blanks reservation of LLC name form may be included, or you may find instructions for preparing one from scratch. A fee schedule in your materials should show how much you must pay for a name reservation, as well as indicate the period of reservation.

If this material is not included, call your state LLC filing office and ask the clerk to send you instructions and a form to reserve your proposed LLC name. If the state LLC filing office requires a written name reservation, but does not provide a form, you can use the tear-out reservation of LLC name letter included in Appendix C. Following is a sample with instructions.

SAMPLE RESERVATION OF LLC NAME LETTER

date

name and address of your state's LLC filing office

LLC Filings Office:

Please reserve the following proposed limited liability company name for my use for the allowable period specified under state law:

insert your proposed LLC name; make sure it conforms to your state's

name requirements as shown in your state sheet in Appendix A

☐ If the above name is not available, please reserve the first available name from the following list of alternative names: ❶

Second Choice: ______________________

Third Choice: ______________________

I enclose a check in payment of the reservation fee. ❷ Please send a certificate, receipt for payment, or other acknowledgment or approval of my reservation request to me at my address shown below.

Thank you for your assistance,

your signature ❸

your name, address and phone number

____

Enclosures: check for reservation fee; stamped, self-addressed envelope

SPECIAL INSTRUCTIONS

❶ You may wish to include alternative names in case your first choice is not available. In that case, check the box and fill in the names in the blanks below.

❷ Include a check or money order for fees. Note that a few states only accept payment in the form of money orders or cashier's checks. We tell you if this applies in your state on your state sheet in Appendix A.

❸ Make sure that the person signing this letter will be available to sign Articles of Organization on behalf of your LLC. The LLC name is reserved for this person's use only. (Although inconvenient, there may be a way around this problem. If the requesting person drops out of the LLC, some states will allow him or her to file a transfer of reservation of name form.)

D. Check Your State's Procedures for Filing Articles

We cover the general procedures and rules below for preparing and filing Articles of Organization for LLCs. Again, make sure you check your state sheet in Appendix A for important rules or procedures that may apply in your state.

1. Some States Have Additional Filing Procedures

The laws and regulations of some states include special requirements prior to or when filing LLC Articles of Organization. Most common are:

- *Supplemental forms.* An additional legal or tax form—such as a separate designation of registered agent and office, a standard industry code form that you check to show the LLC's primary business or a state tax form—may be included in your LLC state materials to be completed and submitted with your Articles.
- *Publication of notice.* Some states require a pre- or post-filing publication in a legal newspaper of your intention to do business as a limited liability company. A local legal newspaper can handle any required publication and filings associated with this formality.

Your state sheet in Appendix A will alert you to extra formalities that apply when filing Articles of Organization in your state. The instructions for any additional forms and special procedures should be included in your LLC state materials. If you have difficulty, the staff at the LLC filing office should be able to provide further information and assistance.

2. Special Requirements for Licensed Professionals

In some states, licensed professionals can form LLCs as long as they comply with additional requirements or filing formalities. For example, some states allow licensed professionals to form an LLC as long as they file a special form of Articles of Organization for a Professional LLC and the LLC name ends with the words "Professional Limited Liability Company" or the abbreviations "PLLC" or P.L.L.C."

Your state sheet and state materials should alert you to special requirements, but double-check with your profession's state licensing board to be doubly sure. Our LLC contact letter in Section A2, above, specifically asks the LLC filing office if the state has a special form for use by professional service LLCs. This is simply another way to find out if you can go ahead in your state and form a professional LLC.

The special state rules that apply to professional LLCs typically limit LLC membership to licensed professionals only (and, generally, to the particular licensed profession only). Other rules may apply as well—for example, minimum malpractice insurance coverage or bonding may be required for each member who practices in the LLC.

Typically, lawyers, doctors, accountants, engineers and healthcare professionals must abide by these extra rules, but other licensed professions may be exempt. To find out whether any special professional LLC rules apply to your licensed profession, call the state board or agency that regulates your profession and ask ("May I form a limited liability company in this state to render licensed professional services of [your field] ?") If the answer is yes, ask whether any special requirements apply to operating your professional LLC in the state. If so, ask to be sent a copy of these special rules.

E. Prepare LLC Articles of Organization

The Articles of Organization form is your primary formation document: your LLC comes into existence on the date you successfully file the Articles with your state LLC filing office. Here's how to go about preparing it.

1. Locate Articles in Your State LLC Materials

Most state LLC filing offices provide LLC Articles of Organization forms that meet the state's basic statutory requirements. Unless you plan to organize an LLC with a complicated organizational structure (with the help of a lawyer, accountant or other specialist), the basic state form will work fine. So, before you do anything else, go through your LLC state materials (Section A2, above) and take out all forms and instructions related to preparing Articles of Organization.

If you're having trouble finding the Articles, a careful look through the materials may prove successful. Sample and tear-out Articles and instructions are occasionally hidden in the back of a general purpose publication, such as *Doing Business in the State of*.... Here's what you can expect to find in your LLC state materials:

- *Ready-to-use Articles of Organization.* Some states provide a printed form that you can fill in and file with the LLC filing office. Instructions for completing the blanks are often provided on the printed form. Special forms for forming an LLC that is doing business as a general or limited partnership, or for forming an LLC to practice a licensed profession, may be included in your state materials. (Our tear-out LLC contact letter in Section A2, above, allows you to request these extra forms.)
- *Sample forms and instructions.* Many states provide a sample Articles of Organization form with instructions. You will need to retype (or word process) your final document following the format and content of the sample form.
- *LLC statutes.* In the few states that do not provide sample or printed Articles of Organization, the LLC filing office may include a copy of the state's LLC Articles statute, which lists the required items of information that must appear in your Articles of Organization. (If this is your situation, see Sections E2 and E5, below, for more on how to use the statute to prepare your Articles.)
- *Filing checklists.* Some LLC filing offices provide helpful checklists of steps involved in filing Articles and preparing other LLC documents and forms (such as an operating agreement, state license and tax filings). Some will even include a list showing common reasons for rejection of Articles—which can help you comply with the less obvious substantive and formal requirements of your state's LLC regulations, such as whether you can show a post office box as an address for your LLC, how to sign and acknowledge the Articles, and even how much space to leave at the top of the first page for the office file stamp.

2. If Your State Does Not Provide Forms: Look Up the Law Yourself

If your state does not provide a fill-in-the-blanks form or sample Articles of Organization, we suggest calling a local law library or business forms supplier to ask if a state-specific LLC Articles of Organization form is available.

If you can't locate a ready-to-use form, you'll need to draft your own Articles of Organization. Fortunately, doing this will be easier than you might think. Start by locating the statute in your state's LLC law that lists the required contents of Articles of Organization. If your state doesn't provide a copy of this statute in its LLC materials (many do), you'll need to find this section of law yourself. You can find your state's LLC law at a local law library or at a larger public library—many public libraries have state legal codes.

Once you have the state LLC act in front of you, it should take just a few minutes to find the relevant section of the LLC act that lists the required information that must be included in LLC Articles of Organization. Almost always, you'll find a section titled "Articles of Organization—Required Contents." You can find it by checking the Index at the end of the act, looking at the Table of Contents at the beginning of the act, or simply by thumbing through the act and scanning the titles of each section of the law.

Once you find the section that lists the required contents for Articles of Organization of an LLC, read each requirement and compare it to each of the provisions contained in our sample Articles of Organization and instructions just below. In most cases, a provision in our sample form can be used verbatim, or with slight word changes, to satisfy each requirement of your state's LLC Articles of Organization statute. We give an example of how to do this in Section E5, below. (For additional information on doing your own legal research, see Chapter 8, Section C.)

3. How to Complete Articles of Organization

The basic clauses required in most states' LLC Articles of Organization are similar. Below, we provide sample language and explanations for provisions you are likely to find in the Articles provided by your LLC filing office and required under your state's LLC statutes. You'll find a tear-out form containing all the provisions discussed here in Appendix C.

By following the material below and referring to the specific instructions for preparing Articles of Organization provided by your LLC office (or the statute that lists the required contents of LLC Articles in your state), you should be able to prepare your own Articles without difficulty. Here are some hints to make this job easier:

- *Scan our sample Articles of Organization.* Glancing through the language of our sample Articles below, before you begin filling in your own Articles, will help you get a general idea of the types of provisions included in standard LLC Articles of Organization. This overview will help you understand the form and instructions provided by your LLC office, or evaluate how each provision can be used to satisfy your state's statutory requirements if you are drafting your own form.
- *Prepare a draft first.* If your state LLC office provides a fill-in-the-blanks form, photocopy it and prepare a draft. If your state provides a sample form that must be retyped, first word process, type or write out a draft copy.
- *Use instructions as guidance.* If you get stuck with a particular article or provision in a state-provided form, refer to our instructions below for a similar item in our sample form.
- *Use the state sheets and state LLC office materials.* To locate any special LLC formation requirements in your state, see your state materials and your state sheet in Appendix A. For example, your state may require you to specify in your Articles whether members of your LLC can vote to continue the legal existence of your LLC after the dissociation (the loss of membership rights) by a member; we show each state's statutory requirements for this "default continuation rule" in the state sheets.
- *Use sample Articles if you are preparing your Articles from scratch.* If you are crafting your own Articles of Organization based upon the requirements listed in your state's LLC Act, you will use one or more of the sample provisions below to prepare your Articles. We show how to use our sample Article provisions to create Articles of Organization for the state of Texas in Section E5.

We'll start at the top of the Articles, and discuss each part of the form separately. Each provision is shown, followed by explanatory text. The bold information contains instructions for filling in blanks in a given provision.

Pay attention to state format requirements. Most state LLC filing offices expect Articles of Organization to be typed or printed on one side of a page only, with letter-size (8½" x 11") now being the customary page size (though many will still accept 8½" x 14" legal-sized paper). Whatever type of typewriter or printer you use—for example, dot-matrix, laser or ink jet—make sure the printed text is legible and of good contrast.

CUSTOMIZING YOUR ARTICLES OF ORGANIZATION

Although the standard Articles of Organization discussed in this chapter and the form normally included in your LLC state materials will be sufficient for most LLCs, you may wish to include special operating rules or provisions. Ordinarily it is preferable to cover such special rules in your operating agreement, which can be adopted and changed with relative ease, rather than in the Articles (amended Articles must be refiled with the state LLC office).

You may, however, need to place certain special provisions in the Articles for them to be effective. For example, if an LLC wants to adopt the following types of provisions, they must often be included in its Articles of Organization:

- management of the LLC by designated managers
- appointment of a manager or member by a designated person or group, rather than by all members, or
- indemnification (payment of legal expenses) of LLC members or managers under special provisions of state law.

You won't normally have reason to be concerned with provisions of this sort—but if you do, your state LLC office materials may indicate any special provisions that must be included in the Articles to be effective. (The state LLC statute that contains the list of required information in Articles almost always lists optional items of information that need to be placed in Articles, rather than in the operating agreement, if the LLC wishes to adopt them. For further information and for help in customizing your Articles with special provisions, check your state's LLC statutes or consult an LLC business lawyer.

a. Heading of Articles

ARTICLES OF ORGANIZATION
OF
__________NAME OF LLC__________

State law does not normally specify any format for the heading of the Articles, but it's common practice to give the title of the document, usually "Articles of Organization," followed by the proposed name of the LLC. Some states use a different title for this document—for example, Delaware and a few other states call this document the "Certificate of Formation." If a name other than "Articles of Organization" is used for this form, it will be shown on your state sheet and in materials from your state's LLC filing office.

In the blank, fill in the correct, full name of your LLC. Make sure the name you list is exactly want you want your LLC to be named. As discussed in Sections C3 and C5, we suggest you check the availability of your proposed name and, if appropriate, reserve it prior to filing your Articles. By reserving your name, you avoid having your Articles returned unfiled because another LLC is already using your proposed name (or a similar one) as the name of its LLC listed with the state LLC office.

b. Statement of Statutory Authority

The undersigned natural person(s), of the age of eighteen years or more, acting as organizer(s) of a limited liability company under the State of **___name of state___** Limited Liability Company Act, adopt(s) the following Articles of Organization **___or other title for form, such as "Certificate of Formation"___** for such limited liability company.

Although not required, it is traditional in many states to include a preliminary statement of statutory authority after the heading to the Articles of Organization and before the first Article. You will normally see language of this sort on state-provided forms.

c. Name of Limited Liability Company

Article 1. Name of Limited Liability Company. The name of this limited liability company is __**name of LLC**__.

Insert the proposed name of your LLC in the blank. This should be identical to the name listed in the heading.

Numbering or lettering of Articles of Organization. State law does not normally specify any particular numbering or lettering scheme for Articles. We employ Arabic numerals, but other number or letter sequences are permissible—such as "Article One," "Article I" or "Article A."

d. Name and Address of Initial Registered Office and Agent

Article 2. Registered Office and Registered Agent. The initial registered office of this limited liability company and the name of its initial registered agent at this address are: __**name and address of LLC initial registered agent and office**__.

Most states require that Articles of Organization include both of the following:

- *The name of the LLC's initial registered agent.* The agent is sometimes called the "agent for service of process." He or she is authorized to receive legal papers on behalf of the LLC. Typically, the agent must be a resident of the state and at least 18 years of age.
- *The address of the initial registered office.* The registered office is the address where the agent maintains a place of business—where papers may be mailed, and where service of process can be personally performed on the agent. The registered office address ordinarily must be located in the state.

Although the registered office may be different from the principal office of the LLC (the actual office or business location of the LLC) in many states, most LLCs keep things simple and appoint one of the members as the initial agent, showing the principal address of the LLC as the registered office address (where the agent can be contacted personally and receive mail). A street address, not a post office box, is normally required as the address of the registered office.

Some states supply a separate Designation of Registered Agent form (or one with a similar title) to be filed with the Articles, which the agent signs to show his or her consent to act as registered agent for the LLC. In other states, a simple statement at the end of the Articles, signed by the initial agent, is needed—such as, "The undersigned hereby accepts appointment as registered agent for the above named limited liability company."

Don't needlessly hire a registered agent company. Most states allow you to designate another business as a registered agent, and, indeed, some companies specialize in acting as registered agents for LLCs and corporations for an annual fee. Because acting as a registered agent simply involves being available to receive mail (and personal service), most readers will handle this task themselves and not bother to hire an outside firm.

Some states also require an LLC to designate the Secretary of State or another state official as the person who is entitled to receive legal notices on behalf of the LLC in case the registered agent resigns, cannot be located or is otherwise unable or unavailable to act as agent for the LLC in the future. In some states, this designation of state official as alternate agent happens automatically as a matter of law; in other states, specific language to this effect must be inserted in the Articles. The ready-to-use or sample Articles in your LLC packet should include any required language.

Example: Here is the alternate-agent language used in Articles of Organization for Utah LLCs (which is included in the state's sample Articles of Organization form): "Appointment of the Director of the Division of Corporations and Commercial Code of the Utah Department of Commerce as Agent for Service of Process. The Director of the Division of Corporations and Commercial Code of the Utah Department of Commerce is hereby appointed the agent of the limited liability company for service of process if the registered agent has resigned, the registered agent's authority has been revoked, or the registered agent cannot be found or served with the exercise of reasonable diligence."

e. Statement of Purposes

> *Article 3. Statement of Purposes.* The purposes for which this limited liability company is organized are: **list purposes of the LLC business, for example, "to operate a computer repair and retail store, and to engage in any other lawful business for which limited liability companies may be organized in this state."**

Almost all states require a statement of purposes in the Articles of Organization. Some say that a general statement of purposes is sufficient—that is, "to engage in any lawful business for which limited liability companies may be organized in this state." Others states require a brief statement of the specific business purposes of the LLC—usually a short and straightforward description of the particular type of business to be operated by the LLC.

If a specific statement of business purposes is required, it is often a good idea to follow it with a general statement of purposes—allowing the LLC "to engage in any other lawful business for which limited liability companies may be organized in this state." Adding this general language helps make it clear to the organizers, future LLC members and others who may read your Articles that your LLC, while formed for one particular purpose, can engage in other business activities. The sample language in the sample above contains a dual-purpose statement of this sort.

Here are some other examples of how to complete this statement:

- "to open and operate a car stereo and security alarm sales and service facility, and to engage in any other lawful business for which limited liability companies may be organized in this state"
- "to purchase, sell and otherwise invest in real property and commercial interests in real property, and to engage in any other lawful business for which limited liability companies may be organized in this state," or
- "to provide financial consulting services to individuals and businesses, and to engage in any other lawful business for which limited liability companies may be organized in this state."

f. Management of the LLC

> *Article 4. Management and Names and Addresses of Initial* **"Members" or "Managers"**. The management of this limited liability company is reserved to the **"members" or "managers."** The names and addresses of its initial **"members" or "managers"** are: **names and addresses of members or managers.**

Articles of Organization usually state whether the LLC will be member-managed or manager-managed (discussed in detail in Chapter 2, Section C1). Here's a recap of what these terms mean:

- *Member-managed LLC.* This simply means that management decisions are made by *all* the members. Member management is the default rule in most states—if you don't specify how your LLC will be managed in your Articles, your LLC will be member-managed. As explained in Chapter 3, Section B2, member-management also helps in obtaining pass-through tax status with the IRS.
- *Manager-managed LLC.* Some LLCs may decide to designate some of the members and/or persons outside the LLC to manage the business. If so, the Articles must usually state that management is reserved to managers, and list the names and addresses of the specially designated managers. Normally, just one manager is required, but even smaller LLCs typically appoint more than one person to manage the company. If managers are listed, members' names and addresses usually are not required, but in some states, you may be asked to list the names and addresses of both members and managers (even if some individuals function in both capacities).

In each of the first sets of blanks, indicate whether your LLC will be run by "members" or "managers." In the indicated space, list the names and addresses of the LLC's initial members or managers. Normally, street (not post office box) addresses must be shown.

If you have selected manager-management, follow this suggestion to help your LLC qualify for pass-through tax status:

- *List at least one member-manager.* The tax rules get a little fuzzy if your LLC does not have at least one member (owner) on your management team when you opt for manager-management. As we have said, most smaller manager-managed LLCs will want at least one member to have a say in management anyway, so following this particular piece of advice should not present a problem.

All LLCs (manager- or member-managed) should follow the next suggestion:

- *Have at least two members.* Most states require the LLC to have two or more members. Even if your state allows one member, you will want at least two to qualify for pass-through tax treatment with the IRS. (We cover this issue in Chapter 2, Section A.)

g. Principal Place of Business

> *Article 5. Principal Place of Business of the Limited Liability Company.* The principal place of business of the limited liability company shall be: **street address of principal office of LLC.**

The Articles of Organization often specify the principal place of business of the LLC. Normally, this location may be within or outside the state, but most LLCs will show the address of its main office located in the state. Technically, the principal place of business listed in the Articles is one of the places where the business may be sued (brought to court), not necessarily the place where most of the business operations of the LLC are performed. For most smaller LLCs, there's only one place of business, and you will list it here.

h. Duration of the LLC

> *Article 6. Period of Duration of the Limited Liability Company.* The period of duration of the limited liability company shall be: **"perpetual" or "from the date these Articles of Organization are filed through and including (give future date or state a period of years)."**

In many states, the Articles of Organization must include a provision specifying the duration of the LLC. Your state's Articles form or its statute for the contents of Articles will tell you if this provision is required for your state, and, if so, how you must fill it in.

In some states, it's permissible to provide for a "perpetual" (unlimited) duration of the LLC in this provision. If you have this option, you probably will want to take it—this way your LLC automatically continues into the future until and unless your members vote to dissolve it.

Some states that require this provision won't let you provide a perpetual duration for your LLC. Instead, you must limit its duration to a number of years from the date the Articles are filed or to a specific date in the future. Some states even say that this date can't be more than 30 or 50 years into the future. Don't worry about any of these limitations. If you must limit the life of your LLC in your Articles under state rules, choose a date that as far in the future as you can—either 30 or 50 years from the date of filing of your Articles, or even further into the future. If permitted, a good date to pick is the end of the 21st century: December 31, 2099. If your LLC is still around after the end of the next century—or whatever termination date you are forced to select—you or your LLC successors can file an amendment extending the legal life of the LLC for another 30, 50, or 100 years more.

i. Signatures of Persons Forming the LLC

In Witness Whereof, the undersigned organizer(s) of this Limited Liability Company has(have) signed these Articles of Organization on the date indicated.

Date: ______________________

Signature(s):

____

typed or printed name, Organizer

____

typed or printed name, Organizer

____

typed or printed name, Organizer

____

typed or printed name, Organizer

____

typed or printed name, Organizer

States have various signature requirements for LLC Articles of Organization. In most states, one person may act as organizer of the LLC by signing the form and submitting the Articles for filing. The usual practice is to have all initial members listed in the Articles of Organization date and sign the form. If managers are listed instead of members in the Articles, one or more managers will usually sign the form and act as organizer of the LLC.

If you have reserved your LLC's name. The person who reserved your LLC name with the state should sign your Articles as one of its (or only) organizers. (If he or she is not available, check with your LLC filing office, which may allow you to file a transfer of reservation of name or similar form, signed by the person who reserved your LLC name.)

The signature statement on your state Articles of Organization may look a little different from the sample form, depending on your state. For example, in some states, people must sign under penalty of perjury with an assertion that the facts stated in the Articles are true based upon the information and belief of the signers.

In a few states, the Articles must be notarized—that is, signed in the presence of a notary public, who fills out a concluding notarization statement and impresses a notarial seal at the bottom of the form (notary statements vary from state to state). Notaries are found in real estate offices and other businesses, or simply by looking up the word "Notary" in a local telephone business directory. Notary fees are usually modest.

If your state does not provide a ready-to-use form, your state materials should tell you who needs to sign your Articles and how this should be done, including any required language or notary procedure.

LLC ORGANIZER DOES NOT HAVE TO BE A MEMBER OR MANAGER

Most states let you choose one person (or a few people) to act as the organizer of your LLC. The organizer can sign and file your Articles on behalf of the LLC (instead of having all the initial members or managers sign the form). Typically, the organizer does not need to be a member or associated with the LLC in any way; he or she probably must be at least 18 years of age.

What the states have in mind here is to allow a lawyer to prepare, sign and file your Articles for you—but you will usually tend to this task yourself by selecting at least one of your initial members or managers as your organizer. Of course, you may want to let everyone join in on the action and have all founding members sign your Articles as organizers of your LLC. This is not legally required, but fine to do if you want.

4. Sample Completed Articles of Organization

To help you tie all this information together, we include a sample completed Articles of Organization form below. The Articles are prepared for a fictitious business, "Luxor Light LLC," a three-member LLC for a lighting fixture business. The sample is relatively standard; note that in Article 4 Luxor Light has opted to be managed by members (the option most LLCs will choose).

ARTICLES OF ORGANIZATION
OF
LUXOR LIGHTING LLC

The undersigned natural persons, of the age of eighteen years or more, acting as organizers of a limited liability company under the Anystate Limited Liability Company Act, adopt the following Articles of Organization for such limited liability company.

Article 1. Name of Limited Liability Company. The name of this limited liability company is **Luxor Light LLC.**

Article 2. Registered Office and Registered Agent. The initial registered office of this limited liability company and the name of its initial registered agent at this address are:
Robert Johnston, 1515 San Estudillo, Anycity, Anystate, 00000.

Article 3. Statement of Purposes. The purposes for which this limited liability company is organized are:
to operate a custom home and commercial lighting and fixture store, and to engage in any other lawful business for which limited liability companies may be organized in this state.

Article 4. Management and Names and Addresses of Initial Members. The management of this limited liability company is reserved to the members. The names and addresses of its initial members are:

Robert Johnston, 1515 San Estudillo, Anycity, Anystate, 00000

Rebecca Johnston, 1515 San Estudillo, Anycity, Anystate, 00000

Gregory Luxor, 3021 Los Avenidos, Anycity, Anystate, 00000.

Article 5. Principal Place of Business of the Limited Liability Company. The principal place of business of the limited liability company shall be:
56 Rue de Campanille, Anycity, Anystate, 00000.

Article 6. Period of Duration of the Limited Liability Company. The period of duration of the limited liability company shall be: **perpetual**.

In Witness Whereof, the undersigned organizer of this Limited Liability Company has signed these Articles of Organization on the date indicated.

Date: **date**

Signature(s): *Gregory Luxor*

Gregory Luxor, Organizer

5. Example of How to Prepare Articles From Scratch

As we've noted, not all states provide ready-to-use forms or sample Articles of Organization. Here is an example of how to use your state's list of requirements for Articles, together with our sample Articles, to craft your own LLC Articles of Organization.

Good news for Texas LLC. For those of you forming a Texas LLC, you won't have to prepare your own Articles from scratch. We do it for you as part of the example below. Our sample Articles of Organization form is based upon the real-life Texas LLC statutes. Just retype the following sample and supply your own information in the blanks.

Although the state of Texas does not provide a ready-to-use form for LLC Articles of Organization, it does mail out a list of the state's requirements for the contents of Articles when you ask for LLC forms and information. (If you peruse the Texas LLC Act as we explain in Section E3, above, you'll find these requirements listed in Article 3.02 of the Texas Act.) Here is the relevant excerpt from a letter that the Texas Secretary of State sends out:

Formation of a Limited Liability Company

To form a liability company, you must file articles of organization pursuant to Article 3.02 of the Texas Limited Liability Company Act. The articles of organization must minimally set forth:

1. The name of the limited liability company. The name must contain the words "Limited Liability Company" or "Limited Company" or the abbreviations "L.L.C.," "LLC," "LC," "L.C." or "Ltd. Co." The name of a limited liability company cannot be the same as or deceptively similar to that of another limited liability company, corporation, limited partnership, name reservation or registration.

2. The period of duration, which may be perpetual, or a specific date of termination.

3. The purpose for which the limited liability company is organized, which may be stated to be, or include, the transaction of any or all lawful business for which limited liability companies may be organized.

4. The street address of its initial registered office in Texas and the name of its initial registered agent at such address.

5. If the limited liability company is to be managed by a manager or managers, a statement that the company is to be managed by a manager or managers and the names and addresses of the initial manager or managers. If the management of a limited liability company is reserved to the members, a statement that the limited liability company will not have managers and the names and addresses of its initial members.

6. The name and address of each organizer.

Our sample Articles of Organization (Section E4, above) contain each of the required Texas provisions. Most of our sample articles can be used word-for-word to meet the statutory requirements, or the blanks can be filled in with the required information.

Here is a summary of changes we've made in the sample Texas Articles:

- The finished version of the Texas Articles uses six of the sample Articles from Section E4. We don't use sample Article 5, which specifies the principal place of business of the LLC, because Texas rules do not require it.
- In Article 4, we add a statement that the LLC shall not have managers. Texas requirements say that this language is necessary if management is reserved to the members (normally, a statement that the management is reserved to members is enough). This is the only substantive change necessary to make our sample Articles work in Texas.

Finally, note that instructions for information to be supplied in blanks in our sample Articles (from Section E4, above) are shown in bold. Additions to the language of our sample Articles are noted in italics.

ARTICLES OF ORGANIZATION
OF

NAME OF LLC

The undersigned natural persons, of the age of eighteen years or more, acting as members of a limited liability company under the Texas Limited Liability Company Act, adopt the following Articles of Organization for such limited liability company.

Article 1. Name of Limited Liability Company. The name of this limited liability company is

name of the Texas LLC.

Article 2. Registered Office and Registered Agent. The initial registered office of this limited liability company and the name of its initial registered agent at this address are:

name and address of registered agent and office.

Article 3. Statement of Purposes. The purposes for which this limited liability company is organized are:

"to engage in any lawful business for which limited liability companies may be organized in this state."

Article 4. Management and Names and Addresses of Initial Members. The management of this limited liability company is reserved to the members, *and it shall not have managers.* The names and addresses of its initial members are:

names and addresses of initial members.

Article 5. Period of Duration of the Limited Liability Company. The period of duration of the limited liability company shall be: **"perpetual."**

Article 6. Names and Addresses of Organizers. The names and addresses of the organizers of this LLC are:

name and address of organizer(s), typically one or more of the initial members.

In Witness Whereof, the undersigned organizer(s) of this Limited Liability Company has (have) signed these Articles of Organization on the date indicated.

Date: **date**

Signature(s): **signature(s) of organizer(s)**

typed or printed name, Organizer

F. Finalize and File Your Articles of Organization

If you prepared a draft of your Articles of Organization, now's the time to transfer the information to a clean blank form. Again, if you're preparing your Articles from scratch, they should be neatly typed or printed with a word processor on one side of letter-size pages (8½" x 11"). Check over your Articles of Organization one last time to make sure they're correct and have been properly signed.

File your Articles of Organization with your state LLC filing office following the instructions in your state LLC materials. (Again, any special filing requirements or procedures are also listed in your state sheet.) Filing is usually done by mail, although many offices will accept Articles in person. If you mail your Articles, remember to keep an extra copy in case the original is lost in the mail.

In Appendix C, we include a tear-out Articles filing letter you may wish to use to submit your Articles of Organization to the state LLC filing office. Complete the tear-out form following the sample and Special Instructions below. The address of your state LLC filing office and the amount of the required filing fee are shown on your state sheet in Appendix A, and in your state materials.

If you have problems filing your Articles. The filing office may return your Articles and indicate which items need correction (your check should be held until you fix the problem). Often the problem is technical, not substantive, and easy to fix. If the problem is more complicated, such as an improper or insufficient LLC purpose clause, you may be able to solve the problem by rereading the instructions earlier in this chapter and those in your LLC materials for preparing Articles. If you get stuck, you will need to do a little research or obtain further help from an LLC lawyer who's experienced in drafting and filing LLC Articles of Organization in your state. (See Chapter 8.)

SAMPLE LLC ARTICLES FILING LETTER

date

name and address of your state's LLC filing office

LLC Filings Office:

I enclose an original and **number** ❶ copies of the proposed Articles of Organization of **name of LLC**, ❷ a proposed domestic limited liability company.

Please file the Articles of Organization and return a file-stamped copy of the original Articles or other receipt, acknowledgment or proof of filing to me at the address below.

A check/money order in the amount of $**filing fee amount—see your state sheet**, ❸ made payable to your office, for total filing and processing fees is enclosed.

☐ The above LLC name was reserved for my use **if applicable, insert "according to reservation number" and the reservation number**, issued on **date of issuance**. ❹

Sincerely,

your signature

your printed or typed name, Organizer

your address and phone number ❺

Enclosures: Articles of Organization; check

SPECIAL INSTRUCTIONS

❶ In some states, you need only submit an original of the Articles—the LLC office will file the original and send you a file-stamped copy or file receipt. In other states, you need to submit the original and one or more copies. The LLC filing office will file the original and file-stamp and return one or more copies to you.

Depending on the state, an additional fee may be charged for submitting more than one copy of your Articles for file-stamping. One copy (plus the original) should be sufficient in most cases; you can always make copies of this file-stamped copy to keep in your LLC records book or give to others as the need arises.

❷ Show the proposed name for your LLC (the name stated in your Articles of Organization). As explained in Section C, above, it can be risky to file Articles with a name that you haven't checked ahead of time. We recommend checking the availability of your proposed name before filing Articles or reserving the name for your exclusive use. If you don't, and the desired name is unavailable, your Articles will be returned unfiled.

❸ Include a check (or money order) for the total fees, made payable to the state or state office. Remember to consult your state sheet in Appendix A for particulars—a few states require payment by cashier's check or postal money order; some allow credit card payment. Also check your LLC state materials carefully to make sure your total fee and method of payment are correct.

❹ If you reserved your LLC name, check the box. Then fill in the blanks to show the certificate number and/or date of issuance of your reservation of LLC name. In some states, the LLC filing office simply sends you a file-stamped copy of your reservation letter—if so, just fill in the file-stamped date of the name reservation letter in the second blank, and include a copy of your file-stamped reservation certificate with this cover letter.

❺ The person (or one of the persons) who is acting as organizer of your LLC—by signing your Articles—should sign this cover letter. If you reserved an LLC name, the person who reserved the name should sign this letter—and the Articles of Organization as well—since the LLC name is reserved for this person's use. (If the person who reserved the name isn't available, again there are some ways around this. For example, some states allow the original reserver to transfer the name over to another LLC member by signing a form supplied by the state LLC office. If this issue applies to you, ask the LLC filing office if it has a transfer of reservation of name form for this purpose.)

G. What to Do After Filing Articles of Organization

Once you've sent in your Articles for filing, your next step is to wait. The LLC filing office will make sure the LLC name is available for use and that your Articles of Organization conform to law. If there are no problems, the office will mail you a file-stamped copy of your Articles or a filing receipt. Don't forget to congratulate yourself. Once your Articles of Organization have been successfully filed, your business is a legally recognized limited liability company.

Before commencing LLC business, we want to issue a few words of advice. Although filing Articles of Organization is all you are legally required to do to establish the legal existence of your LLC, make sure you go at least one step further and prepare an operating agreement for your LLC—see Chapter 5 if your LLC is member-managed or Chapter 6 if your LLC is manager-managed. Among other things, this agreement will help your LLC qualify for pass-through tax treatment with the IRS, an aspect of forming an LLC that is just as critical as establishing its legal credentials.

Finally, don't miss Chapter 7, where we cover some of the ins and outs of tending to your new LLC.

●

CHAPTER 5

Prepare an LLC Operating Agreement for Your Member-Managed LLC

If you've turned to this chapter, we assume you have already formed or are in the process of forming your LLC by preparing and filing Articles of Organization with your state LLC filing office, as explained in Chapter 4. Here, you'll learn how to prepare a fill-in-the-blanks operating agreement for a member-managed LLC.

Manager-managed LLCs. Most LLCs will be member-managed—that is, managed by all members. If, however, you plan to adopt a manager-managed LLC (one managed by only some LLC members and/or by nonmembers), you'll need an operating agreement that provides for manager-management. If yours is a manager-managed LLC, or you're unsure of the type of operating agreement to prepare for your LLC, start by turning to Chapter 6. (Note that even if you create the management operating agreement covered in Chapter 6 (rather than the member-managed agreement in Section C of this chapter), you'll need to read all of Sections A and B below. Section A discusses areas of LLC operation not covered in either of our tear-out operating agreements, and Section B talks a little about making modifications to either agreement.

A. Scope of Our Basic LLC Operating Agreements

The tear-out operating agreements we supply in this book are relatively straightforward forms that cover all major LLC issues. You may discover that our operating agreements are considerably shorter than the typically long-winded LLC agreements available commercially or from a lawyer. Our agreements help you set up your LLC under sensible ground rules and contain necessary reminders about restrictions that apply to most LLCs under state law and federal tax rules.

There are two major areas of LLC operations that our agreements do not cover, however. Let's briefly look at each.

1. Special Capital Account Provisions

Capital account provisions set forth the types and amounts of capital contributed by your original members. If you read a lawyer- or accountant-prepared LLC operating agreement, you'll usually see lists of complicated capital account definitions and provisions (language that specifies how members' capital contributions and distributions are to be handled under a range of circumstances). This special language can be important if you decide to split profits and losses among your LLC members in ratios that are different from the percentage of capital each member contributes to your LLC. (Chapter 3, Section D2 gives a fuller discussion of this issue.)

For our purposes, and for most readers of this book, adding page upon page of special provisions to handle so-called "special allocations" of profits and losses will not be necessary, so we do not include them in our tear-out operating agreements. If you think you'd like to include special allocation provisions in your operating agreement, ask your tax advisor for help. (See Chapter 8 for suggestions on finding a legal or tax advisor.)

Consider getting help drafting other special financial provisions. Of course, a legal or tax advisor can also help you prepare special financial provisions of any sort—for example, to set up a special class of membership that gets a guaranteed share of LLC profits or losses or to establish a special schedule for distribution of LLC profits to members before liquidation.

2. Buy-Sell or Right of First Refusal Provisions

An important and sometimes complicated aspect of forming any business involves deciding whether and how to plan in advance to sell a member's interest in the business to outsiders or other owners. Here are some examples of the kinds of issues that may arise:

- *"Right of first refusal" issues.* Does an owner who wishes to sell out have to offer to sell his or her interest to the other owners before selling to an outsider? Must the other owners buy that interest for the amount an outsider is ready to pay?
- *Valuation questions.* When a member (or his or her estate) wishes to sell to other members, how will the interest be valued? At fair market value (whatever that is—it's often hard to tell with a small, privately held business)? Should an appraiser resolve this issue at the time of sale? Or should the value of membership interests be established ahead of time in the LLC operating agreement—if so, should the value be based upon the book or net asset value of the business, a multiple of the earnings of the business or some other formula?
- *When and how should a departing LLC member be paid?* Should payment be made all in a lump sum or in installments? This is an important question, since your LLC or its other members may not have sufficient cash or borrowing power to come up with the needed buyout funds right away, with the result that a cash sale could only be made to an outsider. On the other hand, a departing LLC member (or his or her estate) will want to be paid as soon as possible. Should interest be charged and paid by the LLC if the buyout is accomplished in installments?
- *Life insurance.* Should the buyout of a deceased owner be funded with life insurance purchased ahead of time by the LLC or each of the other members?
- *Does it matter why or when a member is being bought out?* For example, if a member calls it quits and wishes to transfer his or her interest back to the LLC after only six months with the LLC, should he or she receive a smaller buyback price than a member who hangs in there for five years? What about a member who is expelled? What about a member who suffers a debilitating illness or dies?

Just in case you find all these questions daunting, you should know that most businesses decide to tackle these issues down the road, hopefully with a few years of successful business operations under their belt. They reason that, for now, it's enough to know that an appraiser can be called in to establish a fair value of a member's interests if and when a member wishes to sell out. (You don't even need to say this in your operating agreement; just call in an appraiser when and if the time comes.) Similarly, most small LLCs decide that the transfer restrictions built into the operating agreement to satisfy the tax requirements are adequate to limit sales to outsiders (by requiring the approval of all or a majority of the nontransferring members before admitting a new person as a member in the LLC).

However, other more detail-oriented business owners decide to ask and answer all these questions and spell out their conclusions as part of the membership restrictions in their initial operating agreement. Although we think each approach has its merits, we follow the first one here and do not add buy-sell provisions to our basic LLC operating agreements. One additional reason that we take this approach is that it could take a separate book to show you all the possible choices that can be included in buy-sell provisions.

If you want comprehensive buy-sell provisions. If you decide to go the extra distance and include buy-sell provisions for inclusion in your initial operating agreement, you can ask your LLC legal advisor to put together buy-sell provisions that will work for you. Alternately, you should be able to find several legal workbooks at the local law or business library that cover buy-sell or right of first refusal provisions. If you draft your own provisions, it makes sense to have your LLC legal advisor take a look at them to see if there are any glaring gaps or mistakes.

B. Modifying Your LLC Operating Agreement

As you create your own LLC operating agreement, you will undoubtedly want to add or change provisions to suit your needs. Modifying or writing LLC operating agreement provisions is not akin to brain surgery, and you can ordinarily do much of it yourself—just use common sense and your own sound business judgment.

If you wonder whether state law has established any guidelines you must follow in an area of your LLC's operation, it is a simple matter to check your state's LLC Act to make sure your rule does not conflict with a specific statute. (Chapter 4, Section E2 discusses how to locate and use state statutes.) You may also choose to ask a legal or tax advisor for a second opinion on the validity or effect of your custom-crafted provisions. We think this second opinion is mandatory for any changes that may affect your LLC's eligibility for pass-through tax treatment—for example, changes in the membership vote requirement for approving transferees as new members or to continue the LLC after a member or member-manager leaves. (For guidance on self-help research and finding an LLC legal or tax advisor, see Chapter 8.)

Will you need to retype your operating agreement? Minor changes to your operating agreement ordinarily can be accomplished simply by neatly crossing out a word or two, then typing or printing your changes between the lines or in the margins (with insertion marks, if necessary, to show where the new words go). Have all members initial each of these changes in the margin when they sign the agreement. For more comprehensive changes, you will need to retype one or more pages to substitute for the tear-out pages that you prepare. Don't worry if these "insert" pages don't cover a full page—they don't have to. Just be sure to consecutively renumber all pages of your operating agreement, including any inserted pages.

Here's a brief summary of the different types of changes you can make to the tear-out operating agreement, and a quick assessment of how safe you are in making them on your own:

- *Internal matters.* Happily, internal LLC housekeeping provisions are your own business. For example, you may choose to specify how and when member or manager meetings will be held, who qualifies to be an officer or employee in your LLC, and how to handle numerous other formalities. If you want to put rules such as these in your operating agreement, you should generally be safe doing so; state LLC statutes and the tax rules have little or nothing to say about internal issues of this sort.

- *Legal procedures.* If you wish to change a legal procedure—such as the number of votes necessary to dissolve your LLC, amend your Articles of Organization or effect a similar structural change to your LLC—you need to check to see if legal rules affect your desired change. If you have a copy of your state's LLC act handy, it should take just a few minutes to browse through it to see if state law has placed limitations or restrictions on the provisions you are thinking of adopting. (Many LLC filing offices send out copies of the state LLC Act for a small fee or at no charge.)
- *Tax matters.* Tax matters are a little oilier and may be harder to track down or grasp. Because the tax status of your LLC is so important, we recommend showing your LLC tax advisor any changes to your operating agreement that may have tax effects. This person can tell you if your proposed operating agreement changes are good, bad or indifferent from a tax perspective. You ordinarily won't want to tinker with pass-through tax classification provisions—those that affect your classification as a partnership under the federal tax rules—without guidance from your LLC tax advisor.

Example 1: Hank forms an LLC with friend and former business partner Max. Hank has cash and Max doesn't. Max signs a note, promising to pay his investment to the LLC (together with interest) over time. It's decided that even though each person will contribute equally to the capitalization of the LLC, Hank should get an extra share of the profits for putting up cash in one lump sum at the start of the business operations. They ask their tax advisor to check their operating agreement, since special allocations (a disproportionate division) of profits may have tax consequences and require the addition of special provisions to their operating agreement. Their tax advisor adds IRS special allocations language to the agreement that restates technical tax regulations related to sharing profits and losses disproportionately. (See Chapter 3, Section D2, for more on this special allocations tax issue and adding provisions to your operating agreement to handle it.)

Example 2: Kenneth and Francine decide to change the rules in their LLC member-managed operating agreement involving membership vote requirements for the transfer of LLC interests to outsiders. First, they check their state sheet in Appendix A, where we provide the basic state rules for specific LLC matters with tax consequences (they look under the heading "Operating Rules" and read the "Default Transfer Rule" found in the state's LLC law). Next, they ask their tax advisor to take a look at their operating agreement to make sure their changes do not adversely affect the pass-through tax status of their LLC. They realize that how they handle transfers of membership interests will determine whether the IRS will attribute the corporate characteristic of free transferability of interests to their LLC (as discussed in Chapter 3, Section B4).

C. How to Prepare a Member-Managed LLC Operating Agreement

Appendix C contains a basic Operating Agreement for a Member-Managed Limited Liability Company (the first of two agreements in Appendix C). If you wish to prepare this form, tear it out now, making sure that you don't miss any pages or inadvertently take pages from the other (manager-managed) operating agreement. You may want to photocopy the operating agreement before you get started, in case you make mistakes or want to modify it significantly.

We'll start at the top of the agreement and work our way through it. We provide instructions for filling out items in the blanks of the sample agreement, below. To help you complete some of the more complicated information, we provide additional instructions in the Special Instructions that accompany the sample operating agreement. Special Instructions are numbered sequentially as they occur in the sample agreement.

OPERATING AGREEMENT FOR MEMBER-MANAGED LIMITED LIABILITY COMPANY

I. PRELIMINARY PROVISIONS

Here we address preliminary matters, such as the effective date of the agreement, the name of the LLC and other basic information.

(1) Effective Date: This operating agreement of

__________________ **name of LLC,** ❶ __________________

effective__________ **date** __________, ❷ is adopted by the members whose signatures appear at the end of this agreement. ❸

(2) Formation: This limited liability company (LLC) was formed by filing Articles of Organization, a Certificate of Formation or a similar organizational document with the state of ______ **state of formation** ______'s LLC filing office on ____ **date of filing Articles of Organization, Certificate of Formation or similar organizational document.** ____ ❹ A copy of this organizational document has been placed in the LLC's records book.

(3) Name: The formal name of this LLC is as stated above. However, this LLC may do business under a different name by complying with the state's fictitious or assumed business name statutes and procedures. ❺

(4) Registered Office and Agent: The registered office of this LLC and the registered agent at this address are as follows: ______________________________

name and address of registered agent and office. ______________________________

The registered office and agent may be changed from time to time as the members may see fit, by filing a change of registered agent or office form with the state LLC filing office. It will not be necessary to amend this provision of the operating agreement if and when such a change is made. ❻

(5) Business Purposes: The specific business purposes and activities contemplated by the founders of this LLC at the time of initial signing of this agreement consist of the following:

state the specific business purposes and activities you foresee for your LLC. ❼ ____

It is understood that the foregoing statement of purposes shall not serve as a limitation on the powers or abilities of this LLC, which shall be permitted to engage in any and all lawful business activities. If this LLC intends to engage in business activities outside the state of its formation that require the qualification of the LLC in other states, it shall obtain such qualification before engaging in such out-of-state activities.

SPECIAL INSTRUCTIONS

❶ Insert the name of your LLC exactly as shown in your Articles of Organization. (We discuss how to choose a name in Chapter 4, Section C.)

❷ The key is to insert a date that is on or after the date all your members sign this operating agreement (you'll have your operating agreement signed as the last step in preparing this form). If you aren't sure how long it will take to do this, simply insert the words "the last date of signing shown at the end of this agreement."

❸ All members will need to sign the agreement. This is not just a practical precaution; it also has tax significance. All members must sign for the agreement to be considered a "partnership agreement" by the IRS, thereby helping the LLC qualify for pass-through tax treatment. Again, members will sign the operating agreement at the end of this process.

❹ Insert the date and year your Articles of Organization or Certificate of Formation were filed with your state LLC filing office. In most cases, this date will be shown as the "file-stamped" date on the first page of the filed Articles or Certificate, or on a filing receipt mailed to you from the state LLC filing office.

❺ This paragraph states that your LLC is allowed to do business under another name—one that is different from the formal LLC name stated in your Articles of Organization and operating agreement. In that event, you may need to register a fictitious or assumed business name with the state, as well as each county where you will use the fictitious business name. (See Chapter 7, Section D3, and call your state LLC filing office if you want more information.)

❻ Most Articles of Organization specify the LLC's registered office and agent—just copy the information from your Articles of Organization into the blank. (We cover this in Chapter 4, Section E3d.) Typically, the registered office address must be a street address (not a post office box) located in the state. Most states require the agent to be at least 18 years of age and a state resident. Typically, a founding member of the LLC will act as initial agent and show the principal office address of the LLC as the registered office address.

As this paragraph specifies, you may change your LLC's registered agent and office by filing a form with your state LLC filing office (and paying a small fee). If and when you do so, there is no need to go back and change this information in your operating agreement.

❼ In plain English, specify the business purposes of your LLC. You may have listed specific business purposes in your Articles of Organization (covered in Chapter 4, Section E3e). If so, you can copy that information in these blanks.

Mostly, this statement is meant to let your own members know what your plans are for the LLC's business operations, so feel free to expand your statement of purposes to provide as much detail as you want. Here are some examples:

- "to open and operate a car stereo and security alarm sales and service facility"
- "to purchase, sell and otherwise invest in real property and commercial interests in real property," or
- "to provide financial consulting services to individuals and businesses."

(6) Duration of LLC: The duration of this LLC shall be **specify "perpetual" or any specific termination date or term of years for the LLC specified in the Articles of Organization**. Further, this LLC shall terminate when a proposal to dissolve the LLC is adopted by the membership of this LLC or when this LLC is otherwise terminated in accordance with law. ❽

II. MEMBERSHIP PROVISIONS

Here we cover provisions that deal with the rights and responsibilities of your LLC's members.

(1) Nonliability of Members: No member of this LLC shall be personally liable for the expenses, debts, obligations or liabilities of the LLC, or for claims made against it. ❾

(2) Reimbursement for Organizational Costs: Members shall be reimbursed by the LLC for organizational expenses paid by the members. The LLC shall be authorized to elect to deduct organizational expenses and start-up expenditures ratably over a period of time as permitted by the Internal Revenue Code and as may be advised by the LLC's tax advisor. ❿

(3) Management: This LLC shall be managed exclusively by all of its members. ⓫

(4) Members' Percentage Interests: A member's percentage interest in this LLC shall be computed as a fraction, the numerator of which is the total of a member's capital account and the denominator of which is the total of all capital accounts of all members. This fraction shall be expressed in this agreement as a percentage, which shall be called each member's "percentage interest" in this LLC. ⓬

(5) Membership Voting: Except as otherwise may be required by the Articles of Organization, Certificate of Formation or a similar organizational document, other provisions of this operating agreement, or under the laws of this state, each member shall vote on any matter submitted to the membership for approval in proportion to the member's percentage interest in this LLC. Further, unless defined otherwise for a particular provision of this operating agreement, the phrase "majority of members" means a majority of members whose combined percentage interests in this LLC represent more than 50% of the percentage interests of all members in this LLC. ⓭

(6) Compensation: Members shall not be paid as members of the LLC for performing any duties associated with such membership, including management of the LLC. Members may be paid, however, for any services rendered in any other capacity for the LLC, whether as officers, employees, independent contractors or otherwise. ⓮

❽ Most Articles of Organization specify the duration of the legal existence of the LLC, as discussed in Chapter 4, Section E3h. If so, insert this same time period here. Perhaps you're wondering if your LLC must dissolve if your Articles of Organization set a termination date and the business lasts that long. No—you can always amend your Articles to extend the legal life of your LLC as the termination date approaches. (We cover the process of amending Articles in Chapter 7, Section D4.)

If your Articles are silent on this issue, your state most likely does not require you to limit the duration of your LLC's legal existence, and you can insert the word "perpetual" in the blank. Your state LLC materials should indicate if your state has any special rules for limiting the life of your LLC.

Finally, notice that the concluding sentence of this provision makes it clear that the LLC can always be terminated by a vote of the membership and as otherwise allowed by law. (See "VI. Dissolution Provisions: (1) Events That Trigger Dissolution of the LLC," in this operating agreement, and the corresponding Special Instructions ㊳ through ㊶, below.) We include this sentence as a reminder that members have the ultimate say as to when the LLC will wind up its affairs and dissolve.

❾ Although there is no legal requirement that you insert this statement of nonliability in your agreement, we think it's a good idea to include it as a basic restatement of this important state law protection.

In the extremely unlikely case that you don't want limited liability protection for all members, you would delete this paragraph. (For a discussion of how to make one LLC member personally liable for LLC debts and still qualify for pass-through tax treatment, see Chapter 3, Section B1.)

❿ This paragraph authorizes the LLC to reimburse its founders for LLC formation expenses advanced by members, such as filing fees, legal fees and tax fees.

Also included is a reminder that the Internal Revenue Code allows businesses to amortize (deduct over a period of time, usually a 60-month period) organizational and start-up expenses paid or reimbursed by the LLC. (See Internal Revenue Code Sections 709 and 195.) Your tax advisor should tell you whether you can and should make either or both of these important tax elections, and how to implement each of them on your first LLC informational tax return. If you don't make these elections, you may not be able to deduct start-up expenses and organizational costs paid by the LLC. In other words, you may be forced to wait and deduct them later, when the LLC is sold or liquidated.

⓫ This provision makes it clear that all members will manage your LLC. This is exactly the structure and process founders of most smaller LLCs prefer, since it allows all members a hand in managing the business. As discussed earlier, by being member-managed, you also stand a better chance of qualifying for pass-through tax status with the IRS by avoiding the corporate characteristic of centralized management. (If you want to provide for management by some, but not all, members, you need to adopt the management agreement covered in Chapter 6, not this agreement.)

⓬ This paragraph defines an important LLC formula: the calculation of each member's percentage interest in the LLC. This percentage will be used later in the agreement to:

- allocate profits and losses of the LLC to members
- allocate voting rights among the members
- distribute assets of the LLC when it is liquidated, and
- value a member's interest when it is sold to an outsider or back to the LLC.

This percentage is arrived at by computing a fraction that reflects the proportion of each member's capital account to the total of all members' capital accounts. Each member's capital account starts with the amount of money or value of property he or she contributed at the outset of the LLC, plus any additions to, distributions from or other adjustments to this account.

Example: Barbara, Bill, Fred, Francis and Mike start their LLC by contributing $5,000 cash each. Each member's capital account currently shows a positive $5,000 balance. Each member has a 20% percentage interest in the LLC. This figure is the result of dividing each member's $5,000 capital account balance by the $25,000 total capital account balance for all members, resulting in the fraction 1/5, expressed in the operating agreement as a percentage interest of 20%. (According to subsequent provisions in the agreement, each person is allocated 20% of the profits and losses of the LLC and is entitled to a 20% share of the LLC's total voting power.)

If you want to change this standard approach. You may make changes to this provision and base percentage interests in your LLC disproportionately, or by some other formula. For example, you could decide that anyone who contributes cash to your LLC is entitled to a 10% increase in the standard percentage interest (with other members' interests reduced accordingly). If you wish to come up with your own method, ask your tax advisor to make sure that you will meet the requirements of IRS regulations relating to special allocations of profits and losses. Generally, Internal Revenue Code regulations under Section 704 of the Internal Revenue Code require that special allocations of LLC profits and losses have "substantial economic effect," meaning they are based upon a specific economic reality of your business—for example, perhaps one member devotes more time to a profit making activity or is on the line for its losses. You can, however, pretty much do what you want if you adopt special allocation tax language in your agreement. See Chapter 3, Section D2, for more information on this special tax issue.

⓭ This provision gives each member voting power equal to his or her percentage interest in the LLC—for instance, a 10% member gets a 10% vote on any matter. This is standard practice, although you can base voting rights on some other measure if you wish. Here are some possibilities:

- each member gets one vote on all membership matters—known as per capita voting, or
- each member's vote depends on his or her share in the profits of the LLC (if profits interests differ from percentage interests).

Special tax-critical voting rules. You'll see in later provisions that special membership voting rules are specified in your operating agreement to approve transfers of membership and to agree to continue the LLC after a member leaves. (These tax-critical issues are discussed in Chapter 3.) These special voting rules will take precedence if they conflict with any of the provisions of the basic LLC membership voting rule specified here. For example, this operating agreement's "V. Membership Withdrawal and Transfer Provisions: (2) Restrictions on the Transfer of Membership," requires the approval of all nontransferring members to approve the transfer of membership to a new member. This unanimous vote requirement will take precedence over the membership voting provisions contained in this paragraph.

⓮ This paragraph says that members will not be paid in their capacity as members or member-managers of the LLC. It does, however, allow compensation in any other capacity—for example, the LLC may pay members who also serve as LLC officers, staff, salaried personnel or independent contractors.

Example: Sally and Joe are the only two members of their member-managed LLC. Both actively operate the LLC, Sally as President and Joe as Sales Manager. They receive salaries for their day-to-day work, but don't receive any extra compensation simply for signing up and legally functioning as members (and member-managers) of their LLC.

⓯ Especially if you have previously been involved in a small corporation, you may be surprised that the operating agreement doesn't require regular membership meetings. We don't require meetings for several reasons:

- Most LLC members naturally will prefer to spend their time taking care of business, not holding and documenting formal LLC meetings. After all, you and your business associates can schedule and hold meetings for any purpose when and as you need, without having to treat them as formal LLC membership meetings.
- When you do need a formal meeting to approve an important legal formality that should be recorded in your LLC records, you can call one as provided in this clause.
- We've heard it said that setting up regular meetings of members in an LLC operating agreement may make the LLC look too much like a corporation. Most corporations delight—or at least acquiesce—in the convention of providing for regular and special management (director) and owner (shareholder) meetings in operating provisions in their Bylaws.

Most state statutes are silent as to whether and how members' meetings are called and held. If your state law does deal with this, the state law LLC meeting provisions are usually default rules only—that is, you are usually free to change them in your LLC operating agreement. To learn what, if anything, your state has to say on this subject, scan your state's LLC Act. Particularly, look for a section of law titled "Meetings of Members." Be aware, however, that many meeting requirements only concern meetings by managers in *manager-managed* LLCs (the type of LLC that uses the operating agreement covered in Chapter 6). Manager-meeting provisions of this sort do not apply to a member-managed LLC.

When it comes to calling meetings, we've kept things simple and in line with the kind of flexibility normally accorded LLCs under state law: members can decide to meet at any time with a minimum of pre-meeting formality. Further, our provision says that all members must either attend a meeting or, alternatively, that any nonattending members must agree in writing to the holding of the meeting ahead of time. This is the approach most small, closely held LLCs will wish to take—after all, the holding of a formal membership meeting is infrequent and is usually enough of a big deal to warrant attendance by everyone, or at least to require the pre-meeting consent of any member who can't attend.

We have also added an escape hatch in this provision, which allows the holding of a formal LLC membership meeting with a majority of the membership (percentage) interests in attendance, if it is a second postponed meeting (the second postponement of a members' meeting, whose time and date was announced at the first postponed meeting). You can change this postponement procedure to suit your tastes—for example, you could require two postponements (instead of one) before permitting a meeting with less than unanimous attendance or consent. Similarly, you may wish to change the quorum requirement of such a meeting, such as to two-thirds of the per capita membership in the LLC rather than our majority of percentage interests requirement.

Some LLCs will wish to provide for alternatives to face-to-face member meetings. For example, you can allow for membership action by unanimous written consent of the members (without a meeting), or provide for conference-call, computer bulletin-board or video hookups and other high-tech ways to hold virtual meetings over the phone lines or in cyberspace. Frankly, we think worrying about all of this is probably a bit much for most smaller LLCs. Formal membership meetings are not commonly needed in the first place, unless big structural changes are in the works, such as amending the LLC Articles of Organization or approving a dissolution of the LLC. If you are considering approving a major proposal of this sort, meeting face-to-face makes the most sense anyway.

(7) Members' Meetings: The LLC shall not provide for regular members' meetings. However, any member may call a meeting by communicating his or her wish to schedule a meeting to all other members. Such notification may be in person or in writing, or by telephone, facsimile machine, or other form of electronic communication reasonably expected to be received by a member, and the other members shall then agree, either personally, in writing, or by telephone, facsimile machine or other form of electronic communication to the member calling the meeting, to meet at a mutually acceptable time and place. Notice of the business to be transacted at the meeting need not be given to members by the member calling the meeting, and any business may be discussed and conducted at the meeting.

If all members cannot attend a meeting, it shall be postponed to a date and time when all members can attend, unless all members who do not attend have agreed in writing to the holding of the meeting without them. If a meeting is postponed, and the postponed meeting cannot be held either because all members do not attend the postponed meeting or the nonattending members have not signed a written consent to allow the postponed meeting to be held without them, a second postponed meeting may be held at a date and time announced at the first postponed meeting. The date and time of the second postponed meeting shall also be communicated to any members not attending the first postponed meeting. The second postponed meeting may be held without the attendance of all members as long as a majority of the percentage interests of the membership of this LLC is in attendance at the second postponed meeting. Written notice of the decisions or approvals made at this second postponed meeting shall be mailed or delivered to each nonattending member promptly after the holding of the second postponed meeting. ⓯

Written minutes of the discussions and proposals presented at a members' meeting, and the votes taken and matters approved at such meeting, shall be taken by one of the members or a person designated at the meeting. A copy of the minutes of the meeting shall be placed in the LLC's records book after the meeting. ⓰

(8) Membership Certificates: This LLC shall be authorized to obtain and issue certificates representing or certifying membership interests in this LLC. Each certificate shall show the name of the LLC, the name of the member, and state that the person named is a member of the LLC and is entitled to all the rights granted members of the LLC under the Articles of Organization, Certificate of Formation or a similar organizational document, this operating agreement and provisions of law. Each membership certificate shall be consecutively numbered and signed by one or more officers of this LLC. The certificates shall include any additional information considered appropriate for inclusion by the members on membership certificates.

If and when a member calls a meeting. Note that it is a common requirement under state law that once a meeting is called to discuss a specific proposal, the LLC is not allowed to take action on the matter until the meeting is held. We're sure you'll extend this courtesy to your membership anyway without being told (and without the need to put this provision in your agreement).

If the subject of LLC meetings sparks your interest and you want to include more detailed rules, you ordinarily can let your imagination and good sense be your guide. Following are some examples of issues you may want to address—but before you make any changes, do take a quick look at your state LLC act to be sure there are no special rules to consider:

- You can set a time limit for calling meetings (no more than 60 days or less than 10 days from the date of the call, for example).
- You may want to require verbal or written notice of meetings (our provision allows all sorts of methods for giving and acknowledging notice, including the use of fax machines and other electronic devices).
- You may limit the business to be conducted at a meeting to matters stated in the notice.
- You may wish to set lower quorum requirements to hold member meetings (less than the unanimous presence or consent of members), and the like.

⑯ In Chapter 7, Sections C2, C3 and C4, we show you how to document meetings, and we discuss the importance of keeping good records, preferably in a well-organized LLC records kit. Of course, it's possible to create your own, or you may be interested in ordering an LLC records kit from Nolo Press. (See order page at the back of this book.)

⑰ There is no statutorily required form for LLC membership certificates, and you are not even legally required to issue them to your members. However, most organizers of LLCs like the idea of membership certificates, since the delivery of certificates to members serves as a formal way to welcome members into the LLC and recognize their capital contribution (and a good excuse to hold an LLC party!).

If you prepare your own certificates, you can follow our basic format for the contents of the certificates as stated in this provision, or you can modify the provision to require additional information on each certificate, such as the date of issuance and the percentage interest each member holds in the LLC. Remember to place a membership certificate legend on each of the certificates—see the preceding sidebar, "How to Prepare a Membership Certificate Legend."

You do not have to obtain and impress a seal of the LLC on each certificate, but it is customary to do so. If you wish to order good quality LLC certificates, as well as a seal, you can do so as part of a Nolo Press LLC records kit. (See the order page at the back of this book.)

⑱ This provision limits the ability of members to own interests in, manage or work in competing outside businesses. We don't specify exactly what a competing business is, so you may want to add language that addresses this issue.

Example: Each member shall agree not to own an interest in, manage or work for another computer retail sales or service business, enterprise or endeavor...

You can be more liberal if you wish, and allow members to own, manage or be employed by competing businesses, but we think our provision states a basic restriction that will match the wishes of most smaller LLC owners.

If you wish to expand or otherwise change this provision. You may wish to take a look at noncompetition provisions for LLCs, partnerships, corporations and other businesses in a local law or business library. Noncompetition clauses can be found in various partnership and employment agreements

Fill In at Time of Issuance

Certificate Number ______________________

Issued To:

____

____

Date ______________________ 19 ____

Fill in at Time of Transfer

Transferor ______________________

Transferee ______________________

Date of Transfer ______________________

No. of Transferee's Certificate ______________

Note: Memberships in this LLC are Subject to Restrictions on Transfer Contained in the Company's Operating Agreement

Fill In at Time of Issuance

Received Certificate Number ______________________

This ________ day of ____________ 19 ______

____

SIGNATURE OF MEMBER

- -

Certificate Number ______

THE MEMBERSHIP INTEREST REPRESENTED BY THIS CERTIFICATE IS SUBJECT TO RESTRICTIONS ON TRANSFER, AND MAY NOT BE OFFERED FOR SALE, SOLD, TRANSFERRED OR PLEDGED EXCEPT ACCORDING TO, AND ONLY IF ALLOWED BY, THESE TRANSFER RESTRICTIONS. TO OBTAIN A COPY OF THESE TRANSFER RESTRICTIONS, CONTACT AN OFFICER OF THIS LCC AT THE FOLLOWING ADDRESS: **type main address of LLC**

type name of LLC

A LIMITED LIABILITY COMPANY

Membership Certificate

THIS IS TO CERTIFY THAT ______________________

is a member of the above Limited Liability Company organized under the laws of this state and is entitled to the full rights and privileges of such membership, subject to the duties and restrictions, as more fully set forth in the Limited Liability Company's Articles of Organization and Operating Agreement.

IN WITNESS WHEREOF, the Company has caused this Certificate to be executed by its duly authorized officers.

Dated ______________________

______________________ *, Officer*

______________________ *, Officer*

contained in *Gordon's Modern Annotated Forms of Agreement*, by Saul Gordon, revised and updated by Stephen Kurzman (Prentice Hall, Englewood Cliffs, NJ). An overview of the court-developed rules in this area is contained in a legal reference book commonly found in law libraries: *ALR (American Law Reports)*, 3rd Edition, Volume 61, starting on page 397. Section 28 of this annotation discusses cases dealing specifically with agreements not to compete found in partnership agreements. Other places to look for specific noncompetition clauses are business buy-sell agreements, corporate bylaws, general and limited partnership agreements and employment contracts in legal and business practice books located in law and business libraries. Or, you may wish to ask your LLC legal advisor to help you craft a member noncompetition clause.

⓳ This is a statement of intent paragraph that says you do not wish to have your LLC taxed as a corporation; you prefer the pass-through tax status that applies to partnerships. This provision also makes it clear that you do not intend be bound by legal partnership or joint venture rules when dealing with the other members (or managers) of the LLC. In other words, you want to be treated as a partnership only for tax purposes.

Of course, you still want to be treated as an LLC under state law, with each member (and manager) insulated from the debts and liabilities of the business. The agreement addresses this in "II. Membership Provisions: (1) Nonliability of Members," above.

⓴ The tax year and accounting period options available to LLCs are the same as those available to partnerships. There are several places to look for the most current information on these rules, including IRS publications and commercial tax guides at the local law or business library. (See IRS Publication 538, *Accounting Periods and Methods,* and IRS Publication 541, *Tax Information on Partnerships.*) Of course, your tax advisor should be on top of any recent rules in these areas.

HOW TO PREPARE A MEMBERSHIP CERTIFICATE LEGEND

If you adopt and use one of the two tear-out agreements included with this book without making modifications, you will require the vote of all nontransferring members to admit into membership a transferee of a selling member. See Special Instruction ㊱, below, which covers "V. Membership, Withdrawal and Transfer Provisions: (2) Restrictions on the Transfer of Membership," in this operating agreement.

This operating agreement's "II. Membership Provisions: (8) Membership Certificates," requires your LLC to put members on notice of the existence of these restrictions on transfer—as well as any others you may adopt in your operating agreement or Articles—by including a statement (a legend) on any membership certificates you issue. You don't need to spell out exact transfer restrictions in your LLC membership certificate legend. Instead, you can summarize the restrictions and tell people reading the certificate how to get a copy of the restrictions from the LLC.

Below is a sample of a simple membership certificate legend to accomplish these purposes. (This standard legend is printed on each LLC membership certificate included in the Nolo Press LLC records kit.) To use this legend, type or print the language below on the front of each membership certificate prior to issuing it to a member; printing it in all caps and/or in boldface is a good way to ensure that it is "conspicuous" and will be noticed and read by anyone who looks at the certificate:

THE MEMBERSHIP INTEREST REPRESENTED BY THIS CERTIFICATE IS SUBJECT TO RESTRICTIONS ON TRANSFER, AND MAY NOT BE OFFERED FOR SALE, SOLD, TRANSFERRED OR PLEDGED EXCEPT ACCORDING TO, AND ONLY IF ALLOWED BY, THESE TRANSFER RESTRICTIONS. TO OBTAIN A COPY OF THESE TRANSFER RESTRICTIONS, CONTACT AN OFFICER OF THIS LLC AT THE FOLLOWING ADDRESS: **insert main address of LLC**.

In addition to the above information, all membership certificates shall bear a prominent legend on their face or reverse side stating, summarizing or referring to any transfer restrictions that apply to memberships in this LLC under the Articles of Organization, Certificate of Formation or a similar organizational document and/or this operating agreement, and the address where a member may obtain a copy of these restrictions upon request from this LLC.

The records book of this LLC shall contain a list of the names and addresses of all persons to whom certificates have been issued, show the date of issuance of each certificate, and record the date of all cancellations or transfers of membership certificates. ⓱

(9) Other Business by Members: Each member shall agree not to own an interest in, manage or work for another business, enterprise or endeavor, if such ownership or activities would compete with this LLC's business goals, mission, profitability or productivity, or would diminish or impair the member's ability to provide maximum effort and performance in managing the business of this LLC. ⓲

III. TAX AND FINANCIAL PROVISIONS

These provisions deal with tax and financial aspects of organizing and running your LLC.

(1) Tax Treatment: It is anticipated that this LLC will not be treated as a corporation under state and federal tax law, but instead it will be treated in the same manner as a partnership for tax purposes. It is further understood that the members do not consider each other partners or joint venturers with any other member or manager of this LLC for any purpose other than federal and state tax purposes. ⓳

(2) Tax Year and Accounting Method: The tax year of this LLC shall be **"the calendar year" or specify a noncalendar year period, such as "July 1 to June 30th"**. The LLC shall use the **"cash" or "accrual"** method of accounting. Both the tax year and the accounting period of the LLC may be changed with the consent of all members if the LLC qualifies for such change, and may be effected by the filing of appropriate forms with the IRS and state tax authorities. ⓴

(3) Tax Matters Partner: If this LLC is required under Internal Revenue Code provisions or regulations, it shall designate from among its members a "tax matters partner" in accordance with Internal Revenue Code Section 6231(a)(7) and corresponding regulations, who will fulfill this role by being the spokesperson for the LLC in dealings with the IRS as required under the Internal Revenue Code and Regulations, and who will report to the members on the progress and outcome of these dealings. ㉑

Here is the basic information you can use to delve deeper into tax options for your LLC:

- *Generally, LLCs (like partnerships) must select a tax year that is the same as the tax year of 50% or more of its members.* Most often, LLCs select a calendar tax year (from January 1 to December 31st), which is the normal tax year for individual members. However, your LLC may be able to elect a noncalendar tax year—what's known as a fiscal year—if it can show a good business purpose for the alternate year. (If you're interested, see Revenue Procedure 92-1, Revenue Procedure 87-32, and Revenue Ruling 87-57.) Section 444 of the Internal Revenue Code also allows the election of a noncalendar tax year if it results in the deferral of not more than three months of income for LLC members.
- *LLCs may elect a cash or accrual method of accounting.* Under the cash method, the business deducts expenses when paid and reports income when received. This is the way most individual taxpayers handle income and expenses on their tax returns. Under the accrual method, the business deducts expenses when it becomes legally obligated to pay them, and reports income when the LLC becomes legally entitled to receive the income. Small, closely held LLCs may benefit from the cash method of accounting because it may allow them to defer the reporting of income and give them added flexibility in claiming deductions, so most choose this option. However, your LLC may not be able to use the cash method of accounting if it has a corporation as a member (with some exceptions) or if it is considered a "tax shelter" under IRS rules. Tax shelters include businesses that sell securities that are registered with the SEC (your LLC should be exempt from registration—see Chapter 2, Section E); those set up with the principal purpose of avoiding the payment of federal income taxes (most LLC founders will have a primary purpose of making money from active business operations, not tax avoidance); and those that fall under the definition of a "syndicate" (your LLC will be considered a syndicate—and therefore unable to elect the cash accounting method—if more than 35% of its losses are allocable to members who do not actively participate in the business).

Select a tax year and accounting method with the help of your tax advisor. Because these are important tax elections with significant financial and tax repercussions, it's important to check your conclusions on picking a tax year and accounting method with your tax advisor.

(21) Generally, if you have ten or more LLC members (or if any member uses more than one percentage to figure his or her shares in LLC profits, losses, credits, deductions or other tax items—for example, a member with a 10% profits interest gets a 20% share of losses), you will need to select a "tax matters partner" and file a designation of tax matters partner form with the IRS. (Remember, LLCs are treated like partnerships under federal tax law.)

This provision simply reminds you that your LLC may have to designate a tax matters partner. Even if required, you do not have to specify in your operating agreement who will act in this capacity. You may informally designate someone later as a tax matters partner, and may change this designation when and as needed. There are technical rules on who may serve as a tax matters partner for an LLC (if interested, see Proposed Internal Revenue Code Regulation §301.6231(a)(7)-1, (a)(7)-2). Ask your tax advisor to help you pick a tax matters partner if you are required to do so, and to make the appropriate IRS filing.

(4) Annual Income Tax Returns and Reports: Within 60 days after the end of each tax year of the LLC, a copy of the LLC's state and federal income tax returns for the preceding tax year shall be mailed or otherwise provided to each member of the LLC, together with any additional information and forms necessary for each member to complete his or her individual state and federal income tax returns. This additional information shall include a federal (and, if applicable, state) Form K-1 (Form 1065—Partner's Share of Income, Credits, Deductions) or equivalent income tax reporting form, as well as a financial report, which shall include a balance sheet and profit and loss statement for the prior tax year of the LLC. ㉒

(5) Bank Accounts: The LLC shall designate one or more banks or other institutions for the deposit of the funds of the LLC, and shall establish savings, checking, investment and other such accounts as are reasonable and necessary for its business and investments. One or more members of the LLC shall be designated with the consent of all members to deposit and withdraw funds of the LLC, and to direct the investment of funds from, into and among such accounts. The funds of the LLC, however and wherever deposited or invested, shall not be commingled with the personal funds of any members of the LLC. ㉓

(6) Title to Assets: All personal and real property of this LLC shall be held in the name of the LLC, not in the names of individual members. ㉔

IV. CAPITAL PROVISIONS

These provisions deal with capital contributions, allocations and distributions by and to LLC members, as well as related matters.

(1) Capital Contributions by Members: Members shall make the following contributions of cash, property or services as shown next to each member's name below. Unless otherwise noted, cash and property described below shall be paid or delivered to the LLC on or by **final date or period for contributions**. The fair market values of items of property or services as agreed between the LLC and the contributing member are also shown below. The percentage interest in the LLC that each member shall receive in return for his or her capital contribution is also indicated for each member. ㉕

Name	Contribution	Fair Market Value	Percentage Interest in LLC
______________	______________	$ ________	________
______________	______________	$ ________	________
______________	______________	$ ________	________
______________	______________	$ ________	________
______________	______________	$ ________	________
______________	______________	$ ________	________

㉒ LLC profits and losses are passed along to members, who will need these figures at the end of each year, as well as other LLC information, to prepare their individual income tax returns. To this end, we include a paragraph requiring that within 60 days after the end of each tax year, all members must be provided with:

- LLC income tax returns
- LLC financial statements (you can dispense with the preparation of financial statements, but we think most members will regard this additional information as critical), and
- a completed IRS Form K-1 (Form 1065—*Partner's Share of Income, Credits, Deductions*).

You can change the time frame for the LLC to provide this information—for example, within 30 days after the end of the LLC's tax year (instead of 60 days), but make sure to give your LLC enough time to prepare these forms and statements.

㉓ This is a general authorization paragraph that allows the LLC to establish accounts with banks and other institutions. It allows one or more members to be designated to deposit and withdraw funds into and from these accounts, and to direct the investment of funds held in these accounts.

Note that unanimous consent is required to designate a person or persons to have this depositing/checkwriting authority, but you can lessen this requirement if you wish by simply deleting the words "with the consent of all members" from the second sentence of this paragraph.

Typically, each member of a small, closely held LLC will have depositing and checkwriting authority—although, for added fiscal control, multiple signatures may be required for withdrawals that exceed a specified amount. You don't need to specify these arrangements in your operating agreement. The details of these checkwriting and investment-directing arrangements will be spelled out on the signature cards and paperwork you must fill in when opening accounts on behalf of your LLC.

The final sentence in this paragraph is a reminder that personal funds of the LLC members may not be commingled (mixed) with the funds of the LLC. If you commingle funds, a state court may decide that you and the other members are not entitled to limited liability protection normally afforded an LLC, and may hold you personally liable for its debts and claims.

㉔ This is another one of our "reminder" provisions to make it clear that the LLC will not commingle (mix) or confuse title to property. LLC property will only be owned by and in the name of the LLC.

㉕ Here is an important provision in your agreement, where you specify who pays what to the LLC to get it started. Generally, there are no minimum capitalization requirements for LLCs under state law. You can start an LLC with a large amount of cash or property, or on a shoestring.

Most states allow members to contribute cash, property or a promise to pay cash or property in the future—for example, one member agrees to provide future services as a contribution and another to pay a specified amount of cash to the LLC within a certain time limit. The state sheets in Appendix A indicate if states place restrictions on the types of payment (consideration) that may be made for membership interests; a few prohibit the use of promises to pay money or provide future services as capital contributions.

Capital contributions may have tricky tax consequences. Particularly problematic are contributions of appreciated property and the contribution of future services to an LLC. We discuss potential problems that can occur with these types of capital contributions, such as increased personal income taxes for members, in Chapter 3, Section D1. To avoid problems, we strongly suggest you talk to your tax advisor before settling on the particular capital contribution scenario you will follow to fund your LLC if all members won't be paying cash up front.

Of course, even if your state says a promise to pay or to work for the LLC can't be used to set one up, you may be able to find a way around this limitation. For example, if a state prohibits using promissory notes (a promise to pay money) to capitalize an LLC, one of the cash-rich members may loan funds to another member for the latter to use as his or her capital contribution. Because the loan is made between the members on a personal basis only, and is off the books of the LLC, it should be fine.

Example: Warren has plenty of cash and will contribute $20,000 as his one-half interest in a new LLC. He makes a personal loan of another $20,000 to his buddy Carl, who turns around and pays this $20,000 as his contribution to the LLC. Warren trusts Carl to pay back the $20,000 (plus interest) with Carl's eventual shares in the LLC's profits. Warren asks Carl to sign a personal promissory note that carries an annual interest rate of 7%, and may even require that Carl pledge collateral for payback of the loan if he wants an extra measure of safety.

Use a promissory note for future cash payments. For future cash payments, you should have members sign a promissory note (with or without interest), payable on demand after a certain date or number of months or years, or payable in equal or unequal installments during the term of the note. For simple note forms to use for this purpose, see *Simple Contracts for Personal Use*, by Stephen Elias and Marcia Stewart (Nolo Press).

Once you've ironed out the details of members' contributions, you're ready to fill in the blanks. In the first blank, specify a date or period when capital contributions must be made by the members—such as "30 days from the signing of this agreement." (The date specified for members' contributions in the first paragraph of this provision applies only if you do not specify a later date for future payments on the individual contribution lines below this paragraph.)

Here's how to fill in the remaining blanks:

- *Name.* On separate lines, list the name of each contributing LLC member. We provide space for six members. If your LLC has seven or more members (or you simply find that you need more space), fill in the words "see Attachment 1" and provide the information on a separate sheet of paper that you label Attachment 1.
- *Contribution.* Describe each member's contribution. If a member is contributing cash, fill in the amount. Describe any contributions of property (personal property or real property) in plain language. If a member will make future payments of money, transfer property or contribute services to the LLC as a capital contribution, you must describe the timeline and general terms for those future payments or services. If you wish, you can insert the specifics of members' future payments here (again, the date specified for members' contributions in the first paragraph of this provision applies only if you do not specify a later date for payment here). If you need more room, which is likely, fill in the words, "See the schedule/bill/promissory note attached to this agreement as Attachment 1" (or another numbered attachment, as the case may be). Then attach a separate document that spells out the details of each member's initial capital contribution to the LLC.

Example 1: Jeremy will contribute $10,000 in cash as his capital contribution. He can only come up with half the cash now, and agrees to pay the balance in six months. The description of his capital contribution reads as follows: "$5,000 cash on or by the date indicated above for contributions by members, and payment of an additional $5,000 on or by June 15, 200X."

Example 2: John contributes a promise to pay $10,000 in cash to his LLC as his capital contribution. The description of Tom's contribution is: "$10,000 to be paid per the terms of a promissory note attached to this agreement as Attachment 1."

Example 3: Tom will pay cash of $1,000 to his LLC, plus a promise to contribute $6,000 in future services as his capital contribution. The following statement is inserted: "$1,000 in cash; $6,000 in future services—see schedule of services attached to this agreement as Attachment 1." On an separate page, the following schedule of future services appears:

Attachment 1—Schedule of Future Services
Tom Chan will contribute a total of 300 hours of work for the LLC, for which he normally would be compensated at the hourly rate of $20. This contributed work shall be performed between January 1, 200X and December 31, 200X, and shall consist of services of at least 12 hours per week during this period."

- *Fair Market Value.* For noncash payments, show the fair market value of the property or services to be contributed. You may leave this item blank for cash payments.
- *Percentage Interest in LLC.* Here you specify the percentage interest each member will receive in return for his or her capital contribution. A member's percentage interest may be expressed as a percentage or a fraction—for example, either "50%" or "1/2." A percentage interest—also referred to as the member's capital interest—is the portion of the net assets of the LLC (total assets minus liabilities) that each member is entitled to when the business is sold or used to value a member's interest when a member is bought out. This percentage interest figure is usually also used to determine other financial and managerial rights. In our agreement, it is used to determine each member's share of the LLC's profit and loss, as well as member's voting power in the LLC. In most cases involving smaller LLCs, members will each put up a proportionate amount of cash for a membership interest—that is, each will normally receive a percentage interest in the LLC that equals his or her proportionate cash capital contribution.

Example 1: Judy, Ed and Sharon each contribute $10,000 to their LLC to get it started, reasoning that $30,000 is just about right to begin operations until enough cash starts to flow into the business to make it self-supporting. Each person gets a one-third percentage interest in the LLC in return for his or her initial cash capital contributions.

Example 2: Gail and Lilian form their own LLC. Gail puts up $10,000 in cash, plus a used computer system that will be signed over to the LLC for a fair value of $5,000. Lilian puts up $7,500 in cash, plus signs over the pink slip to her paid-off Honda Accord with a middle blue book resale value of $7,500. Each has a 50% membership interest in the LLC.

Example 3: Sam and Jerry start an LLC. Sam has the cash, Jerry the expertise. Sam puts up $75,000. Jerry agrees to forego his first $25,000 in salary from the LLC as his capital contribution. Sam has a 75% interest in the LLC, and Jerry has a 25% interest. (In addition, Jerry will likely have to pay personal income taxes on the value of his LLC interest in the year the operating agreement is signed, as discussed in Chapter 3, Section D1.)

How much, if any, extra documentation do you need to prepare to back up your capital contributions? In most cases, just filling in these blanks in your operating agreement to describe the type, value and timing of each member's payment will be enough. For instance, stating that a member will contribute future services worth $10,000 to the LLC on or by a particular date, or that a member will pay $10,000 to the LLC within three years of signing the agreement, plus interest at an annual rate of 9%, will ordinarily make the other members comfortable. In some cases, you may feel the need to prepare additional documentation, such as a schedule of future services that describes when and what work a member will do for the LLC, or a promissory note that specifies the repayment terms of a future cash payment. Or you may wish to inventory and separately value various items of property that are being transferred by a member. Here are examples of how this provision can be completed.

Example 1: Jeff will pay $15,000 at an 8% interest rate per the terms of a two-year note to buy a one-quarter stake in a new LLC. His capital contribution is described as follows:

Name	*Contribution*	*Fair Market Value*	*Percentage Interest in LLC*
Jeff Billings	*$15,000 per terms of note attached as Attachment 1*		*25%*

Example 2: Mary plans to contribute $3,000 in cash and $3,000 in property over the first year of a new LLC's life for her 40% share. Here's how she completes this provision:

Name	*Contribution*	*Fair Market Value*	*Percentage Interest in LLC*
Mary Ranier	*$3,000 in cash and $3,000 in property as described on schedule attached as Attachment 2*	*$6,000*	*40%*

(2) Additional Contributions by Members: The members may agree, from time to time by unanimous vote, to require the payment of additional capital contributions by the members, on or by a mutually agreeable date. 26

(3) Failure to Make Contributions: If a member fails to make a required capital contribution within the time agreed for a member's contribution, the remaining members may, by unanimous vote, agree to reschedule the time for payment of the capital contribution by the late-paying member, setting any additional repayment terms, such as a late payment penalty, rate of interest to be applied to the unpaid balance, or other monetary amount to be paid by the delinquent member, as the remaining members decide. Alternatively, the remaining members may, by unanimous vote, agree to cancel the membership of the delinquent member, provided any prior partial payments of capital made by the delinquent member are refunded promptly by the LLC to the member after the decision is made to terminate the membership of the delinquent member. 27

(4) No Interest on Capital Contributions: No interest shall be paid on funds or property contributed as capital to this LLC, or on funds reflected in the capital accounts of the members. 28

(5) Capital Account Bookkeeping: A capital account shall be set up and maintained on the books of the LLC for each member. It shall reflect each member's capital contribution to the LLC, increased by each member's share of profits in the LLC, decreased by each member's share of losses and expenses of the LLC, and adjusted as required in accordance with applicable provisions of the Internal Revenue Code and corresponding income tax regulations. 29

(26) This simple provision requires the unanimous vote of all members before members can be asked to contribute additional capital to the LLC. You may lower the vote requirement if you wish—for example, by specifying a majority vote (majority of members or of profits or capital interests), but if you do, be aware that some members may not be able to come up with the cash on time. What will you do then? Will you let the cash-rich members increase their percentage interests in the LLC while decreasing the percentage interests of the noncontributing members? This seems unfair, particularly to the members who want to contribute but can't come up with the additional capital on time. Especially for small LLCs, this is the reason we think unanimity is best when it comes to additional contributions.

(27) This is a penalty provision for failure to pay contributions to the LLC on time. We don't address what "on time" means—it will follow the timelines established in your capital contributions clause unless you add language to this late payment provision specifying when its voting procedures kick in. For example, you may want this late payment provision to apply if a member fails to make a cash or property contribution within 30 days of its scheduled date. On the other hand, you may give a member who is to provide future services or make installment cash payments over the course of one or more years at least a month or two to remedy a missed installment payment before the late payment procedures go into effect.

You can also vary the penalty terms. Our provision requires a unanimous vote of remaining members to extend the terms for payment of a late capital contribution or terminate a delinquent member's membership. You may decide to require a lesser vote, eliminate entirely the alternate procedure of terminating a membership for failure to pay a capital contribution on time, or make other changes or additions.

(28) It is standard not to pay interest to members on their capital contributions—after all, members are investing money in the business with the hope of making more money, not banking it.

If, however, you wish to pay interest on members' capital contributions, you should delete this paragraph and provide for interest payments instead. You can make a general authorization, which lets members pin down the terms of the interest payments later by themselves, or spell out the terms—such as interest rate, dates and manner of payment:

> *Sample Language:* Interest on Capital Contributions: Interest shall be paid on funds or property contributed as capital to this LLC or on funds reflected in the capital accounts of the members **"as may be agreed by unanimous vote of the members" or specify terms (interest rate, dates and manner of payment).**

(29) This tax language requires the LLC to set up capital accounts for each member, something that is required for federal income tax purposes. We state general rules here for LLC capital account bookkeeping. We don't cite specific sections of the Internal Revenue Code that may affect your LLC's bookkeeping or lay out all the special provisions that may apply to setting up and maintaining LLC capital accounts.

As discussed in Chapter 3, Section D2, if you decide to make special allocations of profits and losses, you (and your tax advisor) may decide to include (a significant amount of) additional language to make sure your allocations of profits and losses will go unchallenged by the IRS.

(6) Consent to Capital Contribution Withdrawals and Distributions: Members shall not be allowed to withdraw any part of their capital contributions or to receive distributions, whether in property or cash, except as otherwise allowed by this agreement and, in any case, only if such withdrawal is made with the written consent of all members. ㉚

(7) Allocations of Profits and Losses: No member shall be given priority or preference with respect to other members in obtaining a return of capital contributions, distributions or allocations of the income, gains, losses, deductions, credits or other items of the LLC. The profits and losses of the LLC, and all items of its income, gain, loss, deduction and credit shall be allocated to members according to each member's percentage interest in this LLC. ㉛

(8) Allocation and Distribution of Cash to Members: Cash from LLC business operations, as well as cash from a sale or other disposition of LLC capital assets, may be distributed from time to time to members in accordance with each member's percentage interest in the LLC, as may be decided by **"all" or "a majority"** of the members. ㉜

(9) Allocation of Noncash Distributions: If proceeds consist of property other than cash, the members shall decide the value of the property and allocate such value among the members in accordance with each member's percentage interest in the LLC. If such noncash proceeds are later reduced to cash, such cash may be distributed among the members as otherwise provided in this agreement. ㉝

(10) Allocation and Distribution of Liquidation Proceeds: Regardless of any other provision in this agreement, if there is a distribution in liquidation of this LLC, or when any member's interest is liquidated, all items of income and loss shall be allocated to the members' capital accounts, and all appropriate credits and deductions shall then be made to these capital accounts before any final distribution is made. A final distribution shall be made to members only to the extent of, and in proportion to, any positive balance in each member's capital account. ㉞

V. MEMBERSHIP WITHDRAWAL AND TRANSFER PROVISIONS

These provisions deal with members deciding to leave the LLC. We specifically require a vote to admit a transferee (someone who buys or is otherwise transferred an LLC interest from a member) as a new member of the LLC. As you know from Chapter 3, Section B4, the vote requirement to admit transferees into membership is an important tax option that helps your LLC qualify for pass-through tax status with the IRS.

(1) Withdrawal of Members: A member may withdraw from this LLC by giving written notice to all other members at least **number of days** days before the date the withdrawal is to be effective. ㉟

(2) Restrictions on the Transfer of Membership: A member shall not transfer his or her membership in the LLC unless all nontransferring members in the LLC first agree to approve the admission of the transferee into this LLC. Further, no member may encumber a part or all of his or her membership in the LLC by mortgage, pledge, granting of a security interest, lien or otherwise, unless the encumbrance has first been approved in writing by all other members of the LLC. ㊱

30 This provision reflects a standard practice of not allowing withdrawals of capital by LLC members prior to a dissolution of the company, unless approved in writing by all members. You can change this provision to allow premature withdrawals of capital in certain instances or with the consent of less than all members. For example, you may want to give yourself and the other members flexibility to withdraw part of the cash balance from positive capital accounts in times of personal financial emergency with less than unanimous membership consent as long as the LLC remains solvent and able to pay its bills. Your tax advisor can help you draft custom provisions of this sort.

31 This paragraph makes it clear that all members have equal participation rights in the tax items and capital returns of the LLC. The last sentence specifies that members will share in LLC profits and losses in accordance with their respective percentage interests in the business—the most common arrangement for smaller LLCs. These percentages, in turn, are established by the capital contributions listed in "IV. Capital Provisions: (1) Capital Contributions by Members" (the first paragraph of this section of the agreement).

As we've mentioned earlier, we think most smaller LLCs will not need or benefit by establishing a complex membership structure in their operating agreement, nor will they wish to adopt disproportionate profit or loss provisions. But if you have special needs and your tax advisor concurs, by all means replace this paragraph with special provisions of your own. For example, you may wish to give a member who contributes $25,000 in cash as capital a greater share of LLC profits than a member who promises to contribute $25,000 over the course of three years. Again, see Chapter 3, Section D2, and consult your tax advisor to make sure any disproportionate allocations of profits will have "substantial economic effect" under the IRS rules.

Example: Dwayne, Blaine and Jane agree to allocate their LLC profits and losses disproportionately. They change this paragraph to read: "No member shall be given priority or preference with respect to other members in obtaining a return of capital contributions, distributions or allocations of the income, gains, losses, deductions, credits or other items of the LLC. Items of its income, gain, loss, deduction and credit shall be allocated to members according to each member's percentage interest in this LLC, except as follows: [here they specify any special (disproportionate) allocations of profits, losses and any other items to particular members]. Their tax advisor adds a significant amount of additional language to have these special allocations respected by the IRS as explained in Chapter 3, Section D2].

Here are other changes you can make to this provision (again, get help from your tax advisor):

- You can adopt multi-class membership provisions, with some members being first in line to receive a return of their capital investment.
- If you want to go even further, you can decide that some LLC members will be entitled to their share of profits and losses (disproportionate or otherwise) before all other members and shall continue to receive the only distributions of LLC profits until they have been paid back their initial capital contribution. The following sample provision, or one similar to it, will accomplish this.

Sample Language: Allocations of Profits and Losses: Notwithstanding any other provision in this agreement, the following members, called "priority members," shall receive all distributions of the LLC's profits and losses before any distributions are made to any other members of the LLC: **list priority members**. Further, the other members of the LLC shall not receive any distributions until each of these priority members has received total distributions equal to each priority member's initial capital contribution to the LLC.

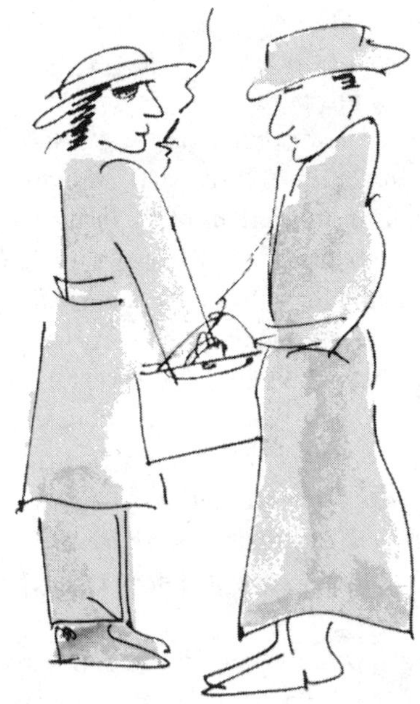

㉜ This provision gives members leeway to distribute cash profits or proceeds of the LLC to members if they vote to do so. Most smaller LLCs will specify a unanimous vote, but some may prefer to allow a majority of the membership to decide this issue—remember, a majority of members is defined earlier in this agreement ("II. Membership Provisions: (5) Membership Voting") as a majority of the percentage interests in the LLC.

Again, we assume that allocations of profits and proceeds will follow each member's percentage interest in the LLC, but you can vary who gets how much if you (and your tax advisor) decide to implement disproportionate (special) allocations of LLC profits.

㉝ This paragraph addresses how any noncash LLC property will be allocated among members. Basically, property gets allocated among the members in proportion to each member's percentage interest in the LLC. If reduced to cash later, it will be distributed to members according to an earlier provision in this operating agreement ("IV. Capital Provisions: (8) Allocation and Distribution of Cash to Members").

Example: Second-Hand Freight and Salvage, Ltd. Liability Co., a five-member company, decides to sell a truck and allocate the current value of this asset to the members, who own the LLC in equal percentages. The truck is worth $30,000, so the capital account of each member is increased by $6,000. The members can vote to distribute this cash according to the cash distribution provision in their agreement.

㉞ This paragraph sets up a special rule to handle a distribution of the cash and other assets of the LLC when the business itself liquidates or when a member's interest is liquidated. It applies the distribution to each member's capital account, then allows for credits and deductions that may need to be made prior to a final distribution. A final distribution of positive account balances is then made to members with positive account balances. Members with negative account balances owe the LLC money, not the other way around.

㉟ This is a liberal provision that lets a member bow out from the LLC by giving prescribed written notice. The period required is up to you—you can allow a quick departure, say in 30 days, or require many months' prior written notice. A typical advance notice period mentioned in LLC statutes is 180 days, but you may wish to shorten this period to 90 days or less.

If you want, you may modify this provision. For example, you may choose to limit the circumstances under which members may withdraw, or you may want to assess a monetary penalty if a member leaves too soon. (One way is to limit the price the member gets for his or her interest under mandatory buyout provisions in your agreement. We don't include buy-sell provisions of this sort in our simple agreement so you'll need to consult a lawyer or tax advisor; see Section A2 in this chapter.)

Problems with imposing significant penalties on departing members. Be careful if you decide to specify a substantial monetary penalty—for example, debiting a member's capital account prior to distributing the balance on departure. Courts can look askance on (decide not to enforce) limitations placed on individuals' abilities to come and go into and out of a business freely; they may decide that the limitations unduly restrict an individual's right to transfer an LLC interest or compete freely in the marketplace. Besides, lawyers love to sue, and your departing member may hook up with a litigious lawyer (or vice versa) upon leaving your LLC.

There are other issues you may want to address in this provision—for example, what will happen if a "service member" leaves the business before fully performing services promised in return for a share in the LLC.

Example: John received a 15% share in Fast Fries LLC in return for a promise to perform $15,000 worth of services for the LLC over a two-year period. However, John leaves prior to completing these promised capital contributions; when he gives notice of withdrawal, he has only worked off $7,500. Can John be forced to report to work for the LLC even though he is no longer a member? No—a court simply won't enforce this requirement. In short, if John is determined to leave, there is no legal remedy available to force him to keep working off his capital contribution.

The simple solution is to require departing "service members" to pay off in cash the amount of services left undone. This can be paid by way of a set-off against the departing member's capital account, with the member agreeing to pay any deficiency in cash or over time according to the terms of a promissory note.

Sample Language: If any member leaves this LLC prior to fully performing services promised as part of the member's capital contribution, his or her capital account shall be debited in an amount equal to the dollar amount of the value of the unpaid services prior to a distribution of any capital account balance to the member. If the capital account balance prior to this deduction is less than the full amount of the value of the unperformed services, the amount of the value of the unperformed services that exceeds the positive capital account balance of the member shall be paid by the departing member as follows: __**specify terms of repayment of any deficiency, for example "in cash within 30 days of departure by the member from the LLC" or "in accordance with the terms of a promissory note payable to the LLC by the departing member, the principal amount of which shall be the value of the unperformed services that were not satisfied from the member's positive capital account balance upon his or her departure from the LLC"**__.

Example: Part of Sam's contribution to Sam & Pam's Sandblasting & Plastering LLC is a promise to perform future services worth $10,000. The LLC operating agreement requires departing service members to convert any unperformed services to a promissory note if they leave the LLC prior to performing all promised services. Sam decides to leave the LLC when he still owes $5,000, and his capital account balance is at $2,000. When he departs, Sam will either be required to pay the remaining $3,000 in cash or under the terms of a promissory note that he signs in favor of the LLC.

For departing members who received a share in the LLC in return for a promise to pay off a note on which they still owe money, you may choose to do nothing. Because these people are still legally bound to pay off the note, you can afford to simply let them leave (not try to renegotiate the note or convert it to a lump-sum payment).

You may, however, decide that any type of long-distance or extended payoff would be too tenuous or uncomfortable after a member leaves the business. Accordingly, you may wish to add language here requiring all persons who owe money on their initial capital contribution to make a lump sum cash payment to the LLC equal to the amount of the unpaid capital contribution at the time of their withdrawal from the LLC.

> *Sample Language:* If a member departs this LLC prior to full payment of his or her capital contribution, whether the unpaid capital contribution consists of cash, payments under a promissory note, the performance of future services or the transfer of property, the member shall be bound to pay a lump sum to the LLC at the time of his or her departure equal to the amount or value of the unpaid cash, unpaid principal and interest under the note, value of unperformed services, or the value of the untransferred property. The lump sum shall be paid to this LLC no later than __**period**__ days after the departing member leaves the LLC, and payment of the lump sum within this period shall extinguish the liability of the departing member for the amount or value of his or her unpaid capital contribution to this LLC.

Our above examples and sample provisions are suggestions only. The best way to anticipate and come to terms with handling unpaid capital contributions upon the departure of a member is to talk with all members and your tax advisor (particularly if you plan to tinker with a member's capital account balance when he or she leaves). Reaching this kind of informed consensus before you add any language to your operating agreement can help avoid bad feelings and uncooperative behavior later—when, for example, a departing member complains he wasn't in on the discussions on how unpaid contributions would be handled when a member leaves, and therefore didn't realize he'd have to pay cash to be let out of the LLC.

This operating agreement provision deals only with a member packing up and quitting the LLC. It does not address a member who wants to sell his or her interest to a new member. The latter issue is an important one with tax consequences, which we deal with separately in the next provision in the agreement," Restrictions on the Transfer of Membership."

36 This provision covers an important tax option that will help determine whether your LLC qualifies for pass-through tax status with the IRS. Here you deal with the issue of the admission of new members who are transferred a membership interest from a former member.

Under IRS Revenue Procedure 95-10, you will avoid the corporate characteristic of "free transferability of interests" if you require the vote of at least a majority of the other members to admit a new member. (See the discussion in Chapter 3, Section B4.) IRS rules say that a "majority" for purposes of this vote may be defined in one of three ways:

- a majority of the capital and profits interests in the LLC (a "majority in interest" under the tax rules)
- a majority of either capital or profits interests, or
- a per capita majority, such as the approval of three of four nontransferring members.

- a per capita majority, such as the approval of three of four nontransferring members.

We neatly avoid having to define the type of majority vote in this operating agreement provision by requiring the LLC to have *all* nontransferring members approve the sale of membership interests to a new member. This more than meets IRS requirements and keeps LLC interests "in the family" unless all existing members approve letting in a new member. This approach also comports with the standard state LLC law default rule, which requires unanimous written consent of non-transferring members unless a different rule is stated in the LLC Articles or operating agreement. (Your state's rule is listed under the "Default Transfer Rule" item in the "Operating Rules" section of your state sheet in Appendix A).

A unanimous vote approach makes sense—after all, the new member will have to get along and work closely with the other managing members. If any member doesn't like or is incompatible with the new member, the LLC's business may suffer significantly and the personal enjoyment the members derive from working together may be lost. If, however, you wish to alter this provision to allow a *majority* of nontransferring members to approve the sale of a membership to a new member (as allowed under IRS rules), you need to do two things:

- Make sure your state lets you adopt a less-than-majority membership vote rule for approving transfers of membership. (Again, this state law is summarized in your state sheet in Appendix A.)
- Decide how to calculate the majority. The three choices available under Revenue Procedure 95-10 are capital *and* profits, capital *or* profits, or per capita membership votes. (Ask your tax advisor for help if you need it.)

Finally, note that this paragraph requires all members to agree before a member encumbers a membership, such as putting it up as collateral for a loan or pledging it as security for the performance of some other legal obligation. You can lessen the vote requirement for encumbrances, but we think unanimous written approval works best here too.

Notwithstanding the above provision, any member shall be allowed to assign an economic interest in his or her membership to another person without the approval of the other members. Such an assignment shall not include a transfer of the member's voting or management rights in this LLC, and the assignee shall not become a member of the LLC. (37)

VI. DISSOLUTION PROVISIONS

This section addresses the dissolution of the LLC, or events that may trigger a dissolution. Some of these provisions have important tax consequences, as we explain below.

(1) Events That Trigger Dissolution of the LLC: The following events shall trigger a dissolution of the LLC, except as provided:

(a) the death, insanity, bankruptcy, retirement, resignation or expulsion of a member, except that within **number of days, typically a maximum of 90 under state LLC default rules** of the happening of any of these events, all remaining members of the LLC may vote to continue the legal existence of the LLC, in which case the LLC shall not dissolve; (38)

(b) the expiration of the term of existence of the LLC if such term is specified in the Articles of Organization, Certificate of Formation or a similar organizational document, or this operating agreement; (39)

(c) the written agreement of all members to dissolve the LLC; (40)

(d) entry of a decree of dissolution of the LLC under state law. (41)

VII. GENERAL PROVISIONS

These provisions cover general items concerning operation of the LLC. You'll also find standard provisions, normally found at the end of LLC agreements, dealing with the enforceability of the agreement.

(1) Officers: The LLC may designate one or more officers, such as a President, Vice President, Secretary and Treasurer. Persons who fill these positions need not be members of the LLC. Such positions may be compensated or noncompensated according to the nature and extent of the services rendered for the LLC as a part of the duties of each office. Ministerial services only as a part of any officer position will normally not be compensated, such as the performance of officer duties specified in this agreement, but any officer may be reimbursed by the LLC for out-of-pocket expenses paid by the officer in carrying out the duties of his or her office. (42)

(2) Records: The LLC shall keep at its principal business address a copy of all proceedings of membership meetings, as well as books of account of the LLC's financial transactions. A list of the names and addresses of the current membership of the LLC also shall be maintained at this address, with notations on any transfers of members' interests to nonmembers or persons being admitted into membership in the LLC.

(37) This paragraph states an exception recognized under state statutes and the IRS tax rules that we touched upon earlier in this book (See Chapter 3, Section B4a. For the technical language, see Income Tax Regulation §301.7701-2(e)(1).) Namely, an LLC can let its members transfer *economic interests* to outsiders without the approval of the other members and still avoid the corporate characteristic of "free transferability of interests." Under this exception, as long as the person getting the interest—the assignee or transferee—does not become a new member with management and voting rights, the transfer is of an economic interest only, and does not count for purposes of complying with state and tax law rules on limiting the sale of membership interests to outsiders.

Example: Katherine owns a one-third interest in a lucrative LLC. She assigns one-quarter of her profits interest in her LLC to a trust set up for the benefit of her niece, Brenda. This transfer of economic rights only is not restricted by the membership transfer restrictions in her LLC's operating agreement.

Of course, you can decide not to permit even these transfers of economic interests by members, simply by deleting this paragraph. (By the way, you don't need to be overly concerned about the possibility of outsiders buying an economic interest in your LLC—there generally is little interest by outsiders in buying a profits-only interest in an LLC without full membership rights.)

(38) This provision covers an important tax and practical issue: what will happen if a member resigns, retires, dies, goes bankrupt or is subject to any of the other conditions listed here. (These are the contingencies listed in Revenue Procedure 95-10, and are the events best to include in your operating agreement. Refer to Chapter 3, Section B3 for a discussion. The ruling is set out in Appendix B.)

Under the tax rules, the way you handle these events has an effect on whether your LLC qualifies for pass-through tax treatment with the IRS. Under Revenue Procedure 95-10, you will avoid the corporate characteristic of "continuity of life," and therefore help your LLC qualify for pass-through tax status, if any one of these listed events will trigger a dissolution of your LLC, pending a vote by the members.

As long as you require the vote of at least a majority in interest of the remaining members (see below) to continue the legal existence of the LLC, you will avoid this corporate tax characteristic. We think you will want to go beyond this, however, and require the vote of all remaining members to continue the LLC, which is what our provision says. By taking this approach, you let all members decide whether or not to keep the business going following any of these dissolution-triggering events.

If you decide to modify the provision in the tear-out operating agreement and lessen the vote requirement, keep these two points in mind:

- *You will need to require the vote of at least a "majority in interest" of the remaining members.* You must define the term in this provision of your operating agreement as it is used in Revenue Procedure 95-10—that is, to mean the vote of remaining members holding a majority of both the capital *and* profits interests in the LLC.
- *You must make sure that your state allows you to lessen the vote requirement if you opt for less than the approval of all remaining LLC members.* Your state's legal rule for this vote requirement is contained in the item "Default Continuation Rule" in the "Operating Rules" section of your state sheet in Appendix A. Even if your state's default rule requires a unanimous vote of all remaining members, it may let you say otherwise in your operating agreement (we tell you whether it does on the state sheet).

Copies of the LLC's Articles of Organization, Certificate of Formation or a similar organizational document, a signed copy of this operating agreement, and the LLC's tax returns for the preceding three tax years shall be kept at the principal business address of the LLC. A statement also shall be kept at this address containing any of the following information that is applicable to this LLC:

- the amount of cash or a description and value of property contributed or agreed to be contributed as capital to the LLC by each member;
- a schedule showing when any additional capital contributions are to be made by members to this LLC;
- a statement or schedule, if appropriate, showing the rights of members to receive distributions representing a return of part or all of members' capital contributions; and
- a description of, or date when, the legal existence of the LLC will terminate under provisions in the LLC's Articles of Organization, Certificate of Formation or a similar organizational document, or this operating agreement.

If one or more of the above items is included or listed in this operating agreement, it will be sufficient to keep a copy of this agreement at the principal business address of the LLC without having to prepare and keep a separate record of such item or items at this address.

Any member may inspect any and all records maintained by the LLC upon reasonable notice to the LLC. Copying of the LLC's records by members is allowed, but copying costs shall be paid for by the requesting member. 43

(3) All Necessary Acts: The members and officers of this LLC are authorized to perform all acts necessary to perfect the organization of this LLC and to carry out its business operations expeditiously and efficiently. The Secretary of the LLC, or other officers, or all members of the LLC, may certify to other businesses, financial institutions and individuals as to the authority of one or more members or officers of this LLC to transact specific items of business on behalf of the LLC. 44

(4) Mediation and Arbitration of Disputes Among Members: In any dispute over the provisions of this operating agreement and in other disputes among the members, if the members cannot resolve the dispute to their mutual satisfaction, the matter shall be submitted to mediation. The terms and procedure for mediation shall be arranged by the parties to the dispute.

Notice that you must fill in the blank in our provision to specify the deadline for voting to continue the legal existence of the LLC after the occurrence of a dissolution-triggering event. In most states, this vote must be taken within 90 days from the triggering event—again, see the "Default Continuation Rule" in your state sheet. If your state does not specify a deadline for taking this vote, or lets you override the state requirements (most states permit this), we suggest putting "90 days" in this blank. You can always vote any time before the 90-day deadline (the language says "within [number of days]" of the happening of one of the membership terminating events). If, however, you are set on a shorter period, we recommend specifying no less than 30 days to give your members a chance to meet and approve the continuance of your LLC.

❸❾ Some states require the Articles of Organization to limit the legal existence of the LLC to a specified term of years or until a particular date. This provision simply states that the LLC will dissolve if a termination date or period is specified in the Articles of Organization or this operating agreement. (See our earlier discussion on filling in "I. Preliminary Provisions: (6) Duration of LLC," Special Instruction ❽, above.)

❹⓿ Your LLC may decide to call it quits at any time by the unanimous approval of all members to dissolve. We think this makes sense—and most LLC owners wouldn't want it any other way. (In fact, most state LLC laws say you can do this even if your operating agreement doesn't specify it.)

❹❶ State statutes may provide for the involuntary dissolution of an LLC should the members reach an impasse or in the case of fraud, illegality or nonpayment of state taxes. This provision simply recognizes that the LLC may dissolve by order of a state court.

❹❷ This paragraph allows, but does not require, the LLC to appoint one or more persons as officers of the LLC, who may be members or nonmembers. Some state LLC statutes mention the officer positions of President, Vice President, Secretary and Treasurer, but even those states don't require that the positions be filled or define the job duties and responsibilities of these offices.

We suggest you not worry too much about specific officer titles ("Treasurer" vs. "Chief Financial Officer" vs. "Chief Poobah in Charge of Payroll"). Pay attention instead to making sure each LLC employee knows the scope and responsibilities of his or her position with your LLC, whether it is as a formal officer or in a regular staff position.

Feel free to modify this provision to have it reflect how you want to handle the designation and compensation of any officers in your LLC. We suggest not being too specific, to allow you to have the maximum leeway to appoint various types of LLC salaried and nonsalaried officers and personnel. Note that you do not need to say that your LLC has the power to hire employees and compensate them for their services; this type of employment authority goes without saying.

❹❸ Your state LLC statute may allow you to restrict when or why members are allowed to look at LLC records, or permit you to restrict access to particular types of LLC legal or financial records. We don't nitpick here, and simply give all members an unrestricted right to view all records at any time.

If you want to restrict membership inspection rights, take a look at your state LLC statute to see how restrictive you are allowed to be under state law, then insert your own provisions.

> *Sample Language:* Any member may inspect the financial or other records of this LLC for a purpose reasonably related to the member's interest in this LLC. The Treasurer of this LLC shall make the determination within one week of the member's request and, if the Treasurer finds that the member's request is related to his or her interest in the LLC, the requesting member shall be allowed to inspect the records during regular business hours of the LLC at its principal place of business.

If good-faith mediation of a dispute proves impossible or if an agreed-upon mediation outcome cannot be obtained by the members who are parties to the dispute, the dispute may be submitted to arbitration in accordance with the rules of the American Arbitration Association. Any party may commence arbitration of the dispute by sending a written request for arbitration to all other parties to the dispute. The request shall state the nature of the dispute to be resolved by arbitration, and, if all parties to the dispute agree to arbitration, arbitration shall be commenced as soon as practical after such parties receive a copy of the written request.

All parties shall initially share the cost of arbitration, but the prevailing party or parties may be awarded attorney fees, costs and other expenses of arbitration. All arbitration decisions shall be final, binding and conclusive on all the parties to arbitration, and legal judgment may be entered based upon such decision in accordance with applicable law in any court having jurisdiction to do so. ㊺

(5) Entire Agreement: This operating agreement represents the entire agreement among the members of this LLC, and it shall not be amended, modified or replaced except by a written instrument executed by all the parties to this agreement who are current members of this LLC as well as any and all additional parties who became members of this LLC after the adoption of this agreement. This agreement replaces and supersedes all prior written and oral agreements among any and all members of this LLC. ㊻

(6) Severability: If any provision of this agreement is determined by a court or arbitrator to be invalid, unenforceable or otherwise ineffective, that provision shall be severed from the rest of this agreement, and the remaining provisions shall remain in effect and enforceable. ㊼

VIII. SIGNATURES OF MEMBERS AND SPOUSES

The final section of the agreement contains signature lines for the members, plus a series of lines for their spouses to sign.

(1) Execution of Agreement: In witness whereof, the members of this LLC sign and adopt this agreement as the operating agreement of this LLC.

Date: ______________________________ ㊽
Signature: ______________________________
Printed Name: ______________________ , Member

Date: ______________________________
Signature: ______________________________
Printed Name: ______________________ , Member

44 This housekeeping provision says that the Secretary of the LLC, or other LLC officers or its members, may sign a statement that certifies to other businesses or to outside persons the capacity of one or more LLC members or officers to engage in particular business on behalf of the LLC. A bank, escrow or title company, or outside person or business may wish to obtain a statement certifying such authority prior to entering into a contract or business transaction with an LLC member or officer. (We provide a Certification of Authority form to use for this purpose in Chapter 7, Section D7c; a tear-out form is also provided in Appendix C.)

45 A mediation approach, followed if necessary by arbitration, is a relatively quick and inexpensive way to settle disputes among members—for example, arguments over the valuation of LLC interests incident to a buyout or disagreements over who gets to use the LLC's name after the business is formally dissolved.

This bare-bones provision says unresolved disputes among LLC members should first be submitted to mediation. Mediation is a voluntary, nonbinding process, in which an impartial mediator tries to get the parties to agree to a settlement. (For an excellent, in-depth coverage of the mediation process, see *How to Mediate Your Dispute,* by Peter Lovenheim (Nolo Press).)

In our provision, if mediation cannot be undertaken or is unsuccessful, the dispute may be submitted to binding arbitration by the parties. This procedure is voluntary, and all parties to the dispute must agree to arbitration. Even this procedure—an out-of-court, informal hearing before an impartial arbitrator that produces a legally enforceable decision—is a better dispute resolution process than a full-blown lawsuit. Arbitration is both quicker and less expensive than going to court.

You may want to make some minor changes, such as choosing a different association as a model for the arbitration rules, requiring three arbitrators instead of one (opposing sides of a dispute each pick one arbitrator, and these two arbitrators pick a third), and other changes you deem appropriate.

46 This is a boilerplate legal provision that negates any prior agreements among the members, whether oral (spoken) or written. This can be important because the general rule is that LLCs, like partnerships, may legally be based on oral agreements.

This provision also requires future changes to the agreement, or the adoption of a new operating agreement, to be signed by all original parties to the agreement who are current members of the LLC, plus any new members. You can change this provision to allow less than unanimous approval of operating agreement changes, but we think these changes are usually important enough to warrant unanimous approval of all current members. (We cover how to amend your operating agreement in Chapter 7, Section C1.)

47 This is a standard legal provision that directs a court or arbitrator to enforce the balance of the agreement even if one or more provisions are held invalid, ambiguous or otherwise unenforceable.

48 Before the members sign the agreement, remember that they must initial crossed-out language and changes that were made to the agreement, if any. (However, they don't need to initial filled-in blank lines.)

Have each member date and sign the operating agreement. Type or print the name of each member under the corresponding signature line, after the words "Printed Name." Make sure every initial member signs the operating agreement. Again, this is not just a practical requirement; it also has technical tax significance. All members must sign for the agreement to be considered a "partnership agreement" under the federal tax rules, thereby helping the LLC qualify for pass-through tax treatment.

Date: ______________________________

Signature: ______________________________

Printed Name: ______________________ , Member

Date: ______________________________

Signature: ______________________________

Printed Name: ______________________ , Member

(2) Consent of Spouses: The undersigned are spouses of members of this LLC who have signed this operating agreement in the preceding provision. These spouses have read this agreement and agree to be bound by its terms in any matter in which they have a financial interest, including restrictions on the transfer of memberships and the terms under which memberships in this LLC may be sold or otherwise transferred. (49)

Date: ______________________________

Signature: ______________________________

Printed Name: ______________________________

Spouse of: ______________________________

Date: ______________________________

Signature: ______________________________

Printed Name: ______________________________

Spouse of: ______________________________

Date: ______________________________

Signature: ______________________________

Printed Name: ______________________________

Spouse of: ______________________________

Date: ______________________________

Signature: ______________________________

Printed Name: ______________________________

Spouse of: ______________________________

Get assistance from a tax advisor. Before you settle on your final agreement, let your tax advisor review your choices, particularly those related to the financial (capital) provisions and tax options for qualifying for LLC pass-through tax treatment.

49 Here is another standard provision that shows spousal consent to the provisions of the operating agreement. We strongly suggest that each married LLC member have his or her spouse date and sign on one of the sets of lines following this spousal consent provision. Doing this can help avoid disputes later, should spouses separate, divorce or die, or should one spouse decide to sell or transfer his or her membership in the LLC.

Leaving interests by means of estate planning devices. You may add provisions that permit spouses of members to use a will or other estate planning device, such as a living trust, to leave their half- or other co-interest in an LLC membership to outsiders. See your tax or legal advisor for guidance if you wish to address issues of this sort in your agreement.

D. Distribute Copies of Your Operating Agreement

Congratulations! You are done with another important organizational task, and your LLC is well on its legal way. Make photocopies of the completed, signed operating agreement and give each member a copy. Finally, place the original, signed operating agreement in your LLC records book.

CHAPTER 6

Prepare an LLC Operating Agreement for Managers

Some LLCs wish to set up a special management structure that does not consist of all LLC members. The management team may be made up of:

- some—but not all—LLC members
- both outside managers and some—but not all—LLC members, or
- only outside managers.

In this chapter, we show you how to prepare an alternate operating agreement for a manager-managed LLC. We assume you are in the process of forming, or have already formed, your LLC by preparing and filing Articles of Organization with your state LLC filing office, as explained in Chapter 4.

If yours is a member-managed LLC, turn to Chapter 5. In Chapter 5, we cover the first LLC operating agreement contained in Appendix C, which provides for management of the LLC by all members. If you're unsure of the type of agreement you will need, read on.

A. Choosing a Manager-Managed LLC

Although most smaller LLCs will choose to be managed by all members (not by managers, as provided in the agreement covered in this chapter), a minority will find a manager-managed LLC more suitable. LLCs usually decide on manager-management for one or both of these reasons:

- At least one member wishes to be a "passive" investor and to hand over the reins and responsibilities of management to others.

  Example: Sole Sisters is a shoe design and distribution partnership owned and operated by three sisters, Julie, Lauri and Ginny. Ginny contributed the cash to get the partnership started, leaving all business management and day-to-day operations to Julie and Lauri, who contributed as their capital contributions portions of past (unpaid) services performed for the partnership. All three sisters decide that converting the business to an LLC makes sense, but they wish to keep the same management arrangement among themselves. What's the solution? Simple: they decide to adopt a manager-management agreement—the kind discussed in this chapter—with Julie and Laurie designated as the managers of the LLC. Ginny will be a nonmanaging member, thus avoiding all management responsibilities.
- The members believe that the LLC will be handled better by outsiders (nonmembers) who have special expertise in managing the business.

  Example: Power-Packed Peanut Products LLC, a food wholesaler, is formed and funded by Tina and Kay, entrepreneurs with an eye for a promising business venture, but with little expertise or interest in managing or running it on a day-to-day basis. They decide to shell out substantial salaries to experienced food wholesalers Jason and Charlotte, who will manage and run the business as its nonmember managers. Jason and Charlotte bring years of prior experience to the newly formed business, having just sold their co-owned food distribution business, J & C Wholesalers, at a substantial profit. They are ready to get involved growing another successful company in exchange for chunky salaries on PPPP's payroll.

1. Limited Liability for All Members of Manager-Managed LLC

In their roles as LLC members, all members—whether managing or nonmanaging—qualify for personal legal immunity from business debts and legal claims made by outsiders against the LLC.

2. Limited Liability for Managers of Manager-Managed LLC

State law may impose slightly stricter standards on LLC managers (regardless of whether or not they're also members). That is, managers will receive the normal personal immunity from business debts and liabilities that the LLC provides, but they may suffer exposure to personal liability if they participate in making exceptionally bad or illegal business decisions in their roles as managers.

Don't get too concerned here if you plan to be an LLC manager. The circumstances where a manager may be found personally liable are the exceptions, not the rule. Circumstances that breed such personal liability tend to involve decisions that are self-interested (where a manager takes personal advantage of a business deal with the LLC without proper disclosure of his or her interest) or situations where the manager acts in an extremely reckless or illegal manner.

Example 1: Suits of Amoré, Limited Liability Company, a haberdasher of formal men's attire for weddings, parties and other black-tie affairs, is on the lookout for top quality Italian suits it can offer to its customers. In the course of his research, Fredo, an LLC manager, spots a phenomenal opportunity to purchase top-of-the-line Santoro suits (normally $2,500 plus retail per unit) at an unheard of discount. He decides to cash out his personal bank account savings and buy up the suits, rather than mention his find to the other LLC managers, who would jump at the chance to acquire the merchandise. Fredo will either find a private buyer or store the suits until he can set himself up in a sideline business selling suits. If another LLC manager gets wind of Fredo's find, and the LLC sues him for lost profits—the amount the LLC could have made had it been allowed to buy and resell the suits—a court would likely find Fredo personally liable. The normal rule is that a manager has a duty of loyalty to disclose opportunities discovered in the course of his or her work that might benefit the business (unless it is obvious that the business would have no interest in the opportunity); only after the business decides not to act is the manager allowed to go ahead and personally pursue the opportunity.

Example 2: The managers of Lowball Construction Ltd. Liability Co. are warned repeatedly by the VP of operations that an electrical panel box installation being performed by the company at one of its worksites is not up to code. The LLC managers disregard his advice to order the substandard work to be redone, insisting that the company can't afford to miss another performance deadline under its contract with the owner of the building. After Lowball completes the installations, the owner rents the building to a computer manufacturer, which moves in and sets up sensitive electronic measurement and test equipment it uses in its operation. When the computer firm flips the switch to fire up its equipment, a short circuit due to faulty ground wiring in the service panel box sends a voltage spike through the outlets on the circuit—and destroys all the computer maker's expensive test equipment. The building owner is sued for the loss, and she immediately sues the LLC and its managers. The LLC's lawyer advises the managers that it is unlikely that their commercial insurance carrier will cover this loss—the electrical panel box at fault was never inspected and approved by the local building inspector. The managers may be held personally liable for the loss due to their gross negligence (and illegality) in not heeding the warnings of their VP to re-do the faulty service panel wiring.

Of course, these are fanciful or extreme examples, mostly used to make the following points. First, the LLC will protect you and your co-managers personally for normal negligence—the kind of business judgment errors humans without 20-20 foresight may make. You'll even be protected if outsiders inadvertently suffer a financial loss due to such faulty decisions (of course, the LLC itself can be forced to pay for these losses). Second, don't be lulled into an unassailable sense of security by the normal limited liability protection afforded by the LLC form. If you engage in truly foolish conduct that is obviously reckless to the safety of other people or their property, or you act illegally or underhandedly in your own self-interest, then the mantle of personal protection that your LLC normally provides may be lifted. In that case, you and the other LLC managers will be exposed to personal liability for the reckless or illegal decisions.

Provide managers with indemnification and/or insurance. If you want to attract outside managers to help run your LLC, you may need to take extra measures to make them feel more comfortable in these lawsuit-happy times. One way is to offer an LLC indemnity agreement, which guarantees direct payment by the LLC for any legal expenses or judgments managers may be asked to pay arising out of their work for the LLC. Another personal safeguard is to cover managers personally with an error and omissions insurance policy for their managerial duties. The two can be combined for complete legal coverage: indemnification can kick in for all amounts not covered by insurance.

3. Tax Aspects of Manager-Management

Your decision to select a management team affects how you qualify for pass-through tax status with the IRS. To recap our analysis in Chapter 3, if an LLC is managed by all members (not by managers, as provided in the agreement covered in this chapter), the IRS says it will avoid the corporate characteristic of "centralized management." This puts the LLC on a surer footing in qualifying for pass-through (partnership) tax status with the IRS, simply because the LLC has to avoid just one more (not two more) corporate characteristics.

If you adopt an LLC management operating agreement, you may not be able to avoid the corporate characteristic of centralized management. The IRS will want to look at all the facts and circumstances of your LLC before it decides this issue one way or the other (mostly, the IRS will want to see if the managers are secure in their management roles or whether they can be removed or voted out of office).

Even if your manager-managed LLC cannot avoid the corporate characteristic of centralized management, it may qualify for pass-through tax status by avoiding the remaining two corporate characteristics (free transferability of interests and continuity of life); it's just that you have a little less room for error. (We cover the rules for qualifying for pass-through tax status in Chapter 3, Sections B and C; reread that material if any of these points are unfamiliar to you.)

B. How to Prepare an LLC Management Operating Agreement

Now let's look at the LLC management operating agreement. Note that this is the second operating agreement in Appendix C, titled Limited Liability Company Management Operating Agreement. Make sure you pick the right agreement and don't miss any pages or inadvertently take pages from the other (member-managed) agreement. You may want to photocopy the management operating agreement before you get started, in case you make mistakes or want to modify it significantly.

1. Read Chapter 5 Material on Basic Operating Agreement Issues

The management operating agreement is similar to the operating agreement provided in Chapter 5, but it is customized to include LLC manager provisions. Before you begin filling in your LLC management operating agreement, spend a few minutes to learn more about these important matters:

- *Scope of our basic LLC operating agreements.* Read Chapter 5, Section A. There you'll find information about capital account provisions and buy-sell and right of first refusal provisions.
- *Modifying your operating agreement.* Also read Chapter 5, Section B, which covers general rules on when and how to make changes to your agreement.

2. Where to Find Instructions for LLC Management Operating Agreement

Below, we provide instructions in the sample agreement to help you fill in the blanks. In addition, we use two different kinds of references to alert you to Special Instructions:

- *Lettered references* accompany provisions that are unique to this operating agreement. Special Instructions Ⓐ through Ⓝ accompany the management operating agreement in this chapter.
- *Numbered references* apply to provisions that are the same as (or almost identical to) those found in the Chapter 5 agreement. Special Instructions ❶ through ㊾ are contained in Chapter 5, Section C. Note that some numbered references will be missing from this agreement. This is because certain provisions in Chapter 5 apply only to member-managed LLCs, so they are not carried over to this management operating agreement.

While this may sound complicated, it really isn't, and you'll get the idea with no trouble at all as you read the provisions below.

3. Line-by-Line Instructions for Management Operating Agreement

We'll start at the top of the Limited Liability Company Management Operating Agreement and work our way through it.

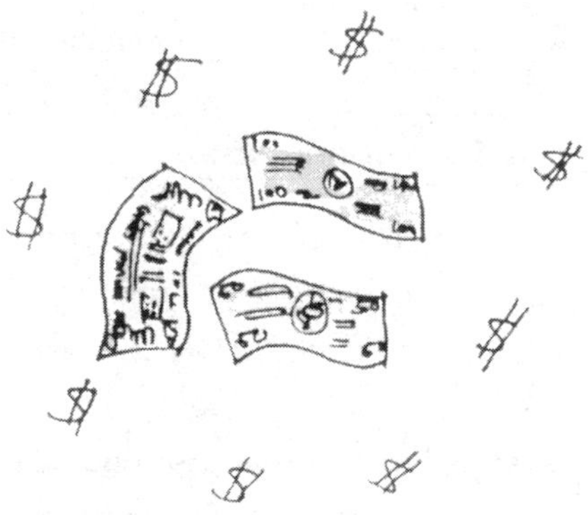

LIMITED LIABILITY COMPANY
MANAGEMENT OPERATING AGREEMENT

I. PRELIMINARY PROVISIONS

Here we address preliminary matters, such as the effective date of the agreement, the name of the LLC and other basic information. These provisions are almost identical to those provided in the basic LLC operating agreement in Chapter 5. Again, where indicated, the numbered Special Instructions for these provisions are in Chapter 5, Section C.

(1) Effective Date: This operating agreement of ____________________ **name of LLC,** ❶ ____________________

effective ________ **date** ________, ❷ is adopted by the members whose signatures appear at the end of this agreement. ❸

(2) Formation: This limited liability company (LLC) was formed by filing Articles of Organization, a Certificate of Formation or a similar organizational document with the state of ________ **state of formation** ________'s LLC filing office on **date of filing Articles of Organization, Certificate of Formation or similar organizational document** ____. ❹ A copy of this organizational document has been placed in the LLC's records book.

(3) Name: The formal name of this LLC is as stated above. However, this LLC may do business under a different name by complying with the state's fictitious or assumed business name statutes and procedures. ❺

(4) Registered Office and Agent: The registered office of this LLC and the registered agent at this address are as follows: ____________________ **name and address of registered agent and office.** ____________________

The registered office and agent may be changed from time to time as the members or managers may see fit, by filing a change of registered agent or office form with the state LLC filing office. It will not be necessary to amend this provision of the operating agreement if and when such a change is made. ❻

(5) Business Purposes: The specific business purposes and activities contemplated by the founders of this LLC at the time of initial signing of this agreement consist of the following: **state the specific business purposes and activities you foresee for your LLC.** ❼ ____________________

It is understood that the foregoing statement of purposes shall not serve as a limitation on the powers or abilities of this LLC, which shall be permitted to engage in any and all lawful business activities. If this LLC intends to engage in business activities outside the state of its formation that require the qualification of the LLC in other states, it shall obtain such qualification before engaging in such out-of-state activities.

(6) Duration of LLC: The duration of this LLC shall be **specify "perpetual" or any specific termination date or term of years for the LLC specified in the Articles of Organization**. Further, this LLC shall terminate when a proposal to dissolve the LLC is adopted by the membership of this LLC or when this LLC is otherwise terminated in accordance with law. ❽

II. MANAGEMENT PROVISIONS

These provisions address the unique management structure of a manager-managed LLC. The lettered Special Instructions for these provisions accompany the agreement in this chapter.

(1) Management by Managers: This LLC will be managed by the managers listed below. All managers who are also members of this LLC are designated as "members"; nonmember managers are designated as "nonmembers." Ⓐ

Name: ______________________________ ☐ Member ☐ Nonmember
Address: ______________________________

Name: ______________________________ ☐ Member ☐ Nonmember
Address: ______________________________

Name: ______________________________ ☐ Member ☐ Nonmember
Address: ______________________________

Name: ______________________________ ☐ Member ☐ Nonmember
Address: ______________________________

Name: ______________________________ ☐ Member ☐ Nonmem
ber
Address: ______________________________

Name: ______________________________ ☐ Member ☐ Nonmember
Address: ______________________________

(2) Nonliability of Managers: No manager of this LLC shall be personally liable for the expenses, debts, obligations or liabilities of the LLC, or for claims made against it. **B**

(3) Authority and Votes of Managers: Except as otherwise set forth in this agreement, the Articles of Organization, Certificate of Organization or similar organizational document, or as may be provided under state law, all management decisions relating to this LLC's business shall be made by its managers. Management decisions shall be approved by **"all" or "a majority"** of the current managers of the LLC, with each manager entitled to cast one vote for or against any matter submitted to the managers for a decision. **C**

(4) Term of Managers: Each manager shall serve until the earlier of the following events:

(a) the manager becomes disabled, dies, retires or otherwise withdraws from management;

(b) the manager is removed from office; or **D**

(c) the manager's term expires, if a term has been designated in other provisions of this agreement.

Upon the happening of any of these events, a new manager may be appointed to replace the departing manager by **"a majority of the members of the LLC" or "a majority of the remaining managers"**. **E**

(5) Management Meetings: Managers shall be able to discuss and approve LLC business informally, and may, at their discretion, call and hold formal management meetings according to the rules set forth in the following provisions of this operating agreement.

Regularly scheduled formal management meetings need not be held, but any manager may call such a meeting by communicating his or her request for a formal meeting to the other managers, noting the purpose or purposes for which the meeting is called. Only the business stated or summarized in the notice for the meeting shall be discussed and voted upon at the meeting.

The meeting shall be held within a reasonable time after a manager has made the request for a meeting, and in no event, later than **period** days after the request for the meeting. A quorum for such a formal managers' meeting shall consist of **"all" or "a majority of"** managers, and if a quorum is not present, the meeting shall be adjourned to a new place and time with notice of the adjourned meeting given to all managers. An adjournment shall not be necessary, however, and a managers' meeting with less than a quorum may be held if all nonattending managers agreed in writing prior to the meeting to the holding of the meeting. All such written consents to the holding of a formal management meeting shall be kept and filed with the records of the meeting.

The proceedings of all formal managers' meetings shall be noted or summarized with written minutes of the meeting and a copy of the minutes shall be placed and kept in the records book of this LLC. **F**

SPECIAL INSTRUCTIONS

Ⓐ Fill in the names and addresses of the managers of the LLC. Check the appropriate box to show whether each manager is a member or nonmember. Remember, managers can be either members or nonmembers.

Ⓑ This paragraph reiterates the basic legal rule that managers (like members) are not personally liable for LLC debts and claims—just in case an overreaching lawyer or other pesky individual tries to argue that your managers have, by signing up as managers, implicitly agreed to be personally responsible for LLC debts.

Ⓒ In the blank, specify the number of management votes necessary to pass or approve decisions submitted to the managers. You may select "all" or "a majority," or specify a particular number or percentage of votes needed to make a management decision, such as "two-thirds, "51%" or "three." We recommend specifying percentages or fractions, rather than numbers, because a specified number may turn out to be too small if you increase the size of your management team later. For example, if you require three management votes for a management team currently consisting of five persons, this number will represent less than a majority if you later add one more manager to your LLC.

Note that this provision states the standard rule that each manager gets one vote, regardless of any percentage interest he or she may hold in the LLC as a member.

Ⓓ You may wish to use your operating agreement to give procedures for the removal of LLC managers. You may want to specify the membership votes needed for removal of a manager, or the automatic grounds for such removal. You can even specify a procedure to have a vote of the managers themselves decide the removal of a manager. (You'll need to retype at least one page of the tear-out form to add this new language.)

Sample Language: Removal of Managers: Managers may be removed by the vote of **"a majority of the members" or "all of the members"**, not counting the vote of any member-manager to be removed. **You may specify one or more automatic reasons for removal of a manager, for example: "A member-manager shall be removed automatically from office upon missing two or more consecutive meetings of the managers without giving reasonable notice of such expected absence to the other managers of the LLC prior to the meeting."**

Be aware of tax consequences. Your LLC may not be able to avoid the corporate characteristic of "centralized management" if the nonmanaging members have an unrestricted right to remove managers. Again, having centralized management would count against you in your quest for pass-through tax status with the IRS. (You may also risk having the corporate characteristic of centralized management if you have procedures to elect managers, as discussed in Special Instruction Ⓔ, just below.)

Ⓔ Our provision gives an unspecified term for managers—that is, it doesn't contain a periodic election procedure for managers. This provision does specify a procedure to fill a vacancy on the management team. In the blank, indicate the vote requirement necessary for the remaining managers or members to accomplish this. If you require a majority vote of members, keep in mind that this is defined in "III. Membership Provisions: (4) Membership Voting," as the vote of a majority of the percentage interests of the members—unless you provide a special formula to use for filling a vacancy by members. A majority of managers normally means the per capita (one person, one vote) majority vote of the current LLC managers (the managers remaining on the management team who are appointing someone to fill the vacancy).

Our provisions simply allow your members or managers to fill a vacancy that is not otherwise handled by your operating agreement; you may consider adding provisions that provide for the periodic election of managers by members. Remember, however, that Revenue Procedure 95-10 says you may not avoid the corporate characteristic of centralized management if you have procedures to elect (and remove) your managers. (See Chapter 3, Section B2, for more on this point.) We think it best, normally, to leave these provisions generalized as they are here, without specifically limiting the term of managers. This will help you avoid the centralized management characteristic in your quest for pass-through tax status, but let you adopt periodic management election procedures later if it is absolutely necessary to do so.

If you operate a larger LLC or will have any outside (nonmember) managers, you may decide to limit their terms by providing for periodic elections of managers. Many LLCs can do this and still avoid pass-through tax status (by avoiding the corporate characteristics of free transferability of interests and continuity of life). Here is an optional management election provision you can add to this provision to require the annual election of managers by the members. (You'll need to retype at least one page of the tear-out form to add this new language.)

Sample Language: Election of Managers: The membership of this LLC shall meet every year on __**date**__ to nominate and elect __**number**__ member-managers and __**number**__ nonmember-managers of the LLC. __**You may specify a procedure for voting and how the number of votes to be cast are to be calculated [for example: "Voting by the membership at this election shall be as follows: according to "capital interests," "per capita voting" (one person, one vote) or specify your own method for calculating votes]".**__ **You may want to exclude member-managers from voting in this election or add other provisions to suit your needs.**

Written or electronic notice of this annual membership meeting, its purpose, and the name of anyone nominated as of the date of the notice, shall be mailed, delivered or personally given to each member of this LLC no later than __**period, typically "30 days"**__ prior to the date of the annual meeting.

The term of office for each manager so elected shall be for one year, and until his or her successor is elected by the membership at the next annual membership meeting and such successor accepts his or her office.

F This provision explains that management decisions may be made either informally or at a formal meeting of managers. This is a flexible provision with the following key points:

- *Managers don't have to call formal meetings to make ordinary business decisions.* A formal meeting is only necessary if you want the managers to meet in person at a pre-arranged time or if you want to make a written record of the decisions reached by your managers.
- *Formal management decisions—those you wish to record in your LLC records book—should be approved by the vote requirement specified in the manager voting provision of your agreement.* The vote requirement is covered in *"II. Management Provisions: (3) Authority and Votes of Managers."*
- *Formal management meetings may be called by any manager.* Formal meetings must be held "within a reasonable time" of the call for the meeting, subject to a final date (no later than a specified number of days after the request for the meeting—for example, 30 or 60 days from the request by a manager for a meeting). You may

change these provisions to specify minimum and maximum timelines—for example, requiring the holding of a meeting no less than 10 or more than 60 days after a request for a meeting.

- *You can set the quorum requirement—the number or percentage of managers who must be present to hold a formal management meeting.* You may specify "all," "a majority" or some other portion of the managers. If you specify a quorum requirement, and a quorum is not in attendance, the meeting must be adjourned unless all nonattending managers sign off on the holding of the meeting ahead of time (sign a written consent before the meeting that says they agree to the holding of the meeting for one or more specified purposes even though they can't attend; a simple signed note to this effect is enough to comply with this formal written consent procedure).
- *Only the business communicated in the call for the formal meeting by the manager may be taken up at the meeting.* We think this makes sense for formally called and held management meetings, but you can be more expansive and change our language to allow any business to be discussed and voted upon at a formal meeting. For example, "Any business may be discussed and voted upon at a formal managers' meeting, whether or not stated or summarized in the notice for the meeting or written consent signed by a nonattending member."

More about manager meetings. See Chapter 7, Section C2, for details on when and how to conduct and document formal LLC meetings.

Our provisions are adequate for most smaller LLCs. If the formal management meeting provisions don't suit your needs, you are free to change them. For example, even though the managers of most smaller LLCs should normally talk, meet and make decisions face-to-face at at formal managers' meeting, you can add language that recognizes state-of-the-art ways for managers to meet and formally make decisions at a distance—such as over the Internet, on other computer bulletin boards, via e-mail, video or telephone conferences and the like. You also can allow your managers to make decisions by written consent of all managers (unanimity is typically required for written management decisions under state law, so check your state LLC Act if this interests you).

Again, bear in mind that if an issue is important enough to require the time and consideration of your managers to make and record a formal decision, it's probably best for the managers to talk with one another in person, not just to mail, fax or e-mail in their votes.

(6) Managers' Commitment to LLC: Managers shall devote their best efforts and energy working to achieve the business objectives and financial goals of this LLC. By agreeing to serve as a manager for the LLC, each manager shall agree not to work for another business, enterprise or endeavor, owned or operated by himself or herself or others, if such outside work or efforts would compete with the LLC's business goals, mission, products or services, or would diminish or impair the manager's ability to provide maximum effort and performance to managing the business of this LLC. Ⓖ

(7) Compensation of Managers: Managers of this LLC may be paid per-meeting or per-diem amounts for attending management meetings, may be reimbursed actual expenses advanced by them to attend management meetings or attend to management business for the LLC, and may be compensated in other ways for performing their duties as managers. Managers may work in other capacities for this LLC and may be compensated separately for performing these additional services, whether as officers, staff, consultants, independent contractors or in other capacities. Ⓗ

III. MEMBERSHIP PROVISIONS

The membership provisions are nearly identical to those provided in the basic LLC operating agreement; where indicated, see the corresponding instructions in Chapter 5, Section C.

(1) Nonliability of Members: No member of this LLC shall be personally liable for the expenses, debts, obligations or liabilities of the LLC, or for claims made against it. ❾

(2) Reimbursement for Organizational Costs: Members shall be reimbursed by the LLC for organizational expenses paid by the members. The LLC shall be authorized to elect to deduct organizational expenses and start-up expenditures ratably over a period of time as permitted by the Internal Revenue Code and as may be advised by the LLC's tax advisor. ❿

(3) Members' Percentage Interests: A member's percentage interest in this LLC shall be computed as a fraction, the numerator of which is the total of a member's capital account and the denominator of which is the total of all capital accounts of all members. This fraction shall be expressed in this agreement as a percentage, which shall be called each member's "percentage interest" in this LLC. ⓬

G This provision expresses the desire of the LLC to obtain maximum energy and effort from each LLC manager, and prohibits managers from working in or for outside businesses that compete with the LLC's business or in any business if doing so detracts from the manager's ability to perform properly for the LLC.

This is a general provision, and you may wish to tighten it up a little. For example, we've carefully avoided saying that managers must work full-time for the LLC (as managers or in other capacities), since this is not always the case. You can add language that requires such full-time effort, or go the other way and permit involvement with outside businesses or personal projects by your managers as long as they don't compete with the LLC's business.

Example: Bird Nest Bed & Breakfast, LLC, is founded by Ted and Jill. They have the money and energy to buy, set up and maintain a few scenically situated bed and breakfast cottages in their home town—a suburban location outside a major metropolitan area. Their community is overrun with summer and spring tourists seeking comfortable accommodations from which to base shopping and sightseeing sorties into the neighboring city. The two members are new to the B & B business and decide to bring in Elaine, an experienced B & B consultant, to help organize and operate the LLC. Elaine will work part-time on a consulting basis, plus be given a small stake in LLC profits for joining Ted and Jill as formal managers of the LLC. They decide to modify this provision in their operating agreement to allow Elaine (the provision can be stated to apply generally to all managers or can be worded to specifically apply to manager Elaine) to do consulting work for other businesses, whether in the B & B or unrelated areas of operation, as long as this outside work does not interfere with a manager's ability to provide best management efforts for the LLC.

Whatever changes you make to this provision, don't go overboard. Courts are often reluctant to enforce over-reaching restrictions on the abilities of individuals to decide how hard to work, and for whom. You may be able to sue a manager who strays from the fold in contravention of your operating agreement provisions or for nonperformance of his or her duties under an employment agreement, but don't expect a court to order a person to return to work for you, or work harder for your LLC—this just won't happen.

Also realize that provisions of this sort are really best viewed as an expression of the parties' expectations, rather than ironclad legal language. If a manager wishes to stray or stay away from your LLC, your best solution is to acquiesce—and find a more suitable replacement on your management team for the errant manager.

H This broad provision says managers may receive per-meeting, per-diem, or other payment or compensation for serving as managers. It allows managers to serve and be paid for performing work for the LLC in other capacities as officers, employees and independent contractors.

Even though this provision allows for a multitude of arrangements, the normal situation for smaller LLCs is that the managers also work for the LLC on a day-to-day basis in an officer or employee position (as President, Sales Manager, Chief Financial Officer) and do not receive payment for also serving as managers of the LLC. But you may wish to make other arrangements if you bring in outside managers who only work part- or full-time as managers. If they do not work in other capacities for your LLC, you may want to pay your managers as managers. The details of these arrangements are up to you; this provision allows you to pay managers in any capacity you wish.

Note that even outside managers may not wish to receive direct payment for managing an LLC. If the outside manager is an investor in the LLC, for example, she can look to her capital and/or profits interest in the LLC for a payback, rather than to direct payment for intermittent or part-time management services.

(4) Membership Voting: Except as otherwise may be required by the Articles of Organization, Certificate of Formation or a similar organizational document, other provisions of this operating agreement, or under the laws of this state, each member shall vote on any matter submitted to the membership for approval by the managers of this LLC in proportion to the member's percentage interest in this LLC. Further, unless defined otherwise for a particular provision of this operating agreement, the phrase "majority of members" means a majority of members whose combined percentage interests in this LLC represent more than 50% of the percentage interests of all members in this LLC. ⓭

(5) Compensation: Members shall not be paid as members of the LLC for performing any duties associated with such membership. Members may be paid, however, for any services rendered in any other capacity for the LLC, whether as officers, employees, independent contractors or otherwise. ⓮

(6) Members' Meetings: The LLC shall not provide for regular members' meetings. However, any member may call a meeting by communicating his or her wish to schedule a meeting to all other members. Such notification may be in person or in writing, or by telephone, facsimile machine, or other form of electronic communication reasonably expected to be received by a member, and the other members shall then agree, either personally, in writing, or by telephone, facsimile machine or other form of electronic communication to the member calling the meeting, to meet at a mutually acceptable time and place. Notice of the business to be transacted at the meeting need not be given to members by the member calling the meeting, and any business may be discussed and conducted at the meeting.

If all members cannot attend a meeting, it shall be postponed to a date and time when all members can attend, unless all members who do not attend have agreed in writing to the holding of the meeting without them. If a meeting is postponed, and the postponed meeting cannot be held either because all members do not attend the postponed meeting or the nonattending members have not signed a written consent to allow the postponed meeting to be held without them, a second postponed meeting may be held at a date and time announced at the first postponed meeting. The date and time of the second postponed meeting shall also be communicated to any members not attending the first postponed meeting. The second postponed meeting may be held without the attendance of all members as long as a majority of the percentage interests of the membership of this LLC is in attendance at the second postponed meeting. Written notice of the decisions or approvals made at this second postponed meeting shall be mailed or delivered to each nonattending member promptly after the holding of the second postponed meeting. ⓯

Written minutes of the discussions and proposals presented at a members' meeting, and the votes taken and matters approved at such meeting, shall be taken by one of the members or a person designated at the meeting. A copy of the minutes of the meeting shall be placed in the LLC's records book after the meeting. ⓰

(7) Membership Certificates: This LLC shall be authorized to obtain and issue certificates representing or certifying membership interests in this LLC. Each certificate shall show the name of the LLC, the name of the member, and state that the person named is a member of the LLC and is entitled to all the rights granted members of the LLC under the Articles of Organization, Certificate of Formation or a similar organizational document, this operating agreement, and provisions of law. Each membership certificate shall be consecutively numbered and signed by each of the current members of this LLC. The certificates shall include any additional information considered appropriate for inclusion by the members on membership certificates.

In addition to the above information, all membership certificates shall bear a prominent legend on their face or reverse side stating, summarizing or referring to any transfer restrictions that apply to memberships in this LLC under the Articles of Organization, Certificate of Formation or a similar organizational document and/or this operating agreement, and the address where a member may obtain a copy of these restrictions upon request from this LLC.

The records book of this LLC shall contain a list of the names and addresses of all persons to whom certificates have been issued, show the date of issuance of each certificate, and record the date of all cancellations or transfers of membership certificates. ⓱

IV. TAX AND FINANCIAL PROVISIONS

The tax and financial provisions below are very similar to those provided in the basic LLC operating agreement, but they are extended to apply to LLC managers. Where indicated, see the corresponding numbered instructions in Chapter 5, Section C.

(1) Tax Treatment: It is anticipated that this LLC will not be treated as a corporation under state and federal tax law, but instead it will be treated in the same manner as a partnership for tax purposes. It is further understood that the members do not consider each other partners or joint venturers with any other member of this LLC for any purpose other than federal and state tax purposes. ⓳

(2) Tax Year and Accounting Method: The tax year of this LLC shall be **"the calendar year" or specify a noncalendar year period, such as "July 1 to June 30th"**. The LLC shall use the **"cash" or "accrual"** method of accounting. Both the tax year and the accounting period of the LLC may be changed with the consent of all members or all managers if the LLC qualifies for such change, and may be effected by the filing of appropriate forms with the IRS and state tax authorities. ⓴

(3) Tax Matters Partner: If this LLC is required under Internal Revenue Code provisions or regulations, it shall designate from among its members or member-managers a "tax matters partner" in accordance with Internal Revenue Code Section 6231(a)(7) and corresponding regulations, who will fulfill this role by being the spokesperson for the LLC in dealings with the IRS as required under the Internal Revenue Code and Regulations, and who will report to the members and managers on the progress and outcome of these dealings. ㉑

(4) Annual Income Tax Returns and Reports: Within 60 days after the end of each tax year of the LLC, a copy of the LLC's state and federal income tax returns for the preceding tax year shall be mailed or otherwise provided to each member of the LLC, together with any additional information and forms necessary for each member to complete his or her individual state and federal income tax returns. This additional information shall include a federal (and, if applicable, state) Form K-1 (Form 1065—Partner's Share of Income, Credits, Deductions) or equivalent income tax reporting form, as well as a financial report, which shall include a balance sheet and profit and loss statement for the prior tax year of the LLC. ㉒

(5) Bank Accounts: The LLC shall designate one or more banks or other institutions for the deposit of the funds of the LLC, and shall establish savings, checking, investment and other such accounts as are reasonable and necessary for its business and investments. One or more employees of the LLC shall be designated with the consent of all managers to deposit and withdraw funds of the LLC, and to direct the investment of funds from, into and among such accounts. The funds of the LLC, however and wherever deposited or invested, shall not be commingled with the personal funds of any members or managers of the LLC. ❶

(6) Title to Assets: All personal and real property of this LLC shall be held in the name of the LLC, not in the names of individual members or managers. ㉔

Example: Sals' Berry Farms, a two-person LLC owned and operated by a married couple, Salvatore and Sally, owns and operates a California berry growing business. The spouses bought the business from the prior owners, who have been kept on as managers of the LLC. Sally and Sal are on the management team too, but they receive compensation as Vice Presidents of Operations, not as managers. The prior owners sold the business for a lump-sum buyout payment, plus a 20% share in future profits for the next five years. These nonmember managers of the LLC are not paid in their capacities as managers—they are content to let their management efforts pay off in a more important and lucrative fashion—namely, by boosting the value of their 20% profits interest in the business.

Finally, note that managers of smaller management-run LLCs normally approve the amount of payment, if any, each person gets for performing management duties. You may, however, let LLC members decide the compensation issue. By adding the sample language that follows to the end of this provision, you allow members who are not managers to approve payments to managers. The managers are still allowed to approve smaller amounts, such as reimbursements or per-meeting or per-diem payments.

> *Sample Language:* Except for per-meeting or per-diem amounts, or reimbursement of actual expenses paid to managers, the nonmanaging members of this LLC shall approve compensation and other payments to managers for performing management duties for this LLC.

I This is a general authorization paragraph that allows the LLC to establish accounts with banks and other institutions. It allows the managers to unanimously designate one or more LLC employees to deposit and withdraw funds into and from these accounts, and to direct the investment of funds held in these accounts.

Note that unanimous consent is required to designate a person or persons to have this depositing/checkwriting authority, but you can lessen this requirement if you wish by simply deleting the words "with the consent of all managers" from the second sentence of this paragraph.

In many businesses, multiple signatures may be required for withdrawals that exceed a specified amount. You don't need to specify these arrangements in your operating agreement. The details of these checkwriting and investment-directing arrangements will be spelled out on the signature cards and paperwork you must fill in when opening accounts on behalf of your LLC.

The final sentence in this paragraph is a reminder that personal funds of the LLC members and managers may not be commingled (mixed) with the funds of the LLC. If you commingle funds, a state court may decide that you and the other members and/or managers are not entitled to limited liability protection normally afforded an LLC, and may hold members and managers personally liable for LLC debts and claims.

J This provision gives members or managers leeway to distribute cash profits or proceeds of the LLC to members if they vote to do so. You can give authority to approve cash distributions exclusively to members and/or managers. Many smaller LLCs will trust their managers to make these allocations and distributions, but some may wish to leave important financial decisions of this sort strictly to the members themselves, or require the approval of both managers and members.

Most smaller LLCs will specify a unanimous vote, but some may prefer to allow a majority of the members and/or managers to decide this issue. Remember, a majority of members is defined in "III. Membership Provisions: (4) Membership Voting," as a majority of the percentage interests in the LLC; whereas a majority of managers is determined on a per capita basis (according to "II. Management Provisions: (3) Authority and Votes of Managers").

V. CAPITAL PROVISIONS

Most of the capital provisions in the tear-out management agreement are almost identical to those provided in the basic LLC operating agreement in Chapter 5, Section C. These provisions should work fine for smaller manager-run LLCs.

(1) Capital Contributions by Members: Members shall make the following contributions of cash, property or services as shown next to each member's name below. Unless otherwise noted, cash and property described below shall be paid or delivered to the LLC on or by **final date or period for contributions** . The fair market values of items of property or services as agreed between the LLC and the contributing member are also shown below. The percentage interest in the LLC that each member shall receive in return for his or her capital contribution is also indicated for each member. ㉕

Name	Contribution	Fair Market Value	Percentage Interest in LLC
________________	____________	$ ________	________
________________	____________	$ ________	________
________________	____________	$ ________	________
________________	____________	$ ________	________
________________	____________	$ ________	________
________________	____________	$ ________	________

(2) Additional Contributions by Members: The members may agree, from time to time by unanimous vote, to require the payment of additional capital contributions by the members, on or by a mutually agreeable date. ㉖

(3) Failure to Make Contributions: If a member fails to make a required capital contribution within the time agreed for a member's contribution, the remaining members may, by unanimous vote, agree to reschedule the time for payment of the capital contribution by the late-paying member, setting any additional repayment terms, such as a late payment penalty, rate of interest to be applied to the unpaid balance, or other monetary amount to be paid by the delinquent member, as the remaining members decide. Alternatively, the remaining members may, by unanimous vote, agree to cancel the membership of the delinquent member, provided any prior partial payments of capital made by the delinquent member are refunded promptly by the LLC to the member after the decision is made to terminate the membership of the delinquent member. ㉗

(4) No Interest on Capital Contributions: No interest shall be paid on funds or property contributed as capital to this LLC, or on funds reflected in the capital accounts of the members. 28

(5) Capital Account Bookkeeping: A capital account shall be set up and maintained on the books of the LLC for each member. It shall reflect each member's capital contribution to the LLC, increased by each member's share of profits in the LLC, decreased by each member's share of losses and expenses of the LLC, and adjusted as required in accordance with applicable provisions of the Internal Revenue Code and corresponding income tax regulations. 29

(6) Consent to Capital Contribution Withdrawals and Distributions: Members shall not be allowed to withdraw any part of their capital contributions or to receive distributions, whether in property or cash, except as otherwise allowed by this agreement and, in any case, only if such withdrawal is made with the written consent of all members. 30

(7) Allocations of Profits and Losses: No member shall be given priority or preference with respect to other members in obtaining a return of capital contributions, distributions or allocations of the income, gains, losses, deductions, credits or other items of the LLC. The profits and losses of the LLC, and all items of its income, gain, loss, deduction and credit shall be allocated to members according to each member's percentage interest in this LLC. 31

(8) Allocation and Distribution of Cash to Members: Cash from LLC business operations, as well as cash from a sale or other disposition of LLC capital assets, may be distributed from time to time to members in accordance with each member's percentage interest in the LLC, as may be decided by **"all" or "a majority"** of the **"members," "managers," "members and managers" or "members or managers"**. J

(9) Allocation of Noncash Distributions: If proceeds consist of property other than cash, the **"members," "managers," "members and managers" or "members or managers"** shall decide the value of the property and allocate such value among the members in accordance with each member's percentage interest in the LLC. If such noncash proceeds are later reduced to cash, such cash may be distributed among the members as otherwise provided in this agreement. K

(10) Allocation and Distribution of Liquidation Proceeds: Regardless of any other provision in this agreement, if there is a distribution in liquidation of this LLC, or when any member's interest is liquidated, all items of income and loss shall be allocated to the members' capital accounts, and all appropriate credits and deductions shall then be made to these capital accounts before any final distribution is made. A final distribution shall be made to members only to the extent of, and in proportion to, any positive balance in each member's capital account. 34

VI. MEMBERSHIP WITHDRAWAL AND TRANSFER PROVISIONS

These provisions, which are similar to those in Chapter 5, deal with members deciding to leave the LLC. We specifically require a vote to admit a transferee (someone who buys or is otherwise transferred an LLC interest from a member) as a new member of the LLC. As you know from Chapter 3, Section B4, the vote requirement to admit transferees into membership is an important tax option that helps your LLC qualify for pass-through tax status with the IRS.

(1) Withdrawal of Members: A member may withdraw from this LLC by giving written notice to all other members at least **number of days** days before the date the withdrawal is to be effective. 35

(2) Restrictions on the Transfer of Membership: A member shall not transfer his or her membership in the LLC unless all nontransferring **"members" or "member-managers"** in the LLC first agree to approve the admission of the transferee into this LLC. Further, no member may encumber a part or all of his or her membership in the LLC by mortgage, pledge, granting of a security interest, lien or otherwise, unless the encumbrance has first been approved in writing by all other members of the LLC. L

Notwithstanding the above provision, any member shall be allowed to assign an economic interest in his or her membership to another person without the approval of the other members or member-managers. Such an assignment shall not include a transfer of the member's voting or management rights in this LLC, and the assignee shall not become a member of the LLC. 37

VII. DISSOLUTION PROVISIONS

This section addresses the dissolution of the LLC, or events that may trigger a dissolution. Note that some of these provisions have important tax consequences, as discussed here and in the corresponding Special Instructions in Chapter 5, Section C.

(1) Events That Trigger Dissolution of the LLC: The following events shall trigger a dissolution of the LLC, except as provided:

(a) the death, insanity, bankruptcy, retirement, resignation or expulsion of a **"member" or "member-manager"**, M except that within **number of days, typically a maximum of 90 under state LLC default rules** of the happening of any of these events, all remaining members of the LLC may vote to continue the legal existence of the LLC, in which case the LLC shall not dissolve; 38

Again, we assume that allocations of profits and proceeds will follow each member's percentage interest in the LLC, but you can vary who gets how much if you (with help from your tax advisor) decide to implement disproportionate (special) allocations of LLC profits.

Ⓚ This paragraph addresses how any noncash LLC property will be allocated among members. As with the previous provision, you may want to leave these decisions to just members or managers, or have either or both approve them.

Whoever decides, this provision says that property gets allocated among members in proportion to each member's percentage interest in the LLC. If reduced to cash later, it will be distributed to members according to the previous provision in this operating agreement.

Example: Second-Hand Freight and Salvage, Ltd. Liability Co., a five-member company with three member-managers, decides (by a unanimous manager vote as provided in its operating agreement) to sell a truck and allocate the current value of this asset to all five members, who own the LLC in equal percentages. The truck is worth $30,000, so the capital account of each member is increased by $6,000. The members and/or managers can vote to distribute this cash according to the cash distribution provision in their agreement.

Ⓛ This provision deals with restrictions on the transfer of memberships. The language is based on Revenue Procedure 95-10 and helps your LLC avoid the corporate characteristic of free transferability of interests.

Most LLCs will want all members to approve the admission of persons who are transferred an LLC interest by members of the LLC. Those LLCs will fill in the word "members" in the blank.

Example: Nester's Bright Idea, LLC, is a three-member Seattle firm owned by Nester, his wife Claire, and his brother-in-law Jeb. According to their operating agreement, all members must approve new transferees. The company's new product line, "solid-state espresso spreads"—cappuccino-flavored jams and jellies marketed in frozen, microwave-thawable packets—get hot, so hot that Jeb decides it's time to cash in his LLC membership interest by selling it to his cousin Faye for a substantial sum. Faye must be approved by vote of the two remaining members before she is granted membership rights in the LLC.

A few manager-managed LLCs may wish to allow LLC member-managers to make this decision (rather than letting all other members vote for approval), and should state "member-managers" in the blank. (Revenue Procedure 95-10 lets you do this; see Chapter 3, Section B4.) Be aware, however, of an important point: If you decide to allow member-managers to approve transfers of membership, you must actually appoint one or more members as managers of your LLC. (Make sure you appoint at least one member-manager in "II. Management Provisions: (1) Management by Managers".)

Example: Penguin Pullovers and Winter Apparel, LLC, has four members, three of whom act as managers together with two nonmembers. If PPWA's operating agreement allows the transfer of membership interests by a member to a new member as long as the sale is approved by the remaining members on the management team, it should meet the tax ruling's vote requirements and the LLC should avoid the corporate tax characteristic of free transferability of interests.

Special steps if you change this provision. If you wish to alter this provision to allow a *majority* of nontransferring members or member-managers to approve the sale of a membership to a new member (as allowed under IRS rules), you need to do two things. First, make sure your state lets you—see the "Default Transfer Rule" in the "Operating Rules" section of your state sheet in Appendix A. Second, decide how to calculate this majority. The three choices available under Revenue Procedure 95-10 are capital *and* profits, capital *or* profits, or per capita membership votes. (For a further discussion of these choices, see Special Instruction ㊱ in Chapter 5, Section C.)

(b) the expiration of the term of existence of the LLC if such term is specified in the Articles of Organization, Certificate of Formation or a similar organizational document, or this operating agreement; 39

(c) the written agreement of all members to dissolve the LLC; 40

(d) entry of a decree of dissolution of the LLC under state law. 41

VIII. GENERAL PROVISIONS

The housekeeping and miscellaneous provisions are almost identical to those provided in the basic LLC operating agreement; see the corresponding instructions in Chapter 5, Section C.

(1) Officers: The managers of this LLC may designate one or more officers, such as a President, Vice President, Secretary and Treasurer. Persons who fill these positions need not be members or managers of the LLC. Such positions may be compensated or noncompensated according to the nature and extent of the services rendered for the LLC as a part of the duties of each office. Ministerial services only as a part of any officer position will normally not be compensated, such as the performance of officer duties specified in this agreement, but any officer may be reimbursed by the LLC for out-of-pocket expenses paid by the officer in carrying out the duties of his or her office. 42

(2) Records: The LLC shall keep at its principal business address a copy of all proceedings of membership meetings, as well as books of account of the LLC's financial transactions. A list of the names and addresses of the current membership of the LLC also shall be maintained at this address, with notations on any transfers of members' interests to nonmembers or persons being admitted into membership in the LLC. A list of the current managers' names and addresses shall also be kept at this address.

Copies of the LLC's Articles of Organization, Certificate of Formation or a similar organizational document, a signed copy of this operating agreement, and the LLC's tax returns for the preceding three tax years shall be kept at the principal business address of the LLC. A statement also shall be kept at this address containing any of the following information that is applicable to this LLC:

- the amount of cash or a description and value of property contributed or agreed to be contributed as capital to the LLC by each member;
- a schedule showing when any additional capital contributions are to be made by members to this LLC;
- a statement or schedule, if appropriate, showing the rights of members to receive distributions representing a return of part or all of members' capital contributions; and

Note a couple more points about our provisions. Even if you allow member-managers to vote on transfers of memberships, the members must approve the pledge or encumbrance of an LLC membership. Also, the members may still transfer economic interests in memberships without approval (this is allowed under the tax rules—see Special Instruction ㊲ in Chapter 5, Section C). We think these collateral provisions work the way most manager-managed LLCs will want as well.

Ⓜ Most LLCs will want to require the vote of all remaining members to continue the LLC following the dissociation of any member. By taking this approach, you let all members decide whether or not to keep the business going following any of the listed dissolution-triggering events. If this applies to your LLC, fill in the word "member" in the blank.

A few manager-managed LLCs may wish to limit the approval process only to the dissociation of members who are also managers, and should fill in the blank with the words "member-manager." This is allowed under Revenue Procedure 95-10—as long as you have, in fact, appointed one or more members to serve as managers. In other words, you can require a membership vote to continue the LLC only when the interest of a member-manager (not just a plain member) is terminated upon the member-manager's death, resignation, expulsion, retirement, bankruptcy or insanity. The tax ruling says that this provision still qualifies the LLC to avoid the corporate characteristic of "continuity of life," which in turn helps the LLC qualify for pass-through tax status with the IRS.

Example: Philly's Putty, LLC, specializes in wall-spackling and touch-up pre-painting work for general contractors. Phil owns and manages the business along with his sister, Felicia, and a third member-investor, Renaldo. Phil and Felicia are the two member-managers; Renaldo is the nonmanaging member. Their operating agreement calls for a vote to continue the LLC following dissociation of member-managers only. Renaldo decides to resign and cash out his membership. Phil and Felicia do not need to vote to continue the legal life of the LLC (although a vote would be required if either of their membership interests is terminated).

You can lower the unanimous vote requirement here to less than all remaining members. If you wish to do so: 1) check your state sheet's "Default Continuation Rule" in the "Operating Rules" section to make sure your state lets you, and 2) make sure you require at least the vote of a "majority in interest" of the remaining members (this means a majority of the capital *and* profits interests owned by remaining members. Your state's "Default Continuation Rule" in your state sheet in Appendix A also tells if you must take this vote within 90 days or some other period. If your state lets you set your own deadline for voting, we suggest no less than 30 days to give your members a chance to meet and approve the continuance of your LLC.

The other paragraphs in this provision cover additional LLC dissolution events, which do not have special tax significance. As indicated, these paragraphs are explained in Chapter 5, Section C, Special Instructions ㊳, ㊴, ㊵ and ㊶.

Ⓝ Your state LLC statute may allow you to restrict when or why members or managers are allowed to look at LLC records, or restrict access to particular types of LLC legal or financial records. We don't nitpick here, and simply give all members and managers an unrestricted right to view all records at any time.

If you want to restrict inspection rights, take a look at your state LLC statute to see how restrictive you are allowed to be under state law, then insert your own provisions. Normally, you will not wish to limit manager's rights—managers may need to look at LLC legal or financial records on a moment's notice to make a management decision—but you may wish to restrict members' inspection rights. Here's some sample language to accomplish this:

- a description of, or date when, the legal existence of the LLC will terminate under provisions in the LLC's Articles of Organization, Certificate of Formation or a similar organizational document, or this operating agreement.

If one or more of the above items is included or listed in this operating agreement, it will be sufficient to keep a copy of this agreement at the principal business address of the LLC without having to prepare and keep a separate record of such item or items at this address.

Any member or manager may inspect any and all records maintained by the LLC upon reasonable notice to the LLC. Copying of the LLC's records by members and managers is allowed, but copying costs shall be paid for by the requesting member or manager. Ⓝ

(3) All Necessary Acts: The members, managers and officers of this LLC are authorized to perform all acts necessary to perfect the organization of this LLC and to carry out its business operations expeditiously and efficiently. The Secretary of the LLC, or other officers, or one or more managers or all members of the LLC, may certify to other businesses, financial institutions and individuals as to the authority of one or more members, managers or officers of this LLC to transact specific items of business on behalf of the LLC. (44)

(4) Mediation and Arbitration of Disputes Among Members: In any dispute over the provisions of this operating agreement and in other disputes among the members, if the members cannot resolve the dispute to their mutual satisfaction, the matter shall be submitted to mediation. The terms and procedure for mediation shall be arranged by the parties to the dispute.

If good-faith mediation of a dispute proves impossible or if an agreed-upon mediation outcome cannot be obtained by the members who are parties to the dispute, the dispute may be submitted to arbitration in accordance with the rules of the American Arbitration Association. Any party may commence arbitration of the dispute by sending a written request for arbitration to all other parties to the dispute. The request shall state the nature of the dispute to be resolved by arbitration, and, if all parties to the dispute agree to arbitration, arbitration shall be commenced as soon as practical after such parties receive a copy of the written request.

All parties shall initially share the cost of arbitration, but the prevailing party or parties may be awarded attorney fees, costs and other expenses of arbitration. All arbitration decisions shall be final, binding and conclusive on all the parties to arbitration, and legal judgment may be entered based upon such decision in accordance with applicable law in any court having jurisdiction to do so. (45)

(5) Entire Agreement: This operating agreement represents the entire agreement among the members of this LLC, and it shall not be amended, modified or replaced except by a written instrument executed by all the parties to this agreement who are current members of this LLC as well as any and all additional parties who became members of this LLC after the adoption of this agreement. This agreement replaces and supersedes all prior written and oral agreements among any and all members of this LLC. (46)

(6) Severability: If any provision of this agreement is determined by a court or arbitrator to be invalid, unenforceable or otherwise ineffective, that provision shall be severed from the rest of this agreement, and the remaining provisions shall remain in effect and enforceable. 47

IX. SIGNATURES OF MEMBERS AND SPOUSES

The execution and consent of spouses, provisions are identical to those provided in the basic LLC operating agreement; see the corresponding instructions in Chapter 5, Section C.

(1) Execution of Agreement: In witness whereof, the members of this LLC sign and adopt this agreement as the operating agreement of this LLC.

Date: ______________________________ 48
Signature: ______________________________
Printed Name: ________________________, Member

Date: ______________________________
Signature: ______________________________
Printed Name: ________________________, Member

Date: ______________________________
Signature: ______________________________
Printed Name: ________________________, Member

Date: ______________________________
Signature: ______________________________
Printed Name: ________________________, Member

Date: ______________________________
Signature: ______________________________
Printed Name: ________________________, Member

Date: ______________________________
Signature: ______________________________
Printed Name: ________________________, Member

(2) Consent of Spouses: The undersigned are spouses of members of this LLC who have signed this operating agreement in the preceding provision. These spouses have read this agreement and agree to be bound by its terms in any matter in which they have a financial interest, including restrictions on the transfer of memberships and the terms under which memberships in this LLC may be sold or otherwise transferred. (49)

Date: ____________________
Signature: ____________________
Printed Name: ____________________
Spouse of: ____________________

Date: ____________________
Signature: ____________________
Printed Name: ____________________
Spouse of: ____________________

Date: ____________________
Signature: ____________________
Printed Name: ____________________
Spouse of: ____________________

Date: ____________________
Signature: ____________________
Printed Name: ____________________
Spouse of: ____________________

Date: ____________________
Signature: ____________________
Printed Name: ____________________
Spouse of: ____________________

Date: ____________________
Signature: ____________________
Printed Name: ____________________
Spouse of: ____________________

Sample Language: Any member may inspect the financial or other records of this LLC for a purpose reasonably related to the member's interest in this LLC. The Treasurer of this LLC shall make the determination within one week of the member's request and, if the Treasurer finds that the member's request is related to his or her interest in the LLC, the requesting member shall be allowed to inspect the records during regular business hours of the LLC at its principal place of business.

C. Distribute Copies of Your Operating Agreement

Congratulations! You are done with another important organizational task, and your LLC is well on its legal way. Make photocopies of the completed, signed management operating agreement and give each member a copy. Finally, place the original, signed agreement in your LLC records book.

●

CHAPTER 7

After Forming Your LLC

In this chapter, we discuss legal and procedural formalities that you may need to tend to after setting up your limited liability company. We suggest you skim through the chapter and get a general sense of the work you may need to do. If any topic seems pertinent, make sure you carefully read the discussion.

It's important to keep in mind that LLCs are relatively new, so trying to anticipate the ongoing issues and concerns particular to LLCs is a bit of a guessing game. For now, we cover operational tasks and issues we believe are most likely to apply. We're sure you'll be on the lookout for other LLC matters, and should be able to handle them successfully using common sense and good business judgment (backed up, if necessary, by a consultation with a small business legal or tax advisor, as discussed in Chapter 8).

General business information. This book can't possibly cover all the ins and outs of small business law. You'll find a wealth of helpful information in *The Legal Guide for Starting and Running a Small Business*, by Fred Steingold (Nolo Press). For tax guidance, see *Tax Savvy for Small Business*, by Fred Daily (Nolo Press).

A. If You Converted an Existing Business to an LLC

If you converted an existing sole proprietorship or partnership to an LLC, you'll need to take a few extra steps, as discussed in this section. (The aftermath of converting a corporation to an LLC is beyond the scope of this book.)

If yours is a new business. If you did not convert a pre-existing business to an LLC, skip to Section B, below.

1. Notify Agencies and Businesses That You're Now an LLC

Make sure you notify the IRS, your state taxing authority and other governmental agencies that you've changed your legal status to an LLC, and provide your new LLC name. As part of this process, you may need to obtain some of the following in your new LLC name:

- federal Employer Identification Number (EIN)
- state employer identification number
- fictitious or assumed business name statement if you run your LLC under a name different from its formal name listed in its Articles (see Section D3, below)
- sales tax permit
- business license, and
- professional license or permit, if the LLC members engage in a licensed profession.

Of course, you'll want to immediately get to work changing your stationery, business cards, brochures, advertisements, signs and other marketing and business miscellany to reflect your new LLC name. In addition, let your bank, suppliers, customers and business associates know your new business name and LLC status.

Review your files and other papers. If you go through the tax returns and other papers for your prior business, you'll likely discover the names and addresses of other agencies and businesses that should be notified of your new business name and form.

2. Special Procedures for Converting a Partnership to an LLC

If you converted an existing general or limited partnership to an LLC, you will probably need to do a little extra paperwork to end the legal existence of the partnership. If you neglect to take these steps, the general partner(s) may remain personally liable for any unpaid partnership business debts (we assume your LLC will pay off any unpaid debts of the prior business anyway; see the sidebar, "Liability for Previous Partnership Debts"):

- *Converting a general partnership to an LLC.* State law may require the publication of a notice of dissolution of partnership. Newspapers handle this requirement as a matter of routine, so call a local paper that publishes legal notices and ask if it provides this service. Not only should the newspaper be able to tell you whether a notice of dissolution of partnership applies in your state, it should be able to mail you a summary of your state's notice requirements in this area if you want to read them yourself. Once you publish your notice, the newspaper should send you a copy of the published notice and an affidavit of publication to place in your files. (If you can't get a satisfactory answer from a newspaper, a law or business library should contain information on terminating the legal existence of a partnership in your state; look up "partnerships" in the card catalog or ask a research librarian for help.)
- *Converting a limited partnership to an LLC.* The conversion usually is not legally effective until you file a cancellation or termination of limited partnership form with your Secretary of State's office. The state filing office should have a fill-in-the-blanks or sample form you can order by phone to use for this purpose, similar to the sample provided below. You generally must attend to this formality even if your state LLC office supplied a special form of Articles to convert a partnership to an LLC. (See your state sheet in Appendix A. Your LLC filing office will normally handle the filing for terminating a limited partnership.)

LIABILITY FOR PREVIOUS PARTNERSHIP DEBTS

If your general or limited partnership has outstanding claims or debts owing at the time of its conversion to an LLC, the general partners of the pre-existing partnership will remain personally liable for these debts. Of course, your new LLC probably plans to assume and pay these bills as they come due. As a courtesy, and to make sure all partnership creditors have personal notice of your new business form, we recommend you send a personal letter to notify each one of the conversion of the partnership to an LLC, and provide the LLC's name and business address where future correspondence may be sent.

If there are significant disputed debts or claims of your prior partnership that your LLC will not automatically pay when it begins doing business, we strongly urge you to check with a business lawyer. You will obviously want to know your legal rights and responsibilities as to these disputed amounts.

SAMPLE CANCELLATION OF LIMITED PARTNERSHIP

Prescribed by
Bob Taft, Secretary of State
30 East Broad Street, 14th Floor
Columbus, Ohio 43266-0418
Form LPC (July 1994)

Registration #________
Approved____________
Date______________
Fee $10

CERTIFICATE OF CANCELLATION OF LIMITED PARTNERSHIP

Pursuant to the provisions of Ohio Revised Code Section 1782.10(B), the undersigned,____
(name of limited partnership)
bearing registration number ________________________, does hereby certify the following:

1. The name of the limited partnership:__________________________________

____

2. The registration number of the limited partnership:____________________

3. The date of the initial filing of its certificate of limited partnership:____________
month day year

4. The date of the filing of its certificate of limited partnership with the Ohio Secretary of State (if different from the date listed in line #3):____________________
month day year

5. The reason for filing the certificate of cancellation is as follows:

(If insufficient space for this item, please attach a separate sheet)

6. The effective date of cancellation: (please check/complete one of the following)

[ ] Upon Filing of Certificate of Cancellation [ ]________________
month day year

(Please note that the effective date of cancellation cannot precede or be earlier than the date of filing)

7. Is a person other than any general partner reflected on the certificate of limited partnership winding up the limited partnership's affairs?

[ ] Yes [ ] No *(please check the applicable box)*

If "Yes" was checked above, the name and the business, residence or mailing address of **each** liquidating trustee must be listed in the following space:

Name Address

____

____

____

____

(if additional space is required for this item, please attach a separate sheet)

8. Other (Optional)

(If additional space is required to complete this item, please attach separate sheet(s); this portion of the certificate may not exceed three (3) additional pages, ORC 1782.10(B)(6))

IN WITNESS WHEREOF, the undersigned have executed this Certificate of Cancellation this _________day of ________________________________, 19____.

Signed:__________________________ Signed:________________________

Signed:__________________________ Signed:________________________

Signed:__________________________ Signed:________________________

INSTRUCTIONS

1. A certificate of cancellation must be signed by all general partners OR, if the general partners are not winding up the affairs of the limited partnership, by all liquidating trustees, provided that if the limited partners are winding up the affairs of the limited partnership, a certificate of cancellation need by signed only by a majority in number of the limited partners.

2. A certificate of cancellation must be filed upon the dissolution and the commencement of the winding up of the partnership, or at any other time there are no limited partners.

[Ohio Revised Code Section 1782.10(B)]

3. Certain Businesses Must File Notice of Bulk Sales

Most states require the publication and mailing of a Notice of Bulk Sales when certain types of businesses—such as retail, wholesale and manufacturing businesses—are sold or converted to another form. The idea behind these notice requirements is to prevent debtor businesses (those owing money when they "go out of business") from changing their business form without arranging to pay their debts.

A local paper that publishes legal notices should know the rules for making this publication if it is required in your state. Ask the newspaper for a copy of your state's bulk sales act rules if you want to read them yourself. If the newspaper can't help you, again, a business or law library should have information and forms that you can use to handle any state requirements.

Your conversion to an LLC may be exempt from notice of bulk sales rules. In many states, bulk notice requirements are simplified or even waived if a business is simply being converted to a new form—such as the conversion of a partnership or sole partnership to an LLC—and the new business will assume and pay off the prior business's debts.

B. Basic Tax Forms and Formalities

Let's look at some tax issues and tasks you will need to keep in mind and tend to when the time comes (and tax time inevitably comes much too soon for most of us).

1. Federal Income Taxes

Although your LLC is a pass-through tax entity, you will need to file a federal LLC informational tax return each year. At the time of this writing, specific LLC forms aren't provided by the IRS. You must file the IRS return that applies to partnerships, IRS Form 1065, and attach a completed Form 1065 Schedule K-1 for each member, which lists the member's share of LLC income, credits and deductions.

Look for LLC-specific forms. It's possible that federal tax forms specially geared to LLCs will be developed. If so, they should be used instead of the partnership tax forms. If this happens, IRS Publication 334 should provide a sample filled-in federal form for you to follow (see sidebar, "Tax Resources for LLCs").

TAX RESOURCES FOR LLCs

Like many small business owners, you may plan to turn your annual tax preparation work over to your tax advisor, rather than handle this task yourself. If you're like many LLC owners, you may also decide to keep yourself informed of tax matters that may affect your business.

Whether you plan to prepare your own tax returns or simply want more information, you'll want to take advantage of the free tax forms and publications provided by the IRS. Call 1-800-TAX-FORM and request copies of:

- the federal *U.S. Partnership Return*, IRS Form 1065
- 1065 Schedule K-1, and
- IRS Publication 334, *Tax Guide for Small Business*. This is one of the best guides for finding and filling in the latest annual tax return form for different types of business, including LLCs (which are treated as partnerships). The final part of this publication contains filled-in sample forms for all types of businesses. Look at the partnership return and schedules, as these apply to your LLC.

2. State Income Taxes

Most states will follow the federal lead and, for state tax purposes, classify your LLC as a partnership (provided you qualify under the federal rules). This normally means you avoid the payment of any entity (business) level income tax charged in your state. In other words, just the members pay state income taxes on LLC profits and salaries, assuming the state has a personal income tax scheme. Even if your LLC is exempt from payment of state income taxes, it may have to file a state informational return, or annually submit a copy of the federal partnership tax return (discussed in Section B1, just above).

If your state doesn't impose corporate or personal income taxes. The states of Nevada, South Dakota, Washington and Wyoming do not impose either personal or corporate state income taxes. Alaska, Florida, New Hampshire, Tennessee and Texas do not impose state tax on individual income (although New Hampshire and Texas impose a special personal tax on interest and dividend income). Except for Florida and Texas (covered below), being treated as a partnership in a state without a personal income tax ordinarily means that the LLC and its members do not pay state income tax on LLC profits. However, don't forget that even if your LLC and members avoid paying income taxes on profits earned in your state, *out-of-state* taxes may be imposed if profits are earned in other states. This is a technical issue, and subject to state-by-state variations. Ask your tax advisor or check the tax section of a business or law library if you are forming an LLC with multi-state operations.

There are exceptions to the rule that states follow the federal tax classification of LLCs. Some state tax offices require LLCs to pay a minimum annual tax each year, sometimes euphemistically called an LLC "renewal fee." Some states go whole hog and subject LLCs to the same or similar business income or franchise tax that is levied on corporations.

The best source for current information on how your state handles the income taxation of LLCs is your state tax office. The main office is usually located in the state capitol city and can be reached in-state through a toll-free telephone number. Your state sheet in Appendix A will tell you if your state is one of the few that charges a separate LLC income or renewal fee each year (other than the small annual report fee typically required in most states). Here are the three primary states that impose annual taxes or fees of this sort (other states in search of revenue may eventually join this list):

- *California* imposes a minimum $800 annual tax on LLCs (the minimum tax also applies to limited partnerships and corporations doing business in the state). California also charges those LLCs with yearly incomes of $250,000 or more additional fees, from $500 to $4,500 annually.
- *Florida* imposes its 5.5% annual corporate income tax on LLCs.
- *Texas* imposes an annual franchise tax on LLCs. It is based on earned surplus, thus has the effect of a state business income tax.

If your LLC must pay a minimum or full state franchise or income tax, make sure you make required estimated payments. Franchise and income taxes must usually be prepaid in four installments during the tax year, with the first payment consisting of any minimum amount charged. If you miss estimated tax payments, you will be charged penalties and interest. In some states, your LLC can be suspended if you fail to pay these taxes for a few years.

3. Employment Taxes

Your LLC will need to register as an employer. For salaried workers, your LLC must withhold, report and pay:

- federal and, if applicable, state incomes taxes
- federal employment taxes (unemployment and social security taxes), and
- state payroll taxes (state unemployment, disability, workers' compensation insurance).

For more information on ongoing federal payroll tax requirements. Call 1-800-TAX-FORM and request IRS Form SS-4 (to get a federal Employer Identification for your LLC), IRS Publication 15, *Circular E, Employer's Tax Guide* and the IRS Publication 15 Supplement (for federal payroll tax information). For state payroll tax requirements, call the state Department of Revenue (or similar state tax office) at its main information number—usually a toll-free number for use within the state—and ask to be transferred to the state employment tax division.

4. Other State and Local Taxes

State sales, use and county property tax payments apply to LLCs. Counties and cities also may impose local and regional taxes in an effort to stay above the red line and provide basic services to residents. Check with your county and city tax offices for current information.

C. Ongoing LLC Legal Paperwork and Procedures

Now let's cover a few legal formalities that may come up from time to time during the life of your LLC. Again, because LLCs are so new, we have done our best to predict the types of procedures that will likely apply to the new LLC legal way of life. By necessity, we provide this information and the forms below as guidelines, not as time-tested material.

1. Changing Your Operating Agreement

During the life of your LLC, you may want to make changes to your operating agreement or draw up a new agreement—for example:

- If a new member joins the LLC, you will want a new agreement to include the new member's capital, profits and losses and voting percentages, and have it signed by new and old members.
- A prospective new member, or his or her legal or tax advisor, may ask for a change to one or more provisions in your old agreement to suit the needs of the new member.

Of course, you can decide to update your operating agreement at any time, not just when a new member joins your LLC. Generally, we think it's a good idea to sit down with your fellow LLC members at least once every two or so years and go over your agreement to see if it continues to meet your needs. If it doesn't, perhaps now is the time to make a few changes.

Example: The Pig in a Poke Ltd. Liability Company, a mail order lottery subscription and award notification service, wants to enlarge its membership base. The current members reason that it will be easier to attract new LLC members if they can be allowed to transfer their membership to others more easily under provisions of their operating agreement. They meet and decide to lessen the current unanimous vote requirement in their agreement to allow transfers to new members by a per capita majority vote of the members. They then amend their operating agreement to reflect this change. (This majority vote still meets the requirements of Revenue Procedure 95-10, having to do with qualifying for pass-through tax treatment for the LLC, as discussed in Chapter 3, Section B4.)

a. How to Update Your Operating Agreement

There are three steps to updating an LLC operating agreement:

- First, have your members formally meet, discuss and formally approve the changes you plan to make to the operating agreement. (We cover LLC meetings in Section C2, below.)
- Next, prepare a new operating agreement. Simply re-create your old agreement, revising it to reflect your LLC's new needs.
- Finally, have all members sign the updated operating agreement, which contains the new provisions plus all unchanged provisions carried over from your previous agreement.

WATCH OUT FOR TAX-IMPACT CHANGES TO YOUR AGREEMENT

Any changes you make to your operating agreement may impact one or more of the important options that determine your eligibility for pass-through tax status with the IRS. (These options are discussed at length in Chapter 3, as well as in Chapters 5 and 6.)

More specifically, if proposed changes to your agreement involve any of the following four tax-related areas, we recommend you have your tax advisor check your changes before you vote to adopt them:

- how the LLC is managed (by members or managers)
- the rules for admitting new members who buy or are otherwise transferred a membership interest in your LLC
- the reasons for canceling a person's membership in your LLC or the vote needed to continue the LLC's legal existence after a membership is relinquished (a member resigns or retires) or is canceled (a member files bankruptcy, is expelled, or is found mentally incompetent by a court), or
- the limited liability status of any member (this is an unlikely change—in which you make one of your LLC members personally liable for LLC liabilities, much like a general partner).

b. How to Prepare a New Agreement for a New Member

As we've said, preparing and signing a new LLC operating agreement is essential to make sure a new member agrees to all rights and responsibilities of LLC membership, and to make sure each current member agrees to the new division of capital, profits, losses and voting that results from bringing in a new member.

To prepare a new operating agreement, you can simply re-create your old agreement, making sure to change the capital contributions clause and other provisions that are affected by admitting the new member. All current members plus the new member sign the new agreement. Place the original in your LLC records book.

Example: Shortly after its formation, Tried & True Triad Music Promotions LLC, a three-owner company, decides to admit a fourth member. The new member will pay $20,000 to the LLC, the same amount each of the original members paid. The company adopts a new operating agreement and changes the ownership percentages of the original three members in the capital contribution clause from 33-1/3% to 25%, also showing a 25% interest for the newly admitted fourth member. No other changes are required, because splitting of profits and losses and voting rights follow the percentage interests shown in the capital contributions clause. The three initial members and the new member sign the new agreement and place it in the LLC records book.

2. Minutes of Meetings of Members and Managers

If your LLC wishes to approve and formally document an important legal, tax or business transaction, you'll normally hold a meeting of your members (or managers, in the more unusual situation where you have opted for manager control by adopting the operating agreement covered in Chapter 6).

Your members or managers may decide to hold a formal LLC meeting to take actions such as the following:

- vote on any matters that require a membership (or manager) vote, as set out in your operating agreement
- change your LLC operating agreement (even in manager-managed LLCs, the members normally are asked to ratify any changes to the operating agreement proposed by managers)
- amend the LLC's Articles of Organization (see Section D4, below)
- make significant capital outlays, such as to purchase real property
- fund a major, recurring LLC expense, such as contributions to an employee pension or profit-sharing plan
- sell real estate or other major capital items
- sell or purchase an operating division within the company, or expand or discontinue a product line or services
- pursue or settle a lawsuit, or
- approve other important legal, business, financial or tax decisions.

You should prepare minutes of formal LLC meetings during or after the meeting, recording the discussions and decisions made. After the meeting, place the signed minutes in your LLC records book.

You don't always have to meet face-to-face to record a formal LLC decision. Even if your LLC operating agreement requires that all or a certain percentage of members or managers approve a particular decision formally, you don't usually need to get together in person to do so. You may hold meetings on paper if all members or managers agree. You do this by preparing minutes that record a decision as though it had been made at a formal meeting. You then circulate these minutes for formal approval (signing and dating) by each member or manager. This sort of "paper meeting" is fine if everyone agrees to approve a decision this way.

a. Give Adequate Notice of Meeting to All Members or Managers

We don't cover all the ins and outs of calling, providing notice of and holding formal LLC meetings in our standard operating agreement. Most state laws are very flexible and allow LLCs to handle these matters in any way the members or managers wish. If, however, you have specified meeting rules in your operating agreement or Articles of Organization, make sure you follow them.

To make sure everyone involved knows the time, date and purpose of each upcoming meeting, make sure you tell, write, fax, phone or otherwise notify all members or managers (or both groups if both will attend the meeting) well in advance. Normally, two to four weeks' mailed notice is adequate. Providing adequate notice is particularly important if some members are not active in the LLC and not part of your LLC's normal network or grapevine of memos, discussions and verbal feedback. Taking the extra step to provide notice of an upcoming meeting may not be legally necessary under your operating agreement or state law, but it can avoid a lot of aggravation later—for example, if a controversial decision is adopted at a meeting without the approval of one or more members or managers.

b. How to Complete Minutes of Meeting

Below, we provide a sample of the simple, ready-to-use LLC Minutes of Meeting form included in Appendix C. Make a copy of the tear-out form and fill it in as you follow the sample and instructions.

MINUTES OF MEETING OF THE
"MEMBERS" OR "MANAGERS" ❶ OF
NAME OF LLC

A meeting of the **"members" or "managers"** of the above named limited liability company was held on **date, including year**, at **time** __.M., at **address,**
State of **state**, for the following purpose(s):
list the items of business discussed or considered by the members or managers. ❷

---

name and title acted as chairperson, and
name and title acted as secretary of the meeting. ❸

The chairperson called the meeting to order.

The following **"members" or "managers"**, were present at the meeting:
names of members or managers. ❹

The following persons were also present at the meeting, and any reports given by these persons are noted next to their names below: ❺

Name and Title	Reports Presented, If Any
__________	__________
__________	__________
__________	__________
__________	__________

After discussion, on motion duly made and carried by the affirmative vote of
"all," "a majority of the percentage interests" or "a majority of the number,"
or whatever voting requirement is used for members or managers in your LLC
of **the "members" or "managers"**, the following resolution(s) was/were adopted:
insert language of proposal(s) passed by members or managers. ❻

There being no further business to come before the meeting, it was adjourned on motion duly made and carried.

Date: **date**

Signature(s): **signature of LLC Secretary, officer or member** ❼

typed or printed name

Title: **LLC title or status**

SPECIAL INSTRUCTIONS

❶ In the first blank, indicate whether the minutes are being prepared for a meeting of members or managers. Remember, most smaller LLCs are managed by members (not managers), so formal meetings will usually be constituted and convened as membership meetings.

❷ Include a brief statement of the nature of the resolutions that are raised for approval at the meeting. For example: "to approve the purchase of property by the LLC" or "to approve a proposed employment contract to be offered to the CEO of the LLC" or "to accept the terms of a construction loan obtained by the Treasurer of the LLC."

❸ Insert the name and title of the persons designated as chairperson and secretary of the meeting. Normally, the CEO or President of the LLC acts as chairperson. The person preparing these minutes will typically be the secretary of the meeting (often the Secretary of the LLC).

If you have not designated officers for your LLC (see the operating agreement instructions in Chapter 5, Section C, Special Instruction ㊷), simply appoint one of the attending members or managers to serve in each of these capacities.

❹ This paragraph indicates which members or managers attended the meeting. Check your operating agreement to see if it states that a specific number of members or managers must attend meetings—technically, this number is called a "quorum." Our standard operating agreement provisions require:

- *Member-managed LLC:* All members must attend meetings unless a nonattending member agrees in writing prior to the meeting that it may be held in his or her absence (or unless the meeting is a second postponed meeting; see Chapter 5, Section C, Special Instruction ⓯).
- *Manager-managed LLC:* You may pick the number of managers who must attend an LLC managers' meeting—see Chapter 6, Section B3, Special Instruction Ⓕ).

❺ List any nonmembers or nonmanagers who attend the meeting. Also show to the right of an attendee's name any report presented by this person (such as an annual written financial report by the LLC Treasurer, an insurance availability and premium quote report by a Vice President or an oral report by the President on the negotiations that led to the drafting of a proposed lease agreement being presented at the meeting for approval by members). Attach to your minutes a copy of any written reports handed out at the meeting.

❻ Here you take care of the primary reason for preparing minutes of your meeting: to show the vote taken and the language of the proposals approved by your members or managers. If different votes are obtained on different resolutions, repeat the wording of this preliminary paragraph before each resolution.

LLC members are normally given voting power equal to their percentage interests in the LLC; see Chapter 5, Section C, Special Instruction ⓭. So, for example, a member who owns 25% of the LLC will normally have 25% of the voting power of the LLC. Managers, on the other hand, normally are given one vote per person in reaching management decisions; see Chapter 6, Section B3, Special Instruction Ⓒ. Check your operating agreement to be sure of your voting rules for members and managers.

Show the vote obtained in favor of the proposal in the first blank. For more significant or controversial decisions, where members or managers dissent or abstain, you may wish to insert a paragraph that shows how each person voted on every individual proposal—for, against or abstained.

Your operating agreement may require a larger vote. On some special matters—particularly those that relate to the pass-through tax status of your LLC, your operating agreement may have stricter voting requirements. For example, unanimous voting approval of members or managers may be required for:

- the approval of structural changes to the LLC, such as a sale of assets
- the admission or departure of members (covered in Section C3, below)
- continuance or dissolution of the business after a member leaves (discussed in Section C3, below), or
- amendments to the Articles of Organization (covered in Section D4).

In the last blanks of the vote-specification paragraph, insert the wording of each resolution approved at the meeting. The language should be nontechnical and clearly state the decision the members or managers reached. If you wish to back up your brief description of the decision, you can attach additional information to your minutes and refer to the attachments here.

Example of Contract Approval: "The members approved a long-term contract for the supplying of goods to the LLC by [name of company]. A copy of the contract approved is attached." (Although routine business contracts are normally not formally approved at a membership meeting, such approval may be sought to avoid the appearance of a conflict of interest—for example, if the supply company is owned or managed by a member's spouse).

Example of Lease Approval: "The managers approved the terms of a ten-year lease of premises by the LLC. A copy of the lease agreement is attached."

Approval of Tax Matter: "The members approved the following tax proposal, recommended for passage by the LLC's accountant, [name of accountant]. Copies of correspondence with the accountant and other relevant documents considered by members before approval of this proposal are attached."

❼ Have the secretary of the meeting, or any other designated LLC officer or member, date and sign the minutes. Type or print the person's name and title under the signature line. Finally, place a copy of the signed minutes in your LLC records book together with any attachment pages.

More on holding and documenting meetings. If you're interested in this subject, a good resource is *Taking Care of Your Corporation, Volume 1—Director and Shareholder Meetings Made Easy*, by Anthony Mancuso (Nolo Press). Although this book is geared toward corporations, it provides a wealth of information on how to schedule, notice, hold and record formal meetings, and applies to all sorts of businesses, including LLCs.

3. Special Approvals for New or Departing Members

When a member joins or leaves an LLC, it is important to comply with the voting requirements in the LLC's operating agreement. As explained in Chapter 3, these voting requirements must be met to maintain the LLC's eligibility for pass-through tax status with the IRS. This means making sure to obtain the formal approval of members (or member-managers) to:

- continue the legal existence of the LLC after a member's (or member-manager's) interest is terminated, either voluntarily or involuntarily, and
- admit new members who have been transferred an interest in the LLC from a prior member.

The specific vote requirements for each of these events is specified in your operating agreement, as discussed below.

a. Check Vote Required to Approve Transfer or Continuance of LLC

You'll need to determine who has to vote, when, and by how many votes, to approve the transfer of membership by a former member to a new member, or to continue the existence of the LLC after a member dies, retires, resigns, goes bankrupt or insane or is expelled.

The accompanying sidebar, "Standard Voting Requirements in Our LLC Operating Agreements," lists the requirements for these two formal matters under provisions in our tear-out operating agreements in Appendix C. Check your operating agreement to make sure of your exact requirements for these matters.

STANDARD VOTING REQUIREMENTS IN OUR LLC OPERATING AGREEMENTS

Here's how the two operating agreements in Appendix C address voting requirements for these two important tax-related LLC matters:

CONTINUANCE OF LLC AFTER DISSOCIATION OF A MEMBER

- **Who Votes:** Remaining members.
- **When:** Typically within 90 days of dissociation of member (or member-manager).
- **Vote Required:** Typically, approval by all remaining members. Some LLCs may opt for approval by majority of capital and profits interests of remaining members as allowed under IRS rules.
- **Other Requirements:** Some manager-managed LLCs only require approval by members after dissociation of a member-manager.
- **Where to Look in Operating Agreement:** If yours is a member-managed LLC, see Chapter 5, Section C, Special Instruction 38. For a manager-managed LLC, refer to Chapter 6, Section B3, Special Instruction M, as well as Chapter 5, Section C, Special Instruction 38.

TRANSFER OF MEMBERSHIP BY FORMER MEMBER TO NEW MEMBER

- **Who Votes:** Typically, nontransferring members. Some manager-managed LLCs may give this vote to nontransferring member-managers instead of to all members.
- **When:** Varies; see your operating agreement.
- **Vote Required:** Typically, approval by all nontransferring members (or member-managers). Some LLCs may opt for approval by another method allowed under IRS rules: by majority of capital and profits interests, by majority of capital or profits interests, or simply by a per capita (one vote per person) majority of nontransferring members (or member-managers).
- **Where to Look in Operating Agreement:** If yours is a member-managed LLC, see Chapter 5, Section C, Special Instruction 36. For a manager-managed LLC, refer to Chapter 6, Section B3, Special Instruction L.

b. Prepare Minutes Approving Transfer of Membership or Continuance of LLC

Once you know the voting rules you must follow, hold a meeting and obtain the required membership (or member-manager) approval. Then prepare written minutes of the meeting to place in your LLC records book. (Instructions for holding and documenting meetings are in Section C2, above).

Here is language you can use in your minutes to show the approval of either of these formal matters at a membership or member-manager meeting:

c. Prepare New Operating Agreement

Follow the instructions in Section C1, above, and have all members (old and new) sign the new agreement.

Sample Language: The **"members" or "member-managers"** of **name of LLC** met to approve the **"transfer of membership by (name of former member) to (name of new member)" or "continuance of the LLC following the (insert dissociation event, such as "resignation," "retirement," "death," "bankruptcy," "mental incompetence" or "expulsion") of (name of dissociated member)"**, which occurred on **date of transfer of membership or dissociation of member**. The **"nontransferring" (use this word to approve transfers) or "remaining" (use this word instead to approve a continuance of the LLC)** **"members" or "member-managers"** of the LLC voted to approve the matter by the following vote:

Name of Member or Member-Manager	LLC Interest ❶	Vote
list each member or member-manager	**% interest**	**"approve," "against" or "abstain"**

SPECIAL INSTRUCTIONS

❶ If your agreement requires (as ours do) a per capita vote to approve these special matters (this means a simple head count for each member or member-manager), leave this "LLC Interest" column blank.

If your operating agreement requires voting approval of these matters by capital and/or profits interests in the LLC, indicate in this column the appropriate percentage(s) for each member. If, for instance, your agreement requires a majority of the LLC's capital and profits interests to approve the continuance of your LLC after a member resigns, you would fill out this column to show these two percentages for each remaining member who attends the meeting and votes. For example, if a remaining voting member holds both a 50% capital and profits interest in your LLC, this column would state "50% capital and 50% profits interest" for the member.

4. Keep LLC Records

You will want to keep your important LLC documents in a safe, convenient place. We recommend setting up an organized system for keeping your LLC records, whether in manila envelopes, file folders or a specially ordered LLC records book. Nolo Press offers the Nolo 2000™ LLC records kit, an LLC records book that includes the following materials:

- a three-ring binder, with a slipcase cover featuring a modern LLC logo
- labeled index dividers for LLC Articles of Organization, Operating Agreement, Membership Register, Minutes of LLC Meetings and Membership Certificates, and
- 20 customized membership certificates with stubs, with your LLC's name printed on the face of each certificate.

If you're interested in purchasing a Nolo LLC records kit, call our Customer Service desk, 800-992-6656.

D. Other Ongoing LLC Formalities

In this section, we cover a number of additional ongoing legal, tax and practical formalities that apply to LLCs.

1. How to Sign Papers on Behalf of Your LLC

We're sure the separate legal existence of your LLC is important to you, particularly as a means of avoiding personal liability for business debts and claims. To make sure you and other LLC members will enjoy limited liability, members should always sign LLC papers, documents, contracts and other commitments clearly in the name of the LLC, not in their own names.

The best way to do this is to first state the name of the LLC, then sign your name on its behalf.

Example: Tom is one of two members of Park Place Plasterers, Ltd. Liability Co. He enters into a long-term contract for the refurbishing of apartments in a high-rise condominium. Tom signs the contract as follows:

Date: November 3, 199X
Park Place Plasterers, Ltd. Liability Co.
By: ______[Tom's signature]______,
Tom Park, LLC Member/Manager

If you sign contracts in your own name. If you don't follow our advice, the other company or party may be able to hold you personally liable under the contract you've signed. To avoid confusion and legal problems, make this simple signing procedure a regular part of your day-to-day business routine.

SAMPLE STATE LLC ANNUAL REPORT

STATE OF MONTANA

ANNUAL LIMITED LIABILITY COMPANY REPORT

Prepare, sign and submit with fee.

(For use by the Secretary of State only)

Filing Fee: Before April 15 $10 -- After April 15 $20
After September 1 $30 Form: ART-L

MAIL TO: **MIKE COONEY**
Secretary of State
PO Box 202801
Helena, MT 59620-2801
Phone: (406)444-3665

In compliance with Section 35-8-208, MCA, the undersigned limited liability company submits the following report:

Exact Name of Limited Liability Company: ______________________

____

Registered Agent Information

Name of Registered Agent: ______________________

Street Address of Registered Office: ______________________

PO Box or Mailing Address: ______________________

City, State, Zip: ______________________

If there is any change in the registered agent or registered office location, please complete a statement of change form and send an additional $5 filing fee. (A PO Box number may be added without the form or fee.)

1. **State of Organization:** ______________________
2. **Address of Principal Office** in state of organization: ______________________

____

3. **Limited liability company is managed by** *(members or member/managers)*: ______________________
4. **The last date when the limited liability company will be dissolved:** ______________________
5. **Names and addresses** (street name and number) **of Individual Managers or Member/Managers of company:**

______________________ ______________________
______________________ ______________________
______________________ ______________________
______________________ ______________________
______________________ ______________________
______________________ ______________________
______________________ ______________________
______________________ ______________________
______________________ ______________________
______________________ ______________________

6. **Names and addresses of registered business** *(managers or member/managers): **These businesses must be registered with the Montana Secretary of State's Office.***

7. ☐ **Professional Limited Liability Companies only.** *(Please check)* All the members and not less than one-half of the managers are qualified with the proper licensing authority in Montana or meet higher standards as specified by that licensing authority.

8. By my signature below, I, a member of the above limited liability company authorized to execute documents on its behalf, do state that any and all statements contained herein are true and based upon actions taken by the LLC in accordance with the statutes or its articles of organization or operating agreement.

   And I further state that the LLC remains in existence and has taken the necessary actions during the past year to preserve the status.

Exact Name of Limited Liability Company

Signature of Member

Printed Name of Member Signing

Address of Member Signing Report

2. File Annual State LLC Reports

Most states require the yearly filing of one-page annual report forms. These forms are filed with the state LLC filing office where you filed your LLC Articles of Organization, typically, the Secretary of State's office in the state capitol. Annual report forms are printed and supplied by the LLC filing office, and should be mailed out annually (although not necessarily on a calendar-year basis).

You usually need to provide minimal information on this form, such as the names and addresses of current LLC members and/or managers, and the name and address of the LLC's registered agent and office for service of legal process. Often, you can leave items blank if there is no change in the information from the previous annual report filing.

Typically, a small fee, in the $10 to $50 range, must be mailed with this form, but some states require significantly more. For example, expect higher LLC annual report fees in Illinois—$300, Pennsylvania—$300, and Wyoming. We alert you on your state sheet in Appendix A if your state asks for more than a small amount for this annual report filing.

3. Filing a Fictitious or Assumed Business Name Statement

You may wish to operate your LLC locally under a name that's different from the formal name of your LLC listed in your Articles of Organization.

Example: The Solar Plexus Flex and Fitness Center Ltd. Liability Co. decides to operate its three franchise locations under the fictitious name Flex and Fitness Center. The LLC owners want to continue to keep the formal name stated in the state-filed LLC Articles of Organization, but prefer operating their fitness centers under this second, shortened version.

Most states let you use a new name by filing a fictitious or assumed business name statement form and paying a small fee. You normally file this paperwork with the Secretary of State's office or the local county clerk or another county office. In some states, both a state and county filing are required. Find out your state's rules by calling your Secretary of State (see your state sheet in Appendix A) or a local county clerk's office.

Some states also require that a notice of use of, or intention to use, the fictitious name be published in a newspaper of general circulation one or more times in each county where the name is or will be used. Newspapers with legal notice classified sections will perform the required publications for you at a moderate fee and file any statements of publication required under your state's fictitious business name statute. Calling a local newspaper is generally your best way to discover whether your state requires the publication of a fictitious name statement, and how to satisfy any state requirements.

4. Amending Articles of Organization

Your original LLC Articles of Organization contain basic information and ordinarily will stay the way they are for a long time to come. But if you need to make a major change to your LLC that alters the information in this document—such as changing the formal name of your LLC or changing whether your LLC is managed by members or managers—you will need to file amended Articles of Organization with your state's LLC filing office. The filing fee for amended Articles is typically the same as the fee paid to file original Articles of Organization.

Upon request, most LLC filing offices will send an amendment form for you to fill in or will provide instructions on how to prepare your own—usually an easy task. Below is a standard amendment form, typical of the type of filing necessary to register amendments to LLC Articles of Organization with the state.

Hold formal membership meeting to approve amendment. Before filing an amendment with the state, your membership should approve any amendment to the LLC's Articles of Organization at a formal meeting. See Section C2, above, on how to hold and prepare minutes of an LLC meeting.

SAMPLE AMENDMENT OF ARTICLES

ARTICLES AMENDING OR RESTATING ARTICLES OF ORGANIZATION
DOMESTIC LIMITED LIABILITY COMPANY
LLC Rev. 10/93

Secretary of the State
30 Trinity Street
Hartford, CT 06106

1. Name of the limited liability Company:

____

2. Date of filing Articles of Organization (month, day, year): ____________

3. The Articles of Organization Are: (Check One Only)

____A. Amended only, pursuant to P.A. No. 93-262 §12(b).

____B. Amended and Restated, pursuant to P.A. No. 93-262 §12(c).

____C. Restated only, pursuant to P.A. No. 93-262 §12(c).

If 3A or 3B checked, complete #4.

4. The amendment is as follows: (Attach plain sheet of 8½x11 paper, if additional space required)

If 3C is checked, read #5.

5. If the Articles of Organization are restated set forth each article including all prior amendments. (Attach plain sheet of 8½x11 paper, if additional space required.)

EXECUTION

6. Dated this________day of________________, 19____

7. ______________________________ 8. ______________________
Name and capacity of signatory (print or type   Signature

For Official Use Only	Rec; CC:
	______________
	______________
	______________
	______________
	______________
	______________

J150.6

5. Changing Registered Agent or Office

The initial registered agent and office of your LLC are usually specified in your Articles of Organization filed with the state LLC filing office, covered in Chapter 4, Section E3d. The registered agent is the person your LLC authorizes to receive legal documents from the state as well as the public on behalf of the LLC. The registered address is the business address of the agent where legal papers may be served.

If you change the name or address of the registered agent, you are normally required to notify the state. In most states, the LLC filing office will, upon request, mail you a standard fill-in-the-blanks form titled "Change of Registered Agent or Address" or something similar. There may be a small filing fee.

It's in your LLC's best interests that the state have the most current registered agent and office information—you don't want to miss any important legal papers sent by the state to an old address. So take care of this small task when and if you change your LLC's registered agent name or registered office address.

Note that the change of registered agent or office is a routine task. In other words, you don't need to hold a formal LLC meeting to approve these changes, nor do you need to amend your Articles of Organization or revise your operating agreement—besides, your operating agreement specifically lists only the name of your first initial agent and registered office, not subsequent agents or offices. Just fill in and file the state-supplied form—that's all there is to it.

6. Certification of LLC Existence

Outside businesses, financial institutions, creditors and individuals may want to see formal legal paperwork to establish the existence of your LLC before deciding to transact other business with it (enter into a contract, sign a lease, agree to sell or buy property or the like). You can normally show these status-seekers a copy of your Articles of Organization or a copy of your operating agreement to help satisfy them that your LLC has handled all the necessary organizational formalities.

Occasionally, you may have to be even more formal and show a certified copy of your LLC Articles of Organization. A certified copy, which should be available for a small fee from your state LLC filing office (typically the Secretary of State), may not only show the file stamp of the office, but may even contain formal language stating that your LLC has met all necessary state formalities to begin doing business in your state.

Some outsiders may be sticklers for detail and may insist that you show them that your legal status is still valid—after all, Articles of Organization and operating agreements only show that you met legal requirements on a past date. Most states will help you with this. One way is to call the status or legal section of the LLC filing office and ask if you can obtain a current certificate of status or good standing for your LLC. For a small fee, some will send you a standard certification form, which shows your LLC meets all state legal and tax requirements on the date of the status request. This should be enough to satisfy most outsiders that your LLC is a bona fide business. (See the state sheets in Appendix A for the address and phone number of your state's LLC filing office.)

SAMPLE CHANGE OF REGISTERED AGENT OR ADDRESS

State of Tennessee

Department of State
Corporations Section
18th Floor, James K. Polk Building
Nashville, TN 37243-0306

CHANGE OF REGISTERED AGENT/OFFICE (BY A LIMITED LIABILITY COMPANY)

For Office Use Only

Pursuant to the provisions of § 48A-8-102(a) of the Tennessee Limited Liability Company Act, the undersigned Limited Liability Company hereby submits this application:

1. The name of the Limited Liability Company is: ______________________

____

2. The street address of its current registered office is: ______________________

____

3. If the current registered office is to be changed, the street address of the new registered office, the zip code of such office, and the county in which the office is located is: ______________________

____

4. The name of the current registered agent is: ______________________

____

5. If the current registered agent is to be changed, the name of the new registered agent is:

____

6. After the change(s), the street addresses of the registered office and the business office of the registered agent will be identical.

______________________	______________________
Signature Date	Name of Limited Liability Company
______________________	______________________
Signer's Capacity	Signature
	______________________
	Name (typed or printed)

SS-4225 RDA Pending

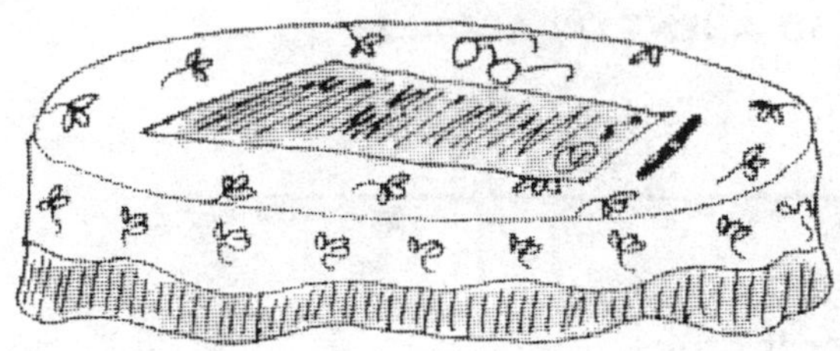

7. Certification of Authority of LLC Members or Officers

It's possible that an outsider may raise a question about the legal authority of your LLC members, managers and/or officers, and want to be sure they really have official status or specific authority for a transaction before proceeding. Typically, this occurs with real estate transactions involving title (and escrow companies that are paid to be fussy), particularly if the property is located in another state.

Complying with a request of this sort involves more than simply checking the legal status of your LLC as discussed in Section D6, just above. You also will need to document the fact that the person acting on behalf of the LLC is properly authorized by the LLC to enter into the transaction. There are a few ways to handle this, as discussed in detail below, namely by providing a:

- copy of your Articles of Organization
- copy of your operating agreement
- certification of authority, or
- state certification form.

Let's look at each of these options.

a. Copy of Articles of Organization

In most states, your Articles of Organization list the *initial* members of your LLC and state whether or not the members will manage the LLC. If your LLC has adopted a manager-managed operating agreement, these individuals should be listed as managers in your Articles of Organization, along with the fact that the LLC is manager-run. To obtain certified copies of Articles of Organization (available for a small fee), contact your state LLC filing office—see your state sheet in Appendix A for the phone number and address.

b. Copy of Operating Agreement

If you need to certify the authority of a member or manager who assumed this role after your Articles of Organization were filed, you can provide a copy of the amended operating agreement signed by the new member or manager.

c. Certification of Authority

If you want to keep your operating agreement private, an alternative approach is to prepare a simple form to certify the authority of any members or managers. We include a tear-out Certification of Authority in Appendix C for this purpose. Below is a sample of this tear-out form, along with instructions.

SAMPLE CERTIFICATION OF AUTHORITY

This LLC is managed by its **"members" or "managers"**. The names and addresses of each of its current **"members" or "managers"** as of **date of certification** are listed below. Each of these persons has managerial authority of the LLC and is empowered to transact business on its behalf.

Name of **"Member" or "Manager"**	Address
____________________	____________________
____________________	____________________
____________________	____________________
____________________	____________________
____________________	____________________

Further, each of the following **"members" or "managers"** is specifically authorized to transact the following business on behalf of the LLC:

describe the specific business transaction. ❶

date of signing—on or after certification date shown above

name of LLC

by **signature**

typed or printed name of signer

LLC title or status ❷

SPECIAL INSTRUCTIONS

❶ Here is a specific designation of authority you can fill in to underscore the member's or manager's authority to transact specific business for your LLC. In the blanks, describe the specific transaction for which the certification is being sought, such as:

- "the signing of a lease for the premises located at *[address]*"
- "entering into a contract with *[name of company or individual]* for *[specify product or services under consideration]*"
- if you don't want to limit the person's authority in any way, "any and all LLC business," or
- if you don't want to complete this blank, insert "N/A" instead.

❷ You can have your LLC Secretary, President or another designated officer prepare and sign this form, or you can have it signed by all current LLC members or managers. These signing procedures are authorized under the standard provisions in the tear-out operating agreements included in this book. (See Chapter 5, Section C, Special Instruction ㊽.) Simply fill in the appropriate title, such as "Secretary," "President," "Member" or "Manager."

d. State Certification Form

Some states let you file a form with the state LLC filing office, which certifies the names and authority of your LLC members and/or managers. They do this because LLCs are a relatively new type of business and the state recognizes that an official form may look better than an internal certification form provided by the LLC. To find out if your state has a form of this type, call your state LLC filing office—see your state sheet in Appendix A for the phone number.

Once filed with the state, file-stamped copies of the statement of authority form can be provided to outside businesses and individuals to let them know who is in charge and has authority to act on behalf of the LLC. Note that some state forms allow the LLC to specify limitations on the members' or managers' authority. Such a statement can come in handy if you want outsiders to know that they must deal with *all* LLC members to transact specific business.

Below is a sample state certification form. This particular form certifies the authority of LLC members and/or managers to transfer real property on behalf of the LLC. This is the typical language found in state-sponsored forms, needed for the typical case where such certification may be necessary—for example, to set up an escrow account or record a real property document on behalf of the LLC.

SAMPLE STATE CERTIFICATION FORM

DOMESTIC
LIMITED LIABILITY COMPANY

STATE OF MAINE

STATEMENT OF LIMITED LIABILITY COMPANY AUTHORITY

____
(Name of Limited Liability Company)

Filing Fee $20.00

____
Deputy Secretary of State

A True Copy When Attested By Signature

____
Deputy Secretary of State

Pursuant to 31 MRSA §626.1., the undersigned limited liability company executes and delivers for filing this statement of limited liability company authority:

FIRST: The street address of its principal place of business:

____
(physical location - street (not P.O. Box), city, state and zip code)

____
(mailing address if different from above)

SECOND: The street address of an office in this State: (if no office, so indicate)

____
(physical location - street (not P.O. Box), city, state and zip code)

____
(mailing address if different from above)

THIRD: ("X" one box only)

☐ A. The names of the members or, if management is vested in a manager or managers, the names of the managers, authorized to execute an instrument transferring real property held in the name of the limited liability company are:

(name and capacity)	(mailing address)
(name and capacity)	(mailing address)
(name and capacity)	(mailing address)

☐ Names of additional members/managers with such authority are attached hereto as Exhibit ____, and made a part hereof.

☐ B. The name of an agent maintaining a list of the names and mailing addresses of members or managers, authorized to execute an instrument transferring real property held in the name of the limited liability company is:

(name)	(mailing address)

CHAPTER 8

Lawyers, Tax Specialists and Legal Research

Much of the work involved in organizing and running an LLC (or other small business) is routine. Any knowledgeable and motivated business person can competently do the work. But there's no way around it—from time to time you are bound to need help from outside sources. One good way to learn more about tax matters and legal issues is to read up on them yourself. You've already taken a big step in this direction by using this book.

Quite likely, you will want to supplement your understanding of the legal and tax consequences of forming an LLC by asking a lawyer or tax professional to double-check your decisions and review your paperwork or advise you on complex areas of law or taxation. At times, you may want to run important business decisions by an experienced advisor who has a mix of business, tax and legal savvy.

Throughout this book, we have flagged instances where a lawyer or tax advisor can provide valuable assistance, such as to:

- review the legal options in your operating agreement
- add special provisions to satisfy the IRS if you will split profits and losses among members disproportionately to capital contributions, or
- customize buy-sell provisions (requirements for transferring interests in your LLC, discussed in Chapter 5, Section A2).

In the sections below, we provide a few tips to help you locate this sort of competent expert assistance and advice. Finally, if you want to do your own research, you'll find valuable suggestions on how to get started.

Consider joining one or more trade groups related to your business. These groups often track legislation in particular areas of business—such as LLC legal and tax developments—and provide sample contracts and other useful legal forms. Some also retain law firms for trade association purposes, which may be able to refer you to competent local lawyers.

A. Finding the Right Tax Advisor

You know that forming an LLC involves understanding and choosing among various tax options. Paramount among these technical issues is making sure that your LLC qualifies under IRS Revenue Procedure 95-10 for pass-through tax status. This book presents a fairly standard and rigid way to achieve this status, but you may wish to come up with your own, more adventuresome, strategy for organizing your LLC and achieving pass-through tax status. (We discuss the various options in Chapter 3, Section B.)

Other LLC business decisions involve tax issues and advice: selecting a tax year and accounting period, setting up financial books and bookkeeping procedures, withholding and reporting payroll taxes, preparing tax returns and schedules that allocate profits, losses, credits and deductions among LLC members. To accomplish these tasks and make informed decisions in these and other tax areas may require help from a tax advisor. Depending on the tax or financial issue, this advisor may be a certified public accountant, financial or investment advisor, loan officer at a bank, pension plan specialist or bookkeeper trained in employment tax reporting and return requirements. To keep costs down, you may be able to take advantage of lower rates offered by newer firms or practitioners.

The best way to find a knowledgeable and helpful tax advisor is to shop around for someone recommended by small business people whose judgment you trust, or someone who is otherwise known to you as qualified for the task. Your tax person should be available over the phone to answer routine questions, or by mail or fax to handle paperwork and correspondence, with a minimum of formality. It is likely that you will spend much more time dealing with your tax advisor than your legal advisor (discussed in Section B, below), so be particularly attentive to the personal side of this relationship.

Tax issues are often cloudy and subject to a range of interpretations and strategies, particularly in the new LLC legal arena, so it is absolutely essential that you discuss and agree to the level of tax-aggressiveness you expect from your advisor. Some LLC owners want to live on the edge, perhaps taking chances with their LLC tax status during the organizational phase or saving every possible tax dollar after the LLC is formed, even at the risk that the LLC's pass-through tax status or its tax practices will be challenged by the IRS. Others are content to forego operational flexibility or questionable tax deductions to gain an extra measure of peace of mind. Whatever your tax strategy, make sure you find a tax advisor who feels the same way you do, or is willing to defer to your more liberal or conservative tax tendencies.

It pays to spend some time learning about LLC and employment taxation. Not only will you have to buy less help from tax professionals, but you'll be in a good position to make good financial and tax planning decisions. IRS publications, business and law library materials, trade groups and countless other sources should provide a growing body of LLC tax information as more businesses avail themselves of this unique business structure. Your accountant or other tax advisor should be able to help you put your hands on good LLC materials. (See the accompanying sidebar, "Resources for Tax and Financial Information.")

RESOURCES FOR TAX AND FINANCIAL INFORMATION

Your tax advisor isn't your only tax and financial resource. For example, banks are an excellent source of general financial advice, particularly if they will be creditors–after all, they will have a stake in the success of your business. The Small Business Administration can be an ideal source of financial and tax information and resources (as well as financing, in some cases).

Following are just a few suggestions for finding additional tax and financial information relevant to operating a business. If you want to get copies of free IRS publications, you can pick them up at your local IRS office or order by phone; call the toll-free IRS forms and publications request telephone number at 1-800-TAX-FORM.

- Start by obtaining IRS Publication 509, *Tax Calendars*, prior to the beginning of each year. This pamphlet contains tax calendars showing the dates for business and employer filings during the year.
- You can find further information on withholding, depositing, reporting and paying federal employment taxes in IRS Publication 15, Circular E, *Employer's Tax Guide*, and the Publication 15 Supplement, as well as IRS Publication 937, *Business Reporting*. Also helpful is IRS Publication 334, *Tax Guide for Small Business.*
- IRS Publication 538, *Accounting Period and Methods*, and IRS Publication 583, *Information for Business Taxpayers*, provide helpful information on accounting methods and bookkeeping procedures.

B. How to Find the Right Lawyer

Most small businesses can't afford to put a lawyer on retainer. Even when consulted on an issue-by-issue basis, lawyer's fees mount up fast—usually way too fast for all but the most pressing legal issues. Just as with individuals, more small businesses are trying to at least partially close this legal affordability gap by doing as much of their own legal research and form preparation as possible. Often a knowledgeable self-helper can sensibly accomplish the whole task. Other times, it makes sense to consult briefly with a lawyer at an interim stage, or have your paperwork or conclusions reviewed, particularly for decisions that are complex or have significant legal consequences.

1. The "Legal Coach" Arrangement

Most readers will not want a lawyer who is programmed to take over all legal decision-making and form-drafting—this just builds up billable hours that few can afford. Instead, we suggest you find someone we call a "legal coach": a professional who is willing to work with you—not just for you—in establishing your LLC and helping with ongoing LLC legal formalities. Under this model, the lawyer helps you take care of many routine legal matters yourself, also being available to consult on more complicated legal issues as the need arises.

Not all lawyers will be comfortable with your taking an active role in your LLC's legal life, so you may need to interview several people before finding a compatible legal advisor. When you call a lawyer, announce your intentions in advance—that you are looking for someone who is willing to review your LLC formation papers or to handle ongoing legal work from time to time. Mention that you are looking for someone who is willing to be flexible, point you in the right direction as the need arises, serve as a legal advisor as circumstances dictate, and tackle particular legal problems if necessary. In exchange for this, let the lawyer know you are willing to pay promptly and fairly.

Some lawyers may find a "legal coach" model unappealing—for example, they may not feel comfortable reviewing documents you have drafted using self-help materials. If so, thank the person for being frank and keep interviewing other lawyers, unless you are willing and able to pay to have a lawyer do all the work for you, from start to finish.

When you find a lawyer who seems agreeable to the arrangement you've proposed, ask to come in to meet for a half hour or so. Expect to pay for this initial consultation. At the in-person interview, reemphasize that you are looking for a "legal coach" relationship. You'll also want to discuss other important issues in this meeting, such as the lawyer's customary charges for services, as explained further below. Pay particular attention to the rapport between you and your lawyer. Remember, you are looking for a legal advisor who will work with you. Trust your instincts and seek a lawyer whose personality and business sense are compatible with your own.

Look elsewhere for tax advice. When it comes to special tax questions, such as seeing how far you can deviate from the safe-harbor rules in Revenue Procedure 95-10 and still qualify for pass-through tax status for your LLC with the IRS, we think a tax advisor with LLC experience is the best person to ask for help. For other tax and financial decisions, such as the best tax year, accounting period, or employee benefit plan for your LLC, you'll find that accountants, financial planners, pension plan specialists and bank officers often have a better grasp of the issues than lawyers. And an added bonus is that although tax advice doesn't come cheap, is usually costs less than legal advice.

WHY TO HIRE A SMALL BUSINESS LAWYER

There is a lawyer surplus these days, and many newer lawyers, especially, are open to non-traditional business arrangements. In your quest for a lawyer, remember:

- *You don't need a big-time business lawyer.* Look for a lawyer with some small business experience, preferably in your field or area of operations. For the most part, you don't want a lawyer who works with big businesses (publicly held corporations, large limited partnerships or investment pools and the like). Not only will this person deal with issues that are far from your concerns, but he or she is almost sure to charge too much.
- *You don't need a legal specialist.* What if you have a very technical legal question? Should you start by seeking out a legal specialist in an area such as insurance, banking or securities law? For starters, the answer is probably no. First, find a good small business lawyer to act as your coach. Then rely on this person to suggest specialized materials or experts as the need arises. Again, finding a lawyer with LLC experience is helpful, but specialized legal involvement in narrower realms of business practice can wait until you actually need advice on a particular legal issue or problem.

2. How to Find a Lawyer

When you're ready to look for a lawyer, talk to people in your community who own or operate businesses of comparable size and scope. Try to get a personal recommendation of a knowledgeable and helpful lawyer. If possible, ask someone who has successfully formed an LLC for the name of the lawyer who helped get the LLC started and what he or she thinks of that person's work.

If you talk to half a dozen business people, chances are you'll come away with several good leads. Other people, such as your banker, accountant, insurance agent or real estate broker may be able to provide the names of lawyers they trust to help them with business matters. Friends, relatives and business associates also may have names of possible lawyers.

How shouldn't you search for a lawyer? Don't conduct a random search of phone books, legal directories or advertisements. Lawyer referral services operated by bar associations are usually equally unhelpful. Often, these simply supply the names of lawyers who have signed onto the service, often accepting the lawyer's word for what types of skills he or she has.

Don't wait until a legal problem arises before seeking out a lawyer. Even if you have all your LLC formation work covered, it's not too early to find a lawyer to use later for ongoing business consultations. Once enmeshed in a crisis, you may not have time to hire a lawyer at affordable rates. Chances are you'll wind up settling for the first person available at a moment's notice—almost a guarantee you'll pay too much for possibly poor service.

3. Set the Extent and Cost of Services in Advance

When you hire a lawyer, get a clear understanding about how fees will be computed. For example, if you call the lawyer from time to time for general advice or to be steered to a good information source, how will you be billed? Some lawyers bill a flat amount for a call or a conference; others bill to the nearest 6-, 10- or 20-minute interval. Whatever the lawyer's system, you need to understand it.

Especially at the beginning of your relationship, when you bring a big job to a lawyer, ask specifically about what it will cost. If you feel it's too much, don't hesitate to negotiate; perhaps you can do some of the routine work yourself, thus reducing the fee.

It's a good idea to get all fee arrangements in writing—especially those for good-sized jobs, such as reviewing your operating agreement. In several states, fee agreements between lawyers and clients must be in writing only if the expected fee is $1,000 or more or is contingent on the outcome of a lawsuit. But whether required or not, it's a good idea to get a written agreement.

Use non-lawyer professionals to cut down on legal costs. Often, non-lawyer professionals perform some tasks better and at less cost than lawyers. For example, look to management consultants for strategic business planning, real estate brokers or appraisers for valuation of properties, financial planners for investment advice, accountants for preparation of financial proposals, insurance agents for advice on insurance protection, independent paralegals for routine legal form-drafting, and CPAs for the preparation of tax returns. Each of these matters is likely to have a legal aspect, and you may eventually want to consult your lawyer, but normally you can wait until you've gathered information on your own.

4. Confront Problems Head-On

If you have any questions about a lawyer's bill or the quality of his or her services, speak up. Buying legal help should be just like purchasing any other consumer service. If you are dissatisfied, seek a reduction in your bill or make it clear that the work needs to be redone properly (a more comprehensive lease, a better contract). If the lawyer runs a decent business, he or she will promptly and positively deal with your concerns. If you don't get an acceptable response, find another lawyer pronto. If you switch lawyers, you are entitled to get your important documents back from the first lawyer.

Even if you fire your lawyer, you may still feel unjustly wronged. If you can't get satisfaction from the lawyer, write to the client grievance office of your state bar association (with a copy to the lawyer, of course). Often, a phone call from this office to your lawyer will bring the desired results.

C. How to Do Your Own Legal Research

Law is information, not magic. If you can look up necessary information yourself, you need not purchase it from a lawyer—although if it involves important issues, you may wish to check your conclusions with a lawyer or use one as a sounding board for your intended course of action.

Much of the research necessary to understand your state's LLC law can be done without a lawyer by spending some time in a local law or business library. Even if you need to go to a lawyer for help in preparing an LLC legal form or to discuss the legal implications of a proposed business transaction, you can give yourself a leg up on understanding the legal issues by reading practice manuals prepared for lawyers and law students.

We've already touched upon how to look up a provision of your state's LLC law in Chapter 4,

Section E2. Let's talk about using libraries a little more here. For starters, the business or reference department of major city and county public libraries often carry LLC statutes, as well as books on LLC law and taxation useful to the small business owner. How do you find a law library open to the public? In many states, you need to look only as far as your county courthouse or, failing that, your state capitol. In addition, publicly funded law schools generally permit the public to use their libraries, and some private law schools grant limited access to their libraries (sometimes for a modest user fee). If you're lucky enough to have access to several law libraries, select one that has a reference librarian to assist you.

In doing legal research for a business, there are a number of sources for legal rules, procedures and issues that you may wish to examine. Here are a few:

- *State limited liability company statutes.* These state laws should be your primary focus for finding the rules for organizing and operating your LLC.

HOW LAWYERS CHARGE FOR LEGAL SERVICES

You can expect your lawyer to bill you in one of these ways:

- *By the hour.* In most parts of the United States, you can get competent services for your small business for $150 to $250 an hour, and often less. Newer attorneys still in the process of building a practice may be available for paperwork review, legal research and other types of legal work at lower rates.
- *Flat fee for a specific job.* Under this arrangement, you pay an agreed-upon amount for a given project, regardless of how much or how little time the lawyer spends. Particularly when you begin working with a lawyer and are worried about hourly costs getting out of control, it can make sense to negotiate a flat fee for a specific job, such as doing a pre-filing review of your LLC paperwork. For example, the lawyer may review your Articles of Organization and operating agreement for $300, or prepare special buy-sell provisions to control the transfer of LLC interests for $500.
- *Retainer.* Some businesses can afford to pay relatively modest amounts, perhaps $1,000 to $2,000 a year, to keep a business lawyer on retainer for ongoing phone or in-person consultations or routine business matters during the year. Of course, your retainer won't cover a full-blown legal crisis, but it may take care of routine contract and other legal paperwork preparation and reviews.
- *Contingent fee based upon settlement amounts or winnings.* This type of fee typically occurs in personal injury, products liability, fraud and employment discrimination disputes, where a lawsuit will likely be filed. The lawyer gets a percentage of the recovery (often 33% to 40%) if you win and nothing if you lose (of course, if your business is the defendant, not the plaintiff, expect to pay an hourly rate to defend the case or settle the dispute—ouch!). Since most small business legal needs involve advice and help with drafting paperwork, a contingency fee approach doesn't normally make sense. However, if you are seeking an award based upon a personal injury claim or lawsuit involving fraud, unfair competition or the infringement of a patent or copyright, you may want to explore the possibility of a contingency fee approach.

- *Other state laws, such as the Corporations, Partnerships, Securities, Commercial, Civil, Labor and Revenue Codes.* These and other laws govern the operation of other types of businesses or specific business transactions; the content, approval and enforcement of commercial contracts; employment practices and procedures, employment tax requirements, and other aspects of doing business in your state. Depending on the type of business operations you engage in, you also may want to research statutes and regulations dealing with legal topics such as environmental law, products liability, real estate, copyrights and so on.
- *Federal laws.* These include the tax laws and procedures found in the Internal Revenue Code and Treasury Regulations implementing these code sections; regulations dealing with advertising, warranties and other consumer matters adopted by the Federal Trade Commission; and equal opportunity statutes such as Title VII of the Civil Rights Act administered by the Justice Department and Equal Employment Opportunities Commission.
- *Administrative rules and regulations (issued by federal and state administrative agencies charged with implementing statutes).* State and federal statutes are often supplemented with regulations that clarify specific statutes and contain rules for an agency to follow in implementing and enforcing them. For example, most states have enacted special administrative regulations under their securities statutes that provide exemptions for businesses registering the offer and sale of interests to others within the state.
- *Case law.* This consists of decisions of federal and state courts interpreting statutes—and sometimes making law, known as "common law," if the subject isn't covered by a statute. Annotated state legal codes contain not only the statutes, but references to court cases interpreting and implementing specific provisions of the states' legal provisions.
- *Secondary sources.* Also important in researching business law are sources that provide background information on particular areas of law. One example is this book. Others are commonly found in the business, legal or reference section of your local library or bookstore.

NOLO PRESS RESOURCES

Below are a few titles published by Nolo Press that we believe offer valuable business information for LLCs:

- *Legal Guide for Starting and Running a Small Business,* by Fred Steingold. This book is an essential resource for every small business owner, whether just starting out or already established. Find out the basics about forming a business, negotiating a favorable lease, hiring and firing employees, writing contracts and resolving business disputes.
- *Tax Savvy for Small Business,* by Frederick Daily. This book gives business owners information about federal taxes and explains how to make the best tax decisions for business, maximize profits and stay out of trouble with the IRS.
- *Taking Care of Your Corporation, Volumes 1 and 2,* by Anthony Mancuso. Although designed specifically for small corporations, these books provide valuable forms for holding meetings and formally approving legal, tax and other important business decisions that arise in the course of operating any business, including an LLC.
- *The Employer's Legal Handbook,* by Fred Steingold. Here's a comprehensive resource that compiles all the basics of employment law in one place. It covers safe hiring practices, wages, hours, tips and commissions, employee benefits, taxes and liability, insurance, discrimination, sexual harassment and termination.
- *How to Write a Business Plan,* by Mike McKeever. If you're thinking of starting a business or raising money to expand an existing one, this book will show you how to write the business plan and loan package necessary to finance your business and make it work. Includes updated sources of financing.
- *Software Development: A Legal Guide* (book with disk: dual PC/Mac format), by Stephen Fishman. A reference bible for people in the software industry, this book explores the legal ins and outs of copyright, trade secrets and patent protection, employment agreements, working with independent contractors and employees, development and publishing agreements and multimedia developments. Sample agreements and contracts are included on disk.

Small business owners often find that they need to learn more about intellectual property issues (patent, copyright, trademark and trade secret law). Whether you're a do-it-yourselfer or simply wish to expand your knowledge of intellectual property law, here are some helpful resources:

- *Patent, Copyright and Trademark: A Desk Reference to Intellectual Property Law,* by Stephen Elias. Written for anyone who needs to understand the terminology of intellectual property law, this book provides overviews and straightforward explanations of the protections offered by patent, copyright, trademark and trade secret laws.
- *Trademark: How to Name Your Business & Product,* by Kate McGrath and Stephen Elias. This book shows small business owners how to choose, use and protect the names and symbols that identify their services and products. Provides step-by-step instructions and all the official forms necessary to register a trademark with the U.S. Patent and Trademark Office.
- *Patent It Yourself,* by David Pressman. This state-of-the-art guide is a must for any inventor who wants to get a patent—from the patent search to the actual application. Patent attorney and former patent examiner David Pressman covers use and licensing, successful marketing and infringement. This best-selling book is also available in software (system requirements: mouse and hard disk, 4 MB RAM, Windows 3.1 or higher, VGA or higher monitor).
- *The Copyright Handbook: How to Protect and Use Written Works,* by Stephen Fishman. Provides fill-in-the-blanks forms and detailed instructions for protecting all types of written expression under U.S. and international copyright law. It also explains copyright infringement, fair use, works for hire and transfers of copyright ownership.

APPENDIX A

State Sheets

The state sheets in this appendix provide the essential, state-specific information necessary to comply with state requirements to form an LLC. You'll also find pertinent information on how to qualify for pass-through tax status with the IRS (and, if applicable, the state tax office).

Locate the material in this appendix for the state in which you plan to form your LLC (the states are listed alphabetically). You'll refer to this information as you prepare your LLC forms according to the instructions in Chapters 4 and 5 or 6 of this book.

Note that your state sheet is divided into four main headings, which we summarize just below:

- LLC Filing Office
- Articles of Organization
- Tax Status, and
- Operating Rules.

LLC Filing Office

Here you'll find the address and phone number (subject to change) of the state office that deals with LLCs and other business entities formed in the state. As discussed in Chapter 4, Section A, you'll contact the LLC filing office to request state-supplied LLC forms and information. The Secretary of State, Corporations Division, is the office that generally handles LLC forms and filings, but some states have a different name for this office.

In the *Forms and Statutes* section, we indicate whether your state's LLC filing office provides a sample or ready-to-use Articles of Organization form or publishes guidelines for preparing your own form. We also point out whether you can obtain a copy of your state's LLC Act from this office (for free or a fee).

Get up-to-date state materials. State-specific information changes frequently and may not always be current on all points in every state. The material you receive from the state LLC filing offices will update you on your state's latest legal requirements and tax rules.

Articles of Organization (or Certificate of Formation)

This section contains information you'll need to complete fill-in-the-blanks Articles of Organization or to prepare your own Articles. When you file this form with the state LLC filing office, your LLC begins its legal existence. (See Chapter 4, Section F.) The Articles of Organization section has several subheadings:

- *Name Requirements.* Each state requires certain words to be included in an LLC's formal name–typically "Limited Liability Company," "Ltd. Liability Co.," "LLC" or "L.L.C." We also indicate the fee and time period for which you may reserve an available LLC name prior to filing your Articles. Unless we say otherwise, name reservations must be obtained by mail, not over the phone. Typically, the state LLC office supplies a form you may use to apply for a name reservation, but a simple written name reservation request will normally work just as well. (We cover name reservations in Chapter 4, Section C5.)
- *Filing Fee.* We list the fee you'll need to pay to file your LLC Articles, plus, if applicable, any special rules for computing and paying the filing fee.
- *Annual Fees.* In some states, we add this section to cover any special (unusually costly) annual fee requirements. For example, in a few states, annual fees in excess of $100 must be paid to the LLC filing office to maintain your LLC's legal status. (See Chapter 7, Section D2.)
- *Special Instructions and Filing Requirements.* This section tells you how many copies of the Articles to send to your state LLC office for filing. It also covers any additional forms that must be filed along with your Articles, as well as any special requirements for preparing and filing Articles of Organization in your state. If you form an LLC in a state that does not provide a printed or sample Articles form, you'll find the statutory requirements for the contents of Articles. In states such as these, we give sample wording if the required information seems particularly tricky or technical. (See Chapter 4, Section E5, for more on preparing Articles from scratch.)

Tax Status

This is a short heading with two tax-related items:

- *IRS Ruling.* You'll find the citation for any official IRS pronouncement—that is, Revenue Ruling—on how a state's LLC Act fits in with the federal tax entity classification scheme. If your state sheet shows a ruling number, you or your tax adviser may want to read the ruling to see how the IRS classifies your state's LLC statute—as flexible or "bulletproof"—and how the options reflected in your state LLC act correspond with the four traditional corporate characteristics you want to avoid to achieve pass-through tax status with the IRS. Most law libraries contain bound sets of IRS Revenue Rulings, and it should take just a minute or two to find and read a ruling if one is listed in this section of your state sheet. (For more on legal research, see Chapter 4, Section E2, and Chapter 8, Section C.)
- *State Tax Office.* We list the location and telephone number of your state's revenue and taxation (or similar) office. We recommend you call this number early on in the LLC formation process, and ask for tax forms and other tax materials relevant to forming and operating an LLC in your state. For example, in states with a corporate income tax scheme, you will want to

know if the state follows the IRS in not taxing your LLC as a corporate entity—or, conversely, if you will be required to estimate, report and pay state corporate franchise or income taxes on LLC profits. You will also want to ask about and comply with any state partnership tax return requirements that apply to LLCs. (See Chapter 7, Section B.)

Operating Rules

Each state sheet covers several important statutory requirements:

- *Default Transfer Rule* and *Default Continuation Rule.* We address each state's rules for how members must vote to approve the transfer of membership to a new member or to continue the legal life of the LLC after a member is dissociated (leaves, dies, is expelled or otherwise loses a membership interest). We summarize and give the legal citation to sections of each state's Limited Liability Company Act that govern these technical LLC operating options. In most cases, the rules shown are "default" rules—that is, they apply only if you do not come up with a different voting or approval rule in your LLC operating agreement. In some states, however, the state rules for these options are mandatory—and we point out when this is the case. Generally, the information given in these sections is essential if you wish to lower the unanimous vote rule that we supply for each of these options in our tear-out operating agreements. (See Chapters 5 and 6.)
- *Special Statutory Rules.* Some state sheets list uncharacteristic legal operating rules that apply (those that vary significantly from LLC operating rules found in most other states). For example, if a state limits the type of payment that may be made as a capital contribution to an LLC, we mention the special capital contribution rule here.

ALABAMA

LLC Filing Office

Secretary of State
Corporate Section
P.O. Box 5616
Montgomery, AL 36103

Telephone: 334-242-5324

Forms and Statutes: Alabama Secretary of State provides an LLC formation summary sheet together with a fill-in-the-blanks Articles of Organization form and a Report of Domestic Limited Liability Company. (See "Special Instructions and Filing Requirements" below.)

Articles of Organization

Name Requirements: Must contain the words "Limited Liability Company" or the abbreviation "L.L.C."

Filing Fee: $40, payable to the "Secretary of State" plus a separate check for $35 for the "Probate Court Judge," who receives and records the original Articles. (See "Special Instructions and Filing Requirements" below.)

Special Instructions and Filing Requirements: Articles of Organization must state the membership voting rule to admit new members and the vote requirement to continue the business of the LLC when a member (or member-manager) leaves. You should insert a summary of these provisions in the space for additional provisions, just before the IN WITNESS clause at the end of the Articles.

Here's how to address two issues in the Articles form:

- *Summary of Rights to Admit New Members:* If you adopt the standard language contained in our Chapter 5 or 6 operating agreements, you may use the following sentence to sum up members' rights to admit additional members and the terms of admission: "The existing members of this LLC must approve the admission of new members by a unanimous vote. Upon such approval, new members shall be accorded all rights associated with membership in this LLC." If yours is a manager-managed LLC that requires only approval by member-managers to admit new members who are transferees of former members, add a sentence to your response noting this exception: "However, the nontransferring member-managers of this LLC are empowered to approve by unanimous vote the admission into membership of a transferee of a former member of this LLC."
- *Rights to Continue LLC:* If you adopt the standard operating agreement provisions in Chapters 5 or 6, the following language should work to summarize members' rights to continue the LLC after the dissociation of a member: "The unanimous approval of the remaining members is required to continue the business of this LLC upon the death, retirement, resignation, expulsion, bankruptcy or dissolution of a member [replace the previous word "member" with "member-manager" if your manager-managed LLC has chosen this option] or the occurrence of any other event that terminates the continued membership of a member in this limited liability company."

Have all initial members sign the Articles. Submit an original plus two copies of completed and signed Articles to the nearest Probate Court judge (check local governmental telephone listing and call for address). The judge will record the original Articles of Organization and forward a copy with fees to the Secretary of State.

After filing Articles of Organization, fill in the Domestic LLC Company Report form and send the original plus two copies of the completed form, together with a check for $5, to the Secretary of State.

Tax Status

IRS Ruling: Revenue Ruling 94-6.

State Tax Office: Department of Revenue, Montgomery, telephone 334-242-1175.

Operating Rules

Default Transfer Rule: Unless otherwise provided in operating agreement, by unanimous written consent of all nontransferring members. [Section 33.]

Default Continuation Rule: Unless otherwise stated in the Articles, by written consent of all remaining members within 90 days after dissociation of a member. [Section 37(b).]

Special Statutory Rules: Unless provided otherwise in operating agreement, managers, if chosen, must be appointed by a vote of at least one-half the number of members. [Section 22(b)(1).]

ALASKA

LLC Filing Office

Department of Commerce & Economic Development
Division of Banking, Securities & Corporations
Corporations Section
P.O. Box 110808
Juneau, AK 99811-0808

Telephone: 907-465-2530

Forms and Statutes: State provides fill-in-the-blanks Articles of Organization with instructions, plus information booklet with requirements for organizing and operating an Alaska LLC.

Articles of Organization

Name Requirements: Must contain the words "Limited Liability Company" or the abbreviations "LLC" or "L.L.C." The word "Limited" may be abbreviated as "Ltd." and the word "Company" as "Co." The name may not contain the words "city" or "borough" or otherwise imply that the company is a municipality. An LLC name may be reserved for 120 days for $15. A proposed LLC name may be registered (kept on the rolls of the LLC filing office) by paying an annual fee of $25.

Filing Fee: $250 fee (includes $100 biennial license fee—due every two years), payable to the "State of Alaska."

Special Instructions and Filing Requirements: Articles need not state a limit on the duration of the LLC. Specify in Article VI of the fill-in-the-blanks form any terms restricting members' ability to transfer their interests. If you adopt the standard language contained in our operating agreements for controlling the transfer of membership rights, you may use the following sentence to sum up the restrictions on assignments of LLC interests: "The unanimous vote of nonassigning members [if yours is a manager-managed LLC that requires member-manager approval only, replace the previous word "members" with "member-managers"] of this LLC is necessary to admit an assignee of a member as a new member of this LLC. Upon such approval, the assignee shall be accorded all rights associated with membership in this LLC."

The Articles must also give a primary and secondary standard industrial code (SIC) that describes the type of business to be operated by the LLC. A list of SIC codes is included in the Alaska LLC filing office materials. File the original and one copy of Articles of Organization.

Tax Status

IRS Ruling: None.

State Tax Office: Department of Revenue, Juneau, telephone 907-465-2300.

Operating Rules

Default Transfer Rule: Unless otherwise provided in agreement, by unanimous consent of nontransferring members. [Section 10.50.165.]

Default Continuation Rule: By approval of all remaining members within 90 days of the membership terminating event. [Section 10.50.400(3)(A).]

Special Statutory Rules: Memberships can be issued to persons in exchange for a promissory note or promise to contribute property or services in the future only if the person has also paid in some property or services to the LLC. [Section 10.50.275.]

ARIZONA

LLC Filing Office

Arizona Corporation Commission
Corporation Filing Section
1200 West Washington
Phoenix, AZ 85007

Telephone: 602-542-3135

Tucson Branch Office: 520-628-6560 (accepts LLC filings)

Forms and Statutes: State provides fill-in-the-blanks Articles of Organization. Also provides a copy of the Arizona LLC Act upon request at no charge.

Articles of Organization

Name Requirements: Must contain the words "Limited Liability Company" or "Limited Company" or the abbreviations "L.L.C." or "L.C." Call the LLC filing office to check name availability. An available LLC name may be reserved for 120 days for $10

Filing Fee: $50, payable to the "Arizona Corporation Commission."

Special Instructions and Filing Requirements: The address of the LLC's statutory agent stated in the Articles must be a street address, and the statutory agent must sign the Articles in the space provided to indicate acceptance of this position. Submit the original and one copy of the Articles for filing.

After filing Articles of Organization, you must publish a Notice of Filing as follows: Within 60 days of filing, publish a Notice of Filing three times in a newspaper of general circulation that publishes legal notices in the county where the LLC has its place of business. The LLC filing office materials contain a Notice of Filing form to use to meet the publication requirement. Within 90 days of filing Articles, an Affidavit of Publication—a form supplied by the newspaper which verifies the Notice was published—must be filed with the Corporation Commission (no fee). The newspaper will handle this requirement.

Tax Status

IRS Ruling: Revenue Ruling 93-93.

State Tax Office: Department of Revenue, Phoenix, telephone 602-542-2076.

Operating Rules

Default Transfer Rule: By consent of all nontransferring members, but operating agreement can give authority to admit new members to one or more members. [Section 29-731(B)(2).]

Default Continuation Rule: By consent of all remaining members within 90 days of termination of a member's membership, but operating agreement may give one or more members or managers the right to vote to continue the LLC after a membership terminating event. [Section 29-781(A)(3).]

ARKANSAS

LLC Filing Office

Arkansas Secretary of State
Corporations Division
State Capitol
Little Rock, Arkansas 72201-1094

Telephone: 501-682-5151

Forms and Statutes: State provides fill-in-the-blanks Articles of Organization (Form LL-01) with instructions.

Articles of Organization

Name Requirements: Must contain the words "Limited Liability Company," "Limited Company" or the abbreviation "L.L.C.," "L.C.," "LLC" or LC." LLCs that perform professional services must have the words "Professional Limited Liability Company," "Professional Limited Company" or the abbreviations "P.L.L.C.," "P.L.C.," "PLLC" or "PLC" in their name. In any of these name variations, the word "Limited" may be abbreviated as "Ltd." and the word "Company" may be abbreviated as "Co." An LLC name may be reserved for 120 days for $25.

Filing Fee: $50 fee, payable to the "Arkansas Secretary of State."

Special Instructions and Filing Requirements: The initial registered agent must accept the designation by signing on the signature line provided in the Third Article of the fill-in-the-blanks form. Insert "N/A" in the Fifth Article if the LLC will be managed by all of the members. Send an original and one copy of completed Articles for filing. A file-stamped copy will be returned to you.

Tax Status

State Tax Status: An LLC with two or more members will be treated as a partnership for state tax purposes. An LLC with only one member will be treated as a sole proprietorship. [Section 4-32-1313.]

IRS Ruling: None.

State Tax Office: Department of Finance & Administration, Revenue Division, Little Rock, telephone 501-682-7250.

Operating Rules

Default Transfer Rule: Unless otherwise stated in operating agreement, by unanimous consent of nontransferring members. [Section 4-32-706.]

Default Continuation Rule: By consent of all remaining members within 90 days of dissociation of member, unless otherwise provided in the operating agreement. [Section 4-32-901.]

Special Statutory Rules: Default membership approval rule is by a vote of one-half or more of the number of members; operating agreement may change this requirement, and special statutory rules may require a greater vote in some matters (unanimous membership is the default rule to amend the operating agreement). [Section 4-32-403.]

CALIFORNIA

LLC Filing Office

California Secretary of State
Limited Liability Company Unit
P.O. Box 944228
Sacramento, CA 94244-2280

Telephone: 916-653-3795

Branch offices of the Secretary of State are located in Fresno, Los Angeles and San Diego. Currently, branch offices provide LLC forms over-the-counter only, and do not accept LLC filings.

Forms and Statutes: State provides fill-in-the-blanks Articles of Organization (Form LLC-1) with instructions, plus a summary of the California LLC Act (called the Beverly-Killea LLC Act). The basic Articles form is all that is legally needed, although you may attach extra provisions to the state-provided form if you wish. The LLC filing office also provides an annual LLC Statement of Information form, which must be filed within 90 days of forming the LLC.

Note for Professionals: Currently, the more than 60 professions licensed by the state cannot form a California LLC—except lawyers and accountants, who may form a Registered Limited Liability Partnership (ask the Secretary of State for RLLP forms and instructions if you are interested). If you are unsure whether you can form a California LLC to render professional services, call your state licensing board.

Articles of Organization

Name Requirements: Must contain the words "Limited Liability Company" or the abbreviation "LLC." The word "Limited" may be abbreviated as "Ltd." and the word "Company" as "Co." The LLC name may contain the names of one or more members, but may not include the words "bank," "insurance," "trust," "trustee," "incorporated" or "corporation," or the abbreviations "inc." or "corp."

An available LLC name may be reserved for 60 days for a $10 fee. Name availability cannot be checked by phone unless you have set up a prepaid account with the LLC office. The best way to secure a name is to reserve it by mail with the LLC filing office (list one or more alternate names in case your first choice for a corporate name is not available for reservation).

Filing Fee: $870 (includes $70 filing fee plus $800 tax payment), payable to the "Secretary of State."

Annual Fees: California charges LLCs (as well as C—regular—corporations, S corporations and limited partnerships) a minimum annual tax of $800, payable to the Franchise Tax Board. You must pay this minimum amount when you form an LLC as noted above and again, within three months after forming your LLC, for your first year of LLC operations. LLCs with total annual incomes of $250,000 or more (defined as gross income plus cost of goods sold) must also estimate and pay the following additional annual amounts:

Annual Total Income Reportable to California	*Additional Annual LLC Fee*
$250,000-$499,999	$500
$500,000-$999,999	$1,500
$1,000,000-$4,999,999	$3,000
$5,000,000 or more	$4,500

Special Instructions and Filing Requirements: Send only original Articles of Organization to the LLC office in Sacramento, together with a check for the filing fee. You will receive a certified copy from the LLC filing office.

Tax Status

IRS Ruling: None.

State Tax Office: Franchise Tax Board, Sacramento, telephone 800-852-5711.

Operating Rules

Default Transfer Rule: Except as otherwise provided in Articles or operating agreement, by consent of all nontransferring members. [Section 17303.]

Default Continuation Rule: Unless otherwise provided in Articles or operating agreement, by a vote of all remaining members within 90 days of the death, withdrawal, resignation, expulsion, bankruptcy or dissolution of a member. [Section 17350.]

COLORADO

LLC Filing Office

Secretary of State
1560 Broadway, Suite 200
Denver, CO 80202

Telephone: 303-894-2251

Forms and Statutes: Provides fill-in-the-blanks Articles of Organization with instructions for new businesses. Provides special Articles of Organization to convert existing general or limited partnership to a Colorado LLC.

Articles of Organization

Name Requirements: Name must include the words "Limited Liability Company." The word "Limited" may be abbreviated as "Ltd." and the word "Company" as "Co." For name availability, call the LLC filing office. The Secretary of State provides an Application for Reservation of Name form; the reservation fee is $10 for a 120-day reservation.

Filing Fee: $50, payable to "Secretary of State." Expedited (quick) filing costs $50 extra. Papers returned to you by fax cost $7 more.

Special Instructions and Filing Requirements: Type or print the information in the blanks on the state-provided form and supply a stamped, self-addressed envelope for the return of file-stamped Articles to you (or have file-stamped Articles faxed back to you for an additional charge). File original and one copy of Articles of Organization.

Tax Status

IRS Ruling: Revenue Ruling 93-6.

State Tax Office: Revenue Department, Denver, telephone 303-866-3091.

Operating Rules

Default Transfer Rule: By written consent of all nontransferring members; provision does not seem to allow this rule to be varied in the operating agreement. If unanimous consent is not obtained, transferee gets only an economic interest in the LLC (rights to profits and losses and return of capital contribution of transferring member), but no voting or management rights. [Section 70-80-702.]

Default Continuation Rule: By consent of all remaining members within 90 days of the membership termination event. Adherence to this rule appears to be mandatory. [Section 7-80-801.]

Special Statutory Rules: LLC Act provides for annual meetings of members; if managers are chosen, they are elected or reelected by majority vote of the number of members at each annual meeting of members. [Section 7-80-402.] In absence of provision in operating agreement, profits and losses and distributions of capital are allocated and distributed to members according to the value of each member's capital contribution. [Sections 7-80-503 and 7-80-504.]

CONNECTICUT

LLC Filing Office

Connecticut Secretary of State
30 Trinity Street
Hartford, CT 06106

Telephone: 203-566-8570

Forms and Statutes: Provides fill-in-the-blanks Articles of Organization, Domestic Limited Liability Company. Cannot form an LLC for a bank, trust, insurance, building and loan, utility (except telephone) or cemetery company.

Articles of Organization

Name Requirements: Must contain the words "Limited Liability Company" or the abbreviations "LLC" or "L.L.C." The word "Limited" may be abbreviated as "Ltd." and the word "Company" as "Co." To reserve LLC name for 120 days, mail state form Application for Reserved Name, Limited Liability Company, with $30 fee, to the Secretary of State.

Filing Fee: $60, payable to "Secretary of State." You only need to send the original Articles. The Secretary will return a mailing receipt to you. Add $25 extra to request a certified copy of your Articles; add $20 for each plain copy of Articles you wish to receive.

Special Instructions and Filing Requirements: Expedited services (quick filing services described in the Secretary of State materials) are not currently available for LLC documents.

Tax Status

IRS Ruling: None.

State Tax Office: Department of Revenue Services, Hartford, telephone 203-566-8520.

Operating Rules

Default Transfer Rule: Unless otherwise provided in the operating agreement, by a majority vote of the number of nontransferring members. [Section 41.]

Default Continuation Rule: Unless otherwise provided in the operating agreement, by the vote of a "majority in interest" of the remaining members within 90 days following the dissociation event. (The term "majority in interest" is not defined in the Connecticut LLC Act, but probably follows the definition found in IRS Revenue Procedure 95-10, namely the vote of remaining members holding a majority of both the capital and profits interests in the LLC.) [Section 42.]

Special Statutory Rules: A promise to contribute future services, cash or property to an LLC is not enforceable unless it is in writing and signed by the member. At the option of the LLC, a member who fails to contribute services or property as promised must pay the LLC an equivalent amount of cash; this rule can only be changed in the operating agreement or by unanimous consent of members. [Section 27.] Profits and losses and cash distributions are split up among members according to the value of their capital contributions, unless otherwise stated in the operating agreement. [Section 28.]

DELAWARE

LLC Filing Office

Department of State
Division of Corporations
P.O. Box 898
Dover, DE 19903

Telephone: 302-739-3073

Forms and Statutes: When you ask for LLC information, Delaware will send you its corporate formation package. Included in this package is a fill-in-the-blanks Limited Liability Company Certificate of Formation (Delaware's version of Articles of Organization). The Mitchie Company, in Charlottesville, Virginia (800-446-3410) publishes the *Delaware Corporation Laws* booklet, which contains the Delaware Limited Liability Company Act.

Certificate of Formation

Name Requirements: Must contain the words "Limited Liability Company" or the abbreviation "L.L.C." May contain the words "Club," "Foundation," "Fund," "Institute," "Society," "Union," "Syndicate," or "Trust." Name availability may be checked by calling 302-727-7283.

An LLC name may be reserved for 120 days by sending two copies of an Application for Reservation of Name together with a fee payment of $10 to the Delaware Division of Corporations. (Delaware LLCs cannot use Delaware's 900-line to reserve a name—a convenience afforded incorporators in Delaware.)

Filing Fee: $70, payable to the "Delaware Department of State." The Department of State, Division of Corporations, also accepts major credit cards.

Annual Fees: A Delaware LLC must pay a flat annual franchise tax of $100. Contact the Franchise Tax Office of the Division of Corporations for more information and for tax forms, telephone 302-739-4225.

Special Instructions and Filing Requirements: Send the Department of State an original plus one copy, and request that the copy be certified and returned to you. Use letter-sized paper only and black ink printer, ribbon or pen to fill in forms. Sign all forms with black ink pen. You may leave the third Article of the state-provided Limited Liability Company Certificate of Formation blank; you do not have to specify a dissolution date for your LLC.

Tax Status

IRS Ruling: Revenue Ruling 93-38.

State Tax Office: Delaware Franchise Tax Office, Dover, telephone 302-739-4225.

Operating Rules

Default Transfer Rule: In addition to any rule stated in operating agreement, by vote of all nontransferring members of the LLC. [Section 18-704(a).]

Default Continuation Rule: By consent of all remaining members within 90 days of termination of membership or as otherwise stated in the operating agreement. [Section 18-801(4).]

Special Statutory Rules: Unless otherwise stated in operating agreement, members are vested with management power according to their percentage interests in the LLC, and are given voting power equal to these interests. A vote of more than 50% of the membership interests is the default rule to approve members' decisions. [Section 18-402.] Profits and losses, and distributions of cash, are allocated to members according to the value of their respective capital contributions, unless otherwise stated in the operating agreement. [Sections 18-503 and 18-504.]

DISTRICT OF COLUMBIA

LLC Filing Office

Department of Consumer & Regulatory Affairs
Corporations Division
614 H Street, N.W., Room 407
Washington, DC 20001

Telephone: 202-727-7278

Forms and Statutes: Provides guidelines and specimen form for Articles of Organization. Use this information to type your own Articles document according to the instructions. Prentice Hall Legal & Financial Services Publishing (212-373-7808) publishes a small booklet containing the corporation laws of Maryland and the District of Columbia (includes the limited liability company statutes) for approximately $20.

Articles of Organization

Name Requirements: Must contain the words "Limited Liability Company" or the abbreviation "L.L.C." If a professional practice is being organized, the name must include the words "Professional Limited Liability Company" or the abbreviation "P.L.L.C." Name availability may be checked by calling 202-727-7283. Available LLC names may be reserved for 60 days for $25.

Filing Fee: $100, payable to the "D.C. Treasurer."

Annual Fees: Domestic and registered foreign LLCs must pay an annual registration fee of $50.

Special Instructions and Filing Requirements: Type Articles of Organization on letter- or legal-sized paper. Submit two originally signed copies (sign each form with a pen) and attach a consent of the registered agent—a fill-in-the-blanks consent form to use for this purpose is included in materials sent out by the LLC filing office. Don't be confused by instructions to the Articles that discuss your LLC operating agreement; you *do not* have to submit a copy of this agreement when you file Articles of Organization.

Tax Status

IRS Ruling: None.

State Tax Office: Finance & Revenue Department, telephone 202-727-6083.

Operating Rules

Default Transfer Rule: Unless otherwise restricted by the Articles or operating agreement (see Section 29-1337 for rules on permissible restrictions), with consent of nontransferring members holding a majority of the interests in profits of the LLC. [Section 29-1336.]

Default Continuation Rule: In addition to any procedure or vote required by Articles or operating agreement, by the unanimous consent of the remaining members with voting rights within 90 days of the dissociation of a member. [Section 29-1347.]

Special Statutory Rules: Unless otherwise stated in Articles or the operating agreement, members vote according to their interests in the profits of the LLC, with the vote of a majority of the profits interests required to approve a membership decision. [Section 29-1317(d).]

A majority of the profits interests of members is also the default vote requirement for filling a vacant manager position. [Section 29-1319(e).] Default rule for allocating profits and losses, and distributing cash of LLC, is according to the value of each member's capital contribution to the LLC. [Sections 29-1324 and 29-1325.]

FLORIDA

LLC Filing Office

Florida Department of State
Division of Corporations
P.O. Box 6327
Tallahassee, FL 32314

Telephone: 904-487-6052

Forms and Statutes: Provides fill-in-the-blanks Articles of Organization with instructions. Also provides an LLC booklet, titled *Florida Limited Liability Company Act*, which contains the Florida LLC Act and a tear-out Articles form. You may use either the separately supplied or the tear-out fill-in-the-blanks form; they are identical.

Articles of Organization

Name Requirements: Must end with the words "Limited Company" or the abbreviation "L.C." A preliminary name availability request can be handled over the phone by calling 904-488-9000. The fee to reserve an available LLC name for 120 days is $35.

Filing Fee: $250 for filing Articles, plus $35 for filing Designation of Registered Agent form for a total of $285, payable to the "Department of State." You can add $52.50 to receive a certified copy of your Articles from the LLC filing office, and/or add $8.75 for a Certificate of Status certifying that your LLC is an active Florida LLC as of its filing date. Payment of the additional fees for these extra forms is optional.

Annual Fees. LLCs must pay an annual report fee of $100.

Special Instructions and Filing Requirements: Note these special instructions for completing Articles of Organization:

- *Article III:* You may state a "perpetual" duration for your LLC.
- *Article V:* If you adopt the standard language contained in our operating agreements, you may use the following sentence to sum up the rights of members to admit additional members and the terms of admission: "The existing members of this LLC must approve the admission of new members by a unanimous vote. Upon such approval, new members shall be accorded all rights associated with membership in this LLC." If your manager-managed LLC requires only approval by member-managers to admit new members who are transferees of former members, add a sentence to your response noting this exception: "However, the nontransferring member-managers of this LLC are empowered to approve by unanimous vote the admission into membership of a transferee of a former member of this LLC."
- *Article VI:* If you adopt the standard operating agreement provisions in Chapter 5 or 6 of this book, the following language should work here: "The unanimous approval of the remaining members is required to continue the business of this LLC upon the death, retirement, resignation, expulsion, bankruptcy or dissolution of a member [replace the previous word "member" with "member-manager" if your manager-managed LLC has chosen this option] or the occurrence of any other event that terminates the continued membership of a member in this limited liability company."

Submit the signed original and one copy of Articles of Organization to the LLC filing office. Include a filled-in transmittal letter and the following completed and signed forms, both of which are included with the LLC materials sent out by the LLC filing office:

- *Certificate of Designation of Registered Agent.* Have this form dated and signed by the person named as intial agent of the LLC.
- Affidavit of Membership and Contributions. This form certifies that your Florida LLC has at least two members, and discloses the cash and/or property contributed by the initial LLC members. On line 4 of this form, you must total these figures together with all future anticipated capital you expect to receive from members in the future. If a later annual report filed by your LLC shows contributions in excess of this anticipated amount, you will be charged a special fee (see instructions to the state-supplied Affidavit of Membership and Contributions form).

Tax Status

IRS Ruling: Revenue Ruling 93-53.

State Tax Office: Revenue Department, Tallahassee, telephone 904-488-5050.

Operating Rules

Default Transfer Rule: Unless otherwise stated in the Articles, by unanimous consent of nontransferring members. [Section 608-433.]

Default Continuation Rule: By unanimous consent of remaining members, or by a right to continue the LLC as stated in the Articles (no time limit for approval given in statute). [Section 608.441(c).]

Special Statutory Rules: In manager-managed LLCs, managers must be elected annually. [Section 608.422.]

GEORGIA

LLC Filing Office

Secretary of State
Corporations Division
Suite 315, West Tower
2 Martin Luther King Jr. Drive
Atlanta, GA 30334

Telephone: 404-656-2817

Forms and Statutes: Provides sample Articles of Organization with two articles. Type or word process Articles on letter-sized paper following the format and content of the sample form. This short format produces minimal, though legally sufficient, Articles of Organization to form a Georgia LLC.

Articles of Organization

Name Requirements: The proposed LLC name *must* be reserved before filing Articles. Call the LLC filing office at the above telephone number to check the availability and reserve your LLC name over the phone (there is no fee for an LLC name reservation). If name reservation approval is given, you will be mailed a name reservation certificate and a Transmittal Form—these documents must be filed with your Articles (as explained in "Special Instructions and Filing Requirements," below).

Filing Fee: $75, payable to "Secretary of State." Attach check to completed Transmittal Form.

Special Instructions and Filing Requirements: File original and one copy of Articles of Organization. Include the original name reservation certificate with your papers. Also include a completed Transmittal Form, with a check for the filing fee attached. The Transmittal Form should be completed to show the name of your LLC and your name reservation number. If your papers are in order, the LLC filing office will attach a certificate of organization to the file copy of your Articles and mail them to you.

Tax Status

IRS Ruling: None.

State Tax Office: Department of Revenue, Atlanta, telephone 404-656-4071.

Operating Rules

Default Transfer Rule: Except as otherwise stated in Articles or operating agreement, by unanimous consent of nontransferring members. [Section 14-11-503.]

Default Continuation Rule: Unless otherwise provided in Articles or operating agreement, by unanimous written consent of remaining members within 90 days of dissociation event. [Section 14-11-602(4).]

HAWAII

At the time this book went to press, Hawaii LLC legislation was pending, but not approved. Call the Department of Commerce and Commercial Affairs, Business Registration Division, at 808-586-2727 to check the progress of this LLC legislation and to ask for LLC materials and forms once it is approved and signed into law.

IDAHO

LLC Filing Office

Idaho Secretary of State
Corporations Division
P.O. Box 83720
Boise, ID 83720-0080

Telephone: 208-334-2300

Forms and Statutes: State provides fill-in-the-blanks Articles of Organization with instructions, and free handbook containing the Idaho Limited Liability Company Act.

Note for Professionals: State also provides Articles for organizing a professional limited liability company (under Section 53-615 of the Idaho LLC Act). This special professional form applies to LLCs formed to render licensed professional services in the fields of architecture, chiropractic, dentistry, engineering, landscape architecture, law, medicine, nursing, occupational therapy, optometry, physical therapy, podiatry, professional geology, psychology, certified or licensed public accountancy, social work, surveying and veterinary medicine.

Articles of Organization

Name Requirements: An LLC name may be reserved for four months for $20. The name must contain the words "Limited Liability Company," "Limited Company" or the abbreviation "L.L.C.," "L.C.," "LLC" or "LC." The word "Limited" may be abbreviated as "Ltd." and the word "Company" may be abbreviated as "Co." A professional services limited liability company name must *end* with the words "Professional Company" or the abbreviation "P.L.L.C." or "PLLC."

Filing Fee: $100 fee, payable to the "Idaho Secretary of State."

Special Instructions and Filing Requirements: Submit the original and two copies for filing to the Corporations Division. The filing fee is increased to $120 if Articles of Organization are not typed or if they include attachments. (To save money, type your responses on the fill-in-the-blanks Articles form.)

Tax Status

IRS Ruling: None.

State Tax Office: State Tax Commission, telephone 208-334-7660.

Operating Rules

Default Transfer Rule: Unless otherwise stated in the operating agreement, by unanimous written consent of nontransferring members. [Section 53-638.]

Default Continuation Rule: Unless otherwise stated in the operating agreement, by unanimous consent of remaining members within 90 days of the dissociation of a member. [Section 53-642(3).]

ILLINOIS

LLC Filing Office

Illinois Secretary of State
Department of Business Services
Limited Liability Company Division
Room 359, Howlett Building
Springfield, IL 62756

Telephone: 217-524-8008

Forms and Statutes: State provides fill-in-the-blanks Articles of Organization. Also includes copy of the Illinois LLC Act, plus a pamphlet summarizing the legal and tax requirements and features of Illinois LLCs, including a copy of the IRS Revenue Ruling that approved the partnership tax status of an Illinois LLC.

Articles of Organization

Name Requirements: Must contain the words "Limited Liability Company" or the abbreviation "L.L.C." The abbreviations "Ltd." and "Co." are *not* allowed in Illinois LLC names. Call 217-782-9520 to check availability of up to three proposed LLC names.

An available LLC name may be reserved for 90 days for (a whopping) $300! A corporate name may be reserved for $25 in Illinois, so why so much for an LLC name reservation? We don't know, but this is what the statute currently requires. Perhaps this fee will be lowered to a more modest amount by future LLC legislation, but for now, you may want to skip reserving your name; just check name availability by calling the above number, then take your chances by promptly filing Articles with your proposed name.

Filing Fee: $500, payable to the "Secretary of State." Payment must be made by certified check, cashier's check, money order or Illinois attorney's or CPA's check (don't send a personal check).

Annual Fees: LLCs do not pay state franchise taxes, but must pay an annual LLC renewal fee of $300.

Special Instructions and Filing Requirements: Submit the original and one copy of the signed Articles of Organization form. The fill-in-the-blanks Articles form must be completed with a typewriter. Note these specifics:

- *Article 2.* Attach Form LLC-1.20, available from the LLC Division, to your Articles if you will do business under a name other than the one stated in the Articles (under an assumed business name).

- *Article 4.* Apply for a Federal Employer Identification Number (EIN) prior to filing the Articles, and show this number in Article 4. To apply for an EIN, file IRS Form SS-4—call 800-TAX-FORM to order this form. In some areas, you can obtain a federal EIN over the phone—call your local IRS tax office to find out if this phone service is available.
- *Article 7.* A Standard Industrial Code (SIC) sheet is included with state materials to specify principal activity of LLC in Article 7. You may also wish to include a statement in this Article that says, "The purpose of this company is to transact any or all lawful business for which limited liability companies may be organized under the Illinois Limited Liability Company Act."
- *Articles 8 and 9.* In Article 8, show the latest date on which the LLC will automatically dissolve (it's fine to specify a date well into the future, such as December 31, 2099). You can leave the second part of Article 8 and the entire Article 9 blank (check "No" to Article 9).

Tax Status

IRS Ruling: Revenue Ruling 93-49. (See copy of ruling set out in Summary of Illinois LLC Act provided by the Secretary of State.)

State Tax Office: For annual tax information, contact Department of Business Services at 217-782-7808. For other tax information, contact the Department of Revenue, Springfield, at 217-785-3336.

Operating Rules

Default Transfer Rule: Unless otherwise stated in Articles or operating agreement, by unanimous consent of nontransferring members. [Section 180/30-5.]

Default Continuation Rule: Unless otherwise provided in Articles or operating agreement, by unanimous consent of remaining members within 90 days of terminating event. [Section 180/35-1(3).]

INDIANA

LLC Filing Office

Indiana Secretary of State
Corporations Division
302 W. Washington, Room E018
Indianapolis, IN 46204

Telephone: 317-232-6576

Forms and Statutes: Sample Articles of Organization are not provided, but office sends out a *Limited Liability Company Guide* pamphlet summarizing LLC formation procedures and legal requirements in Indiana. This material includes a list of information that must be included in Articles under the Indiana statute. (See "Special Instructions and Filing Requirements," below.)

Articles of Organization

Name Requirements: Must include "Limited Liability Company" or abbreviations "L.L.C." or "LLC." Name availability can be checked by phone, and an available name may be reserved for 120 days for $20.

Filing Fee: $90, payable to "Secretary of State" (staple check to Articles).

Special Instructions and Filing Requirements: File original and one copy of Articles; file-stamped copy will be returned to you.

Below is a summary of the requirements for the contents of Indiana Articles of Organization, taken from the Indiana LLC Act. (See Chapter 4, Section E5, for an example of how to draft your own Articles based upon similar state statutory requirements.)

Section 23-18-2-4

(b) Articles of Organization must contain the following:

(1) The name of the limited liability company (see "Name Requirements," above).

(2) The street address of the LLC's registered office in Indiana and its registered agent at that office. (Post office boxes are not allowed, although a box number with a rural route is OK. The agent must be an Indiana resident.)

(3) The latest date upon which the LLC is to dissolve or a statement that the duration of the LLC is perpetual.

(4) If managers rather than members will manage the LLC, a statement to that effect (namely, that "the LLC will be managed by managers" [or "will be managed by a manager" if you'll have just one manager]).

Tax Status

IRS Ruling: None.

State Tax Office: Department of Revenue, Indianapolis, telephone 317-232-2103.

Operating Rules

Default Transfer Rule: Unless otherwise stated in operating agreement, by unanimous written consent of nontransferring members. [Section 23-18-6-4.]

Default Continuation Rule: Unless otherwise provided in Articles or operating agreement, by unanimous consent of remaining members within 90 days of dissociation event. [Section 23-18-9-1.]

IOWA

LLC Filing Office

Iowa Secretary of State
Corporations Division
Hoover Building, 2nd Floor
Des Moines, IA 50319

Telephone: 515-281-5204
Fax: 515-242-5953

Forms and Statutes: Does not provide fill-in-the-blanks Articles of Organization, but provides a copy of the LLC Act, including Section 490A.303 of the Iowa LLC law, which lists the required contents of Articles (see "Special Instructions and Filing Requirements," below).

Articles of Organization

Name Requirements: Must contain the words "Limited Company" or the abbreviation "L.C." An available LLC name may be reserved for 120 days for $10.

Filing Fee: $50, payable to the "Iowa Secretary of State."

Special Instructions and Filing Requirements: Type or word process Articles in black ink. You need to file the original Articles only. The Secretary will return the document, endorsed filed, to you together with a receipt for payment of the filing fee.

Below is a summary of the requirements for the contents of Iowa Articles of Organization, taken from the Iowa LLC Act. (See Chapter 4, Section E5, for an example of how to draft your own Articles based upon similar state statutory requirements.)

Section 490A.303.

1. The Articles of Organization must set forth all of the following:

a. A name that satisfies the requirements of section 490A.401 (see "Name Requirements," above).

b. The street address of the LLC's initial registered office and the name of its initial registered agent at that office.

c. The street address of the principal office of the LLC, which may be the same as the registered office, but need not be within the state.

d. The period of the LLC's duration, which may not be perpetual.

Tax Status

IRS Ruling: None.

State Tax Office: Department of Revenue & Finance, Des Moines, telephone 515-281-3135.

Operating Rules

Default Transfer Rule: Unless otherwise stated in Articles or operating agreement, by unanimous written consent or vote at meeting of nontransferring members. [Section 490A.903.]

Default Continuation Rule: Unless otherwise provided in Articles or operating agreement, by unanimous consent of remaining members (no time limit for approval given in statute). [Section 490A.1301(3).]

KANSAS

LLC Filing Office

Kansas Secretary of State
Corporation Division
2nd Floor, State Capitol
300 S.W. 10th
Topeka, KS 66612-1594

Telephone: 913-296-2236

Forms and Statutes: State provides instructions for preparing Articles of Organization, including a list of required contents, but no fill-in-the-blanks form. You need to prepare a form yourself following the state's instructions (see the "Special Instructions and Filing Requirements" below). The LLC filing office will also provide a photocopy of the Kansas Limited Liability Act upon request.

Articles of Organization

Name Requirements: Must contain the words "Limited Liability Company" or "Limited Company" or the abbreviation "LLC," "L.L.C.," "LC" or "L.C."

Filing Fee: $150 fee, payable to the "Kansas Secretary of State."

Special Instructions and Filing Requirements: Submit original signed Articles and one copy.

Below is a summary of the requirements for the contents of Kansas Articles of Organization, taken from the Kansas LLC Act. (See Chapter 4, Section E5, for an example of how to draft your own Articles based upon similar state statutory requirements.)

Section 17-7607.

(a) The articles of organization of a limited liability company shall set forth:

(1) The name of the LLC (see "Name Requirements" above).

(2) The period of duration of the LLC, or the latest date upon which it will dissolve (Kansas LLCs may have a "perpetual" duration).

(3) The purpose(s) for which the LLC is formed (which may be "...to engage in any lawful business for which limited liability companies may be organized in this state").

(4) The address of the registered office in Kansas and the name and address of the initial resident agent for service of process. (You must list these three items of information; the two addresses must be identical, and the agent must be a resident of Kansas.)

(5) The right, if given, of the members to admit additional members and the terms and conditions of the admissions. (If you adopt the standard language contained in our operating agreements, you may use the following sentence to sum up these rights: "The existing members of this LLC must approve the admission of new members by a unanimous vote. Upon such approval, new members shall be accorded all rights associated with membership in this LLC." If yours is a manager-managed LLC that requires only approval by member-managers to admit new members who are transferees of former members, add a sentence to this article noting the exception: "However, the nontransferring member-managers of this LLC are empowered to approve by unanimous vote the admission into membership of a transferee of a former member of this LLC.")

(6) The right, if any, of the remaining members to continue the business upon the death, retirement, resignation, expulsion, bankruptcy or dissolution of a member, or the occurrence of any other event that terminates the continued membership of a member. If you adopt the standard operating agreement provisions in Chapters 5 or 6 in this book, the following language should work here: "The unanimous approval of the remaining members is required to continue the business of this LLC upon the death, retirement, resignation, expulsion, bankruptcy or dissolution of a member [replace the previous word "member" with "member-manager" if your manager-managed LLC has chosen this option] or the occurrence of any other event that terminates the continued membership of a member in this limited liability company."

(7) If the LLC is to be managed by a manager or managers, a statement to this effect, and the names and addresses of the initial managers who are to serve until their successors are elected and qualified.

(8) If, as is usually the case, the LLC's management is reserved to members, the names and addresses of the members. (You don't need to specifically say that the management of the LLC is reserved to members, but you may include such a statement if you wish, just before the list of the members' names and addresses.)

Tax Status

IRS Ruling: Revenue Ruling 94-30.

State Tax Office: Department of Revenue, Topeka, telephone 913-296-3909.

Operating Rules

Default Transfer Rule: By unanimous written consent of nontransferring members. [Section 17-7618.] (It is unclear whether the operating agreement may vary this approval requirement. The LLC statute says membership interests may be transferred as provided in the operating agreement, but apparently withholds full membership rights to new members unless all nontransferring members approve the transfer.)

Default Continuation Rule: By unanimous consent of remaining members (no time limit for approval stated in statute), or under a right to continue the LLC stated in the Articles—see explanation of Section 17-7607, paragraph (a)(6) under "Special Instructions and Filing Requirements" to Articles above. [Section 17-7622.]

KENTUCKY

LLC Filing Office

Kentucky Secretary of State
P.O. Box 718
Frankfort, KY 40602

Telephone: 502-564-2848

Forms and Statutes: Kentucky Secretary of State does not provide a fill-in form for Articles (see "Special Instructions below and Filing Requirements" below), but does provide other statutory forms for LLCs (Amendment of Articles, Change of Registered Agent or Office, Certificate of Existence or Authorization, Articles of Dissolution, etc.). A copy of the Kentucky LLC Act can be obtained upon request from the Secretary of State for $10.

Articles of Organization

Name Requirements: Must contain the words "Limited Liability Company" or "Limited Company" or the abbreviation "LLC" or "LC." Professional LLCs must contain the words "Professional Limited Liability Company" or Professional Limited Company" or "PLLC" or PLC." The word "Limited" may be abbreviated as "Ltd." and the word "Company" may be abbreviated as "Co." in any limited liability company name. An available LLC name can be reserved for _ days for $15.

Filing Fee: $40, payable to the "Secretary of State"

Special Instructions and Filing Requirements: Type or print Articles in black ink. Form can be signed by one or more members or managers or by an organizer of the LLC. Submit singed original plus *two* copies for filing. One file-stamped copy will be returned to you; the other copy is filed with the county clerk of the county where the registered office of the LLC is located.

You must draft your own Articles of Organization form based upon the requirements of the LLC statute cited below. We provide a sample form below which should meet the minimum standards of the statute (also see Chapter 4, Section E5 for another example of drafting your own form from similar statutory requirements; a local law or business library may contain a legal reference book with a ready-to-use LLC Articles of Organization form).

Sec. 275.005 (1) The articles of organization shall set forth:

(a) A name that satisfies the requirements of law (see "Name Requirements" above)

(b) The street address of the LLC's initial registered office, and the name of its registered agent at that office

(c) The mailing address of the initial principal office of the LLC

(d) A statement that the LLC has at least two (2) members

(e) A statement that the LLC is to be managed by managers or that the LLC is to be managed by its members, and

(f) If the LLC is to have a specific date of dissolution, the latest date on which the LLC is to dissolve.

If a professional LLC is being formed, the Articles must designate the professionals services to be practiced through the professional LLC.

A written statement of the initial registered agent consenting to serve in that capacity must accompany the Articles.

Below is a sample Articles form that should meet the requirements of the above section of the Kentucky LLC Act:

ARTICLES OF ORGANIZATION
OF
NAME OF LLC

One: The name of this limited liability company is name of LLC.

Two: The street address of the limited liability company's initial registered office, and the name of its registered agent at that office, are: name of agent and address of agent's registered office address.

Three: The mailing address of the initial principal office of the limited liability company is mailing address of LLC.

Four: This limited liability company has at least two (2) members.

Five: This limited liability company is to be managed by "its members" or "managers".

[Professional LLCs only—add Article Six below:]

Six: The professionals services to be practiced through this professional limited liability company are insert type of professional services, such as "accounting," "legal services," or type of professional medical practice.

Dated: ______________________

Signature: ______________________

type name of person signing, and title as "member," "manager" or "organizer"

On a separate page, type and fill in the following Consent to Appointment form and submit signed original with the Articles of Organization for filing:

CONSENT TO APPOINTMENT AS REGISTERED AGENT

The undersigned hereby accepts his/her appointment as initial registered agent of name of LLC, a Kentucky limited liability company, and agrees to serve in that capacity.

Dated: ______________________

Signature: ______________________

typed name, Registered Agent

Tax Status

IRS Ruling: None

State Tax Office: Kentucky Revenue Cabinet, Frankfort, telephone 502-564-3658

Operating Rules

Default Transfer Rule: Unless otherwise provided in operating agreement, by unanimous written consent of all nontransferring members. [Section 33.]

Default Continuation Rule: Unless otherwise stated in the Articles, by written consent of all remaining members within 90 days after dissociation of a member. [Section 37(b).]

LOUISIANA

LLC Filing Office

Louisiana Secretary of State
Corporations Division
P.O. Box 94125
Baton Rouge, LA 70804-9125

Telephone: 504-925-4704

Forms and Statutes: State does not provide fill-in-the-blanks Articles of Organization with instructions. You'll need to draft your own based upon the Articles statute found in the Louisiana LLC Act (see "Special Instructions and Requirements" below).

Articles of Organization

Name Requirements: Must contain the words "Limited Liability Company" or the abbreviation "L.L.C." or "L.C." Check LLC name availability by calling the Corporations Division. LLC names may be reserved for 60 days for $20.

Filing Fee: $60, payable to "Secretary of State."

Special Instructions and Filing Requirements: The statutory list of required provisions for Louisiana Articles of Organization is short and sweet, and consists of two standard items of information (although additional matters may be added to Articles). Here is the relevant excerpt from the statute, with our comments:

Section 12:1305.

A. The Articles of Organization shall be written in the English language and shall be executed by at least one person, who need not be a member or manager of the limited liability company. The Articles shall be acknowledged by the person or one of the persons who signed the Articles of Organization or may be executed by authentic act. (Basically, this means signing your Articles in front of a notary or attaching a separate notarized page to previously signed Articles.)

B. The Articles of Organization shall set forth the following:

(1) The name of the limited liability company. (See "Name Requirements," above.)

(2) The purposes for which the limited liability company is formed or that its purpose is to engage in any lawful activity for which limited liability companies may be formed. (A purpose clause you can use is "to engage in any lawful business for which limited liability companies may be organized in this state.")

Other provisions relating to management of the LLC by members or managers, its duration or other provisions need not be included in the Articles, so you can draft your Articles quickly just by showing its name and its lawful purpose as shown in the sample language above. Below are minimum Louisiana Articles, followed by a standard execution and notarization section. Have the person(s) signing your Articles do so in the presence of a notary. Here are sample Articles of Organization for Louisiana:

ARTICLES OF ORGANIZATION

The name of this limited liability company is
________ name of LLC ________.

The purposes for which this limited liability company is organized are to engage in any lawful activity for which limited liability companies may be formed under the laws of this state.

In Witness Whereof, the following person(s) has/have signed these Articles of Organization on
________ date ________:

__________________________.

State of Louisiana)
) ss.
Parish of ________________)

Before me personally appeared
____________________________ who is/are known to me to be the person(s) who executed the foregoing Articles of Organization.

In Witness Whereof, I have hereunto set my hand and seal on this____________ day of
__________________________.

Notary Public Signature:
____

My commission expires:
____

A Limited Liability Company Initial Report must accompany your Articles when submitted for filing. This form must be signed by each person who signs your Articles, and by a person whom you designate to act as your LLC's registered agent. Sign this form in the presence of a notary (you can have your Articles notarized at the same time).

Mail the completed Initial Report plus your original signed and notarized Articles, with any additional copies of Articles you wish certified (for an additional $10 charge per copy) to the LLC filing office. You can request expedited (one-day) filing service for an additional $20 fee.

Tax Status

IRS Ruling: Revenue Ruling 94-5.

State Tax Office: Department of Revenue & Taxation, Baton Rouge, telephone 504-925-7537.

Operating Rules

Default Transfer Rule: Unless otherwise stated in Articles or operating agreement, by unanimous written consent of nontransferring members. [Section 12:1332.]

Default Continuation Rule: Unless otherwise provided in Articles or operating agreement, by unanimous consent of remaining members within 90 days of dissociation event. [Section 12:1334(3).]

MAINE

LLC Filing Office

Secretary of State
Bureau of Corporations, Elections & Commissions
State House, Station #101
Augusta, ME 04333-0101
ATTN: Corporate Examining Section

Telephone: 207-287-4195

Forms and Statutes: State provides fill-in-the-blanks forms for most LLC statutory filings, including Articles of Organization.

Articles of Organization

Name Requirements: Must contain the words "Limited Liability Company." If a professional LLC, must contain the word(s) "Chartered," "Professional Association" or abbreviation "P.A." Use the state-furnished LLC Application for Reservation of Name form and include $20 fee to reserve an LLC name.

Filing Fee: $250, payable to the "Secretary of State."

Special Instructions and Filing Requirements: If forming a professional service LLC, check box at beginning of fill-in-the-blanks Articles of Organization. Have the initial registered agent named in Articles date and sign in space provided on the Articles form.

Tax Status

IRS Ruling: None.

State Tax Office: Bureau of Taxation, Augusta, telephone 207-287-2076.

Operating Rules

Default Transfer Rule: By unanimous written consent of nontransferring members and as may otherwise be provided in Articles or operating agreement. [Section 687.]

Default Continuation Rule: By unanimous consent of remaining members within 90 days of dissociation event or as may otherwise be provided in Articles or operating agreement. [Section 701.]

MARYLAND

LLC Filing Office

Maryland Department of Assessments & Taxation
Charter Division
Room 809
301 West Preston Street
Baltimore, MD 21201-2392
Telephone: 410-225-1340

Forms and Statutes: Provides guidelines to prepare your own Articles. Call the above LLC office to request a copy of these guidelines and a copy of the Maryland LLC Act. (We cover the guidelines in "Special Instructions and Filing Requirements," below.)

Articles of Organization

Name Requirements: Must contain the words "Limited Liability Company" or one of the following abbreviations: "LLC," "LC," "L.L.C." or "L.C." Call the LLC filing office at 410-225-1340 to check name availability. An available name may be reserved for 30 days for a $7 fee.

Filing Fee: $50, payable to "SDAT" (this is the acronym for the State Department of Assessments & Taxation).

Annual Filing: Every five years, the LLC must file a statement (by September 15th) affirming that it is still actively engaged in the business for which it was formed. (Presumably, you may change or expand the original line of business stated in your Articles.)

Special Instructions and Filing Requirements: Articles must be typed or printed using a printer; they cannot be handwritten. Submit the signed original for filing. You may ask for a certified copy of the original Articles to be returned to you by including an additional $6 plus $1 per page in your filing fee check.

Below is a summary of the guidelines for the contents of the Articles. See Chapter 4, Section E5, for an example of how to draft your own Articles based upon similar state statutory requirements.

Maryland Articles of Organization must contain the following information:

- the name of the LLC (see "Name Requirements," above).
- the latest date on which the LLC will dissolve (this must be a specific date; a term of years or perpetual existence is not allowed).

- the purpose of the LLC ("...to engage in any lawful business for which limited liability companies may be organized in this state" is an acceptable purpose).
- the address of the LLC in Maryland (post office boxes are not allowed).
- the name and address of the LLC's resident agent (an adult over 18 with a street address in Maryland).
- the signature of an LLC organizer over the age of 18 (notarization is not required).

Tax Status

IRS Ruling: None.

State Tax Office: Department of Assessments & Taxation, Baltimore, telephone 410-225-1340.

Operating Rules

Default Transfer Rule: By unanimous written consent of nontransferring members and as may otherwise be specified in the operating agreement. [Section 4A-604.]

Default Continuation Rule: Except as may otherwise be provided in the operating agreement, by unanimous consent of remaining members within 90 days of dissociation event. [Sections 4A-902(3) and 4A-904.]

MASSACHUSETTS

LLC Filing Office

Commonwealth of Massachusetts
Corporations Division
One Ashburton Place, 17th Floor
Boston, MA 02108

Telephone: 617-727-2853

Forms and Statutes: The Massachusetts LLC Act went into effect January 1, 1996. Forms were not provided as of the date this book went to press. Please supplement our information by calling the Corporations Division of the Secretary of State (at the above telephone number) and asking for any current forms, instructions and other material for forming a domestic Massachusetts LLC. As part of these materials, the office should send you a copy of the LLC regulations (rules implementing the state LLC Act). To draft your own Certificate of Organization based upon these regulations, see "Special Instructions and Requirements" below.

Note for Professionals: Existing Massachusetts professional practice general partnerships can register as Registered Limited Liability Partnership instead of converting their general partnerships to LLCs (the registration process is simple and provides some limited liability protection). For more information, see the Massachusetts Secretary of the Commonwealth regulations that cover the registration of RLLPs.

Certificate of Organization

Name Requirements: Must contain the words "Limited Liability Company," "Limited Company" or the abbreviation "LLC," "LC," "L.L.C." or "L.C." Available LLC names may be reserved for 30 days for $15.

Filing Fee: $500 fee, payable to the "Commonwealth of Massachusetts."

Annual Fees: You must pay an annual report fee of $500.

Special Instructions and Filing Requirements: Prepare and submit an original and one copy of a completed, signed Certificate of Organization (the Massachusetts name for Articles of Organization). Type or print on only one side of 8½" x 11" paper.

Here is a list of the required contents of the Certificate of Organization for Massachusetts LLCs (see Chapter 4, Section E5, for an example of how to draft your own Articles based upon similar state statutory requirements):

1. Federal Employer Identification Number (EIN), if available. To apply for an EIN, file IRS Form SS-4—call 800-TAX-FORM to order this form. In some areas, you can obtain a federal EIN over the phone; call your local IRS tax office to find out if this phone service is available. If you have not yet received your federal EIN, just state in this paragraph of your Articles: "The federal Employer Identification Number of this limited liability company has been applied for, but has not yet been assigned."

2. The name of the LLC. (See "Name Requirements," above.)

3. The street address in Massachusetts where LLC records will be maintained. (Normally, this is the principal business office of the LLC.)

4. The general nature of the LLC's business. A statement that you plan to engage in any and all lawful business allowed LLCs under state law is not enough. You must indicate the nature of the LLC's actual business—for example, "The general nature of the business of this LLC is real estate sales" or "securities investments."

If your LLC plans to render licensed professional services, such as law, medicine or accounting, you must include the following information: (1) the service to be rendered; (2) the names and addresses of each member or manager who will render the service; and (3) a statement that "The limited liability company will abide by and be subject to any conditions or limitations established by any applicable regulating board, including the provisions of liability insurance required under state law." A professional service LLC also must obtain a certificate from the state board that regulates the profession, which states that each member or manager who will render a professional service is duly licensed. Your state professional board should be able to provide this statement and help you prepare a Certificate of Organization for your professional LLC if you have any questions about these requirements.

5. The date the LLC will dissolve, if applicable. If your LLC wishes to have a perpetual existence (to dissolve only when the members or managers decide), simply don't include this statement in your Certificate.

6. The name and business address of the agent for service of process of the LLC. (If an individual, the agent must be a Massachusetts resident.)

7. If the LLC is manager-managed, the name and the business address of each LLC manager (member-managed LLCs should ignore this item). The business address of a manager may be omitted if it is identical to the LLC's address.

8. The names and business addresses (again, only non-LLC business office addresses are required) of any nonmanagers who are authorized to execute documents on behalf of the LLC for filing with the Corporations Division of the Secretary of the Commonwealth. If you have a member-managed LLC, you must list at least one person here. Normally, member-managed LLCs will show the name of the member who prepares and files the Certificate of Organization–for example, "The name and business address of the person who is authorized to execute documents to be filed with the Corporations Division of the Secretary of the Commonwealth is [name and address of member who is preparing the Certificate]."

9. The name and business address (again, if different from the LLC business address) of any person specifically authorized to execute, acknowledge, deliver and record any recordable instrument purporting to affect an interest in real property. Include this optional statement if your LLC may engage in real property transactions. (The LLC filing office will, for a fee, prepare a Certificate of Good Standing, which shows the names of persons listed in this clause as persons authorized to sign real property papers for your LLC). You may use wording such as: "The names and addresses of persons who are authorized to execute, acknowledge, deliver and record any recordable instrument affecting an interest in real property are: [names and business addresses of one or more managers and/or members]."

10. The Certificate can contain any additional information you wish to include—for example, the names and addresses of the initial members of your LLC.

The certificate of Organization may be signed by any manager (if the LLC is manager-managed), any other person authorized to file papers for the LLC with the Corporations Division (see Item 8 above) or the organizer of the LLC (the person who is forming the LLC, whether or not listed in the Certificate). Generally, member-managed LLCs will list one of the members under Item 8 in the Certificate as a person who may make filings with the Division, and this member will sign the Certificate immediately after an execution paragraph included at the end of the Certificate:

In Witness Whereof, the undersigned affirms, under penalty of perjury, that the facts stated in this Certificate of Organization are true.
Dated: ______________________________
Signed ______________________________,
[show capacity as "Manager," "Member" or "Organizer"]

Tax Status

IRS Ruling: None

State Tax Office: Department of Revenue, Boston, telephone 617-626-2299.

Operating Rules

Default Transfer Rule: By unanimous consent of nontransferring members or as provided in operating agreement. [Section 39]

Default Continuation Rule: By unanimous consent of nontransferring members within 90 days of dissociation event or as provided in operating agreement. [Section 43(4)]

MICHIGAN

LLC Filing Office

Michigan Department of Commerce
Corporation & Securities Bureau
Corporation Division
P.O. Box 30054
Lansing, MI 48909-7554

Telephone: 517-334-6302

Forms and Statutes: State provides fill-in-the-blanks Articles of Organization (Form 700) with instructions, and will send out copy of the Michigan Limited Liability Company Act upon request at no charge. Use separate Form 701 to file Articles for an LLC rendering licensed professional services.

Articles of Organization

Name Requirements: Must contain the words "Limited Liability Company" or the abbreviation "L.L.C." or "L.C."

Filing Fee: $50 nonrefundable fee, payable to the "State of Michigan."

Special Instructions and Filing Requirements: You are only required to submit original Articles. This document will be returned to you after it is copied and stored in the Bureau's LLC database.

Tax Status

IRS Ruling: None

State Tax Office: State Treasurer's Office, Revenue Bureau, Lansing, telephone 517-373-3196.

Operating Rules

Note: Michigan uses two section-number reference systems for its Limited Liability Company Act. Below, we use the section numbers that correspond to the MCL (Michigan Corporations Law).

Default Transfer Rule: By unanimous written consent of nontransferring members. The operating agreement may provide otherwise as long as the LLC is member-managed and at least a majority of its remaining members must vote to continue the business of the LLC after the dissociation of a member. [Section 450.4506.]

Default Continuation Rule: By at least a majority of remaining members within 90 days of a dissociation event. The operating agreement may provide otherwise as long as the LLC is member-managed and unanimous consent is required for an assignee of a member to be admitted to membership. [Section 450.4801(d).]

Here's how the two sections of Michigan law mentioned above work together. A member-managed LLC may use its operating agreement to:

- *require less than unanimous consent of nontransferring members to admit as a new member the assignee of a former member.* If so, the LLC must require at least majority consent of remaining members to continue the life of the LLC after a member is dissociated; *or*

- *require less than a majority of remaining members to vote to continue the existence of the LLC after a member is dissociated.* If so, the LLC must require the unanimous consent of nontransferring members to admit an assignee into membership.

MINNESOTA

LLC Filing Office

Minnesota Secretary of State
Business Services Division
180 State Office Building
100 Constitution Avenue
St. Paul, MN 55155-1299

Telephone: 612-297-1455

Forms and Statutes: State provides fill-in-the-blanks Articles of Organization with instructions.

Articles of Organization

Name Requirements: Must contain the words "Limited Liability Company" or the abbreviation "LLC." Cannot include the words "incorporated" or "corporation" or their abbreviations. Check name availability by calling 612-296-2803. An LLC name may be reserved for a fee of $35.

Filing Fee: $135, payable to the "Minnesota Secretary of State." For fee questions, call 612-296-2803.

Special Instructions and Filing Requirements: Here's how to address several particulars in the state Articles form:

- *Articles 2 and 3:* Although you must specify a registered office in Article 2, designating a registered agent at this address in Article 3 is optional.
- *Article 5:* The duration of the LLC must be given in years (why not use 75 years?).
- *Article 6:* You must indicate a Standard Industrial Code (SIC) that best matches the primary business of your LLC. A list of codes is given in the instructions to the Articles.
- *Article 7:* Indicate whether your members have the ability to avoid automatic termination of the LLC (under a section of Minnesota law covered in the Default Continuation Rule, below). A copy of the relevant law is included with the Articles, and the terminating events under the law include the death, retirement, resignation, expulsion or bankruptcy of a member. Most LLCs will answer "Yes" here, since they will allow the LLC to continue by the unanimous vote of the remaining members. (This vote helps the LLC qualify for pass-through tax treatment with the IRS, discussed in Chapter 3, Section B3). The approval to continue the LLC must be given within 90 days of the terminating event.
- *Article 8:* Specify whether the members have the power to enter into a business continuation agreement. The agreement referred to here goes into effect *after* the legal dissolution of the LLC, and most LLCs will not give members this power.
- *Article 9:* If your LLC will own or lease agricultural or farm land, look at Minnesota Statutes Section 500.24 to make sure you meet the legal requirements before checking the "Yes" box.

Tax Status

IRS Ruling: None

State Tax Office: Department of Revenue, St. Paul, telephone 800-297-5309.

Operating Rules

Default Transfer Rule: Unless otherwise stated in Articles, by unanimous written consent of nontransferring members. [Section 322B.313.]

Default Continuation Rule: By unanimous consent of remaining members within 90 days of dissociation event; the right to vote to continue existence of an LLC must be stated in its Articles (you do this by checking a box in Article 7 of the state-provided form as explained above) or in your operating agreement. [Section 322B.80(5).]

Special Statutory Rules: The Minnesota LLC scheme presupposes management by a board of governors (management by governors is an anachronistic concept carried over by older nonprofit statutes still in force in some states). The LLC law specifies that LLCs must have one or more governors, elected by the members, who serve for an indefinite term of office. Section 322B.606 of the Minnesota LLC Act, however, recognizes that LLCs may wish to adopt membership management. That section says that the LLC members may act in the place of the governors as long as they make management decisions by unanimous vote; this is usually easy to achieve in smaller LLCs and we assume most smaller Minnesota LLCs will opt for membership management. To make sure you satisfy this vote requirement, you'll need to specify a unanimous membership vote requirement in your member-managed LLC operating agreement in Chapter 5.

By the way, you may decide to go along with the statutory scheme and opt for management by governors. Use the manager-management operating agreement in Chapter 6, but change all occurrences of the word "manager" to "governor" and "managers" to "board of governors." Although our general management provisions should work fine (in most cases, you can override the state law management rules with management rules of your own in your operating agreement), take a look at the Board of Governors section of the Minnesota LLC Act to learn more about the default statutory management scheme.

MISSISSIPPI

LLC Filing Office

Mississippi Secretary of State
Corporate Division
P.O. Box 136
Jackson, MS 39205

Telephone: 601-359-1350

Forms and Statutes: The Mississippi Secretary of State provides a fill-in Certificate of Formation to use to form a Mississippi LLC..

Certificate of Formation

Name Requirements: Must contain the words "Limited Liability Company" or the abbreviation "LLC" or "L.L.C." An available LLC name can be reserved for _ days for $25.

Filing Fee: $50, payable to the "Secretary of State"

Tax Status

IRS Ruling: None

State Tax Office: Mississippi State Tax Commission, Jackson 601-359-1141

Operating Rules

Default Transfer Rule: By unanimous consent of all nontransferring members or as provided in Certificate of Formation or operating agreement. [Section 46.]

Default Continuation Rule: Unless otherwise provided in Certificate of Formation or operating agreement, by written consent of all remaining members within 90 days after dissociation of a member. [Section 48(d).]

MISSOURI

LLC Filing Office

Secretary of State
Corporation Division
P.O. Box 778
Jefferson City, MO 65102

Telephone: 314-751-4153

Forms and Statutes: State provides fill-in-the-blanks Articles of Organization with instructions, and will send out a copy of the Missouri Limited Liability Company Act upon request at no charge. Professionals should form a Limited Liability Partnership (LLP) instead of an LLC; ask the filing office for the LLP organization form.

Articles of Organization

Name Requirements: Must contain the words "Limited Liability Company," "Limited Company" or the abbreviations "L.L.C." or "L.C." To reserve a name, submit an Application for Reservation of Name (available from the LLC filing office), together with a check for $25. To check on name availability, call 314-751-3317.

Filing Fee: $105, payable to the "Director of Revenue."

Special Instructions and Filing Requirements: Submit completed Articles in duplicate. Note these instructions for the Missouri Articles:

- *Article 6:* Indicate the rights, if any, of members to continue the existence of the LLC after a member withdraws. Typically, the remaining members are given this right—see the tear-out operating agreement dissolution provisions explained in Chapters 5 and 6. You can fill in this article as follows: "The remaining members have the power to avoid dissolution of the LLC after withdrawal of a member by their unanimous approval to continue the LLC's existence."

- *Article 8:* Make sure you check the "No" box in response to the question, "For tax purposes, is the limited liability company considered a corporation?"

Tax Status

IRS Ruling: None

State Tax Office: Department of Revenue, Jefferson City, telephone 314-751-4450.

Operating Rules

Default Transfer Rule: Unless otherwise stated in the operating agreement, by unanimous written consent of nontransferring members. [Section 347.113.]

Default Continuation Rule: As may be provided in the Articles or operating agreement, and by unanimous consent of remaining members within 90 days of a dissociation event. [Section 347.137.]

MONTANA

LLC Filing Office

Montana Secretary of State
Corporation Bureau
P.O. Box 202801
Helena, MT 59620-2801

Telephone: 406-444-3665

Forms and Statutes: State provides fill-in-the-blanks form for Articles of Organization plus LLC fact sheet booklet containing instructions on forming a Montana LLC. LLC office also provides an annual limited liability company report form.

Articles of Organization

Name Requirements: Must contain the words "Limited Liability Company" or "Limited Company" or, if formed to render licensed professional services, "Professional Limited Liability Company." Permitted abbreviations are "LLC," "L.L.C.," "LC" or "L.C." An available LLC name may be reserved for $10.

Filing Fee: $70 fee, payable to the "Montana Secretary of State."

Special Instructions and Filing Requirements: Submit original signed Articles and one copy.

Tax Status

IRS Ruling: None

State Tax Office: Department of Revenue, Helena, telephone 406-444-3696.

Operating Rules

Default Transfer Rule: Unless otherwise stated in Articles or operating agreement, by unanimous consent of nontransferring members. [Section 35-8-706.]

Default Continuation Rule: Unless otherwise provided in Articles or operating agreement, by unanimous consent of remaining members within 90 days of dissociation event. [Section 35-8-901(3).]

NEBRASKA

LLC Filing Office

Nebraska Secretary of State
Corporate Division
P.O. Box 94608
Lincoln, NE 68509-4608

Telephone: 402-471-4079

Forms and Statutes: State provides fill-in-the-blanks form, "Articles of Organization Limited Liability Company." State material does not include instructions for all items; see below for this information.

Articles of Organization

Name Requirements: Must contain the words "Limited Liability Company" or the abbreviation "L.L.C." An available LLC name may be reserved for 120 days for $20.

Filing Fee: $100 (higher for LLCs with more than $50,000 in capital), plus $3 per page, payable to the "Secretary of State." Add $10 more to request a certificate of organization from the Secretary of State.

Special Instructions and Filing Requirements: Submit original and copy of signed Articles for filing. Following is specific information for filling in the state-provided form. If a particular item in the fill-in-the-blanks form does not apply, fill in "N/A" in the blank.

- *Article 2:* State regulations say you must show a duration for the LLC that is no more than 30 years from the date of filing of the Articles. A sufficient duration is "30 years from the date of filing of these Articles."
- *Article 3:* Show the purpose of the LLC. You can simply indicate "to transact any or all lawful business for which limited liability companies may

be organized in this state."

- *Article 5:* In the first blank, show the total amount of cash all initial members will contribute as capital to the LLC. (If no cash will be contributed, show "0"; if you are unsure whether all initial cash contributions will be reflected in the stated capital account in the LLC's books, ask your tax advisor.) In the second part of this article, describe any noncash capital contributions to be made by the initial members and state the fair market value of these noncash contributions.
- *Article 6:* If LLC members will be required to make additional contributions after your LLC is formed (beyond the initial contributions listed in Article 5), list them here. Indicate the dates or circumstances when the additional contributions must be made.
- *Article 7:* If you adopt the standard language in our operating agreements, you may use this sentence to sum up the rights of members to admit additional members: "The existing members of this LLC must approve the admission of new members by a unanimous vote. Upon such approval, new members shall be accorded all rights associated with membership in this LLC." If yours is a manager-managed LLC that requires approval only by member-managers to admit new members who are transferees of former members, add a sentence here that notes this exception, as follows: "However, the nontransferring member-managers of this LLC are empowered to approve by unanimous vote the admission into membership of a transferee of a former member of this LLC."
- *Article 8:* If you adopt the standard language contained in our operating agreements, add the following sentence to sum up the rights of remaining members to continue the LLC after dissociation of a member: "The unanimous approval of the remaining members is required to continue the business of this LLC upon the death, retirement, resignation, expulsion, bankruptcy or dissolution of a member [replace the previous word "member" with "member-manager" if yours is a manager-managed LLC that chooses this option], or the occurrence of any other event that terminates the continued membership of a member [again, replace the word "member" with "member-manager" if appropriate to your manager-managed LLC] in this limited liability company."
- *Article 9:* If you are forming a manager-managed LLC, list the names and addresses of one or more initial managers of the LLC.
- *Article 10:* If you are forming a member-managed LLC, list the names and addresses of at least two initial members of the LLC.

Tax Status

IRS Ruling: None

State Tax Office: Department of Revenue, Lincoln, telephone 800-742-7474.

Operating Rules

Default Transfer Rule: By written consent of two-thirds of a majority in interest (presumably, a majority of capital and profits interests in the LLC) of nontransferring members. Statute allows operating agreement to set its own rules for the transfer of memberships, but apparently withholds voting and management rights associated with membership from transferees until the two-thirds vote of remaining members is obtained. [Section 21-2621.]

Default Continuation Rule: By unanimous consent of at least two-thirds of a majority in interest of remaining members (or any greater vote requirement stated in the Articles) within 90 days of dissociation event. [Section 21-2622(3).]

NEVADA

LLC Filing Office

Secretary of State
Limited Liability Division
State Capitol Complex
Carson City, NV 89710

Telephone: 702-687-3451

Forms and Statutes: State provides fill-in-the-blanks Articles of Organization with instructions. LLC filing office also sends out a copy of Nevada's LLC statutes at no charge.

Articles of Organization

Name Requirements: Must contain the words "Limited Liability Company," "Limited Company" or "Limited" or the abbreviations "L.L.C.," "L.C.," "LLC" or LC." The word "Company" may be abbreviated as "Co." To check name availability or reserve a name for 90 days, call the LLC filing office.

Filing Fee: $125, payable to the "Secretary of State."

Special Instructions and Filing Requirements: Articles must be acknowledged before a notary. Submit two copies of notarized Articles. Twenty-four-hour expedited filing service costs $50 extra. Here are specific instructions for completing the more complex Articles on the state form:

- *Article 3:* You may state the specific business purpose of your LLC or provide the following general statement: "Any lawful business, except banking and insurance."
- *Article 6:* If you adopt the standard language contained in our operating agreements, check the "Yes" box and insert the following sentence, which sums up the rights of members to admit additional members: "The existing members of this LLC can approve the admission of new members by a unanimous vote. Upon such approval, new members shall be accorded all rights associated with membership in this LLC." If yours is a manager-managed LLC that requires only approval by member-managers to admit new members who are transferees of former members, add a sentence noting this exception, as follows: "However, the nontransferring member-managers of this LLC are empowered to approve by unanimous vote the admission into membership of a transferee of a former member of this LLC."
- *Article 7:* If you adopt the standard language contained in our operating agreements, check the "Yes" box, and insert the following sentence to sum up the rights of remaining members to continue the LLC after dissociation of a member: "The unanimous approval of the remaining members is required to continue the business of this LLC upon the death, retirement, resignation, expulsion, bankruptcy or dissolution of a member [replace the previous word "member" with "member-manager" if yours is a manager-managed LLC that chooses this option], or the occurrence of any other event that terminates the continued membership of a member [again, replace the word "member" with "member-manager" if appropriate to your manager-managed LLC] in this limited liability company."
- *Article 8:* Most smaller LLCs can ignore this article; it contains space for additional provisions you may wish to add to the standard provisions.
- *Article 9:* Check the appropriate box to show whether you opt for member-management or manager-management. List the names and addresses of managers or members as required.

Member-managed LLCs will check the box on the last line of this article to show that all members may contract debts on behalf of the LLC. Check "No" only if your member-managed LLC will prohibit members from contracting debts on behalf of the LLC.

Tax Status

IRS Ruling: Revenue Ruling 93-30.

State Tax Office: Department of Taxation, Carson City, telephone 702-687-4892.

Operating Rules

Default Transfer Rule: By unanimous written consent of nontransferring members; this vote requirement appears to be mandatory. [Section 86:351.]

Default Continuation Rule: By unanimous consent of remaining members. This vote requirement appears unalterable and, moreover, must be stated in the Articles to be effective. (See "Special Instructions and Filing Requirements," Article 7, above.) [Section 86:491(c).]

NEW HAMPSHIRE

LLC Filing Office

New Hampshire Secretary of State
State House, Room 204
107 North Main Street
Concord, NH 03301-4989

Telephone: 603-271-3246

Forms and Statutes: State provides fill-in-the-blanks Certificate of Formation with instructions, Addendum to Certificate of Formation, copies of the New Hampshire statutes covering requirements for forming and naming LLCs, as well as the state's securities laws requirements. The state is in the process of creating other LLC forms, such as a reservation of LLC name and dissolution of LLC; call the Secretary of State at the above number to check the availability of new forms.

You can order a copy of the New Hampshire LLC Law for approximately $20 by calling the New Hampshire State Library at 603-271-2144 (it will cost approximately $10 if you go to the library and make copies yourself). As an alternative, a copy of New Hampshire's Corporations, Partnerships and Associations law, which includes the LLC statutes, is available from Butterworth Legal Publishers in Orford, New Hampshire, for $30 (603-353-4223).

Certificate of Formation

Name Requirements: Must contain the words "Limited Liability Company" or the abbreviations "LLC" or "L.L.C." The state specifically says that an additional space may be inserted between the letters or periods in each of these abbreviations—namely, "L. L. C." and "L L C" are also allowed. The name may contain the words "company," "association," "club," "foundation," "fund," "institute," "society," "union," "syndicate," "limited" or "trust" or abbreviations of these words. An available LLC name may be reserved for 120 days for $15. The name of a professional LLC in New Hampshire must end with the words "Professional Limited Liability Company" or the abbreviation "P.L.L.C."

Filing Fee: $85, payable to the "Secretary of State." This fee includes $50 for filing an Addendum form, discussed in "Special Instructions and Filing Requirements," below.

Annual Fees: LLCs must pay an annual report fee of $100.

Special Instructions and Filing Requirements: When completing the fill-in-the-blanks Certificate of Formation, keep the following points in mind:

- *Second Article:* Be precise and state the nature of your LLC's specific business—for example, "real estate sales" or "automotive repair." You may add a general statement to your specific purposes if you wish: "...and to engage in any lawful businesses permitted to limited liability companies under state law." New Hampshire LLCs may be formed for any lawful business purpose except banking, the construction or maintenance of railroads (unless a special permit is granted), the business of making contracts for the payment of money (loan agreements) or the business of a trust, surety, indemnity or safe deposit company.
- *Fifth Article:* Insert the word "None" in this blank if, as is usually the case, you do not want to specify an automatic dissolution date for your LLC.
- *Sixth Article:* Most smaller LLCs—those without specially-designated managers—will insert the words "is not" in the blank in this article.

Submit original and copy of signed Certificate for filing. You must include an Addendum to Certificate of Formation form that is signed by all LLC members in the presence of a notary. This form states that the offer and sale of interests in the LLC will be made according to specific New Hampshire security law requirements. Most smaller LLCs will be able to fill in Item A on the form, which shows that the LLC is eligible for an exemption from the New Hampshire securities laws. Otherwise, you must complete Item B. You may need to call the New Hampshire Division of Securities Regulation or a lawyer for help in preparing this form.

Tax Status

IRS Ruling: None

State Tax Office: Revenue Administration Department, Concord, telephone 603-271-6121.

Operating Rules

Default Transfer Rule: Unless otherwise stated in operating agreement, by unanimous consent of nontransferring members. [Section 304-C:46.]

Default Continuation Rule: Unless otherwise provided in operating agreement, by unanimous consent of remaining members within 90 days of dissociation event. [Section 304-C:50(IV).]

NEW JERSEY

LLC Filing Office

Department of State
Division of Commercial Recording
CN 308
Trenton, NJ 08625

Telephone: 609-530-6400

Forms and Statutes: Provides fill-in-the-blanks "Certificate of Formation, Limited Liability Company," with instructions for completing each item.

Certificate of Formation

Name Requirements: Must include "Limited Liability Company" or the abbreviation "L.L.C."

Filing Fee: Check or money order for $100, payable to "Secretary of State." Expedited filing is $10 extra.

Special Instructions and Filing Requirements: Type the information in the blanks on the state-provided form. File original and one copy of Certificate; file-stamped copy will be returned to you.

Tax Status

IRS Ruling: None

State Tax Office: Division of Taxation, Trenton, telephone 609-292-5185.

Operating Rules

Default Transfer Rule: By unanimous written consent of nontransferring members and by any other procedure provided in the operating agreement. [Section 42:2B-46.]

Default Continuation Rule: By unanimous consent of remaining members within 90 days of dissociation event or by any other procedure stated in operating agreement. [Section 42:2B-48(d).]

NEW MEXICO

LLC Filing Office

State Corporation Commission
Corporation Department
Chartered Documents Bureau
P.O. Drawer 1269
Santa Fe, NM 87504-1269

Telephone: 505-827-4511

Forms and Statutes: Provides fill-in-the-blanks Articles of Organization with instructions.

Articles of Organization

Name Requirements: Must contain the words "Limited Liability Company" or "Limited Company." The word "Limited" may be abbreviated as "Ltd." and the word "Company" may be abbreviated as "Co." An available LLC name may be reserved for 120 days for $20.

Filing Fee: $50, payable to the "State Corporation Commission."

Special Instructions and Filing Requirements: Member-managed LLCs should leave Article Four of the state-provided Articles of Organization blank. All LLCs can leave Articles Five and Six of the form blank. Submit the original and one copy of Articles for filing.

A signed affidavit of the LLC's initial registered agent showing acceptance of the position must be included; this form is provided in the materials mailed by the LLC filing office. The affidavit must be signed by the agent in the presence of a notary.

Tax Status

IRS Ruling: None

State Tax Office: Taxation & Revenue Department, Santa Fe, telephone 505-827-0700.

Operating Rules

Default Transfer Rule: Unless otherwise stated in Articles or operating agreement, by unanimous written consent of nontransferring members. [Section 53-19-33.]

Default Continuation Rule: By unanimous written consent of remaining members within 90 days of dissociation event, according to a right to do so (presumably stated in Articles or operating agreement). This unanimous voting approval rule appears to be mandatory. [Section 53-19-39(3).]

NEW YORK

LLC Filing Office

Department of State
Bureau of Corporations
162 Washington Avenue
Albany, NY 12231-0001

Telephone: 518-473-2492

Forms and Statutes: Upon request, state provides sample Articles of Organization with instructions and a copy of the New York Limited Liability Company Law at no charge. If you wish to change a general or limited partnership to a New York LLC, the state provides a sample Certificate of Conversion form instead. (If converting a limited partnership, you must also file a certificate of cancellation for the limited partnership with the Department of State.)

Note for Professionals: Use the state-provided sample Articles of Organization for a Professional Service Company if your LLC will perform licensed legal or medical professional services. Other licensed professionals, such as those licensed in the field of education, also need to use this special form. Call the state board that regulates your profession to see if you must form a professional service company, rather than a regular LLC, under Section 1203 of the New York Limited Liability Company Law. If you must form a professional service company, use the state's professional LLC Articles form.

Articles of Organization

Name Requirements: Must contain the words "Limited Liability Company" or the abbreviations "LLC" or "L.L.C." An available LLC name may be reserved for 60 days for $20.

Words related to the finance, banking, trust or insurance business cannot be used without prior approval (see Section 204 of the New York LLC Law). Here is a partial list of such restricted words: acceptance, annuity, assurance, bank, benefit, bond, casualty, endowment, exchange, fidelity, finance, guaranty, indemnity, insurance, investment, loan, mortgage, savings, surety, title, trust, underwriter.

Filing Fee: $200, payable to the "Department of State." Fee must be paid by postal money order, certified check or attorney's check not to exceed $500. Don't send a personal check.

Special Instructions and Filing Requirements: Use the state-supplied sample Articles of Organization form as a guide to word process or type your own form. Following are some recommendations on what to include in your Articles.

You may omit these sample articles:

- *Third Article*—automatic dissolution date of LLC
- *Fifth Article*—street address of registered agent (the Second Article designates the secretary of state as the LLC agent for service), and
- *Eighth Article*—which states that one or more members of the LLC will be personally liable for LLC debts!

Use the sample Sixth Article, but insert "N/A" in the blank if you do not wish to delay the filing date to a date in the future. Most smaller LLCs will use and check the first box of the sample Seventh Article to show that the LLC will be managed by one or more members. If, however, you have decided to form a manager-managed LLC, you will likely find the third box the most appropriate choice (managed by one or more managers).

Make sure you consecutively number your final Articles; your numbering will differ from the sample Articles if you omit any sample Articles as suggested.

You must also prepare a facing sheet to attach to the first page of your original Articles (this is a New York Department of State requirement for all filings). This sheet should have the title:

ARTICLES OF ORGANIZATION
OF
NAME OF YOUR LLC

Also include the following line at the bottom of the facing page: "Send receipt for filing to: [name and address of one of your LLC organizers]."

If you reserved your LLC name prior to filing your Articles, include a copy of the certificate of name reservation you received earlier from the Department of State.

Tax Status

IRS Ruling: None

State Tax Office: Taxation & Finance Department, Albany, telephone 518-438-8581.

Operating Rules

Default Transfer Rule: Unless otherwise stated in operating agreement, by unanimous vote or written consent of a majority in interest (under Section 102(o), this is a majority of profits interests unless the operating agreement contains a different definition) of nontransferring members. [Section 604.]

Default Continuation Rule: Unless otherwise provided in operating agreement, by vote or written consent of majority in interest (majority of profits interests) of remaining members within 180 days of a dissociation event. [Section 701(d).]

NORTH CAROLINA

LLC Filing Office

North Carolina Department of the Secretary of State
Corporations Division
300 North Salisbury Street
Raleigh, NC 27603-5909

Telephone: 701-328-4284

Forms and Statutes: Provides fill-in-the-blanks Articles of Organization.

Articles of Organization

Name Requirements: Must end with the words "Limited Liability Company" or the abbreviation "LLC" or "L.L.C." The words "Limited" and "Company" may be abbreviated to "Ltd." and "Co." An available LLC name may be reserved for $10.

Filing Fee: $100, payable to "Secretary of State."

Annual Fees: LLCs must pay an annual report fee of $200.

Special Instructions and Filing Requirements: Submit original and one copy of state Articles form. Following are instructions for specific Articles:

- *Article 2:* Specify the dissolution date of the LLC. You must indicate a specific date here, though it can be far into the future, such as December 31, 2099.
- *Article 7:* Member-managed LLCs (the majority of smaller LLCs) should check the first box. LLCs adopting a management structure should check the second box.

Tax Status

IRS Ruling: None

State Tax Office: Department of Revenue, Raleigh, telephone 919-733-3991.

Operating Rules

Default Transfer Rule: Unless otherwise stated in Articles or operating agreement, by unanimous vote at a members' meeting or by unanimous written consent of nontransferring members. [Section 57C-5-04.]

Default Continuation Rule: By unanimous written consent of all members (the remaining members *and* the dissociated member or the member's successor) within 90 days of dissociation event, or by a separate procedure specified in the Articles or operating agreement. [Section 57C-6-01(4).]

NORTH DAKOTA

LLC Filing Office

North Dakota Secretary of State
Corporations Division
60 East Boulevard Avenue
Bismarck, ND 58505-0500

Telephone: 701-328-4284

Forms and Statutes: State provides sample Articles of Organization form that you can use to prepare your own form, along with a Registered Agent Consent to Serve form and a brochure summarizing state LLC requirements. You may order the North Dakota LLC Act from the LLC filing office for $27. LLCs formed to render licensed professional services should obtain and file Articles of Organization for a Professional Limited Liability Company; a sample form is available from the LLC filing office together with a separate law summary brochure.

Articles of Organization

Name Requirements: Must contain the words "Limited Liability Company" or the abbreviation "L.L.C." Cannot contain the words "bank," "banker" or "banking." An available LLC name may be reserved for $10.

Filing Fee: $135 ($125 for filing Articles, plus $10 for filing Registered Agent Consent to Serve form), payable to the "Secretary of State."

Special Instructions and Filing Requirements: Submit completed Registered Agent Consent to Serve form with Articles.

Follow these guidelines when preparing your Articles:

- *Article V:* The duration of the legal existence of the LLC stated in the Articles of Organization cannot be longer than 30 years from the date the Articles are filed.
- *Article VI:* LLCs will normally state that members have the right to continue the existence of the LLC after termination of a member's membership. Make sure you type out the full sentence here, including the reference in the sample article to Section 10-32-109. Specify that the remaining members have the right to continue the existence of the LLC by giving dissolution avoidance consent. (For operating agreement provisions giving members these rights, see the dissolution provisions covered in Chapters 5 and 6.)
- *Article VII:* You may show that the members have the power enter into a business continuation agreement (an agreement among themselves to continue the business of the LLC in another form after the LLC dissolves).This statement simply says that your members have the power to enter into such an agreement if they later choose to do so.

Note that special requirements apply to LLCs formed for banking, insurance, farming or ranching; see the Secretary of State LLC summary brochure.

Tax Status

IRS Ruling: None

State Tax Office: Office of State Tax Commission, Bismarck, telephone 701-328-3700.

Operating Rules

Default Transfer Rule: By unanimous written consent of nontransferring members. This approval rule appears to be mandatory. [Section 10-32-32(2).]

Default Continuation Rule: By unanimous consent of remaining members within 90 days of a dissociation event—the right of the members to avoid dissolution must be stated in the Articles (see "Special Instructions and Filing Requirements" for Article VI, above). [Section 10-32-109(1).]

OHIO

LLC Filing Office

Ohio Secretary of State
30 East Broad Street, 14th Floor
Columbus, OH 43266-0418

Telephone: 614-466-3910

Forms and Statutes: State provides fill-in-the-blanks Articles of Organization (Form LCA) with instructions, along with an Original Appointment of Agent (form LCO).

Articles of Organization

Name Requirements: Must contain the words "Limited Liability Company" or "Limited" or the abbreviation "Ltd" or "Ltd." Call the LLC filing office for name availability. Names may be reserved for 60 days for a $5 fee.

Filing Fee: $85 fee, payable to the "Ohio Secretary of State."

Special Instructions and Filing Requirements: In the Second Article, you may show a "perpetual duration" for your LLC (alternatively, if you leave this Article blank, the law assumes your LLC has a perpetual duration). In the Third Article, list the address where members of the public may request copies of the LLC's operating agreement (this document must be made available for public inspection)—normally, the principal address of the LLC. At least two people—usually members—must sign the Articles.

You need to file original Articles only (copies are not required). Attach a completed and signed Original Appointment of Agent (form LCO) when filing Articles.

Tax Status

IRS Ruling: None

State Tax Office: Taxation Department, Columbus, telephone 614-466-2166.

Operating Rules

Default Transfer Rule: Unless otherwise stated in Articles or operating agreement, by unanimous consent of nontransferring members. [Section 1705:20.]

Default Continuation Rule: By unanimous consent of remaining members and as may be stated in the operating agreement. [Section 1705:43(4).]

OKLAHOMA

LLC Filing Office

Oklahoma Secretary of State
101 State Capitol
Oklahoma City, OK 73105-4897

Telephone: 405-521-3911

Forms and Statutes: Provides sample Articles of Organization with instructions.

Articles of Organization

Name Requirements: Must contain the words "Limited Liability Company" or "Limited Company" or the abbreviations "L.L.C." or "L.C." The word "Limited" may be abbreviated as "Ltd." and "Company" may be abbreviated as "Co." Call the LLC filing office to check name availability. An available LLC name may be reserved for 60 days for $10.

Filing Fee: $100, payable to the "Secretary of State."

Special Instructions and Filing Requirements: An ending date of the LLC's existence must be given in the Articles (perhaps December 31, 2099). Send one signed original Articles plus one copy.

Tax Status

IRS Ruling: Revenue Ruling 93-92.

State Tax Office: Tax Commission, Oklahoma City, telephone 405-521-2035.

Operating Rules

Default Transfer Rule: Either as stated in Articles or operating agreement, or by consent of majority of membership interests (this term seems to mean a majority of the percentage interests held by all members, including the transferring member) in writing or by vote at a membership meeting. [Section 2035.]

Default Continuation Rule: Unless otherwise provided in Articles or operating agreement, by unanimous consent of remaining members. The statute does not mention a time limit for obtaining this consent, and this vote requirement appears mandatory. [Section 2037(4).]

OREGON

LLC Filing Office

Oregon Secretary of State
Corporate Division
255 Capitol Street, NE, Suite 151
Salem, OR 97310-1327

Telephone: 503-986-2200

Forms and Statutes: State provides sample Articles of Organization with instructions, and a copy of the Oregon Limited Liability Company Act upon request (the Secretary of State may provide a copy of the Act free or for a $5 fee).

Articles of Organization

Name Requirements: Must contain the words "Limited Liability Company" or the abbreviation "L.L.C." May not contain the words "Cooperative," "Limited Partnership" or the abbreviation "L.P." An available LLC name may be reserved for 120 days for $10.

Filing Fee: $40, payable by check to the "Corporation Division" or by charging to a credit card (include card information at the bottom of Articles of Organization).

Annual Fees: Oregon LLCs must pay an annual fee of $30.

Special Instructions and Filing Requirements: In Article 1, specify the Standard Industrial Code of the LLC's principal business activity (SIC codes are listed on back of the state-provided Articles form). Most organizers will check the box in Article 2 that specifies a perpetual duration for the LLC. The box in Article 6 should not be checked unless the LLC will be managed by managers.

Articles may be filed by fax (503-378-4381) if paying by credit card. If filed by mail, send one signed original plus one copy.

Tax Status

IRS Ruling: None

State Tax Office: Department of Revenue, Salem, telephone 503-945-8738.

Operating Rules

Default Transfer Rule: Unless otherwise stated in Articles or operating agreement, by unanimous consent of nontransferring members. [Section 63.255.]

Default Continuation Rule: Unless otherwise provided in Articles or operating agreement, by consent of remaining members within 120 days of dissociation event. This right to vote to continue the legal life of the LLC after the dissociation of a member *must* be granted to members in the Articles or operating agreement. The statute does not impose a default vote rule—your continuation provision is expected to do this. Finally, the statute says that the admission of an assignee as a member into the LLC, in and of itself, constitutes the requisite consent of the remaining members—no actual vote or written consent is technically necessary. However, we think obtaining and recording such formal consent to the admission of a transferee of a former member is the best way to go. [Section 163.621(4).]

PENNSYLVANIA

LLC Filing Office

Commonwealth of Pennsylvania
Department of State
Corporation Bureau
P.O. Box 8722
Harrisburg, PA 17105-8722

Telephone: 717-787-1057

Forms and Statutes: State provides fill-in-the-blanks "Certificate of Organization—Domestic Limited Liability Company" with instructions, as well as an LLC office Docketing Statement. Call the Legislative Reference Bureau of the Pennsylvania Legislature to request a free copy of Pennsylvania's Limited Liability Company Act (passed in December 1994) at 717-787-7385.

Certificate of Organization

Name Requirements: Must contain the words "Company," "Limited" or "Limited Liability Company," or an abbreviation of one of these three choices. The statute does not provide examples of acceptable abbreviations for these words—our guess is that "Ltd." and "Co." can be used, but not "Liab."

Filing Fee: $100 fee, payable to the "Department of State."

Annual Fees: An annual registration fee of $300, payable to the Department of State.

Special Instructions and Filing Requirements: Here's how most LLCs will complete these blanks on the state-provided form:

- *Article 4:* Smaller LLCs normally will not issue membership certificates and can strike out this language.
- *Article 5:* Most smaller LLCs will be managed by members and should strike out this language.
- *Article 6:* Insert "Not Applicable" in the blank unless you want the LLC office to file your Articles on a particular day after your Articles are received by the office for filing. This would only be applicable if you want to start the legal life of your LLC on a particular day—for example, the first of the month.
- *Article 7:* Strike out the language of this article unless you are forming an LLC to render licensed professional services. In that case, you may need to submit written approval of the state professional board that oversees your profession with your Articles. Such a requirement applies to the following types of practices: chiropractic, dentistry, law, medicine and surgery, optometry, osteopathic medicine and surgery, podiatric medicine, public accounting, psychology and veterinarian medicine. It may also apply to others—so if you are forming an LLC to practice a licensed profession, check with your state board and make sure you can form a Pennsylvania LLC and how to deal with this Article (whether to strike it out or fill it in).

Submit original Articles and three copies of the LLC office Docketing Statement. Also enclose a stamped, self-addressed postcard (or envelope containing a copy of the Articles) to obtain a receipt (or file-stamped copy of your Articles) from the LLC filing office.

Tax Status

IRS Ruling: None

State Tax Office: Department of Revenue, Harrisburg, telephone 717-783-3682.

Operating Rules

Default Transfer Rule: Unless otherwise stated in Articles or operating agreement, by unanimous written consent of nontransferring members. [Section 8924.]

Default Continuation Rule: Either as provided in operating agreement or by unanimous consent of remaining members within 90 days of dissociation event. [Section Sec. 8971(4).]

RHODE ISLAND

LLC Filing Office

Rhode Island Secretary of State
Corporations Division
100 North Main Street
Providence, RI 02903-1335

Telephone: 401-277-3040

Forms and Statutes: Provides fill-in-the-blanks form for Articles of Organization (Form LLC-1A).

Articles of Organization

Name Requirements: Must *end* with the words "Limited Liability Company" or the abbreviations "LLC" or "L.L.C." (upper or lower case are specifically permitted). Call the LLC filing office to check name availability. An available name may be reserved for 120 days for a fee of $50.

Filing Fee: $50, payable to the "Secretary of State."

Special Instructions and Filing Requirements: The state provides a second form titled "Duplicate Articles of Organization" that contains the same information as the original Articles of Organization. Fill out and sign both of these forms and file them with the LLC office.

Follow these guidelines when preparing your Articles:

- *Third Article:* In the blank, specify a month, date and year upon which the LLC will automatically dissolve. A date far into the future is OK, such as December 31, 2099.
- *Fourth Article:* Have the person who is named as registered agent—usually a member—sign on the line at the bottom of this article.
- *Fifth Article:* Organizers will check the second box, which indicates that the LLC wishes to be treated as a partnership for purposes of federal taxation.

Annual Fees: An annual report form must be filed each year with the LLC office with a check for the annual filing fee of $50.

Tax Status

IRS Ruling: Revenue Ruling 93-81.

State Tax Office: Division of Taxation, Providence, telephone 401-277-3934.

Operating Rules

Default Transfer Rule: Unless otherwise stated in operating agreement, by unanimous consent of nontransferring members obtained by written consent or vote at members' meeting. [Section 7-16-36.]

Default Continuation Rule: No default continuation rule given in the LLC Act. An LLC must provide its own rule in its Articles or operating agreement to avoid dissolution of the LLC upon dissociation of a member. [Section 7-16-39(d).]

SOUTH CAROLINA

LLC Filing Office

South Carolina Secretary of State
Corporations Department
P.O. Box 11350
Columbia, SC 29211

Telephone: 803-734-2158

Forms and Statutes: State LLC office provides fill-in-the-blanks Articles of Organization, Articles of Organization for Professional LLC and other LLC forms. Here are two ways to order forms:

- Call Kitco, a legal forms supplier, at 800-351-1244. Kitco provides printed fill-in-the-blank Articles (as well as state tax and other business forms) for a fee.
- Send a check to the LLC filing office for $2 and ask for LLC forms on an IBM PC compatible computer disk (WordPerfect 5.1 format). Articles of Organization with instructions are in the ARTICLES.LLC file. Forms for LLC name reservation as well as Articles of Organization of Professional Service LLC are also included on disk.

Articles of Organization

Name Requirements: Must include "Limited Liability Company" or the abbreviation "LLC." An LLC name may be reserved for 120 days by filing two copies of an Application to Reserve an LLC Name along with a $25 fee.

Filing Fee: $110 fee, payable to the "South Carolina Secretary of State."

Special Instructions and Filing Requirements: File original and one copy of Articles. In Article 3 of the state form, you must provide a real date upon which the LLC will dissolve (unless, of course, you amend your Articles to extend the date just before you reach it). A date we favor is December 31, 2099.

Tax Status

IRS Ruling: None

State Tax Office: Tax Commission, Columbia, telephone 803-737-9881.

Operating Rules

Default Transfer Rule: By nontransferring members' unanimous written consent—or other method of consent specified in operating agreement (for example, by vote at a members' meeting). This unanimous approval rule is mandatory, and the statute specifically allows a member to withhold consent to a transfer of another member's interest "for any reason whatsoever." [Section 33-43-706.]

Default Continuation Rule: By written consent of a majority in interest (defined in this section of law as a majority of capital, profits and loss interests in the LLC) of remaining members within 90 days of a dissociation event. The state statute allows operating agreement to require a greater than majority in interest approval of remaining members, but does not allow other changes to this default statutory rule. [Section 33-43-901(C).]

SOUTH DAKOTA

LLC Filing Office

South Dakota Secretary of State
500 East Capitol
Pierre, SD 57501-5070

Telephone: 605-773-4845

Forms and Statutes: State provides fill-in-the-blanks Articles of Organization for Domestic Limited Liability Company with instructions, plus a copy of the South Dakota Limited Liability Company Act (Chapter 47-34 of the South Dakota Codified Laws) upon request at no charge.

Articles of Organization

Name Requirements: Must end with the words "Limited Liability Company" or the abbreviation "L.L.C."

Filing Fee: $50, if the initial LLC capital is $50,000 or less, payable to the "Secretary of State." Fees increase if the LLC has additional capital, as follows: $50,001 to $100,000 capital—$100 filing fee; in excess of $100,000 capital—filing fee of $100 for the first $100,000 plus 50 cents for each additional $1,000 of capital.

Annual Fees: South Dakota LLCs pay an annual tax of $50 each January 2nd. A penalty of $50 is added if not paid by February 1st.

Special Instructions and Filing Requirements: Here's how to complete some of the less straightforward articles:

- *Article 6:* Articles must show the amount of cash and value of any property contributed as initial capital.
- *Article 7:* If additional contributions are required (normally they are not), specify it here.
- *Article 8:* Show the membership voting rule to admit new members. If you adopt the standard language contained in our operating agreements, the following sentence can be used to sum up the rights of members to admit additional members:

"The existing members of this LLC must approve the admission of new members by a unanimous vote. Upon such approval, new members shall be accorded all rights associated with membership in this LLC." If yours is a manager-managed LLC that requires only approval by member-managers to admit new members who are transferees of former members, add a sentence noting this exception, as follows: "However, the nontransferring member-managers of this LLC are empowered to approve by unanimous vote the admission into membership of a transferee of a former member of this LLC."

- *Article 9:* If you adopt the standard language contained in our operating agreements, you can use the following sentence to sum up the rights of remaining members to continue the LLC after dissociation of a member: "The unanimous approval of the remaining members is required to continue the business of this LLC upon the death, retirement, resignation, expulsion, bankruptcy or dissolution of a member [replace the previous word "member" with "member-manager" if your manager-managed LLC chooses this option], or the occurrence of any other event that terminates the continued membership of a member [again, replace the word "member" with "member-manager" if appropriate to your manager-managed LLC] in this limited liability company."
- *Articles 10 and 11:* Member-managed LLCs should complete Article 11 (and skip Article 10). Manager-managed LLCs should do the opposite.

Original Articles must be signed by two or more members in the presence of a notary. Send the original Articles and one copy to the LLC filing office. Make sure the registered agent named in the Articles signs the consent portion of the form (on the second page of the form).

Tax Status

IRS Ruling: None

State Tax Office: Department of Revenue, Pierre, telephone 605-773-3311.

Operating Rules

Default Transfer Rule: By unanimous written consent of nontransferring members; this rule appears to be mandatory. [Section 47-34-21.]

Default Continuation Rule: If the right to do so is granted in the Articles (see Special Instructions and Filing Requirements, Article 9, above), by unanimous consent of remaining members. No time limit for obtaining this approval is specified in the statute. [Section 47-34-29(3).]

TENNESSEE

LLC Filing Office

Tennessee Department of State
Corporations Section
18th Floor, James Polk Building
Nashville, TN 37243-0306

Telephone: 615-741-0537

Forms and Statutes: State provides fill-in-the-blanks Articles of Organization with instructions, plus copy of Tennessee Limited Liability Company Act upon request. Existing general or limited partnerships convert to a Tennessee LLC by filing special Form SS-4248, Articles of Conversion of Limited Liability Company.

Articles of Organization

Name Requirements: Must contain the words "Limited Liability Company" or the abbreviations "L.L.C." or "LLC." An available LLC name may be reserved for $10.

Filing Fee: $50 per LLC member as of the date of filing, with a minimum fee of $300 (maximum fee is $3,000). Make check payable to the "Tennessee Secretary of State."

Special Instructions and Filing Requirements: Here's how to complete some of the less straightforward articles:

- *Article 5:* Check the appropriate box to indicate whether your LLC is member-managed (this is normally the case) or "board managed." In Tennessee, persons selected to a special management team are called "governors," not "managers" as is normally the case. If you plan to select a special management team to run your LLC (and will adopt the management operating agreement covered in Chapter 6), check the "board managed" box. (By the way, in the Tennessee LLC Act, the term "manager" is used to refer to two special officer—not management—positions. For more on this odd use of LLC nomenclature, see "Special Statutory Rules," below.)

- *Article 9:* Section 48A-16-101(b) of the LLC Act says that an LLC cannot expel a member unless the power to do so is granted in the Articles (by checking the appropriate box in this article). Our operating agreements do not specifically provide for the expulsion of a member, but you may decide you want your LLC to have this power—if so, check the first box. In this case, you probably will want to add language to your operating agreement (which you will prepare as part of Chapters 5 or 6), which specifies the procedure and, perhaps, the grounds for the expulsion of a member from your LLC. If you don't want your LLC to have the power to expel a member, check the second box in this article.
- *Article 10:* Insert "Perpetual" unless you wish to insert a date or term of years to limit the duration of your LLC.
- *Article 12:* This article asks if the members or other parties to a contribution agreement have preemptive rights. Generally, this means that the existing members have first rights to acquire additional interests in the LLC by making additional capital contributions. In other words, the existing member can preempt others who may want to purchase an interest in the LLC. Under Section 48A-21-101 of the Tennessee LLC Act, members and other parties to contribution agreements cannot be given preemptive rights unless you allow them in your Articles (by checking the "Yes" box in this Article). Smaller LLCs will normally not provide for preemptive rights in their Operating Agreement, and will check "No" here. Our tear-out agreements do not contain preemptive rights language.

Articles should be signed by a member or manager; show the person's title as member or manager in the line marked "signer's capacity." Submit original of completed signed Articles for filing.

Tax Status

IRS Ruling: None

State Tax Office: Department of Revenue, Nashville, telephone 615-741-2461.

Operating Rules

Default Transfer Rule: Unless the Articles allow transfers by a majority of the voting power of the LLC (including the votes of parties to any contribution agreements), by unanimous written consent of nontransferring members (including the consent of parties to any contribution agreements). [Section 48A-18-102(b).]

Default Continuation Rule: Unless Articles allow the LLC to be continued by a vote of a majority in interest (apparently not defined in the LLC Act) of remaining members, by unanimous consent of remaining members. Approval must be obtained within 90 days of a dissociation event. [Sections 48A-44-101(a)(5) and 48A-16-101; also see 48A-38-105.]

If yours is a member-managed LLC, you have more leeway to vary the above default continuation rule. Note, however, that every member must be an agent of the LLC (this is how it normally works unless you say otherwise in your Articles). In this event, you are not restricted to a majority in interest vote requirement as stated above. You may go even lower or come up with an entirely different approval vote or procedure for continuing the business of the LLC after a member is dissociated.

Special Statutory Rules: Tennessee has an unusual statutory scheme and nomenclature for management of the LLC. As with all other states, it allows for management of the LLC by all members—you elect this standard management option by checking the "Member Managed" box in Article 5 of the state-provided Articles of Organization.

Now, here is where it begins to get complicated. Member-managed (and other) LLCs are expected to appoint at least two "managers"; a chief manager and a secretary. In reality, these are officer—not manager—positions. The chief manager functions as President of the LLC, and is charged under Section 48A-41-102 with making sure that management orders are carried out (a typical CEO day-to-day responsibility). The Secretary is charged with maintaining the records of the LLC (again, a typical day-to-day officer job).

The people who can be selected in place of the members to manage the LLC are not called managers as they are in most other states—they are called "governors" and they are selected to serve on the board of governors. If you want to select a special management team not consisting of all members, you check the "board managed" box in Article 5 of the state form as explained above.

Where does this nonstandard statutory terminology leave you when selecting and filling in the tear-out operating agreements in this book? Here's what we suggest.

If you opt, as most smaller LLCs do, for member-management, the standard tear-out operating agreement covered in Chapter 5 will work fine for you, with two minor changes.

First, make it clear in your agreement that your members are taking the place of the board of governors as allowed under law in managing your LLC. To do this, add a second sentence to Provision II(3), Management, so that it reads in full as follows (the new sentence is italicized):

(3) Management: This LLC shall be managed exclusively by all of its members. *Any action that would require the action of the Board of Governors under law shall be made by the members.*

Second, change Provision VII (1), Officers, of the standard agreement so that it requires the two "manager" (officer) positions to be filled as required under the LLC Act. You do this by replacing the first sentence with the italicized material below:

(1) Officers: *The LLC shall designate persons to fill the officer positions of chief manager and secretary. The duties associated with these positions shall include those responsibilities listed under law for these officers, plus any additional duties the members shall prescribe for these offices. The duties of the office of chief manager shall include seeing that all orders and resolutions of the members are carried into effect. The duties of the office of secretary shall include keeping accurate membership records and records of the proceedings of meetings of members of this LLC. This LLC may have such other officers, such as President, Vice President and Treasurer, with such duties as the members shall decide.*

Persons who fill these positions need not be members of the LLC. Such positions may be compensated or noncompensated according to the nature and extent of the services rendered for the LLC as a part of the duties of each office. Ministerial services only as a part of any officer position will normally not be compensated, such as the performance of officer duties specified in this agreement, but any officer may be reimbursed by the LLC for out-of-pocket expenses paid by the officer in carrying out the duties of his or her office.

If you form a manager-managed LLC by preparing the management operating agreement covered in Chapter 6, make the following changes to the tear-out agreement.

First, change Provision II(1) so to make it clear that your managers will act as "governors" under Tennessee law (again, changes are noted below in italics):

(1) Management by Managers: This LLC will be managed by the managers listed below. *Managers shall function under law as the "governors" of this LLC as this term is defined and used in the Tennessee Limited liability Company Act.* All managers who are also members of this LLC are designated as "members"; nonmember managers are designated as "nonmembers."

Second, add a new paragraph to the Officer provision—Provision VIII(1)—in your agreement, as shown in italics below:

(1) Officers: The managers of this LLC may designate one or more officers, such as a President, Vice President, Secretary and Treasurer. Persons who fill these positions need not be members or managers of the LLC. Such positions may be compensated or noncompensated according to the nature and extent of the services rendered for the LLC as a part of the duties of each office. Ministerial services only as a part of any officer position will normally not be compensated, such as the performance of officer duties specified in this agreement, but any officer may be reimbursed by the LLC for out-of-pocket expenses paid by the officer in carrying out the duties of his or her office.

The LLC shall designate persons to fill the officer positions of chief manager and secretary. The chief manager shall be an officer, not a "manager" of this LLC as the term "manager" is used in Provision II(1) of this agreement, and shall not, as chief manager, take part in the management of this LLC. The duties associated with these officer positions shall include those responsibilities listed under law for these officers, plus any additional duties the managers shall prescribe for these offices. The duties of the office of chief manager shall include seeing that all orders and resolutions of the managers are carried into effect. The duties of the office of secretary shall include keeping accurate membership records and records of the proceedings of the meetings of members and managers of this LLC.

TEXAS

LLC Filing Office

Texas Secretary of State
Statutory Filings Division
Corporations Section
P.O. Box 13697
Austin, TX 78711-3697

Telephone: 512-463-5586

Forms and Statutes: State provides guidelines to draft your own Articles of Organization. See "Special Instructions and Filing Requirements" below. For $25, you can order the Filing Guide from the Corporations Section, which contains instructions and other forms for Texas LLCs, corporations and partnerships.

Articles of Organization

Name Requirements: Must contain the words "Limited Liability Company" or "Limited Company" or the abbreviations "L.L.C.," "LLC," "LC," "L.C." or "Ltd. Co." Name availability may be checked over the phone by calling 512-463-5555. An available LLC name may be reserved for 120 days for $25.

Filing Fee: $200, payable to the "Secretary of State."

Special Instructions and Filing Requirements: Submit an original Articles of Organization and one copy for filing. See Chapter 4, Section E5, for an example that uses the Texas guidelines to show you how to prepare Articles of Organization to file with the Secretary of State.

Tax Status

IRS Ruling: None

State Tax Office: Texas LLCs are subject to payment of a state franchise tax. For information, call the Comptroller of Public Accounts in Austin at 800-252-5555.

Operating Rules

Default Transfer Rule: By unanimous consent of nontransferring members or as the operating agreement may provide. [Section 4.07.]

Default Continuation Rule: By unanimous vote of remaining members within 90 days of a dissociation event. Articles or operating agreement may specify a different vote requirement or date by which the vote must be made, or operating agreement may say that the dissociation of a member does not trigger dissolution of LLC at all. [Section 6.01(5).]

Special Statutory Rules: Texas LLC law refers to operating provisions adopted by an LLC as its "regulations." [Section 2.09.] In other words, references in the Texas LLC Act to "regulations" mean the provisions contained in your operating agreement. An amendment of Articles to continue the LLC's existence beyond a duration ending date for the LLC specified in the Articles must be filed with the Secretary of State within three years of the duration ending date. [Section 6.01(B).]

UTAH

LLC Filing Office

Department of Commerce
Division of Corporations & Commercial Code
160 East 300 South
P.O. Box 45801
Salt Lake City, UT 84145-0801

Telephone: 801-530-4849

Forms and Statutes: State provides sample Articles of Organization for member-managed LLCs and a photocopy of Utah Limited Liability Company Act on request (typically at no charge). See "Special Instructions and Filing Requirements," below.

Articles of Organization

Name Requirements: Must contain "Limited Liability Company," "Limited Company" or "L.C."

Filing Fee: $75, payable to "State of Utah."

Special Instructions and Filing Requirements: To prepare Articles, follow the format and content of the sample LLC Articles provided by the Division of Corporations.

If you opt for manager-management, rather than member-management, change sample Article 7 as follows (changes are noted in italics):

*7. Management of the Limited Liability Company **by Managers**; Names and Street Address of **Each Manager**: The limited liability company is to be managed by managers.* The name and street address of each manager of the limited liability company are as follows: [List name and address of one or more managers].

Submit signed original and one photocopy of the Articles. At least two members or managers must sign the Articles.

Tax Status

IRS Ruling: Revenue Ruling 93-91.

State Tax Office: Utah State Tax Commission, Salt Lake City, telephone 801-530-4848.

Operating Rules

Default Transfer Rule: By consent of a majority of the profits interests in the LLC of nontransferring members; this consent rule appears mandatory. [Section 48-2b-131.]

Default Continuation Rule: Unless otherwise provided in operating agreement, by consent of members. Statute does not say "all" remaining members, but we think this is a logical and safe interpretation of the default consent requirement. [Section 48-2b-137(3).]

VERMONT

At the time this book went to press, Vermont had not adopted LLC legislation. Call the Secretary of State at 802-828-2386 to check the progress of LLC legislation and to ask for LLC materials and forms once LLC legislation is adopted.

VIRGINIA

LLC Filing Office

Commonwealth of Virginia
State Corporation Commission
P.O. Box 1197
First Floor
Richmond, VA 23209-1197

Telephone: 804-371-9733

Forms and Statutes: Provides fill-in-the-blanks Articles of Organization, Articles of Organization to Convert Existing Partnership to an LLC and Articles of Organization for a Professional LLC with instructions for each form. Persons forming an LLC practice in medicine, law, dentistry, accounting, pharmacy, optometry, behavioral sciences, veterinary medicine or insurance consulting should form a professional LLC. All others should form a regular LLC. A copy of the *Virginia Corporation Law*, which includes Virginia's limited liability company statutes, is available from the State Corporation Commission for $20.

Articles of Organization

Name Requirements: Must contains the words "Limited Liability Company" or "Limited Company" or the abbreviations "L.L.C." or "L.C." To reserve an LLC name, mail state form LLC-1013, Application for Reserved Name, with a $10 fee.

Filing Fee: $100, payable to "State Corporation Commission."

Special Instructions and Filing Requirements: You only need to send original Articles for filing. Type or print in blanks of state form in black ink only. In Article 5, indicate the date when the LLC will terminate—you can specify a date far into the future, or simply state a term of years, such as "75 years from the date of filing of these Articles."

Tax Status

IRS Ruling: Revenue Ruling 93-5.

State Tax Office: Department of Taxation, Richmond, telephone 804-367-2062.

Operating Rules

Default Transfer Rule: By unanimous consent of nontransferring members; this rule appears to be mandatory. [Section 13.1-1040.]

Default Continuation Rule: By unanimous consent of remaining members within 90 days of a dissociation event; this rule appears to be mandatory. [Section 13.1-1046(3).]

WASHINGTON

LLC Filing Office

Washington Secretary of State
Corporations Division
P.O. Box 40234
Olympia, WA 98504-0234

Telephone: 360-753-7115

Forms and Statutes: State provides fill-in-the-blanks Certificate of Formation form.

Certificate of Formation

Name Requirements: Must contains the words "Limited Liability Company," "Limited Liability Co." or the abbreviation "L.L.C." The fee to reserve an available LLC name for 180 days is $30.

Filing Fee: $175, payable to "Secretary of State."

Special Filing Instructions and Requirements: In Article 2 of the Certificate of Formation, you must specify a dissolution date for your LLC (even though the statute seems to make this item optional, the Attorney General has told the Secretary of State a dissolution date is mandatory). You can make this a date far into the future, say "December 31, 2099," or you may wish to state "50 years," "75 years" or a similar term of years. Make sure the registered agent signs the Certificate in the space provided at the bottom of page 1 on the Certificate of Formation form. Submit original and one copy of the Certificate to the LLC filing office.

Annual Fees: You must file an annual report form (provided by the Secretary of State) within 120 days of filing the Certificate of Formation. There is a $10 filing fee.

Tax Status

IRS Ruling: None

State Tax Office: Department of Revenue, Olympia, telephone 800-647-7706.

Operating Rules

Default Transfer Rule: Unless otherwise stated in Articles or operating agreement, by unanimous consent of nontransferring members. [Section 704.]

Default Continuation Rule: By unanimous consent of remaining members within 90 days of dissociation event and as may be provided in the operating agreement. [Section 801(4).]

WEST VIRGINIA

LLC Filing Office

West Virginia Secretary of State
State Capitol, W-139
Charleston, WV 25305-0770

Telephone: 304-558-8000

Forms and Statutes: Provides sample Articles of Organization, plus a copy of the West Virginia LLC Act upon request.

Articles of Organization

Name Requirements: Must contain the words "Limited Liability Company." An available LLC name may be reserved for 120 days for $5.

Filing Fee: $10, payable to the "Secretary of State."

Special Instructions and Filing Requirements: Here are instructions for some of the less straightforward articles:

- *Article 3:* Specify a particular business activity or operation, such as "real estate sales" or "office management services." A general purpose to conduct any and all lawful business is not sufficient.
- *Article 4:* The address of the LLC's registered agent will often be the same as the LLC's principal office specified in Article 2.
- *Article 6:* The period of duration of the LLC can be specified as a date or term of years, but in either

case, may not exceed 50 years. If you specify a term of years, it will run from the date of filing of the Articles. (By the way, this 50-year LLC duration limit does not appear in the statute, but is a policy guideline enforced by the LLC filing office. If you wish to insert a date or term more than 50 years from the date of filing, we suggest you call the office and double-check the status of this Secretary of State guideline.)

- *Article 7:* You'll need to add an Article 7 on the state form. There's not much room for this statement, so print or type in a small typeface to make this statement fit in the space just below Article 6. A statement of this sort appears to be necessary under the state's default continuation rule (see below) so that members can vote to continue the legal life of the LLC after a member is dissociated. This new Article should read as follows:

  7. Members' Right to Continue LLC. Under Section 31-1A-35 of the West Virginia Limited Liability Company Act, the remaining members of this limited liability company have the right to consent to continue the business of this company upon the death, retirement, resignation, expulsion, bankruptcy or dissolution of a member, or the occurrence of any other event that terminates the continued membership of a member in this limited liability company.

There must be at least two organizers, who need not be members of the LLC. They must sign the form in the presence of a notary, who will complete the portion of the form on the back of the first page. Make sure you show the name and mailing address of the person who prepared the form at the very end of the Articles—normally one of the LLC organizers. Make a copy of the completed notarized form and file both with the LLC filing office.

After filing your Articles, the LLC office will send you a certificate of organization. A copy of this form must be filed in the office of the county clerk of the county commission of the county where the principal office of the LLC is located.

Tax Status

IRS Ruling: Revenue Ruling 93-50.

State Tax Office: Department of Tax & Revenue, Charleston, telephone 304-558-3333.

Operating Rules

Default Transfer Rule: By unanimous consent of nontransferring members; this rule appears to be mandatory. [Section 31-1A-34.]

Default Continuation Rule: By unanimous consent of remaining members—the Articles must give the members this right to vote to continue the LLC after the dissociation of a member. [Section 31-1A-35(3).]

WISCONSIN

LLC Filing Office

Wisconsin Secretary of State
Corporations Division
P.O. Box 7846
Madison, WI 53707-7846

Telephone: 608-266-3590

Forms and Statutes: Provides fill-in-the-blanks Articles of Organization with instructions, plus a free booklet titled, "Starting a Business? Here's Help." Send $1.50 to the Wisconsin Secretary of State to request a copy of the Wisconsin LLC Act (ask for a copy of Chapter 183).

Articles of Organization

Name Requirements: Must contain the words "Limited Liability Company" or "Limited Liability Co." or end with the abbreviations "LLC" or "L.L.C." You may specify a second name in the blank in the instructions to Article 1 (on the back page of the printed form) in case the name you show in Article 1 is not available for your use. An available LLC name may be reserved for 120 days by calling the LLC filing office at the telephone number shown above for $30 or by mail for $15.

Filing Fee: $90, payable to the "Secretary of State."

Special Instructions and Filing Requirements: Show the name of the person filling in the Articles in the blank at the bottom of the page (this is the person who "drafted" your Articles). Send one signed original plus one copy.

Tax Status

IRS Ruling: None

State Tax Office: Department of Revenue, Madison, telephone 608-266-6466.

Operating Rules

Default Transfer Rule: Unless otherwise stated in the operating agreement, by unanimous written consent of nontransferring members. [Section 183.0706.]

Default Continuation Rule: By unanimous consent of remaining members within 90 days of a dissociation event or as may otherwise be provided in the operating agreement. [Section 183.0901(4).]

WYOMING

LLC Filing Office

Wyoming Secretary of State
State Capitol
Cheyenne, WY 82002-0020

Telephone: 307-777-5334

Forms and Statutes: State provides fill-in-the-blanks Articles of Organization and a copy of the Wyoming Limited Liability Company Act for free on request.

Articles of Organization

Name Requirements: Must contain the words "Limited Liability Company," "Limited Company," the abbreviations "LLC," "L.L.C.," "LC" or "L.C." or one of the following combination forms: "Ltd. Liability Company," "Ltd. Liability Co." or "Limited Liability Co." (Any of these nine forms is acceptable.) The fee to reserve an LLC name is $30.

Filing Fee: $100, if capital of the LLC does not exceed $50,000. Higher fees apply if the LLC will have larger amounts of capital.

Annual Fees: Annual LLC tax is $100.

Special Instructions and Filing Requirements: Submit an original plus one copy of Articles for filing.

Here are instructions for some of the less straightforward articles:

- *Article II:* State the period of duration of the LLC. You can specify a date, or a term of years, such as 50 or 75. If no duration is given in this blank, the law says your LLC's duration is 30 years from the date of filing.
- *Article III:* Fill in the purpose(s) of your LLC. Rather than referring to the specific business of the LLC (for example, "real estate sales"), you can provide a general statement—but you must specifically exclude the banking and insurance business in such a statement. For example, the following general statement of purpose will work fine: "any lawful business except the business of banking or insurance."
- *Article V:* Specify the cash and value of property to be contributed to start up the LLC.
- *Article VI:* Indicate the amount or circumstances for any additional contributions required of members of your LLC.
- *Article VII:* If you adopt the standard language contained in our operating agreements, you can use the following sentence to sum up the rights of members to admit additional members, and the terms of such admission: "The existing members of this LLC must approve the admission of new members by a unanimous vote. Upon such approval, new members shall be accorded all rights associated with membership in this LLC." If yours is a manager-managed LLC that requires only approval by member-managers to admit new members who are transferees of former members, add a sentence to this article noting this exception, as follows: "However, the nontransferring member-managers of this LLC are empowered to approve by unanimous vote the admission into membership of a transferee of a former member of this LLC."
- *Article VIII:* If you adopt the standard language contained in our operating agreements, the following sentence will sum up the rights of remaining members to continue the LLC after dissociation of a member: "The unanimous approval of the remaining members is required to continue the business of this LLC upon the death, retirement, resignation, expulsion, bankruptcy or dissolution of a member [replace the previous word "member" with "member-manager" if your manager-managed LLC chooses this option], or the occurrence of any other event that terminates the continued membership of a member [again, replace the word "member" with "member-manager" if appropriate to your manager-managed LLC] in this limited liability company."

- *Articles IX and X:* Fill out either Article IX or X, depending on whether your LLC is manager-managed (show names and addresses of initial managers in Article IX) or member-managed (show names and addresses of members in Article X).

The written consent of the registered agent to his/her appointment in this capacity must accompany the Articles. Simply print or type the following statement on a separate sheet of paper. Then have it dated and signed by the agent named in Article IV of your Articles of Organization, and mail it along with your Articles to the LLC filing office.

ACCEPTANCE OF APPOINTMENT OF
REGISTERED AGENT OF

NAME OF LLC

I understand the duties associated with serving in the capacity of registered agent, and I hereby consent to my appointment as registered agent for the above named LLC.

Dated: ______________________

Signed: ______________________,
typed name

Tax Status

IRS Ruling: Revenue Ruling 88-76.

State Tax Office: Department of Revenue, Cheyenne, telephone 307-777-7961.

Operating Rules

Default Transfer Rule: By unanimous written consent of nontransferring members; this consent requirement appears to be mandatory. [Section 17-15-122.]

Default Continuation Rule: By unanimous consent of remaining members; this right of remaining members to consent to continue the LLC after the dissociation of a member must be stated in the Articles (see "Special Instructions and Filing Requirements," above, Article VIII). [Section 17-15-123(iii).]

APPENDIX B

Revenue Rulings and Notices

REVENUE RULING 88-76

§12:01. Revenue Ruling 88–76: Partnership Classification (Wyoming Limited Liability Company) (1988–2 IRB 360).

Section 7701.—Definitions

26 CFR 301.7701–1: Classification of organizations for tax purposes.

Partnership classification. An unincorporated organization operating under the Wyoming Limited Liability Company Act is classified as a partnership for federal tax purposes under section 301.7701–2 of the regulations.

Rev Rul 88–76

ISSUE

Whether a Wyoming limited liability company, none of whose members or designated managers are personally liable for any debts of the company, is classified for federal tax purposes as an association or as a partnership.

FACTS

M was organized as a limited liability company pursuant to the provisions of the Wyoming Limited Liability Company Act (Act). The purpose of M is to acquire, own, and operate improved real property. M has 25 members, including A, B, and C.

The Act provides that a limited liability company may be managed by a designated manager or managers, or by its members. If the limited liability company is managed by its members, management authority is vested in its members in proportion to their capital contributions to the company. M is managed by its designated managers, A, B, and C.

Under the Act, neither the members nor the designated managers of a limited liability company are liable for any debts, obligations, or liabilities of the limited liability company.

The Act also provides that the interest of a member in a limited liability company is part of the personal estate of the member; however, each member can assign or transfer the member's respective interest in the limited liability company only upon the unanimous written consent of all the remaining members. In the event that the remaining members fail to approve the assignment or transfer, the assignee or transferee has no right to participate in the management or become a member of the limited liability company. However, the assignee or transferee is entitled to receive the share of profits or other compensation and the return of contributions to which the transferring member would otherwise be entitled.

A limited liability company formed under the Act is dissolved upon the occurrence of any of the following events: (1) when the period fixed for the duration of the company expires; (2) by the unanimous written consent of all the members; or (3) by the death, retirement, resignation, expulsion, bankruptcy, dissolution of a member or occurrence of any other event that terminates the continued membership of a member, unless the business of the company is continued by the consent of all the remaining members under a right to do so stated in the articles of organization of the company. Under M's articles of organization, the business of M is continued by the consent of all the remaining members.

LAW AND ANALYSIS

Section 7701(a)(2) of the Internal Revenue Code provides that the term "partnership" includes a syndicate, group, pool, venture, or other unincorporated organization, through or by means of which any business, financial operation, or venture is carried on, and which is not a trust or estate or a corporation.

Section 7701(a)(3) of the Code provides that the term "corporation" includes associations, joint-stock companies, and insurance companies.

Section 301.7701–1(b) of the Procedure and Administration Regulations states that the Code prescribes certain categories, or classes, into which various organizations fall for purposes of taxation. These categories, or classes, include associations (which are taxable as corporations), partnerships, and trusts. The tests, or standards, that are to be applied in determining the classification of an organization are set forth in sections 301.7701–2 through 301.7701–4.

Section 301.7701–2(a)(1) of the regulations sets forth the following basic characteristics of a corporation: (1) associates, (2) an objective to carry on business and divide the gains therefrom, (3) continuity of life, (4) centralization of management, (5) liability for corporate debts limited to corporate property, and (6) free transferability of interests. Whether a particular organization is to be classified as an association must be determined by taking into account the presence or absence of each of these corporate characteristics. In addition to the six major characteristics, other factors may be found in some cases which may be significant in classifying an organization as an association, a partnership, or a trust.

Section 301.7701–2(a)(2) of the regulations further provides that characteristics common to partnerships and corporations are not material in attempting to distinguish between an association and a partnership. Since associates and an objective to carry on business and divide the gains therefrom are generally common to corporations and partnerships, the determination of whether an organization which has such characteristics is to be treated for tax purposes as a partnership or as an association depends on whether there exists centralization of management, continuity of life, free transferability of interests, and limited liability.

Section 301.7701–2(a)(3) of the regulations provides that if an unincorporated organization possesses more corporate characteristics than noncorporate characteristics, it constitutes an association taxable as a corporation.

In interpreting section 301.7701–2 of the regulations, the Tax Court, in Larson v. Commissioner, 66 TC 159 (1976), acq., 1979–1 CB 1, concluded that equal weight must be given to each of the four corporate characteristics of continuity of life, centralization of management, limited liability, and free transferability of interests.

In the present situation, M has associates and an objective to carry on business and divide the gains therefrom. Therefore, M must be classified as either an association or a partnership. M is classified as a partnership for federal tax purposes unless the organization has a preponderance of the remaining corporate characteristics of continuity of life, centralization of management, limited liability, and free transferability of interests.

Section 301.7701–2(b)(1) of the regulations provides that if the death, insanity, bankruptcy, retirement, resignation, or expulsion of any member will cause a dissolution of the organization, continuity of life does not exist. Section 301.7701–2(b)(2) provides that an agreement by which an organization is established may provide that the business will be continued by the remaining members in the event of the death or withdrawal of any member, but such agreement does not establish continuity of life if under local law the death or withdrawal of any member causes a dissolution of the organization.

Under the Act, unless the business of M is continued by the consent of all the remaining members, M is dissolved upon the death, retirement, resignation, expulsion, bankruptcy, dissolution of a member or occurrence of any other event that terminates the continued membership of a member in the company. If a member of M ceases to be a member of M for any reason, the continuity of M's not assured, because all remaining members must agree to continue the business. Consequently, M lacks the corporate characteristic of continuity of life.

Under section 301.7701–2(c)(1) of the regulations an organization has the corporate characteristic of centralized management if any person (or group of persons that does not include all the members) has continuing exclusive authority to make management decisions necessary to the conduct of the business for which the organization was formed.

Under the Act, a limited liability company has the discretion to be managed either by a designated manager or managers, or to be managed by its members. Because M is managed by its designated managers, A, B, and C, M possesses the corporate characteristic of centralized management.

Section 301.7701–2(d)(1) of the regulations provides that an organization has the corporate characteristic of limited liability if under local law there is no member who is personally liable for the debts of, or claims against, the organization. Personal liability means that a creditor of an organization may seek personal satisfaction from a member of the organization to the extent that the assets of such organization are insufficient to satisfy the creditor's claim.

Under the Act, neither the managers nor the members of M are personally liable for its debts and obligations. Consequently, M possesses the corporate characteristic of limited liability.

Under section 301.7701–2(e)(1) of the regulations, an organization has the corporate characteristic of free transferability of interests if each of the members or those members owning substantially all of the interests in the organization have the power, without the consent of other members, to substitute for themselves in the same organization a person who is not a member of the organization. In order for this power of substitution to exist in the corporate sense, the member must be able, without the consent of other members, to confer upon the member's substitute all the attributes of the member's interest in the organization. The characteristic of free transferability does not exist if each member can, without the consent of the other members, assign only the right to share in the profits but cannot assign the right to participate in the management of the organization.

Under the Act, neither the managers nor the members of M are personally liable for its debts and obligations. Consequently, M possesses the corporate characteristic of limited liability.

Under section 301.7701–2(e)(1) of the regulations, an organization has the corporate characteristic of free transferability of interests if each of the members or those members owning substantially all of the interests in the organization have the power, without the consent of other members, to substitute for themselves in the same organization a person who is not a member of the organization. In order for this power of substitution to exist in the corporate sense, the member must be able, without the consent of other members, to confer upon the member's substitute all the attributes of the member's interest in the organization. The characteristic of free transferability does not exist if each member can, without the consent of the other members, assign only the right to share in the profits but cannot assign the right to participate in the management of the organization.

Under the terms of the Act, a member of M can assign or transfer that member's interest to another who is not a member of the organization. However, the assignee or transferee does not become a substitute member and does not acquire all the attributes of the member's interest in M unless all the remaining members approve the assignment or transfer. Therefore, M lacks the corporate characteristic of free transferability of interests.

M has associates and an objective to carry on business and divide the gains therefrom. In addition, M possesses the corporate characteristic of centralized management and limited liability. M does not, however, possess the corporate characteristics of continuity of life and free transferability of interests.

HOLDING

M has associates and an objective to carry on business and divide the gains therefrom, but lacks a preponderance of the four remaining corporate characteristics. Accordingly, M is classified as a partnership for federal tax purposes.

REVENUE RULING 95-10

§ 2.07 Text of Revenue Procedure 95-10

Rev. Proc. 95-10, 1995-3 I.R.B. 20

Publication Date: January 17, 1995

SECTION 1. PURPOSE

.01 This revenue procedure specifies the conditions under which the Internal Revenue Service (Service) will consider a ruling request that relates to classification of a domestic or foreign limited liability company (LLC) as a partnership for federal tax purposes. This revenue procedure modifies Rev. Proc. 89-12, 1989-1 C.B. 798, which specifies the conditions under which the Service will consider a ruling request that relates to the classification of an organization as a partnership for federal tax purposes. Rev. Proc. 89-12 applies to organizations formed as partnerships and also applies to other organizations seeking partnership classification. It also provides that any reference to a "limited partnership" includes an organization formed as a limited partnership under applicable state law and any other organization formed under a law that limits the liability of any member for the organization's debts and other obligations to a determinable fixed amount. Rev. Proc. 89-12 no longer applies to LLCs. See section 6 of this revenue procedure.

.02 This revenue procedure applies to all organizations that are formed as LLCs under the laws of the United States or of any State or the District of Columbia (domestic law) providing for or allowing limited liability to any of their members and that are not incorporated organizations, trusts, or partnerships formed under statutes corresponding to the Uniform Partnership Act or the Revised Uniform Limited Partnership Act. This revenue procedure also applies to all organizations formed under a law other than domestic law (foreign law or foreign statute), where the foreign law or foreign statute provides for or allows limited liability to any of their members (whether or not the foreign organization is "incorporated" under a foreign statute). See Rev. Rul. 88-8, 1988-1 C.B. 403. This revenue procedure does not apply to a publicly traded LLC treated as a corporation under Section 7704 of the Internal Revenue Code.

.03 Unless the context clearly indicates otherwise, references to the LLC's operating agreement include the articles of organization and all other controlling documents, however designated, entered into by the members of the LLC. If the applicable statute allows for management by one or more designated persons, managers are those persons designated or elected by the members to act on behalf of the LLC.

.04 The Service may decline to issue a ruling under this revenue procedure when warranted by the facts and circumstances of a particular case and when appropriate in the interest of sound tax administration.

SECTION 2. BACKGROUND

.01 Section 7701(a)(2) defines the term partnership to include a syndicate, group, pool, joint venture, or other unincorporated organization, through or by means of which any business, financial operation, or venture is carried on, and which is not, within the meaning of the Code, a trust or estate or a corporation. Sections 301.7701-2 and 301.7701-3 of the Procedure and Administration Regulations set forth rules for determining whether an organization is classified as a partnership or as an association taxable as a corporation for federal tax purposes.

.02 Rev. Rul. 73-254, 1973-1 C.B. 613, provides that the classification of a foreign unincorporated business organization for federal tax purposes will be determined under Section 7701 and the regulations thereunder. However, it is the local law of the foreign jurisdiction that must be applied in determining the legal relationships of the members of the organization among themselves and with the public at large, as well as the interests of the members of the organization in its assets. Rev. Rul. 88-8 provides that an entity organized under foreign law is considered to be "unincorporated" for purposes of Section 301.7701-2(a)(3) and, therefore, is classified for federal tax purposes solely on the basis of the characteristics set forth in Section 301.7701-2.

.03 Rev. Proc. 94-1, 1994-1 C.B. 378, as updated annually, sets forth procedures for taxpayer requests and Service issuance of advance rulings; however, Rev. Proc. 94-3, 1994-1 C.B. 447, and Rev. Proc. 94-7, 1994-1 C.B. 542, as updated annually, list areas in which the Service will not issue, or will not ordinarily issue, advance rulings.

SECTION 3. INFORMATION TO BE SUBMITTED WITH RULING REQUEST

.01 Section 8 of Rev. Proc. 94-1 outlines general requirements concerning the information to be submitted as part of a ruling request, including a classification ruling request. For example, an LLC classification ruling request must contain a complete statement of all facts relating to the classification issue. Among those facts to be included in the statement are the items of information specified in this revenue procedure; therefore, the ruling request must provide all items of information specified below, or at least account for all the items. For example, if no registration statement is required to be filed with the U.S. Securities and Exchange Commission (SEC), the ruling request should so state.

.02 Submission of the documents and supplementary materials required by section 3.04 of this revenue procedure does not satisfy the information requirements contained in section 3.03 of this revenue procedure or in section 8 of Rev. Proc. 94-1. All material facts in documents, including those items required by section 3.03 of this revenue procedure, must be included in the ruling request and may not merely be incorporated by reference therein. All submitted documents and supplementary materials must contain applicable exhibits, attachments, and amendments.

.03 Required General Information. The following information must be included in the request for a ruling:

(1) The name and taxpayer identification number (if any) of the LLC;

(2) The business of the LLC;

(3) The date and place of filing of the LLC's articles of organization, or the anticipated date and place of filing;

(4) The identification of the domestic or foreign jurisdiction whose law controls the formation and operation of the LLC;

(5) A representation that the LLC has been, and will be at all times, in conformance with the controlling laws of the domestic or foreign jurisdiction;

(6) The nature, amount, and timing of capital contributions made and to be made by the members to the LLC;

(7) The extent of participation of the members and the managers in profits and losses of the LLC, including any possible shift in the profit and loss sharing ratios over time;

(8) A description of the relationships, direct and indirect, between the members and the managers (whether or not also members) that would suggest that the managers, individually or in the aggregate, may not at all times act independently of the members (because of individual or aggregate influence or control by the members in their capacity as such over the managers). These relationships include: (a) ownership by non-manager members of 5 percent or more of the stock or other beneficial interests in a manager; (b) control by non-manager members of 5 percent or more of the voting power in a manager; (c) ownership of 5 percent or more of the stock or other beneficial interests in any manager and in any non-manager members by the same person or persons acting as a group; and (d) control of 5 percent or more of the voting power in any manager and in any non-manager members by

the same person or persons acting as a group. A person is considered to own any beneficial interest owned by a related person and is considered to control any voting power controlled by a related person. A person is treated as related to another person if they bear a relationship to each other specified in Section 267(b) or 707(b)(1). The relationships defined in the first sentence of this section 3.03(8) may also include a debtor-creditor relationship and an employer-employee relationship;

(9) If it is asserted that the LLC lacks the corporate characteristic of limited liability: (a) a description of the legal arrangements supporting the assertion that the LLC lacks limited liability, (b) a representation of the net worth (based on assets at current fair market value) of the member or members assuming personal liability for all obligations of the LLC (assuming member), excluding interests in the LLC held by that member or members, (c) a description of the assuming member's or members' assets and liabilities arising from transactions with the LLC or with a person related to any member or members under Section 267(b) or 707(b)(1), and (d) a description of all other organizations in which the member or members have an interest;

(10) A detailed description of how each of the applicable provisions of section 5 of this revenue procedure are satisfied;

(11) If the Service has issued a revenue ruling on the applicable domestic or foreign law, a discussion of how the revenue ruling applies to the taxpayer's ruling request.

.04 Required Copies of Documents and Supplementary Materials. The following copies of documents and materials must be submitted with the ruling request:

(1) The LLC's articles of organization filed or to be filed with the domestic or foreign jurisdiction in which the LLC is formed;

(2) The LLC's operating agreement (exclusive of the articles of organization);

(3) The registration statement (or comparable document under foreign law) filed or to be filed with the SEC or comparable foreign regulatory body. (A draft that is final in all material respects is acceptable.);

(4) If a registration statement (or comparable document under foreign law) is not required to be filed with the SEC or comparable foreign regulatory body, the documents filed or to be filed with any domestic federal or state (or comparable foreign) agency engaged in the regulation of securities and any private offering

memorandum (or comparable documents under foreign law). (Drafts that are final in all material respects are acceptable.);

(5) A copy of the applicable domestic or foreign law, and amendments, under which the LLC was or will be formed;

(6) An outline or copies of all promotional material used to sell interests in the LLC, highlighting statements about probable domestic and foreign tax consequences and the effect of the requested ruling upon the tax consequences;

(7) An English translation of all documents in a foreign language.

SECTION 4. GENERAL PROVISIONS AND OWNERSHIP TESTS

.01 General. The Service will consider a ruling request that relates to classification of an LLC as a partnership for federal tax purposes only if the LLC has at least two members and, to the extent applicable, the conditions in sections 4 and 5 of this revenue procedure are satisfied. The determination of whether the LLC has at least two members is based on all the facts and circumstances. Section 5.01 relates solely to the corporate characteristic of continuity of life described in Section 301.7701-2(b); section 5.02 relates solely to the corporate characteristic of free transferability of interests described in section 301.7701-2(e); section 5.03 relates solely to the corporate characteristic of centralized management described in section 301.7701-2(c); and section 5.04 relates solely to the corporate characteristic of limited liability described in section 301.7701-(d). Sections 4.02 through 4.05 of this revenue procedure provide minimum ownership requirements that must be satisfied if the taxpayer requests a ruling that the LLC lacks continuity of life under section 5.01(1) (pertaining to dissolution events relating solely to member-managers), free transferability of interests under section 5.02(1) (pertaining to consent to transfer solely by member-managers), or limited liability under section 5.04. Failure to satisfy any of the above sections only precludes a ruling that the LLC lacks the particular corporate characteristic addressed by the relevant section and does not necessarily preclude the issuance of a partnership classification ruling by the Service. If the LLC is issued a ruling under this revenue procedure that it is classified as a partnership and the LLC subsequently has only one member, the letter ruling ceases to be effective because the LLC's status as a partnership for federal tax purposes terminates as of the relevant date specified in Sections 708 and 736.

.02 General Rule as to Profit and Loss Interests. Unless section 4.03 of this revenue procedure applies, if the taxpayer requests a ruling that the LLC lacks continuity of life under section 5.01(1) or free transferability of interests under section 5.02(1), the member-managers in the aggregate must own, pursuant to the express terms of the operating agreement, at least a one percent interest in each material item of the LLC's income, gain, loss, deduction, or credit during the entire existence of the LLC. Further, unless section 4.03 applies, if the taxpayer requests a ruling that the LLC lacks limited liability under section 5.04, the assuming member or members must in the aggregate own, pursuant to the express terms of the operating agreement, at least a one percent interest in each material item of the LLC's income, gain, loss, deduction, or credit during the entire existence of the LLC. However, it will generally not be considered a violation of this section 4.02 if a required allocation under either Section 704(b) or 704(c), or corresponding Income Tax Regulations, temporarily causes less than one percent of the LLC's income, gain, loss, deduction, or credit to be allocable to the party otherwise required under this section 4.02 to receive the allocation; in these cases, the ruling request must describe any required allocations and explain why the allocation is required under Section 704(b) or 704(c), as appropriate. Any other temporary allocation causing less than one percent of any material item of the LLC's income, gain, loss, deduction, or credit to be allocable to the necessary parties will be considered a violation of this section 4.02, unless the LLC clearly establishes in the ruling request that the member-managers or the assuming members (as the case may be) have a material interest in net profits and losses over the LLC's anticipated life. For this purpose, a profits interest generally will not be considered material unless it substantially exceeds one percent and will be in effect for a substantial period of time during which the LLC reasonably expects to generate profits. For example, a 20 percent interest in profits that begins four years after the LLC's formation and continues for the life of the LLC generally would be considered material if the LLC is expected to generate profits for a substantial period of time beyond the initial four-year period.

.03 Exception to General Rule as to Minimum Profits and Loss Interests. If the LLC has total contributions exceeding $50 million, the member-managers (or assuming members) need not meet the one percent standard in section 4.02 of this revenue procedure. However, except for a temporary allocation or nonconformance specified in section 4.02, the member-managers (or assuming members) in the aggregate must maintain an interest at all times during the existence of the LLC in each material item of at least one percent divided by the ratio of total contributions to $50 million, and the LLC's operating agreement must expressly incorporate at least the computed percentage. For example, if total contributions are $125 million, the interest in each material item must be at least .4 percent, that is, one percent divided by 125/50. In no event, however, other than as a result of a temporary allocation or nonconformance specified in section 4.02, may the member-managers' (or assuming members') aggregate interest at any time during the existence of the LLC in any material item be less than .2 percent.

.04 General Rule as to Capital Account Balances. Unless section 4.05 of this revenue procedure applies, if the taxpayer requests a ruling that the LLC lacks continuity of life under section 5.01(1), or free transferability of interests under section 5.02(1), the member-managers, in the aggregate, must maintain throughout the entire existence of the LLC a minimum capital account balance equal to the lesser of one percent of total positive capital account balances or $500,000. Further, unless section 4.05 applies, if the taxpayer requests a ruling that the LLC lacks limited liability under section 5.04, the assuming member or members must maintain a minimum capital account balance in accordance with the rules of the preceding sentence. Whenever a non-managing member (or non-assuming member) makes a capital contribution, the member-managers (or assuming members) must be obligated, pursuant to the express terms of the operating agreement, to contribute immediately to the LLC capital equal to 1.01 percent of the non-managing members' (or non-assuming members') capital contributions or a lesser amount (including zero) that causes the sum of the member-managers' (or assuming members') capital account balances to equal the lesser of one percent of total positive capital account balances for the LLC or $500,000. If no member has a positive capital account balance, then the member-managers (or assuming members) in the LLC need not have a positive capital account balance to satisfy this section 4.04. Capital accounts and the value of contributions are determined under the rules of Section 1.704-1(b)(2)(iv) of the Income Tax Regulations.

.05 Exception to General Rule of Minimum Capital Account Balances. If at least one member-manager (or assuming member) otherwise required under section 4.04 of this revenue procedure to have and maintain a minimum capital account balance has contributed or will contribute substantial services in the capacity as a member, apart from services for which guaranteed payments under Section 707(c) are made, the capital account standard in section 4.04 does not apply to any of the member-managers (or assuming members). However, the operating agreement of the LLC must expressly provide that, upon the dissolution and termination of the LLC, the member-managers (or assuming members) will contribute capital to the LLC in an amount equal to the lesser of: (1) the aggregate deficit balance, if any, in their capital accounts, or (2) the excess of 1.01 percent of the total capital contributions of the non-managing members (or non-assuming members) over the aggregate capital previously contributed to the LLC by the member-managers (or assuming members). Those services that do not relate to day-to-day operations in the LLC's primary business activity, such as services related to the organization and syndication of the

LLC, accounting, financial planning, general business planning, and services in the nature of investment management, will be closely scrutinized by the Service to determine if they are in fact substantial services. In making this determination, the nature of the LLC and its activities will be taken into account.

SECTION 5. RULING GUIDELINES FOR SPECIFIC CORPORATE CHARACTERISTICS

.01 Continuity of Life.

(1) Dissolution Events Relating Solely to Member-Managers. If the members of the LLC designate or elect one or more members as managers and the controlling statute, or the operating agreement pursuant to the controlling statute, provides that the death, insanity, bankruptcy, retirement, resignation, or expulsion of any member-manager causes a dissolution of the LLC without further action of the members, unless the LLC is continued by the consent of not less than a majority in interest of the remaining members, the Service will generally rule that the LLC lacks continuity of life. For purposes of the preceding sentence, all the member-managers must be subject to the specified dissolution events. For example, if the LLC is managed by A, B, and C, it must be provided that a dissolution event with respect to A, B, or C will dissolve the LLC, and not a dissolution event with respect to only one of the named managers (i.e., a dissolution event only with respect to A but not B or C).

(2) Dissolution Events Relating to Members. If the members of the LLC do not designate or elect one or more members as managers (or if the LLC requests a ruling under this section 5.01(2) despite the presence of member-managers) and the controlling statute, or the operating agreement pursuant to the controlling statute, provides that the death, insanity, bankruptcy, retirement, resignation, or expulsion of any member dissolves the LLC without further action of the members, unless the LLC is continued by the consent of not less than a majority in interest of the remaining members, the Service generally will rule that the LLC lacks continuity of life. For purposes of the preceding sentence, all the members must be subject to the specified dissolution events.

(3) Majority in Interest. See Rev. Proc. 94-46, 1994-28 I.R.B. 129, pertaining to majority in interest, for purposes of applying sections 5.01(1) and (2) of this revenue procedure.

(4) Limitation on Dissolution Events. If the controlling statute, or the operating agreement pursuant to the controlling statute, provides that less than all of the dissolution events listed above with respect to the member-managers (when

applying section 5.01(1)) or the members (when applying section 5.01(2)) dissolves the LLC, the Service will not rule that the LLC lacks continuity of life unless the taxpayer clearly establishes in the ruling request that the event or events selected provide a meaningful possibility of dissolution.

.02 Free Transferability of Interests.

(1) Consent to Transfer Solely by Member-Managers. If the members of the LLC designate or elect one or more members as managers, and the controlling statute, or the operating agreement pursuant to the controlling statute, provides that each member, or those members owning more than 20 percent of all interests in the LLC's capital, income, gain, loss, deduction, and credit, does not have the power to confer upon a non-member all the attributes of the member's interests in the LLC without the consent of not less than a majority of the non-transferring member-managers, the Service will generally rule that the LLC lacks free transferability of interests. See Rev. Proc. 92-33, 1992-1 C.B. 782.

(2) Consent to Transfer by Members. If the members of the LLC do not designate or elect one or more members as managers (or if the LLC requests a ruling under this section 5.02(2) despite the presence of member-managers), and the controlling statute, or the operating agreement pursuant to the controlling statute, provides that each member, or those members owning more than 20 percent of all interests in the LLC's capital, income, gain, loss, deduction, and credit, does not have the power to confer upon a non-member all the attributes of the member's interests in the LLC without the consent of not less than a majority of the non-transferring members, the Service will generally rule that the LLC lacks free transferability of interests. See Rev. Proc. 92-33.

(3) Majority Defined. For purposes of applying sections 5.02(1) and 5.02(2) of this revenue procedure, consent of a majority includes either a majority in interest (see Rev. Proc. 94-46 pertaining to majority in interest), a majority of either the capital or profits interests in the LLC, or a majority determined on a per capita basis.

(4) Meaningful Consent. The Service will not rule that the LLC lacks free transferability of interests unless the power to withhold consent to the transfer constitutes a meaningful restriction on the transfer of the interests. For example, a power to withhold consent to a transfer is not a meaningful restriction if the consent may not be unreasonably withheld.

.03 Centralization of Management.

(1) Members Manage LLC Without Managers. If the controlling statute, or the operating agreement pursuant to the controlling statute, provides that the LLC

is managed by the members exclusively in their membership capacity, the Service generally will rule that the LLC lacks centralized management.

(2) Members Designated or Elected as Managers. If the members of the LLC designate or elect one or more members as managers of the LLC, the Service will not rule that the LLC lacks centralized management unless the member-managers in the aggregate own at least 20 percent of the total interests in the LLC. However, even if the aggregate ownership requirement is satisfied, the Service will consider all the relevant facts and circumstances, including, particularly, member control of the member-managers (whether direct or indirect), in determining whether the LLC lacks centralized management. The Service will not rule that the LLC lacks centralized management if the member-managers are subject to periodic elections by the members or, alternatively, the non-managing members have a substantially non-restricted power to remove the member-managers.

.04 Limited Liability. The Service generally will not rule that an LLC lacks limited liability unless at least one assuming member validly assumes personal liability for all (but not less than all) obligations of the LLC, pursuant to express authority granted in the controlling statute. In addition, the Service generally will not rule that an LLC lacks limited liability unless the assuming members have an aggregate net worth that, at the time of the ruling request, equals at least 10 percent of the total contributions to the LLC and is expected to continue to equal at least 10 percent of total contributions to the LLC throughout the life of the LLC. In the case of an LLC in which the assuming members do not satisfy the safe harbor described in the preceding sentence, close scrutiny will be applied to determine whether the LLC lacks limited liability. In that connection, it must be demonstrated that an assuming member has (or the assuming members collectively have) substantial assets (other than the member's interest in the LLC) that could be reached by a creditor of the LLC. In determining the net worth of the assuming member (or assuming members), the principles contained in section 4.03 of Rev. Proc. 92-88, 1992-2 C.B. 496, are to be applied.

SECTION 6. EFFECT ON OTHER REVENUE PROCEDURES

Rev. Proc. 89-12 is modified so that it does not apply to ruling requests submitted by LLCs described in this revenue procedure.

SECTION 7. EFFECTIVE DATE

This revenue procedure applies to all ruling requests received in the National Office on or after January 17, 1995.

DRAFTING INFORMATION

The principal author of this revenue procedure is D. Lindsay Russell of the Office of Assistant Chief Counsel (Passthroughs & Special Industries). For further information regarding this revenue procedure contact Mr. Russell at (202) 622-3050 (not a toll-free call).

REVENUE RULING 95-14

I.R.S. Notice 95-14, 1994-14 I.R.B. 7

Simplification of Entity Classification Rules

Publication Date: April 3, 1995

The Internal Revenue Service and the Treasury Department are considering simplifying the classification regulations to allow taxpayers to treat domestic unincorporated business organizations as partnerships or as associations on an elective basis. The Service and Treasury also are considering adopting similar rules for foreign business organizations. Comments are requested regarding this and other possible approaches to simplifying the regulations.

BACKGROUND

Section 7701(a)(2) of the Internal Revenue Code defines a partnership to include a syndicate, group, pool, joint venture, or other unincorporated organization, through or by means of which any business, financial operation, or venture is carried on, and which is not a trust or estate or a corporation. Section 7701(a)(3) defines a corporation to include associations, joint-stock companies, and insurance companies. In addition, certain business entities are taxed as corporations under various sections of the Code, such as publicly traded partnerships under Section 7704 and taxable mortgage pools under Section 7701(i).

Sections 301.7701-2 and 301.7701-3 of the Procedure and Administration Regulations (the classification regulations) provide rules for determining whether an unincorporated organization that has associates and an objective to carry on business and divide the gains therefrom is classified as a partnership or as an association for federal tax purposes. These regulations classify such an organization as an association if it has a preponderance of four specified corporate characteristics: (1) continuity of life; (2) centralization of management; (3) liability for organization debts limited to the organization's assets; and (4) free transferability of interests. The classification regulations, together with numerous revenue rulings and revenue procedures, provide guidance in determining when an unincorporated organization possesses these characteristics.

The existing classification regulations are based on the historical differences under local law between partnerships and corporations. However, many states recently have revised their statutes to provide that partnerships and other unincorporated organizations may possess characteristics that have traditionally been associated with corporations, thereby narrowing considerably the traditional distinctions between corporations and partnerships. For example, some partnership statutes have been modified to provide that no partner is unconditionally liable for all of the debts of the partnership. Similarly, almost all states have enacted statutes allowing the formation of limited liability companies. These entities are designed to provide liability protection to all members and to otherwise resemble corporations, while generally qualifying as partnerships for federal tax purposes. See, e.g., Rev. Rul. 88-76, 1988-2 C.B. 360.

One consequence of the narrowing of the differences under local law between corporations and partnerships is that taxpayers can achieve partnership tax classification for a non-publicly traded organization that, in all meaningful respects, is virtually indistinguishable from a corporation. Taxpayers and the Service, however, continue to expend considerable resources in determining the proper classification of domestic unincorporated business organizations. For example, since the issuance of Rev. Rul. 88-76, the Service has issued seventeen revenue rulings analyzing individual state limited liability company statutes, and has issued several revenue procedures and numerous letter rulings relating to classification of various unincorporated organizations under the classification regulations. In addition, small unincorporated organizations may not have sufficient resources and expertise to apply the current classification regulations to achieve the tax classification they desire.

POSSIBLE SIMPLIFICATION OF THE CURRENT CLASSIFICATION RULES

A. Domestic Unincorporated Business Organizations

The Service and Treasury are considering simplifying the existing classification regulations to allow taxpayers to elect to treat certain domestic unincorporated business organizations as partnerships or as associations for federal tax purposes. This approach would apply to all such organizations that have two or more associates and an objective to carry on business and divide the gains therefrom, unless the organization's classification is determined under another Code provision. For example, an entity that is treated as a partnership, but which is publicly traded and is taxed as a corporation under Section 7704, would continue to be taxed as a corporation under this approach. Similarly, a taxable mortgage pool under Section 7701(i) would continue to be taxed as a corporation, and an entity that makes an election to be a real estate mortgage investment conduit (REMIC) under Section 860D(b) would continue to be taxed under the REMIC rules. This approach generally would not affect the existing rules for classifying trusts (other than trusts that are classified as associations or partnerships under Sections 301.7701-2 and 301.7701-3).

Under this approach, all affirmative elections would be prospective from the date the election is filed or a later date designated in the election. Retroactive elections would not be permitted. The elections would have to be executed by all members of the organization and would be binding on all members thereafter, until superseded by a subsequent election.

The Service and Treasury recognize that there is considerable flexibility under the current rules to effectively change the classification of an organization at will (for example, by forming a new organization with different factors that would result in a different classification, and merging the old organization into it). On the other hand, the purpose of this approach is to simplify the rules in order to reduce the burdens on both taxpayers and the Service. The Service and Treasury are concerned that allowing taxpayers to change their classification simply by filing an election could result in a significant increase in the number of organizations changing their classification, thereby increasing burdens for some taxpayers and the Service. Accordingly, the Service and Treasury will consider whether the elections provided under this approach should be restricted.

Under this approach, an election to change the classification of an organization would have the same federal tax consequences as a change in classification under current law. For example, if an organization were classified as an association taxable as a corporation and later elected to be classified as a partnership, the election would be treated as a complete liquidation of the corporation and a formation of a new partnership. Thus, a final return for the corporation and a first-year return for the partnership each would have to be filed. In addition, the new partnership would have to ensure that its allocations were in compliance with Section 704(b) and the regulations thereunder.

This approach would include mechanisms for classifying organizations that do not make affirmative classification elections. Because the Service and Treasury believe that domestic unincorporated business organizations typically are formed to obtain partnership classification, those organizations generally would be classified as partnerships for federal tax purposes unless the organization files an election to be classified as an association taxable as a corporation. However, because the Service and Treasury believe that the current classification of existing organizations should be altered only by affirmative election, those organizations that are in existence on or prior to the effective date of the revised regulations would retain their current classification unless an affirmative election to be classified differently is filed.

B. Foreign Business Organizations

All foreign business organizations are currently considered unincorporated for federal tax purposes and, therefore, must be analyzed under the regulations that apply to domestic unincorporated business organizations. See Rev. Rul. 88-8, 1988-1 C.B. 403. The classification of a foreign organization involves not only a review of organizational agreements, but also a thorough understanding of the governing foreign law. Because the complexities and resources devoted to classification of domestic unincorporated business organizations are mirrored in the foreign context, the Service and Treasury are considering simplifying the classification rules for foreign organizations in a manner consistent with the approach described above for domestic organizations.

The Service and Treasury must, however, take into account a number of special considerations that arise in the foreign area. The first is that presently there is no foreign analogue to a state-law corporation and, therefore, no foreign organization that is automatically treated as a corporation for federal tax purposes. Thus, an elective system that follows exactly the approach described above for domestic unincorporated organizations would apply to all foreign organizations, without exception. The Service and Treasury are considering the appropriateness and feasibility of identifying particular forms of foreign organizations that, like state-law corporations, would automatically be treated as corporations.

A second consideration in the foreign area is the possibility of inconsistent, or hybrid, entity classification; that is, classification as a taxable entity in one country but as a flow-through entity (e.g., a partnership) under the tax laws of another country. An elective approach could expand the potential that exists under the current classification regulations for hybrid structures. The Service and Treasury are considering whether it is appropriate to address inconsistent classification in any rules to be proposed and also are considering how the tax benefits or detriments that may result from inconsistent classification can be addressed through the tax treaty process.

A third consideration in the foreign area is that a purely elective approach could have a substantive effect on entity classification by increasing taxpayers' flexibility to achieve their desired classification of certain foreign organizations. Under the present rules, taxpayers holding interests in foreign organizations are not always as able as those holding interests in domestic organizations to achieve their desired result. Because any change in the existing classification regulations is intended generally to simplify the rules without resulting in a substantial change in the classification of unincorporated organizations, the Service and Treasury must consider whether an elective approach should be modified with respect to foreign organizations.

To the extent the Service and Treasury determine that taxpayers may elect the classification of a foreign organization for federal tax purposes, consideration also must be given to the appropriate mechanism for classifying organizations that do not make affirmative elections. While domestic unincorporated organizations are typically formed to obtain partnership classification, the desired classification of foreign organizations is likely to be less uniform. The classification of a foreign organization as an association for federal tax purposes can be beneficial in many circumstances, while the classification as a partnership can be beneficial in others. Because of compliance requirements and excise tax provisions that apply to foreign partnerships and their partners, the Service and Treasury believe that it would be appropriate to treat a foreign organization that fails to make an affirmative election as an association, subject to a rule for existing organizations similar to that described above for domestic organizations. This rule would avoid inadvertently subjecting taxpayers to the partnership compliance rules and excise tax provisions and is likely in many circumstances to coincide with taxpayers' desired classification.

REQUEST FOR COMMENTS AND HEARING

The Service and Treasury invite comments on simplification of the current classification regulations, including alternate methods for simplifying those regulations. In addition, comments are invited on the approach described in this notice, including (1) whether adoption of the simplified approach described in this notice would be appropriate; (2) whether this approach would result in a greater proportion of newly formed businesses choosing unincorporated organizations rather than state-law corporations; (3) the mechanics of this approach, including the election requirements, the classification of organizations that do not file an affirmative election, and transition issues; (4) whether the ability to elect to change the classification of an organization should be restricted and, if so, in what manner; and (5) the proper treatment of unincorporated organizations that have a single owner or member.

In the international context, comments also are invited on (1) whether the approach should be extended to the classification of foreign organizations and, if so, whether the approach should be modified with respect to those organizations; (2) the appropriateness and feasibility of identifying foreign entities that, like state-law corporations, should automatically be classified as corporations; (3) the likely effect of the approach on the ability to achieve hybrid classification of foreign and domestic organizations and the appropriateness and viability of achieving international consistency in the classification of these organizations; (4) whether this approach would substantially change the federal tax classification of foreign organizations; and (5) whether the mechanics of the approach described for domestic organizations should be modified with respect to foreign organizations.

Written comments (a signed original and eight (8) copies) should be addressed to: Internal Revenue Service, Room 5228, P.O. Box 7604, Ben Franklin Station, Attn: CC:CORP:T:R (Notice 95-14), Washington, D.C. 20044. In the alternative, comments may be hand delivered between the hours of 8:00a.m. and 5:00p.m. to: CC:DOM:CORP:T:R (Notice 95-14), Courier's Desk, Internal Revenue Service, 1111 Constitution Avenue, N.W., Washington, D.C. Comments must be received on or before July 3, 1995. All comments will be available for public inspection and copying.

A public hearing has been scheduled for July 20, 1995, at 10:00a.m. in the Auditorium of the Internal Revenue Building, 1111 Constitution Avenue, N.W., Washington, D.C. Because of access restrictions, visitors will not be admitted beyond the Internal Revenue Building lobby more than 15 minutes before the hearing starts.

Persons who wish to present oral comments at the hearing must submit written comments by July 3, 1995, and submit an outline of the topics to be discussed and the time to be devoted to each topic (signed original and eight (8) copies) by July 6, 1995. A period of ten minutes will be allotted for each person making comments. An agenda showing the scheduling of the speakers will be prepared after the deadline for receiving outlines has passed. Copies of the agenda will be available free of charge at the hearing.

The Service and Treasury will consider scheduling additional hearings in other locations if taxpayers so request and there is sufficient interest.

EFFECT ON CURRENT LAW

While the Service and Treasury consider simplifying the current classification regulations, the Service will continue to apply the current rules without regard to the approach described in this notice. No inference is intended concerning the proper interpretation and application of the current rules.

DRAFTING INFORMATION

The principal authors of this notice are Armando Gomez of the Office of Assistant Chief Counsel (Passthroughs & Special Industries) and Ronald M. Gootzeit of the Office of Associate Chief Counsel (International). For further information regarding this notice contact Mr. Gomez, (202) 622-3050; concerning foreign organizations, Mr. Gootzeit, (202) 622-3880; concerning submissions and the hearing, Mike Slaughter, (202) 622-7190 (not toll-free numbers).

APPENDIX C

Tear-Out LLC Forms

LLC Contact Letter

Reservation of LLC Name Letter

Articles of Organization

Articles Filing Letter

Operating Agreement for Member-Managed Limited Liability Company

Limited Liability Company Management Operating Agreement

Minutes of Meeting

Certification of Authority

____

____

____

____

____

LLC Filings Office:

I am in the process of forming a domestic limited liability company (LLC). Please note:

- ☐ I am *or* ☐ I am not converting an existing ________________ partnership to an LLC.
- ☐ I am *or* ☐ I am not forming an LLC to perform the professional services of ____, which are licensed by the state.

Please send me the following forms, material and other information:

(1) printed, sample or specimen LLC Articles of Organization, with instructions. If your office reviews Articles of Organization for correctness prior to filing, please advise me of the procedure I should follow to obtain this pre-filing review;

(2) the telephone number or address I can contact to determine if a proposed limited liability company name is available for my use, plus any forms necessary to reserve an LLC name;

(3) a current schedule of fees for LLC filings;

(4) other LLC forms and publications provided by your office (or a list of these) that may be helpful in understanding the requirements for forming, operating and dissolving an LLC in this state; and

(5) the name and price of a publication that contains the limited liability company statutes of this state. Please indicate whether it may be ordered from your office or, if applicable, another office or supplier.

If there is a fee for any of the above materials, please advise. Enclosed is a self-addressed, stamped envelope for your reply.

Thank you for your assistance,

____

____

____

____

Enclosure: self-addressed, stamped envelope

____

____

____

____

____

LLC Filings Office:

Please reserve the following proposed limited liability company name for my use for the allowable period specified under state law:

____

☐ If the above name is not available, please reserve the first available name from the following list of alternative names:

Second Choice: ______________________________

Third Choice: ______________________________

I enclose a check in payment of the reservation fee. Please send a certificate, receipt for payment, or other acknowledgment or approval of my reservation request to me at my address shown below.

Thank you for your assistance,

____

____

____

____

Enclosures: check for reservation fee; stamped, self-addressed envelope

ARTICLES OF ORGANIZATION
OF

____

The undersigned natural person(s), of the age of eighteen years or more, acting as organizers of a limited liability company under the State of ____________________ Limited Liability Company Act, adopt(s) the following Articles of Organization ________________________________ for such limited liability company.

Article 1. Name of Limited Liability Company. The name of this limited liability company is ____.

Article 2. Registered Office and Registered Agent. The initial registered office of this limited liability company and the name of its initial registered agent at this address are:

____

____

____.

Article 3. Statement of Purposes. The purposes for which this limited liability company is organized are: ____

____

____

____

____

____.

Article 4. Management and Names and Addresses of Initial ____________________.
The management of this limited liability company is reserved to the ________________.
The names and addresses of its initial ______________________________ are:

____

____

____

____

____

____

Article 5. Principal Place of Business of the Limited Liability Company. The principal place of business of the limited liability company shall be: ______________________________

____.

Article 6. Period of Duration of the Limited Liability Company. The period of duration of the limited liability company shall be: ______________________________

____.

In Witness Whereof, the undersigned organizer(s) of this limited liability company has(have) signed these Articles of Organization on the date indicated.

Date: ______________________________

Signature(s):

______________________________	______________________________
Organizer	Typed or Printed Name
______________________________	______________________________
Organizer	Typed or Printed Name
______________________________	______________________________
Organizer	Typed or Printed Name
______________________________	______________________________
Organizer	Typed or Printed Name
______________________________	______________________________
Organizer	Typed or Printed Name
______________________________	______________________________
Organizer	Typed or Printed Name

____

____

____

____

____

LLC Filings Office:

I enclose an original and __________ copies of the proposed Articles of Organization of ____, a proposed domestic limited liability company. Please file the Articles of Organization and return a file-stamped copy of the original Articles or other receipt, acknowledgment or proof of filing to me at the address below.

A check/money order in the amount of $ ______________ , made payable to your office, for total filing and processing fees is enclosed.

☐ The above LLC name was reserved for my use ____, issued on ____.

Sincerely,

____

________________________________ , Organizer

____

____

____

Enclosures: Articles of Organization; check

OPERATING AGREEMENT FOR
MEMBER-MANAGED LIMITED LIABILITY COMPANY

I. PRELIMINARY PROVISIONS

(1) Effective Date: This operating agreement of ______________________________

____,

effective ____, is adopted by the members whose signatures appear at the end of this agreement.

(2) Formation: This limited liability company (LLC) was formed by filing Articles of Organization, a Certificate of Formation or a similar organizational document with the state of ____'s LLC filing office on

____.

A copy of this organizational document has been placed in the LLC's records book.

(3) Name: The formal name of this LLC is as stated above. However, this LLC may do business under a different name by complying with the state's fictitious or assumed business name statutes and procedures.

(4) Registered Office and Agent: The registered office of this LLC and the registered agent at this address are as follows: ____

____.

The registered office and agent may be changed from time to time as the members may see fit, by filing a change of registered agent or office form with the state LLC filing office. It will not be necessary to amend this provision of the operating agreement if and when such a change is made.

(5) Business Purposes: The specific business purposes and activities contemplated by the founders of this LLC at the time of initial signing of this agreement consist of the following:

____

____

____.

It is understood that the foregoing statement of purposes shall not serve as a limitation on the powers or abilities of this LLC, which shall be permitted to engage in any and all lawful business activities. If this LLC intends to engage in business activities outside the state of its formation that require the qualification of the LLC in other states, it shall obtain such qualification before engaging in such out-of-state activities.

(6) Duration of LLC: The duration of this LLC shall be ___________________________

____.

Further, this LLC shall terminate when a proposal to dissolve the LLC is adopted by the membership of this LLC or when this LLC is otherwise terminated in accordance with law.

II. MEMBERSHIP PROVISIONS

(1) Nonliability of Members: No member of this LLC shall be personally liable for the expenses, debts, obligations or liabilities of the LLC, or for claims made against it.

(2) Reimbursement for Organizational Costs: Members shall be reimbursed by the LLC for organizational expenses paid by the members. The LLC shall be authorized to elect to deduct organizational expenses and start-up expenditures ratably over a period of time as permitted by the Internal Revenue Code and as may be advised by the LLC's tax advisor.

(3) Management: This LLC shall be managed exclusively by all of its members.

(4) Members' Percentage Interests: A member's percentage interest in this LLC shall be computed as a fraction, the numerator of which is the total of a member's capital account and the denominator of which is the total of all capital accounts of all members. This fraction shall be expressed in this agreement as a percentage, which shall be called each member's "percentage interest" in this LLC.

(5) Membership Voting: Except as otherwise may be required by the Articles of Organization, Certificate of Formation or a similar organizational document, other provisions of this operating agreement, or under the laws of this state, each member shall vote on any matter submitted to the membership for approval in proportion to the member's percentage interest in this LLC. Further, unless defined otherwise for a particular provision of this operating agreement, the phrase "majority of members" means a majority of members whose combined percentage interests in this LLC represent more than 50% of the percentage interests of all members in this LLC.

(6) Compensation: Members shall not be paid as members of the LLC for performing any duties associated with such membership, including management of the LLC. Members may be paid, however, for any services rendered in any other capacity for the LLC, whether as officers, employees, independent contractors or otherwise.

(7) Members' Meetings: The LLC shall not provide for regular members' meetings. However, any member may call a meeting by communicating his or her wish to schedule a meeting to all other members. Such notification may be in person or in writing, or by telephone, facsimile machine, or other form of electronic communication reasonably expected to be received by a member, and the other members shall then agree, either personally, in writing, or by telephone, facsimile machine or other form of electronic communication to the member calling the meeting, to meet at a mutually acceptable time and place. Notice of the business to be transacted at the meeting need not be given to members by the member calling the meeting, and any business may be discussed and conducted at the meeting.

If all members cannot attend a meeting, it shall be postponed to a date and time when all members can attend, unless all members who do not attend have agreed in writing to the holding of the meeting without them. If a meeting is postponed, and the postponed meeting cannot be held either because all members do not attend the postponed meeting or the nonattending members have not signed a written consent to allow the postponed meeting to be held without them, a second postponed meeting may be held at a date and time announced at the first postponed meeting. The date and time of the second postponed meeting shall also be communicated to any members not attending the first postponed meeting. The second postponed meeting may be held without the attendance of all members as long as a majority

of the percentage interests of the membership of this LLC is in attendance at the second postponed meeting. Written notice of the decisions or approvals made at this second postponed meeting shall be mailed or delivered to each nonattending member promptly after the holding of the second postponed meeting.

Written minutes of the discussions and proposals presented at a members' meeting, and the votes taken and matters approved at such meeting, shall be taken by one of the members or a person designated at the meeting. A copy of the minutes of the meeting shall be placed in the LLC's records book after the meeting.

(8) Membership Certificates: This LLC shall be authorized to obtain and issue certificates representing or certifying membership interests in this LLC. Each certificate shall show the name of the LLC, the name of the member, and state that the person named is a member of the LLC and is entitled to all the rights granted members of the LLC under the Articles of Organization, Certificate of Formation or a similar organizational document, this operating agreement and provisions of law. Each membership certificate shall be consecutively numbered and signed by one or more officers of this LLC. The certificates shall include any additional information considered appropriate for inclusion by the members on membership certificates.

In addition to the above information, all membership certificates shall bear a prominent legend on their face or reverse side stating, summarizing or referring to any transfer restrictions that apply to memberships in this LLC under the Articles of Organization, Certificate of Formation or a similar organizational document and/or this operating agreement, and the address where a member may obtain a copy of these restrictions upon request from this LLC.

The records book of this LLC shall contain a list of the names and addresses of all persons to whom certificates have been issued, show the date of issuance of each certificate, and record the date of all cancellations or transfers of membership certificates.

(9) Other Business by Members: Each member shall agree not to own an interest in, manage or work for another business, enterprise or endeavor, if such ownership or activities would compete with this LLC's business goals, mission, profitability or productivity, or would diminish or impair the member's ability to provide maximum effort and performance in managing the business of this LLC.

III. TAX AND FINANCIAL PROVISIONS

(1) Tax Treatment: It is anticipated that this LLC will not be treated as a corporation under state and federal tax law, but instead it will be treated in the same manner as a partnership for tax purposes. It is further understood that the members do not consider each other partners or joint venturers with any other member or manager of this LLC for any purpose other than federal and state tax purposes.

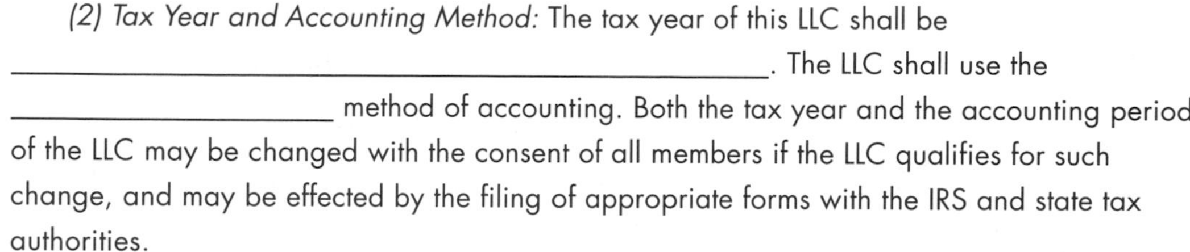

(2) Tax Year and Accounting Method: The tax year of this LLC shall be ____. The LLC shall use the ______________________ method of accounting. Both the tax year and the accounting period of the LLC may be changed with the consent of all members if the LLC qualifies for such change, and may be effected by the filing of appropriate forms with the IRS and state tax authorities.

(3) Tax Matters Partner: If this LLC is required under Internal Revenue Code provisions or regulations, it shall designate from among its members a "tax matters partner" in accordance with Internal Revenue Code Section 6231(a)(7) and corresponding regulations, who will fulfill this role by being the spokesperson for the LLC in dealings with the IRS as required under the Internal Revenue Code and Regulations, and who will report to the members on the progress and outcome of these dealings.

(4) Annual Income Tax Returns and Reports: Within 60 days after the end of each tax year of the LLC, a copy of the LLC's state and federal income tax returns for the preceding tax year shall be mailed or otherwise provided to each member of the LLC, together with any additional information and forms necessary for each member to complete his or her individual state and federal income tax returns. This additional information shall include a federal (and, if applicable, state) Form K-1 (Form 1065—Partner's Share of Income, Credits, Deductions) or equivalent income tax reporting form, as well as a financial report, which shall include a balance sheet and profit and loss statement for the prior tax year of the LLC.

(5) Bank Accounts: The LLC shall designate one or more banks or other institutions for the deposit of the funds of the LLC, and shall establish savings, checking, investment and other such accounts as are reasonable and necessary for its business and investments. One or more members of the LLC shall be designated with the consent of all members to deposit and withdraw funds of the LLC, and to direct the investment of funds from, into and among such accounts. The funds of the LLC, however and wherever deposited or invested, shall not be commingled with the personal funds of any members of the LLC.

(6) Title to Assets: All personal and real property of this LLC shall be held in the name of the LLC, not in the names of individual members.

IV. CAPITAL PROVISIONS

(1) Capital Contributions by Members: Members shall make the following contributions of cash, property or services as shown next to each member's name below. Unless otherwise noted, cash and property described below shall be paid or delivered to the LLC on or by ____. The fair market values of items of property or services as agreed between the LLC and the contributing member are also shown below. The percentage interest in the LLC that each member shall receive in return for his or her capital contribution is also indicated for each member.

Name	Contribution	Fair Market Value	Percentage Interest in LLC
____________________	____________	$ ________	________
____________________	____________	$ ________	________
____________________	____________	$ ________	________
____________________	____________	$ ________	________
____________________	____________	$ ________	________
____________________	____________	$ ________	________

(2) Additional Contributions by Members: The members may agree, from time to time by unanimous vote, to require the payment of additional capital contributions by the members, on or by a mutually agreeable date.

(3) Failure to Make Contributions: If a member fails to make a required capital contribution within the time agreed for a member's contribution, the remaining members may, by unanimous vote, agree to reschedule the time for payment of the capital contribution by the late-paying member, setting any additional repayment terms, such as a late payment penalty, rate of interest to be applied to the unpaid balance, or other monetary amount to be paid by the delinquent member, as the remaining members decide. Alternatively, the remaining members may, by unanimous vote, agree to cancel the membership of the delinquent member, provided any prior partial payments of capital made by the delinquent member are refunded promptly by the LLC to the member after the decision is made to terminate the membership of the delinquent member.

(4) No Interest on Capital Contributions: No interest shall be paid on funds or property contributed as capital to this LLC, or on funds reflected in the capital accounts of the members.

(5) Capital Account Bookkeeping: A capital account shall be set up and maintained on the books of the LLC for each member. It shall reflect each member's capital contribution to the LLC, increased by each member's share of profits in the LLC, decreased by each member's share of losses and expenses of the LLC, and adjusted as required in accordance with applicable provisions of the Internal Revenue Code and corresponding income tax regulations.

(6) Consent to Capital Contribution Withdrawals and Distributions: Members shall not be allowed to withdraw any part of their capital contributions or to receive distributions, whether in property or cash, except as otherwise allowed by this agreement and, in any case, only if such withdrawal is made with the written consent of all members.

(7) Allocations of Profits and Losses: No member shall be given priority or preference with respect to other members in obtaining a return of capital contributions, distributions or allocations of the income, gains, losses, deductions, credits or other items of the LLC. The profits and losses of the LLC, and all items of its income, gain, loss, deduction and credit shall be allocated to members according to each member's percentage interest in this LLC.

(8) Allocation and Distribution of Cash to Members: Cash from LLC business operations, as well as cash from a sale or other disposition of LLC capital assets, may be distributed from time to time to members in accordance with each member's percentage interest in the LLC, as may be decided by ____________________ of the members.

(9) Allocation of Noncash Distributions: If proceeds consist of property other than cash, the members shall decide the value of the property and allocate such value among the members in accordance with each member's percentage interest in the LLC. If such noncash proceeds are later reduced to cash, such cash may be distributed among the members as otherwise provided in this agreement.

(10) Allocation and Distribution of Liquidation Proceeds: Regardless of any other provision in this agreement, if there is a distribution in liquidation of this LLC, or when any member's interest is liquidated, all items of income and loss shall be allocated to the members' capital accounts, and all appropriate credits and deductions shall then be made to these capital accounts before any final distribution is made. A final distribution shall be made to members only to the extent of, and in proportion to, any positive balance in each member's capital account.

V. MEMBERSHIP WITHDRAWAL AND TRANSFER PROVISIONS

(1) Withdrawal of Members: A member may withdraw from this LLC by giving written notice to all other members at least ________________________ days before the date the withdrawal is to be effective.

(2) Restrictions on the Transfer of Membership: A member shall not transfer his or her membership in the LLC unless all nontransferring members in the LLC first agree to approve the admission of the transferee into this LLC. Further, no member may encumber a part or all of his or her membership in the LLC by mortgage, pledge, granting of a security interest, lien or otherwise, unless the encumbrance has first been approved in writing by all other members of the LLC.

Notwithstanding the above provision, any member shall be allowed to assign an economic interest in his or her membership to another person without the approval of the other members. Such an assignment shall not include a transfer of the member's voting or management rights in this LLC, and the assignee shall not become a member of the LLC.

VI. DISSOLUTION PROVISIONS

(1) Events That Trigger Dissolution of the LLC: The following events shall trigger a dissolution of the LLC, except as provided:

(a) the death, insanity, bankruptcy, retirement, resignation or expulsion of a member, except that within ______________________________ of the happening of any of these events, all remaining members of the LLC may vote to continue the legal existence of the LLC, in which case the LLC shall not dissolve;

(b) the expiration of the term of existence of the LLC if such term is specified in the Articles of Organization, Certificate of Formation or a similar organizational document, or this operating agreement;

(c) the written agreement of all members to dissolve the LLC;

(d) entry of a decree of dissolution of the LLC under state law.

VII. GENERAL PROVISIONS

(1) Officers: The LLC may designate one or more officers, such as a President, Vice President, Secretary and Treasurer. Persons who fill these positions need not be members of the LLC. Such positions may be compensated or noncompensated according to the nature and extent of the services rendered for the LLC as a part of the duties of each office. Ministerial services only as a part of any officer position will normally not be compensated, such as the performance of officer duties specified in this agreement, but any officer may be reimbursed by the LLC for out-of-pocket expenses paid by the officer in carrying out the duties of his or her office.

(2) Records: The LLC shall keep at its principal business address a copy of all proceedings of membership meetings, as well as books of account of the LLC's financial transactions. A list of the names and addresses of the current membership of the LLC also shall be maintained at this address, with notations on any transfers of members' interests to nonmembers or persons being admitted into membership in the LLC.

Copies of the LLC's Articles of Organization, Certificate of Formation or a similar organizational document, a signed copy of this operating agreement, and the LLC's tax returns for the preceding three tax years shall be kept at the principal business address of the LLC. A statement also shall be kept at this address containing any of the following information that is applicable to this LLC:

- the amount of cash or a description and value of property contributed or agreed to be contributed as capital to the LLC by each member;
- a schedule showing when any additional capital contributions are to be made by members to this LLC;

- a statement or schedule, if appropriate, showing the rights of members to receive distributions representing a return of part or all of members' capital contributions; and
- a description of, or date when, the legal existence of the LLC will terminate under provisions in the LLC's Articles of Organization, Certificate of Formation or a similar organizational document, or this operating agreement.

If one or more of the above items is included or listed in this operating agreement, it will be sufficient to keep a copy of this agreement at the principal business address of the LLC without having to prepare and keep a separate record of such item or items at this address.

Any member may inspect any and all records maintained by the LLC upon reasonable notice to the LLC. Copying of the LLC's records by members is allowed, but copying costs shall be paid for by the requesting member.

(3) All Necessary Acts: The members and officers of this LLC are authorized to perform all acts necessary to perfect the organization of this LLC and to carry out its business operations expeditiously and efficiently. The Secretary of the LLC, or other officers, or all members of the LLC, may certify to other businesses, financial institutions and individuals as to the authority of one or more members or officers of this LLC to transact specific items of business on behalf of the LLC.

(4) Mediation and Arbitration of Disputes Among Members: In any dispute over the provisions of this operating agreement and in other disputes among the members, if the members cannot resolve the dispute to their mutual satisfaction, the matter shall be submitted to mediation. The terms and procedure for mediation shall be arranged by the parties to the dispute.

If good-faith mediation of a dispute proves impossible or if an agreed-upon mediation outcome cannot be obtained by the members who are parties to the dispute, the dispute may be submitted to arbitration in accordance with the rules of the American Arbitration Association. Any party may commence arbitration of the dispute by sending a written request for arbitration to all other parties to the dispute. The request shall state the nature of the dispute to be resolved by arbitration, and, if all parties to the dispute agree to arbitration, arbitration shall be commenced as soon as practical after such parties receive a copy of the written request.

All parties shall initially share the cost of arbitration, but the prevailing party or parties may be awarded attorney fees, costs and other expenses of arbitration. All arbitration decisions shall be final, binding and conclusive on all the parties to arbitration, and legal judgment may be entered based upon such decision in accordance with applicable law in any court having jurisdiction to do so.

(5) Entire Agreement: This operating agreement represents the entire agreement among the members of this LLC, and it shall not be amended, modified or replaced except by a written instrument executed by all the parties to this agreement who are current members of this LLC as well as any and all additional parties who became members of this LLC after the adoption of this agreement. This agreement replaces and supersedes all prior written and oral agreements among any and all members of this LLC.

(6) Severability: If any provision of this agreement is determined by a court or arbitrator to be invalid, unenforceable or otherwise ineffective, that provision shall be severed from the rest of this agreement, and the remaining provisions shall remain in effect and enforceable.

VIII. SIGNATURES OF MEMBERS AND SPOUSES

(1) Execution of Agreement: In witness whereof, the members of this LLC sign and adopt this agreement as the operating agreement of this LLC.

Date: ______________________________
Signature: ______________________________
Printed Name: ______________________, Member

Date: ______________________________
Signature: ______________________________
Printed Name: ______________________, Member

Date: ______________________________
Signature: ______________________________
Printed Name: ______________________, Member

Date: ______________________________
Signature: ______________________________
Printed Name: ______________________, Member

Date: ______________________________
Signature: ______________________________
Printed Name: ______________________, Member

Date: ______________________________
Signature: ______________________________
Printed Name: ______________________, Member

(2) Consent of Spouses: The undersigned are spouses of members of this LLC who have signed this operating agreement in the preceding provision. These spouses have read this agreement and agree to be bound by its terms in any matter in which they have a financial interest, including restrictions on the transfer of memberships and the terms under which memberships in this LLC may be sold or otherwise transferred.

Date: ____

Signature: ____

Printed Name: _______________________________________

Spouse of: ____

Date: ____

Signature: ____

Printed Name: _______________________________________

Spouse of: ____

Date: ____

Signature: ____

Printed Name: _______________________________________

Spouse of: ____

Date: ____

Signature: ____

Printed Name: _______________________________________

Spouse of: ____

Date: ____

Signature: ____

Printed Name: _______________________________________

Spouse of: ____

Date: ____

Signature: ____

Printed Name: _______________________________________

Spouse of: ____

LIMITED LIABILITY COMPANY
MANAGEMENT OPERATING AGREEMENT

(1) Effective Date: This operating agreement of ______________________________

____,

effective ____, is adopted by the members whose signatures appear at the end of this agreement.

(2) Formation: This limited liability company (LLC) was formed by filing Articles of Organization, a Certificate of Formation or a similar organizational document with the state of ____'s LLC filing office on ____.

A copy of this organizational document has been placed in the LLC's records book.

(3) Name: The formal name of this LLC is as stated above. However, this LLC may do business under a different name by complying with the state's fictitious or assumed business name statutes and procedures.

(4) Registered Office and Agent: The registered office of this LLC and the registered agent at this address are as follows: ____

____.

The registered office and agent may be changed from time to time as the members or managers may see fit, by filing a change of registered agent or office form with the state LLC filing office. It will not be necessary to amend this provision of the operating agreement if and when such a change is made.

(5) Business Purposes: The specific business purposes and activities contemplated by the founders of this LLC at the time of initial signing of this agreement consist of the following:

____

____

____.

It is understood that the foregoing statement of purposes shall not serve as a limitation on the powers or abilities of this LLC, which shall be permitted to engage in any and all lawful business activities. If this LLC intends to engage in business activities outside the state of its formation that require the qualification of the LLC in other states, it shall obtain such qualification before engaging in such out-of-state activities.

(6) Duration of LLC: The duration of this LLC shall be ______________________________

____.

Further, this LLC shall terminate when a proposal to dissolve the LLC is adopted by the membership of this LLC or when this LLC is otherwise terminated in accordance with law.

II. MANAGEMENT PROVISIONS

(1) Management by Managers: This LLC will be managed by the managers listed below. All managers who are also members of this LLC are designated as "members"; nonmember managers are designated as "nonmembers."

Name: ______________________________ ☐ Member ☐ Nonmember
Address: ______________________________

Name: ______________________________ ☐ Member ☐ Nonmember
Address: ______________________________

Name: ______________________________ ☐ Member ☐ Nonmember
Address: ______________________________

Name: ______________________________ ☐ Member ☐ Nonmember
Address: ______________________________

Name: ______________________________ ☐ Member ☐ Nonmember
Address: ______________________________

Name: ______________________________ ☐ Member ☐ Nonmember
Address: ______________________________

(2) Nonliability of Managers: No manager of this LLC shall be personally liable for the expenses, debts, obligations or liabilities of the LLC, or for claims made against it.

(3) Authority and Votes of Managers: Except as otherwise set forth in this agreement, the Articles of Organization, Certificate of Organization or similar organizational document, or as may be provided under state law, all management decisions relating to this LLC's business shall be made by its managers. Management decisions shall be approved by ____________ of the current managers of the LLC, with each manager entitled to cast one vote for or against any matter submitted to the managers for a decision.

(4) Term of Managers: Each manager shall serve until the earlier of the following events:

(a) the manager becomes disabled, dies, retires or otherwise withdraws from management;

(b) the manager is removed from office; or

(c) the manager's term expires, if a term has been designated in other provisions of this agreement.

Upon the happening of any of these events, a new manager may be appointed to replace the departing manager by ______________________________.

(5) Management Meetings: Managers shall be able to discuss and approve LLC business informally, and may, at their discretion, call and hold formal management meetings according to the rules set forth in the following provisions of this operating agreement.

Regularly scheduled formal management meetings need not be held, but any manager may call such a meeting by communicating his or her request for a formal meeting to the other managers, noting the purpose or purposes for which the meeting is called. Only the business stated or summarized in the notice for the meeting shall be discussed and voted upon at the meeting.

The meeting shall be held within a reasonable time after a manager has made the request for a meeting, and in no event, later than ______________________ days after the request for the meeting. A quorum for such a formal managers' meeting shall consist of ______________________ managers, and if a quorum is not present, the meeting shall be adjourned to a new place and time with notice of the adjourned meeting given to all managers. An adjournment shall not be necessary, however, and a managers' meeting with less than a quorum may be held if all nonattending managers agreed in writing prior to the meeting to the holding of the meeting. All such written consents to the holding of a formal management meeting shall be kept and filed with the records of the meeting.

The proceedings of all formal managers' meetings shall be noted or summarized with written minutes of the meeting and a copy of the minutes shall be placed and kept in the records book of this LLC.

(6) Managers' Commitment to LLC: Managers shall devote their best efforts and energy working to achieve the business objectives and financial goals of this LLC. By agreeing to serve as a manager for the LLC, each manager shall agree not to work for another business, enterprise or endeavor, owned or operated by himself or herself or others, if such outside work or efforts would compete with the LLC's business goals, mission, products or services, or would diminish or impair the manager's ability to provide maximum effort and performance to managing the business of this LLC.

(7) Compensation of Managers: Managers of this LLC may be paid per-meeting or per-diem amounts for attending management meetings, may be reimbursed actual expenses advanced by them to attend management meetings or attend to management business for the LLC, and may be compensated in other ways for performing their duties as managers. Managers may work in other capacities for this LLC and may be compensated separately for performing these additional services, whether as officers, staff, consultants, independent contractors or in other capacities.

III. MEMBERSHIP PROVISIONS

(1) Nonliability of Members: No member of this LLC shall be personally liable for the expenses, debts, obligations or liabilities of the LLC, or for claims made against it.

(2) Reimbursement for Organizational Costs: Members shall be reimbursed by the LLC for organizational expenses paid by the members. The LLC shall be authorized to elect to deduct organizational expenses and start-up expenditures ratably over a period of time as permitted by the Internal Revenue Code and as may be advised by the LLC's tax advisor.

(3) Members' Percentage Interests: A member's percentage interest in this LLC shall be computed as a fraction, the numerator of which is the total of a member's capital account and the denominator of which is the total of all capital accounts of all members. This fraction shall be expressed in this agreement as a percentage, which shall be called each member's "percentage interest" in this LLC.

(4) Membership Voting: Except as otherwise may be required by the Articles of Organization, Certificate of Formation or a similar organizational document, other provisions of this operating agreement, or under the laws of this state, each member shall vote on any matter submitted to the membership for approval by the managers of this LLC in proportion to the member's percentage interest in this LLC. Further, unless defined otherwise for a particular provision of this operating agreement, the phrase "majority of members" means a majority of members whose combined percentage interests in this LLC represent more than 50% of the percentage interests of all members in this LLC.

(5) Compensation: Members shall not be paid as members of the LLC for performing any duties associated with such membership. Members may be paid, however, for any services rendered in any other capacity for the LLC, whether as officers, employees, independent contractors or otherwise.

(6) Members' Meetings: The LLC shall not provide for regular members' meetings. However, any member may call a meeting by communicating his or her wish to schedule a meeting to all other members. Such notification may be in person or in writing, or by telephone, facsimile machine, or other form of electronic communication reasonably expected to be received by a member, and the other members shall then agree, either personally, in writing, or by telephone, facsimile machine or other form of electronic communication to the member calling the meeting, to meet at a mutually acceptable time and place. Notice of the business to be transacted at the meeting need not be given to members by the member calling the meeting, and any business may be discussed and conducted at the meeting.

If all members cannot attend a meeting, it shall be postponed to a date and time when all members can attend, unless all members who do not attend have agreed in writing to the holding of the meeting without them. If a meeting is postponed, and the postponed meeting cannot be held either because all members do not attend the postponed meeting or the nonattending members have not signed a written consent to allow the postponed meeting to be held without them, a second postponed meeting may be held at a date and time announced at the first postponed meeting. The date and time of the second postponed meeting shall also be communicated to any members not attending the first postponed meeting. The second

postponed meeting may be held without the attendance of all members as long as a majority of the percentage interests of the membership of this LLC is in attendance at the second postponed meeting. Written notice of the decisions or approvals made at this second postponed meeting shall be mailed or delivered to each nonattending member promptly after the holding of the second postponed meeting.

Written minutes of the discussions and proposals presented at a members' meeting, and the votes taken and matters approved at such meeting, shall be taken by one of the members or a person designated at the meeting. A copy of the minutes of the meeting shall be placed in the LLC's records book after the meeting.

(7) Membership Certificates: This LLC shall be authorized to obtain and issue certificates representing or certifying membership interests in this LLC. Each certificate shall show the name of the LLC, the name of the member, and state that the person named is a member of the LLC and is entitled to all the rights granted members of the LLC under the Articles of Organization, Certificate of Formation or a similar organizational document, this operating agreement, and provisions of law. Each membership certificate shall be consecutively numbered and signed by one or more officers of this LLC. The certificates shall include any additional information considered appropriate for inclusion by the members on membership certificates.

In addition to the above information, all membership certificates shall bear a prominent legend on their face or reverse side stating, summarizing or referring to any transfer restrictions that apply to memberships in this LLC under the Articles of Organization, Certificate of Formation or a similar organizational document and/or this operating agreement, and the address where a member may obtain a copy of these restrictions upon request from this LLC.

The records book of this LLC shall contain a list of the names and addresses of all persons to whom certificates have been issued, show the date of issuance of each certificate, and record the date of all cancellations or transfers of membership certificates.

IV. TAX AND FINANCIAL PROVISIONS

(1) Tax Treatment: It is anticipated that this LLC will not be treated as a corporation under state and federal tax law, but instead it will be treated in the same manner as a partnership for tax purposes. It is further understood that the members do not consider each other partners or joint venturers with any other member of this LLC for any purpose other than federal and state tax purposes.

(2) Tax Year and Accounting Method: The tax year of this LLC shall be ______________ ____ . The LLC shall use the ______________________ method of accounting. Both the tax year and the accounting period of the LLC may be changed with the consent of all members or all managers if the LLC qualifies for such change, and may be effected by the filing of appropriate forms with the IRS and state tax authorities.

(3) Tax Matters Partner: If this LLC is required under Internal Revenue Code provisions or regulations, it shall designate from among its members or member-managers a "tax matters partner" in accordance with Internal Revenue Code Section 6231(a)(7) and corresponding regulations, who will fulfill this role by being the spokesperson for the LLC in dealings with the IRS as required under the Internal Revenue Code and Regulations, and who will report to the members and managers on the progress and outcome of these dealings.

(4) Annual Income Tax Returns and Reports: Within 60 days after the end of each tax year of the LLC, a copy of the LLC's state and federal income tax returns for the preceding tax year shall be mailed or otherwise provided to each member of the LLC, together with any additional information and forms necessary for each member to complete his or her individual state and federal income tax returns. This additional information shall include a federal (and, if applicable, state) Form K-1 (Form 1065—Partner's Share of Income, Credits, Deductions) or equivalent income tax reporting form, as well as a financial report, which shall include a balance sheet and profit and loss statement for the prior tax year of the LLC.

(5) Bank Accounts: The LLC shall designate one or more banks or other institutions for the deposit of the funds of the LLC, and shall establish savings, checking, investment and other such accounts as are reasonable and necessary for its business and investments. One or more employees of the LLC shall be designated with the consent of all managers to deposit and withdraw funds of the LLC, and to direct the investment of funds from, into and among such accounts. The funds of the LLC, however and wherever deposited or invested, shall not be commingled with the personal funds of any members or managers of the LLC.

(6) Title to Assets: All personal and real property of this LLC shall be held in the name of the LLC, not in the names of individual members or managers.

V. CAPITAL PROVISIONS

(1) Capital Contributions by Members: Members shall make the following contributions of cash, property or services as shown next to each member's name below. Unless otherwise noted, cash and property described below shall be paid or delivered to the LLC on or by ____. The fair market values of items of property or services as agreed between the LLC and the contributing member are also shown below. The percentage interest in the LLC that each member shall receive in return for his or her capital contribution is also indicated for each member.

Name	Contribution	Fair Market Value	Percentage Interest in LLC
____________	____________	$ ________	________
____________	____________	$ ________	________
____________	____________	$ ________	________
____________	____________	$ ________	________
____________	____________	$ ________	________
____________	____________	$ ________	________

(2) Additional Contributions by Members: The members may agree, from time to time by unanimous vote, to require the payment of additional capital contributions by the members, on or by a mutually agreeable date.

(3) Failure to Make Contributions: If a member fails to make a required capital contribution within the time agreed for a member's contribution, the remaining members may, by unanimous vote, agree to reschedule the time for payment of the capital contribution by the late-paying member, setting any additional repayment terms, such as a late payment penalty, rate of interest to be applied to the unpaid balance, or other monetary amount to be paid by the delinquent member, as the remaining members decide. Alternatively, the remaining members may, by unanimous vote, agree to cancel the membership of the delinquent member, provided any prior partial payments of capital made by the delinquent member are refunded promptly by the LLC to the member after the decision is made to terminate the membership of the delinquent member.

(4) No Interest on Capital Contributions: No interest shall be paid on funds or property contributed as capital to this LLC, or on funds reflected in the capital accounts of the members.

(5) Capital Account Bookkeeping: A capital account shall be set up and maintained on the books of the LLC for each member. It shall reflect each member's capital contribution to the LLC, increased by each member's share of profits in the LLC, decreased by each member's share of losses and expenses of the LLC, and adjusted as required in accordance with applicable provisions of the Internal Revenue Code and corresponding income tax regulations.

(6) Consent to Capital Contribution Withdrawals and Distributions: Members shall not be allowed to withdraw any part of their capital contributions or to receive distributions, whether in property or cash, except as otherwise allowed by this agreement and, in any case, only if such withdrawal is made with the written consent of all members.

(7) Allocations of Profits and Losses: No member shall be given priority or preference with respect to other members in obtaining a return of capital contributions, distributions or allocations of the income, gains, losses, deductions, credits or other items of the LLC. The profits and losses of the LLC, and all items of its income, gain, loss, deduction and credit shall be allocated to members according to each member's percentage interest in this LLC.

(8) Allocation and Distribution of Cash to Members: Cash from LLC business operations, as well as cash from a sale or other disposition of LLC capital assets, may be distributed from time to time to members in accordance with each member's percentage interest in the LLC, as may be decided by ______________________________ of the

____ .

(9) Allocation of Noncash Distributions: If proceeds consist of property other than cash, the ____ shall decide the value of the property and allocate such value among the members in accordance with each member's percentage interest in the LLC. If such noncash proceeds are later reduced to cash, such cash may be distributed among the members as otherwise provided in this agreement.

(10) Allocation and Distribution of Liquidation Proceeds: Regardless of any other provision in this agreement, if there is a distribution in liquidation of this LLC, or when any member's interest is liquidated, all items of income and loss shall be allocated to the members' capital accounts, and all appropriate credits and deductions shall then be made to these capital accounts before any final distribution is made. A final distribution shall be made to members only to the extent of, and in proportion to, any positive balance in each member's capital account.

VI. MEMBERSHIP WITHDRAWAL AND TRANSFER PROVISIONS

(1) Withdrawal of Members: A member may withdraw from this LLC by giving written notice to all other members at least ______________________________ days before the date the withdrawal is to be effective.

(2) Restrictions on the Transfer of Membership: A member shall not transfer his or her membership in the LLC unless all nontransferring _____________________________________ in the LLC first agree to approve the admission of the transferee into this LLC. Further, no member may encumber a part or all of his or her membership in the LLC by mortgage, pledge, granting of a security interest, lien or otherwise, unless the encumbrance has first been approved in writing by all other members of the LLC.

Notwithstanding the above provision, any member shall be allowed to assign an economic interest in his or her membership to another person without the approval of the other members or member-managers. Such an assignment shall not include a transfer of the member's voting or management rights in this LLC, and the assignee shall not become a member of the LLC.

VII. DISSOLUTION PROVISIONS

(1) Events That Trigger Dissolution of the LLC: The following events shall trigger a dissolution of the LLC, except as provided:

(a) the death, insanity, bankruptcy, retirement, resignation or expulsion of a ______________________________, except that within ____________________ of the happening of any of these events, all remaining members of the LLC may vote to continue the legal existence of the LLC, in which case the LLC shall not dissolve;

(b) the expiration of the term of existence of the LLC if such term is specified in the Articles of Organization, Certificate of Formation or a similar organizational document, or this operating agreement;

(c) the written agreement of all members to dissolve the LLC;

(d) entry of a decree of dissolution of the LLC under state law.

VIII. GENERAL PROVISIONS

(1) Officers: The managers of this LLC may designate one or more officers, such as a President, Vice President, Secretary and Treasurer. Persons who fill these positions need not be members or managers of the LLC. Such positions may be compensated or noncompensated according to the nature and extent of the services rendered for the LLC as a part of the duties of each office. Ministerial services only as a part of any officer position will normally not be compensated, such as the performance of officer duties specified in this agreement, but any officer may be reimbursed by the LLC for out-of-pocket expenses paid by the officer in carrying out the duties of his or her office.

(2) Records: The LLC shall keep at its principal business address a copy of all proceedings of membership meetings, as well as books of account of the LLC's financial transactions. A list of the names and addresses of the current membership of the LLC also shall be maintained at this address, with notations on any transfers of members' interests to nonmembers or persons being admitted into membership in the LLC. A list of the current managers' names and addresses shall also be kept at this address.

Copies of the LLC's Articles of Organization, Certificate of Formation or a similar organizational document, a signed copy of this operating agreement, and the LLC's tax returns for the preceding three tax years shall be kept at the principal business address of the LLC. A statement also shall be kept at this address containing any of the following information that is applicable to this LLC:

- the amount of cash or a description and value of property contributed or agreed to be contributed as capital to the LLC by each member;

- a schedule showing when any additional capital contributions are to be made by members to this LLC;
- a statement or schedule, if appropriate, showing the rights of members to receive distributions representing a return of part or all of members' capital contributions; and
- a description of, or date when, the legal existence of the LLC will terminate under provisions in the LLC's Articles of Organization, Certificate of Formation or a similar organizational document, or this operating agreement.

If one or more of the above items is included or listed in this operating agreement, it will be sufficient to keep a copy of this agreement at the principal business address of the LLC without having to prepare and keep a separate record of such item or items at this address.

Any member or manager may inspect any and all records maintained by the LLC upon reasonable notice to the LLC. Copying of the LLC's records by members and managers is allowed, but copying costs shall be paid for by the requesting member or manager.

(3) All Necessary Acts: The members, managers and officers of this LLC are authorized to perform all acts necessary to perfect the organization of this LLC and to carry out its business operations expeditiously and efficiently. The Secretary of the LLC, or other officers, or one or more managers or all members of the LLC, may certify to other businesses, financial institutions and individuals as to the authority of one or more members, managers or officers of this LLC to transact specific items of business on behalf of the LLC.

(4) Mediation and Arbitration of Disputes Among Members: In any dispute over the provisions of this operating agreement and in other disputes among the members, if the members cannot resolve the dispute to their mutual satisfaction, the matter shall be submitted to mediation. The terms and procedure for mediation shall be arranged by the parties to the dispute.

If good-faith mediation of a dispute proves impossible or if an agreed-upon mediation outcome cannot be obtained by the members who are parties to the dispute, the dispute may be submitted to arbitration in accordance with the rules of the American Arbitration Association. Any party may commence arbitration of the dispute by sending a written request for arbitration to all other parties to the dispute. The request shall state the nature of the dispute to be resolved by arbitration, and, if all parties to the dispute agree to arbitration, arbitration shall be commenced as soon as practical after such parties receive a copy of the written request.

All parties shall initially share the cost of arbitration, but the prevailing party or parties may be awarded attorney fees, costs and other expenses of arbitration. All arbitration decisions shall be final, binding and conclusive on all the parties to arbitration, and legal judgment may be entered based upon such decision in accordance with applicable law in any court having jurisdiction to do so.

(5) Entire Agreement: This operating agreement represents the entire agreement among the members of this LLC, and it shall not be amended, modified or replaced except by a written instrument executed by all the parties to this agreement who are current members of this LLC as well as any and all additional parties who became members of this LLC after the adoption of this agreement. This agreement replaces and supersedes all prior written and oral agreements among any and all members of this LLC.

(6) Severability: If any provision of this agreement is determined by a court or arbitrator to be invalid, unenforceable or otherwise ineffective, that provision shall be severed from the rest of this agreement, and the remaining provisions shall remain in effect and enforceable.

IX. SIGNATURES OF MEMBERS AND SPOUSES

(1) Execution of Agreement: In witness whereof, the members of this LLC sign and adopt this agreement as the operating agreement of this LLC.

Date: ____

Signature: ____

Printed Name: ______________________________ , Member

Date: ____

Signature: ____

Printed Name: ______________________________ , Member

Date: ____

Signature: ____

Printed Name: ______________________________ , Member

Date: ____

Signature: ____

Printed Name: ______________________________ , Member

Date: ____

Signature: ____

Printed Name: ______________________________ , Member

Date: ____

Signature: ____

Printed Name: ______________________________ , Member

(2) Consent of Spouses: The undersigned are spouses of members of this LLC who have signed this operating agreement in the preceding provision. These spouses have read this agreement and agree to be bound by its terms in any matter in which they have a financial interest, including restrictions on the transfer of memberships and the terms under which memberships in this LLC may be sold or otherwise transferred.

Date: ______________________________________
Signature: __________________________________
Printed Name: _______________________________
Spouse of: __________________________________

Date: ______________________________________
Signature: __________________________________
Printed Name: _______________________________
Spouse of: __________________________________

Date: ______________________________________
Signature: __________________________________
Printed Name: _______________________________
Spouse of: __________________________________

Date: ______________________________________
Signature: __________________________________
Printed Name: _______________________________
Spouse of: __________________________________

Date: ______________________________________
Signature: __________________________________
Printed Name: _______________________________
Spouse of: __________________________________

Date: ______________________________________
Signature: __________________________________
Printed Name: _______________________________
Spouse of: __________________________________

MINUTES OF MEETING OF THE

____

OF

____

A meeting of the ____________________ of the above named limited liability company was held on ____________________________________, at ________________ __.M., at ____

________________________________, State of _________________________________,

for the following purpose(s):

____

____

____

____.

____ acted as chairperson, and ____ acted as secretary of the meeting.

The chairperson called the meeting to order.

The following _______________________ were present at the meeting:

____

____

____

____

____

____.

The following persons were also present at the meeting, and any reports given by these persons are noted next to their names below:

Name and Title	Reports Presented, If Any
____	_________________________
____	_________________________
____	_________________________
____	_________________________
____	_________________________
____	_________________________

After discussion, on motion duly made and carried by the affirmative vote of

________________________ of the __________________________________,

the following resolution(s) was/were adopted:

____

____

____

____

____

____

____

____

____

____

____

____

____

____

There being no further business to come before the meeting, it was adjourned on motion duly made and carried.

Date: __________________________________

Signature(s): ______________________________

____

Title: ___________________________________

CERTIFICATION OF AUTHORITY

This LLC is managed by its ______________________________ . The names and addresses of each of its current ________________________ as of ________________________________ are listed below. Each of these persons has managerial authority of the LLC and is empowered to transact business on its behalf.

Name of ___________________________	Address
___________________________________	___________________________________
	___________________________________
___________________________________	___________________________________
	___________________________________
___________________________________	___________________________________
	___________________________________
___________________________________	___________________________________
	___________________________________
___________________________________	___________________________________
	___________________________________
___________________________________	___________________________________
	___________________________________

Further, each of the following _____________________________ is specifically authorized to transact the following business on behalf of the LLC:

____

____

____

Date: ____

Name of LLC: ____________________________________

by____

Printed Name: ___________________________________

Title: ____

APPENDIX C

Membership Certificates

Fill In at Time of Issuance

Certificate Number ______________

Issued To:

____

____

Date ______________ 19 ____

Fill in at Time of Transfer

Transferor ______________

Transferee ______________

Date of Transfer ______________

No. of Transferee's Certificate ______________

Note: Memberships in this LLC are Subject to Restrictions on Transfer Contained in the Company's Operating Agreement

Fill In at Time of Issuance

Received Certificate Number ______________

This ________ day of ________ 19 ____

____

SIGNATURE OF MEMBER

Certificate Number ______

THE MEMBERSHIP INTEREST REPRESENTED BY THIS CERTIFICATE IS SUBJECT TO RESTRICTIONS ON TRANSFER, AND MAY NOT BE OFFERED FOR SALE, SOLD, TRANSFERRED OR PLEDGED EXCEPT ACCORDING TO, AND ONLY IF ALLOWED BY, THESE TRANSFER RESTRICTIONS. TO OBTAIN A COPY OF THESE TRANSFER RESTRICTIONS, CONTACT AN OFFICER OF THIS LCC AT THE FOLLOWING ADDRESS: ______________

____

A LIMITED LIABILITY COMPANY

MEMBERSHIP CERTIFICATE

THIS IS TO CERTIFY THAT ______________

is a member of the above Limited Liability Company organized under the laws of this state and is entitled to the full rights and privileges of such membership, subject to the duties and restrictions, as more fully set forth in the Limited Liability Company's Articles of Organization and Operating Agreement.

IN WITNESS WHEREOF, the Company has caused this Certificate to be executed by its duly authorized officers.

Dated ______________

______________ *, Officer*

______________ *, Officer*

Fill In at Time of Issuance	Fill in at Time of Transfer	Fill In at Time of Issuance
Certificate Number ______	Transferor ______	Received Certificate Number ______
Issued To:	Transferee ______	This ______ day of ______ 19 ______
______	Date of Transfer ______	______
______	No. of Transferee's Certificate ______	SIGNATURE OF MEMBER
Date ______ 19 ______	Note: Memberships in this LLC are Subject to Restrictions on Transfer Contained in the Company's Operating Agreement	

Certificate Number ______

THE MEMBERSHIP INTEREST REPRESENTED BY THIS CERTIFICATE IS SUBJECT TO RESTRICTIONS ON TRANSFER, AND MAY NOT BE OFFERED FOR SALE, SOLD, TRANSFERRED OR PLEDGED EXCEPT ACCORDING TO, AND ONLY IF ALLOWED BY, THESE TRANSFER RESTRICTIONS. TO OBTAIN A COPY OF THESE TRANSFER RESTRICTIONS, CONTACT AN OFFICER OF THIS LCC AT THE FOLLOWING ADDRESS: ______

______

A LIMITED LIABILITY COMPANY

MEMBERSHIP CERTIFICATE

THIS IS TO CERTIFY THAT ______

is a member of the above Limited Liability Company organized under the laws of this state and is entitled to the full rights and privileges of such membership, subject to the duties and restrictions, as more fully set forth in the Limited Liability Company's Articles of Organization and Operating Agreement.

IN WITNESS WHEREOF, the Company has caused this Certificate to be executed by its duly authorized officers.

Dated ______

______ *, Officer*

______ *, Officer*

Fill In at Time of Issuance

Certificate Number ____________________

Issued To:

____

____

Date ____________________ 19 ____

Fill in at Time of Transfer

Transferor ____________________

Transferee ____________________

Date of Transfer ____________________

No. of Transferee's Certificate ____________

Note: Memberships in this LLC are Subject to Restrictions on Transfer Contained in the Company's Operating Agreement

Fill In at Time of Issuance

Received Certificate Number ____________________

This ________ day of ____________ 19 ____

____

SIGNATURE OF MEMBER

Certificate Number ______

THE MEMBERSHIP INTEREST REPRESENTED BY THIS CERTIFICATE IS SUBJECT TO RESTRICTIONS ON TRANSFER, AND MAY NOT BE OFFERED FOR SALE, SOLD, TRANSFERRED OR PLEDGED EXCEPT ACCORDING TO, AND ONLY IF ALLOWED BY, THESE TRANSFER RESTRICTIONS. TO OBTAIN A COPY OF THESE TRANSFER RESTRICTIONS, CONTACT AN OFFICER OF THIS LCC AT THE FOLLOWING ADDRESS: ____________________

____

A LIMITED LIABILITY COMPANY

MEMBERSHIP CERTIFICATE

THIS IS TO CERTIFY THAT ____________________

is a member of the above Limited Liability Company organized under the laws of this state and is entitled to the full rights and privileges of such membership, subject to the duties and restrictions, as more fully set forth in the Limited Liability Company's Articles of Organization and Operating Agreement.

IN WITNESS WHEREOF, the Company has caused this Certificate to be executed by its duly authorized officers.

Dated ____________________

____________________ *, Officer*

____________________ *, Officer*

Fill In at Time of Issuance

Certificate Number ______________

Issued To:

____

____

Date ______________ 19 ____

Fill in at Time of Transfer

Transferor ______________

Transferee ______________

Date of Transfer ______________

No. of Transferee's Certificate ______________

Note: Memberships in this LLC are Subject to Restrictions on Transfer Contained in the Company's Operating Agreement

Fill In at Time of Issuance

Received Certificate Number ______________

This ________ day of ______________ 19 ____

____

SIGNATURE OF MEMBER

Certificate Number ______

THE MEMBERSHIP INTEREST REPRESENTED BY THIS CERTIFICATE IS SUBJECT TO RESTRICTIONS ON TRANSFER, AND MAY NOT BE OFFERED FOR SALE, SOLD, TRANSFERRED OR PLEDGED EXCEPT ACCORDING TO, AND ONLY IF ALLOWED BY, THESE TRANSFER RESTRICTIONS. TO OBTAIN A COPY OF THESE TRANSFER RESTRICTIONS, CONTACT AN OFFICER OF THIS LCC AT THE FOLLOWING ADDRESS: ______________

____

A LIMITED LIABILITY COMPANY

MEMBERSHIP CERTIFICATE

THIS IS TO CERTIFY THAT ______________

is a member of the above Limited Liability Company organized under the laws of this state and is entitled to the full rights and privileges of such membership, subject to the duties and restrictions, as more fully set forth in the Limited Liability Company's Articles of Organization and Operating Agreement.

IN WITNESS WHEREOF, the Company has caused this Certificate to be executed by its duly authorized officers.

Dated ______________

______________ *, Officer*

______________ *, Officer*

Fill In at Time of Issuance

Certificate Number ______________________

Issued To:

____

____

Date ______________________ 19 ____

Fill in at Time of Transfer

Transferor ______________________

Transferee ______________________

Date of Transfer ______________________

No. of Transferee's Certificate ______________

Note: Memberships in this LLC are Subject to Restrictions on Transfer Contained in the Company's Operating Agreement

Fill In at Time of Issuance

Received Certificate Number ______________

This ________ day of __________ 19 ____

____

SIGNATURE OF MEMBER

Certificate Number ______

THE MEMBERSHIP INTEREST REPRESENTED BY THIS CERTIFICATE IS SUBJECT TO RESTRICTIONS ON TRANSFER, AND MAY NOT BE OFFERED FOR SALE, SOLD, TRANSFERRED OR PLEDGED EXCEPT ACCORDING TO, AND ONLY IF ALLOWED BY, THESE TRANSFER RESTRICTIONS. TO OBTAIN A COPY OF THESE TRANSFER RESTRICTIONS, CONTACT AN OFFICER OF THIS LCC AT THE FOLLOWING ADDRESS: ______________________

____

A LIMITED LIABILITY COMPANY

MEMBERSHIP CERTIFICATE

THIS IS TO CERTIFY THAT ______________________

is a member of the above Limited Liability Company organized under the laws of this state and is entitled to the full rights and privileges of such membership, subject to the duties and restrictions, as more fully set forth in the Limited Liability Company's Articles of Organization and Operating Agreement.

IN WITNESS WHEREOF, the Company has caused this Certificate to be executed by its duly authorized officers.

Dated ______________________

______________________ *, Officer*

______________________ *, Officer*

Fill In at Time of Issuance

Certificate Number ______________________

Issued To:

____

____

Date ______________________ 19 ____

Fill in at Time of Transfer

Transferor ______________________

Transferee ______________________

Date of Transfer ______________________

No. of Transferee's Certificate ______________

Note: Memberships in this LLC are Subject to Restrictions on Transfer Contained in the Company's Operating Agreement

Fill In at Time of Issuance

Received Certificate Number ______________________

This ________ day of __________ 19 ____

____

SIGNATURE OF MEMBER

Certificate Number ______

THE MEMBERSHIP INTEREST REPRESENTED BY THIS CERTIFICATE IS SUBJECT TO RESTRICTIONS ON TRANSFER, AND MAY NOT BE OFFERED FOR SALE, SOLD, TRANSFERRED OR PLEDGED EXCEPT ACCORDING TO, AND ONLY IF ALLOWED BY, THESE TRANSFER RESTRICTIONS. TO OBTAIN A COPY OF THESE TRANSFER RESTRICTIONS, CONTACT AN OFFICER OF THIS LCC AT THE FOLLOWING ADDRESS: ______________________________

____

A LIMITED LIABILITY COMPANY

MEMBERSHIP CERTIFICATE

THIS IS TO CERTIFY THAT ______________________________

is a member of the above Limited Liability Company organized under the laws of this state and is entitled to the full rights and privileges of such membership, subject to the duties and restrictions, as more fully set forth in the Limited Liability Company's Articles of Organization and Operating Agreement.

IN WITNESS WHEREOF, the Company has caused this Certificate to be executed by its duly authorized officers.

Dated ______________________

______________________ *, Officer*

______________________ *, Officer*

Fill In at Time of Issuance	Fill in at Time of Transfer	Fill In at Time of Issuance
Certificate Number ______	Transferor ______	Received Certificate Number ______
Issued To:	Transferee ______	This ______ day of ______ 19 ______
______	Date of Transfer ______	
______	No. of Transferee's Certificate ______	______
Date ______ 19 ____	Note: Memberships in this LLC are Subject to Restrictions on Transfer Contained in the Company's Operating Agreement	SIGNATURE OF MEMBER

Certificate Number ______

THE MEMBERSHIP INTEREST REPRESENTED BY THIS CERTIFICATE IS SUBJECT TO RESTRICTIONS ON TRANSFER, AND MAY NOT BE OFFERED FOR SALE, SOLD, TRANSFERRED OR PLEDGED EXCEPT ACCORDING TO, AND ONLY IF ALLOWED BY, THESE TRANSFER RESTRICTIONS. TO OBTAIN A COPY OF THESE TRANSFER RESTRICTIONS, CONTACT AN OFFICER OF THIS LCC AT THE FOLLOWING ADDRESS: ______

______

A LIMITED LIABILITY COMPANY

MEMBERSHIP CERTIFICATE

THIS IS TO CERTIFY THAT ______

is a member of the above Limited Liability Company organized under the laws of this state and is entitled to the full rights and privileges of such membership, subject to the duties and restrictions, as more fully set forth in the Limited Liability Company's Articles of Organization and Operating Agreement.

IN WITNESS WHEREOF, the Company has caused this Certificate to be executed by its duly authorized officers.

Dated ______

______ *, Officer*

______ *, Officer*

Fill In at Time of Issuance

Certificate Number ______________________

Issued To:

____

____

Date ______________________ 19 ____

Fill in at Time of Transfer

Transferor ______________________

Transferee ______________________

Date of Transfer ______________________

No. of Transferee's Certificate ______________________

Note: Memberships in this LLC are Subject to Restrictions on Transfer Contained in the Company's Operating Agreement

Fill In at Time of Issuance

Received Certificate Number ______________________

This ________ day of ______________ 19 ____

____

SIGNATURE OF MEMBER

Certificate Number ______

THE MEMBERSHIP INTEREST REPRESENTED BY THIS CERTIFICATE IS SUBJECT TO RESTRICTIONS ON TRANSFER, AND MAY NOT BE OFFERED FOR SALE, SOLD, TRANSFERRED OR PLEDGED EXCEPT ACCORDING TO, AND ONLY IF ALLOWED BY, THESE TRANSFER RESTRICTIONS. TO OBTAIN A COPY OF THESE TRANSFER RESTRICTIONS, CONTACT AN OFFICER OF THIS LCC AT THE FOLLOWING ADDRESS: ______________________

____

A LIMITED LIABILITY COMPANY

MEMBERSHIP CERTIFICATE

THIS IS TO CERTIFY THAT ______________________

is a member of the above Limited Liability Company organized under the laws of this state and is entitled to the full rights and privileges of such membership, subject to the duties and restrictions, as more fully set forth in the Limited Liability Company's Articles of Organization and Operating Agreement.

IN WITNESS WHEREOF, the Company has caused this Certificate to be executed by its duly authorized officers.

Dated ______________________

______________________ *, Officer*

______________________ *, Officer*

Fill In at Time of Issuance

Certificate Number ______________________

Issued To:

____

____

Date ______________________ 19 ____

Fill in at Time of Transfer

Transferor ______________________

Transferee ______________________

Date of Transfer ______________________

No. of Transferee's Certificate ______________

Note: Memberships in this LLC are Subject to Restrictions on Transfer Contained in the Company's Operating Agreement

Fill In at Time of Issuance

Received Certificate Number ______________________

This ________ day of ____________ 19 ____

____

SIGNATURE OF MEMBER

Certificate Number ______

THE MEMBERSHIP INTEREST REPRESENTED BY THIS CERTIFICATE IS SUBJECT TO RESTRICTIONS ON TRANSFER, AND MAY NOT BE OFFERED FOR SALE, SOLD, TRANSFERRED OR PLEDGED EXCEPT ACCORDING TO, AND ONLY IF ALLOWED BY, THESE TRANSFER RESTRICTIONS. TO OBTAIN A COPY OF THESE TRANSFER RESTRICTIONS, CONTACT AN OFFICER OF THIS LCC AT THE FOLLOWING ADDRESS: ______________________________

____

A LIMITED LIABILITY COMPANY

Membership Certificate

THIS IS TO CERTIFY THAT ______________________________

is a member of the above Limited Liability Company organized under the laws of this state and is entitled to the full rights and privileges of such membership, subject to the duties and restrictions, as more fully set forth in the Limited Liability Company's Articles of Organization and Operating Agreement.

IN WITNESS WHEREOF, the Company has caused this Certificate to be executed by its duly authorized officers.

Dated ______________________

______________________ *, Officer*

______________________ *, Officer*

Fill In at Time of Issuance

Certificate Number ______________________

Issued To:

____

____

Date ______________________ 19 ____

Fill in at Time of Transfer

Transferor ______________________

Transferee ______________________

Date of Transfer ______________________

No. of Transferee's Certificate ______________

Note: Memberships in this LLC are Subject to Restrictions on Transfer Contained in the Company's Operating Agreement

Fill In at Time of Issuance

Received Certificate Number ______________________

This __________ day of ____________ 19 ____

____

SIGNATURE OF MEMBER

Certificate Number ______

THE MEMBERSHIP INTEREST REPRESENTED BY THIS CERTIFICATE IS SUBJECT TO RESTRICTIONS ON TRANSFER, AND MAY NOT BE OFFERED FOR SALE, SOLD, TRANSFERRED OR PLEDGED EXCEPT ACCORDING TO, AND ONLY IF ALLOWED BY, THESE TRANSFER RESTRICTIONS. TO OBTAIN A COPY OF THESE TRANSFER RESTRICTIONS, CONTACT AN OFFICER OF THIS LCC AT THE FOLLOWING ADDRESS: ______________________

____

A LIMITED LIABILITY COMPANY

MEMBERSHIP CERTIFICATE

THIS IS TO CERTIFY THAT ______________________ *is a member of the above Limited Liability Company organized under the laws of this state and is entitled to the full rights and privileges of such membership, subject to the duties and restrictions, as more fully set forth in the Limited Liability Company's Articles of Organization and Operating Agreement.*

IN WITNESS WHEREOF, the Company has caused this Certificate to be executed by its duly authorized officers.

Dated ______________________

______________________ *, Officer*

______________________ *, Officer*

Index

A

B

C

D

E

F

G

H

I

L

M

	BUSINESS	EDITION	PRICE	CODE
	Business Plans to Game Plans	1st	$29.95	GAME
	Helping Employees Achieve Retirement Security	1st	$16.95	HEAR
▣	Hiring Indepedent Contractors: The Employer's Legal Guide	1st	$29.95	HICI
	How to Finance a Growing Business	4th	$24.95	GROW
▣	How to Form a CA Nonprofit Corp.—w/Corp. Records Binder & PC Disk	1st	$49.95	CNP
▣	How to Form a Nonprofit Corp., Book w/Disk (PC)—National Edition	3rd	$39.95	NNP
▣	How to Form Your Own Calif. Corp.—w/Corp. Records Binder & Disk—PC	1st	$39.95	CACI
	How to Form Your Own California Corporation	8th	$29.95	CCOR
▣	How to Form Your Own Florida Corporation, (Book w/Disk—PC)	3rd	$39.95	FLCO
▣	How to Form Your Own New York Corporation, (Book w/Disk—PC)	3rd	$39.95	NYCO
▣	How to Form Your Own Texas Corporation, (Book w/Disk—PC)	4th	$39.95	TCI
	How to Handle Your Workers' Compensation Claim (California Edition)	1st	$29.95	WORK
	How to Market a Product for Under $500	1st	$29.95	UN500
	How to Write a Business Plan	4th	$21.95	SBS
	Make Up Your Mind: Entrepreneurs Talk About Decision Making	1st	$19.95	MIND
	Managing Generation X: How to Bring Out the Best in Young Talent	1st	$19.95	MANX
	Marketing Without Advertising	1st	$14.00	MWAD
	Mastering Diversity: Managing for Success Under ADA and Other Anti-Discrimination Laws	1st	$29.95	MAST
▣	OSHA in the Real World: (Book w/Disk—PC)	1st	$29.95	OSHA
▣	Taking Care of Your Corporation, Vol. 1, (Book w/Disk—PC)	1st	$26.95	CORK
▣	Taking Care of Your Corporation, Vol. 2, (Book w/Disk—PC)	1st	$39.95	CORK2
	Tax Savvy for Small Business	1st	$26.95	SAVVY
	The California Nonprofit Corporation Handbook	7th	$29.95	NON
	The California Professional Corporation Handbook	5th	$34.95	PROF
	The Employer's Legal Handbook	1st	$29.95	EMPL
	The Independent Paralegal's Handbook	3rd	$29.95	PARA
	The Legal Guide for Starting & Running a Small Business	2nd	$24.95	RUNS
	The Partnership Book: How to Write a Partnership Agreement	4th	$24.95	PART
	Rightful Termination	1st	$29.95	RITE
	Sexual Harassment on the Job	2nd	$18.95	HARS
	Trademark: How to Name Your Business & Product	2nd	$29.95	TRD

▣ Book with disk

CALL 800-992-6656 OR USE THE ORDER FORM IN THE BACK OF THE BOOK

	EDITION	PRICE	CODE
Workers' Comp for Employers	2nd	$29.95	CNTRL
Your Rights in the Workplace	2nd	$15.95	YRW
CONSUMER			
Fed Up With the Legal System: What's Wrong & How to Fix It	2nd	$9.95	LEG
Glossary of Insurance Terms	5th	$14.95	GLINT
How to Insure Your Car	1st	$12.95	INCAR
How to Win Your Personal Injury Claim	1st	$24.95	PICL
Nolo's Pocket Guide to California Law	4th	$10.95	CLAW
Nolo's Pocket Guide to Consumer Rights	2nd	$12.95	CAG
The Over 50 Insurance Survival Guide	1st	$16.95	OVER50
True Odds: How Risk Affects Your Everyday Life	1st	$19.95	TROD
What Do You Mean It's Not Covered?	1st	$19.95	COVER
ESTATE PLANNING & PROBATE			
How to Probate an Estate (California Edition)	8th	$34.95	PAE
Make Your Own Living Trust	2nd	$19.95	LITR
Nolo's Simple Will Book	2nd	$17.95	SWIL
Plan Your Estate	3rd	$24.95	NEST
The Quick and Legal Will Book	1st	$15.95	QUIC
Nolo's Law Form Kit: Wills	1st	$14.95	KWL
FAMILY MATTERS			
A Legal Guide for Lesbian and Gay Couples	8th	$24.95	LG
Child Custody: Building Agreements That Work	1st	$24.95	CUST
Divorce & Money: How to Make the Best Financial Decisions During Divorce	2nd	$21.95	DIMO
How to Adopt Your Stepchild in California	4th	$22.95	ADOP
How to Do Your Own Divorce in California	21st	$21.95	CDIV
How to Do Your Own Divorce in Texas	6th	$19.95	TDIV
How to Raise or Lower Child Support in California	3rd	$18.95	CHLD
Nolo's Pocket Guide to Family Law	4th	$14.95	FLD
Practical Divorce Solutions	1st	$14.95	PDS
The Guardianship Book (California Edition)	2nd	$24.95	GB
The Living Together Kit	7th	$24.95	LTK
GOING TO COURT			
Collect Your Court Judgment (California Edition	2nd	$19.95	JUDG
Everybody's Guide to Municipal Court (California Edition)	1st	$29.95	MUNI
Everybody's Guide to Small Claims Court (California Edition)	12th	$18.95	CSCC
Everybody's Guide to Small Claims Court (National Edition)	6th	$18.95	NSCC
Fight Your Ticket ... and Win! (California Edition)	6th	$19.95	FYT

Book with disk

CALL 800-992-6656 OR USE THE ORDER FORM IN THE BACK OF THE BOOK

	EDITION	PRICE	CODE
How to Change Your Name (California Edition)	6th	$24.95	NAME
Represent Yourself in Court: How to Prepare & Try a Winning Case	1st	$29.95	RYC
The Criminal Records Book (California Edition)	5th	$21.95	CRIM
HOMEOWNERS, LANDLORDS & TENANTS			
Dog Law	2nd	$12.95	DOG
▣ Every Landlord's Legal Guide (National Edition)	1st	$29.95	ELLI
For Sale by Owner (California Edition)	2nd	$24.95	FSBO
Homestead Your House (California Edition)	8th	$9.95	HOME
How to Buy a House in California	3rd	$24.95	BHCA
Neighbor Law: Fences, Trees, Boundaries & Noise	2nd	$16.95	NEI
Safe Homes, Safe Neighborhoods: Stopping Crime Where You Live	1st	$14.95	SAFE
Tenants' Rights (California Edition)	12th	$18.95	CTEN
The Deeds Book (California Edition)	3rd	$16.95	DEED
The Landlord's Law Book, Vol. 1: Rights & Responsibilities (California Edition)	5th	$34.95	LBRT
The Landlord's Law Book, Vol. 2: Evictions (California Edition)	5th	$34.95	LBEV
HUMOR			
29 Reasons Not to Go to Law School	1st	$9.95	29R
Poetic Justice	1st	$9.95	PJ
IMMIGRATION			
How to Become a United States Citizen	5th	$14.95	CIT
How to Get a Green Card: Legal Ways to Stay in the U.S.A.	2nd	$24.95	GRN
U.S. Immigration Made Easy	5th	$39.95	IMEZ
MONEY MATTERS			
Building Your Nest Egg With Your 401(k)	1st	$16.95	EGG
Chapter 13 Bankruptcy: Repay Your Debts	2nd	$29.95	CH13
How to File for Bankruptcy	6th	$26.95	HFB
Money Troubles: Legal Strategies to Cope With Your Debts	4th	$19.95	MT
Nolo's Law Form Kit: Personal Bankruptcy	1st	$14.95	KBNK
Nolo's Law Form Kit: Rebuild Your Credit	1st	$14.95	KCRD
Simple Contracts for Personal Use	2nd	$16.95	CONT
Smart Ways to Save Money During and After Divorce	1st	$14.95	SAVMO
Stand Up to the IRS	2nd	$21.95	SIRS

▣ Book with disk

CALL 800-992-6656 OR USE THE ORDER FORM IN THE BACK OF THE BOOK

PATENTS AND COPYRIGHTS			
Copyright Your Software	1st	$39.95	CYS
Patent, Copyright & Trademark: A Desk Reference to Intellectual Property Law	1st	$24.95	PCTM
Patent It Yourself	4th	$39.95	PAT
Software Development: A Legal Guide (Book with disk—PC)	1st	$44.95	SFT
The Copyright Handbook: How to Protect and Use Written Works	2nd	$24.95	COHA
The Inventor's Notebook	1st	$19.95	INOT
RESEARCH & REFERENCE			
Law on the Net	1st	$39.95	LAWN
Legal Research: How to Find & Understand the Law	4th	$19.95	LRES
Legal Research Made Easy (Video)	1st	$89.95	LRME
SENIORS			
Beat the Nursing Home Trap: A Consumer's Guide	2nd	$18.95	ELD
Social Security, Medicare & Pensions	6th	$19.95	SOA
The Conservatorship Book (California Edition)	2nd	$29.95	CNSV
SOFTWARE			
California Incorporator 2.0—DOS	2.0	$47.97	INCI2
Living Trust Maker 2.0—Macintosh	2.0	$47.97	LTM2
Living Trust Maker 2.0—Windows	2.0	$47.97	LTWI2
Small Business Legal Pro—Macintosh	2.0	$39.95	SBM2
Small Business Legal Pro—Windows	2.0	$39.95	SBW2
Nolo's Partnership Maker 1.0—DOS	1.0	$47.97	PAGI1
Nolo's Personal RecordKeeper 3.0—Macintosh	3.0	$29.97	FRM3
Patent It Yourself 1.0—Windows	1.0	$149.97	PYW1
WillMaker 6.0—Macintosh	6.0	$41.97	WM6
WillMaker 6.0—Windows	6.0	$41.97	WIW6

SPECIAL UPGRADE OFFER

Get 25% off the latest edition of your Nolo book

It's important to have the most current legal information. Because laws and legal procedures change often, we update our books regularly. To help keep you up-to-date we are extending this special upgrade offer. Cut out and mail the title portion of the cover of your old Nolo book and we'll give you 25% off the retail price of the NEW EDITION when you purchase directly from us. For more information call us at 1-800-992-6656. This offer is to individuals only.

ORDER FORM

Code	Quantity	Title	Unit price	Total

Subtotal

California residents add Sales Tax

Basic Shipping (*$5 for 1 item; $6 for 2-3 items, $7 for 4 or more*)

UPS RUSH delivery $7–any size order*

TOTAL

Name

Address

(UPS to street address, Priority Mail to P.O. boxes)

* Delivered in 3 business days from receipt of order. S.F. Bay area use regular shipping.

FOR FASTER SERVICE, USE YOUR CREDIT CARD AND OUR TOLL-FREE NUMBERS

Order 24 hours a day	1-800-992-6656
Fax your order	1-800-645-0895
e-mail	NoloInfo@nolopress.com
General Information	1-510-549-1976
Customer Service	1-800-728-3555, Mon.-Sat. 9am-5pm, PST

METHOD OF PAYMENT

☐ Check enclosed

☐ VISA ☐ MasterCard ☐ Discover Card ☐ American Express

Account # Expiration Date

Authorizing Signature

Daytime Phone

Prices subject to change.

Visit our store

If you live in the Bay Area, be sure to visit the Nolo Press Bookstore on the corner of 9th and Parker Streets in West Berkeley. You'll find our complete line of books and software, all at a discount. We also have t-shirts, posters and a selection of business and legal self-help books from other publishers. Open every day.

NOLO PRESS 950 PARKER ST., BERKELEY, CA 94710

more from

NOLO PRESS

THE LEGAL GUIDE FOR STARTING & RUNNING A SMALL BUSINESS

By Attorney Fred S. Steingold

Get the information you need to decide whether to form a sole proprietorship, partnership, corporation or limited liability company, hire and fire employees, negotiate a favorable lease, write contracts, resolve business disputes, cope with financial problems and much more.

$24.95 / RUNS

"This is a must-have and must-have handy for would-be and practicing entrepreneurs . . . Keep it close to your desk for ready reference."

—Reuters Financial Report

TAX SAVVY FOR SMALL BUSINESS

By Tax Attorney Frederick W. Daily

Virtually every decision a small business makes has tax consequences that can affect its bottom line.

For small business owners, this book tells you what you need to know about federal taxes, and shows you how to make the best decisions for your business, maximize your profits and stay out of trouble with the IRS.

And if you are already in trouble, it explains, step-by-step, how to survive an audit.

$26.95 / SAVVY

HIRING INDEPENDENT CONTRACTORS

The Employer's Legal Guide
Book with disk

By Attorney Stephen Fishman

Using independent contractors can save you a bundle in payroll taxes, health insurance costs, workers' compensation premiums and overtime pay. But the rules about who qualifies are complicated, and the IRS and state revenue agencies keep a close eye on businesses that hire independent contractors. Misclassifying a worker can result in serious financial penalties in a state or federal audit. A legal guide for employers, this book clearly lays out:

- what the risks and benefits are of hiring independent contractors
- who qualifies as an independent contractor for the purposes of the IRS, state unemployment insurance, workers' compensation insurance, federal labor laws and other laws
- how to hire independent contractors without risking an IRS or state audit
- how to make good agreements and retain ownership of intellectual property when using independent contractors.

Includes independent contractor agreements on disk.

$29.95 / HICI

CALL 800-992-6656 OR USE THE ORDER FORM IN THIS BOOK

m o r e f r o m

NOLO PRESS

Small Business Legal Pro Deluxe CD

A complete reference library for small business owners, this CD contains the complete text of four of Nolo's bestselling books: *The Legal Guide for Starting and Running a Small Business*, *Tax Savvy for Small Business*, *The Employer's Legal Handbook* and *Everybody's Guide to Small Claims Court*. Now you can get instant access to information on hiring and firing, leases, deductions, wages, buying or selling a business, audits, preparing a winning small claims case and more.

- create over 50 business letters and documents
- find information in a snap with random-access text searching, keyword index, multi-level table of contents and hypertext links
- printout and copy text, create book marks for quick and easy access and attach your own notes to any section.

$35.97/SBCD2 • *List price $59.95*

Small Business Legal Pro

The Legal Guide for Starting and Running a Small Business is also available on Disk. Now you can get straightforward answers to the legal questions that come up in your business, straight form your computer. *Small Business Legal Pro* features random access text searching, key-word index, hyper-text linking, and "Law in the Real World" examples from businesses just like yours.

Windows Version 2.0 $25.97/SBWI2

Macintosh Version 2.0 $25.97/SBM2

CALL 800-992-6656 OR USE THE ORDER FORM IN THIS BOOK